The OFFICIAL Handbook for the

Clep®

EXAMINATIONS

REVISED EDITION

THE COLLEGE BOARD

The College-Level Examinations are offered by the College Board, a nonprofit membership organization that provides tests and other educational services for students, schools, and colleges. The membership is composed of more than 2,700 colleges and universities, secondary schools, and education associations. Representatives of the members serve on the Board of Trustees and on advisory councils and committees that consider the programs of the College Board and participate in the determination of its policies and activities.

This book was prepared and produced by Educational Testing Service (ETS), which develops and administers the tests of the College-Level Examination Program for the College Board. Additional copies of this book may be obtained by sending $15 to College Board Publications, Box 886, New York, NY 10101-0886. Please allow two to four weeks for delivery. For faster delivery, call 1-800-323-7155 and charge your order to a Visa or MasterCard credit card.

If you have questions about the College-Level Examinations that are not answered in this or other publications, write to the Director, College-Level Examination Program, The College Board, 45 Columbus Avenue, New York, NY 10023-6992.

ISBN: 0-87447-527-9

Library of Congress Catalog Card Number: 94-072220

Printed in the United States of America

9 8 7 6 5 4 3 2 1

Contents

VII. Examination Guides

Appendixes

Introduction

This guide to the College-Level Examination Program (CLEP) examinations has been written mainly for adults who are making plans to enroll in college. If you've been out of school for a while and haven't taken a college-level test recently, it's important that you read through all the chapters of this handbook.

The handbook contains information of interest to others as well. College-bound high school students, military personnel, professionals seeking certification, and persons of all ages who have learned or wish to learn college-level material outside the college classroom will find the handbook helpful as they strive to accomplish their goals.

CLEP is based on the premise that some individuals enrolling in college have already learned part of what is taught in college courses through noncredit adult courses, job training, independent reading and study, and advanced high school courses. Often, their job and life experiences have enhanced and reinforced their learning. CLEP provides these individuals the opportunity to demonstrate their college-level learning by taking examinations that assess the knowledge and skills taught in college courses.

The first few sections of this handbook explain how CLEP can help you earn credit for the college-level learning you have acquired, and provide suggestions for preparing for the examinations. The guides to the individual examinations include test descriptions, sample questions, and suggested resources for preparing for the examinations.

If you still have general questions about continuing or adult education after reading this handbook, the following associations can provide advice and information:

American Council on Education
1 DuPont Circle, N.W.
Washington, D.C. 20036
(202) 939-9475

American Association for Adult and Continuing Education
Suite 700
1101 Connecticut Avenue, N.W.
Washington, D.C. 20036
(202) 429-5131

I. The College-Level Examination Program

How the Program Works

CLEP examinations are administered at more than 1,200 colleges and universities nationwide, and approximately 2,800 institutions award college credit to those who do well on them. The 34 examinations allow people who have acquired knowledge outside the usual educational settings to show that they have learned college-level material so that they can bypass certain college courses.

The CLEP examinations cover material that is taught in introductory-level courses at many colleges and universities. Faculties at individual colleges review the exams to ensure that they cover the important material currently taught in their courses. Colleges differ in the CLEP examinations for which they award credit; some colleges accept only two or three of the examinations while others accept all of them.

Although CLEP is sponsored by the College Board and the examinations are scored by Educational Testing Service (ETS), neither of these organizations can award college credit. Only accredited colleges may grant credit toward a degree. When you take a CLEP examination, you may request that a copy of your score report be sent to the college you are attending or planning to attend. After evaluating your scores, the college will decide whether or not to award you credit for a certain course or courses, or to exempt you from them.

If the college gives you credit, it will record the number of credits on your permanent record, thereby indicating that you have completed work equivalent to a course in that subject. If the college decides to grant exemption without giving you credit for a course, you will be permitted to omit a course that would normally be required of you and to take a course of your choice instead.

The General Examinations

Each of the five General Examinations covers material taught in courses that most students take as requirements during their first two years of college. Most colleges require all their students to take three or six semester hours (or the equivalent) in each of the five areas. They may grant credit in the area in which a satisfactory test score is earned rather than for a specific course. General Examinations are available in the following areas: English Composition (with or without Essay), Humanities, Mathematics, Natural Sciences, and Social Sciences and History.

The Subject Examinations

Each Subject Examination includes material usually covered in an undergraduate course with a similar title. On the basis of a satisfactory test score, each institution grants credit equal to the amount it gives to students who successfully complete that course. Twenty-nine Subject Examinations in several curriculum areas are offered (see the Contents pages for a list).

What the Examinations Are Like

The examinations consist of multiple-choice questions to be answered within a 90-minute time limit. There are two versions of the General Examination in English Composition: One is made up entirely of multiple-choice questions; the other has a 45-minute multiple-choice section and a 45-minute essay section. (Additional information about the length, timing, and content of each CLEP examination is given in the examination guides in chapter 7.)

Optional 90-minute free-response sections are available for the four Subject Examinations in Composition and Literature. These sections are required by some colleges in addition to the 90-minute multiple-choice test. The optional sections are not graded at Educational Testing Service (ETS); rather, they are sent to the college designated by the candidate and graded there by faculty. Before registering for a CLEP examination, find out whether the college that is to receive your score requires the optional free-response section.

Where to Take the Examinations

CLEP examinations are administered throughout the year at more than 1,200 test centers in the United States and can be arranged for candidates outside the U.S. on request. Arrangements for foreign administrations take between six weeks and four months, depending on the site. Contact CLEP, P.O. Box 6600, Princeton, NJ 08541-6600 for further information about special administrations.

In Appendix C you will find a list of institutions that award credit for satisfactory scores on CLEP examinations. Some colleges only administer CLEP examinations to their own students. If your college does not administer the exams, contact the test center in your area for information about its testing schedule.

After you have been tested, your answer sheet will be sent to ETS for scoring. Once the answer sheet is received at ETS, it is scored within 48 hours. Because of mailing considerations and certain unavoidable delays, however, you can expect to receive your score report in about two weeks.

Your score report is mailed to you and to the recipient you designate. CLEP scores are kept on file at ETS for 20 years. During this period, for a small fee, you may have your transcript sent to another college or to anyone else you specify. (Your scores will never be sent to anyone without your approval.)

Active military personnel may take CLEP examinations without charge through the Defense Activity for Non-Traditional Education Support (DANTES) program. At military installations, information about CLEP may be obtained from the Education Officer.

II. Approaching a College about CLEP

The following sections provide a step-by-step approach to learning about the CLEP policy at a particular college or university. The person or office that can best assist students desiring CLEP credit may have a different title at each institution, but the following guidelines will lead you to information about CLEP at any institution.

Adults returning to college often benefit from special assistance when they approach a college. Opportunities for adults to return to formal learning in the classroom are now widespread, and colleges and universities have worked hard to make this a smooth process for older students. Many colleges have established special offices that are staffed with trained professionals who understand the kinds of problems facing adults returning to college. If you think you might benefit from such assistance, be sure to find out whether these services are available at your college.

How to Apply for College Credit

Step 1. *Obtain the general information catalog and a copy of the CLEP policy from the colleges you are considering. If you have not yet applied for admission, ask for an admission application form, too.*

Information about admission and CLEP policies can be obtained by writing or visiting college admission offices. Tell the admission officer that you are a prospective student and that you are interested in applying for admission and CLEP credit. Ask for a copy of the publication in which the college's complete CLEP policy is explained. Also get the name and the telephone number of the person to contact in case you have further questions about CLEP.

At this stage, you may wish to obtain information from external degree colleges. Many adults find that such colleges suit their needs exceptionally well. External degrees are discussed later in this chapter.

Step 2. *If you have not already been admitted to the college you are considering, look at its admission requirements for undergraduate students to see whether you can qualify.*

Virtually all public community colleges and a number of four-year state colleges have "open admission" policies for in-state students. This usually means that they admit anyone who has graduated from high school or has earned a high school equivalency diploma.

If you think you do not meet the admission requirements, contact the admission office for an interview with a counselor. Colleges do sometimes make exceptions, particularly for adult applicants. State why you want the interview and ask what documents you should bring with you or send in advance. (These materials may include a high school transcript, transcript of previous college work, completed application for admission, etc.) Make an extra effort to have all the information requested in time for the interview.

During the interview, relax and be yourself. Be prepared to state honestly why you think you are ready and able to do college work. If you have already taken CLEP examinations and scored high enough to earn credit, you have shown that you are able to do college work. Mention this achievement to the admission counselor because it may increase your chances of being accepted. If you have not taken a CLEP examination, you can still improve your chances of being accepted by describing how your job training or independent study has helped prepare you for college-level work. Tell the counselor what you have learned from your work and personal experiences.

Step 3. *Evaluate the college's CLEP policy.*

Typically, a college lists all its academic policies, including CLEP policies, in its general catalog. You will probably find the CLEP policy statement under a heading such as Credit-by-Examination, Advanced Standing, Advanced Placement, or External Degree Program. These sections can usually be found in the front of the catalog.

Many colleges publish their credit-by-examination policy in a separate brochure, which is distributed through the campus testing office, counseling center, admission office, or registrar's office. If you find a very general policy statement in the college catalog, seek clarification from one of these offices.

Review the material in the section of this chapter entitled "Questions to Ask about a College's CLEP Policy." Use these guidelines to evaluate the college's CLEP policy. If you have not yet taken a CLEP examination, this evaluation will help you decide which examinations to take and whether or not to take the free-response portion. Because individual colleges have different CLEP policies, a review of several policies may help you decide which college to attend.

Step 4. *If you have not yet applied for admission, do so early.*

Most colleges expect you to apply for admission several months before you enroll, and it is essential that you meet the published application deadlines. It takes time to process your application for admission. If you have yet to take a CLEP examination, you may want to take one or more CLEP examinations while you are waiting for your application to be processed. Be sure to check the college's CLEP policy beforehand so that you are taking examinations your college will accept for credit. You should also find out from the college when to submit your CLEP scores.

Complete all forms and include all documents requested with your application(s) for admission. Normally, an admission decision cannot be reached until all documents have been submitted and evaluated. Unless told to do so, do not send your CLEP scores until you have been officially admitted.

Step 5. *Arrange to take CLEP examination(s) or to submit your CLEP score(s).*

You may want to wait to take your CLEP examinations until you know definitely which college you will be attending. Then you can make sure you are taking exams your college will accept for credit. You will also be able to request that your scores be sent to the college, free of charge, when you take the exams.

If you have already taken a CLEP examination but did not have a copy of your score report sent to your college, you may have an official transcript sent at any time for a small fee by filling out the Transcript Request Form that was sent to you with your score report. If you do not have the form, send the following information to CLEP Transcript Service, P.O. Box 6600, Princeton, New Jersey 08541-6600: your name (as it appeared on your answer sheet), social security number, birth date, the name of the test and test center, and the test date. Also include a check or money order made payable to CLEP for $15 (this fee is subject to change).

Your CLEP scores will be evaluated, probably by someone in the admission office, and sent to the registrar's office to be posted on your permanent record once you are enrolled. Procedures vary from college to college, but the process usually begins in the admission office.

Step 6. *Ask to receive a written notice of the credit you receive for your CLEP score(s).*

A written notice may save you problems later, when you submit your degree plan or file for graduation. In the event that there is a question about whether or not you earned CLEP credit, you will have an official record of what credit was awarded. You may also need this verification of course credit if you go for academic counseling before the credit is posted on your permanent record.

Step 7. *Before you register for courses, seek academic counseling.*

A discussion with your academic adviser can prevent you from taking unnecessary courses and can tell you specifically what your CLEP credit will mean to you. This step may be accomplished at the time you enroll. Most colleges have orientation sessions for new students prior to each enrollment period. During orientation, students are usually assigned an academic adviser who then gives them individual help in developing long-range plans and a course schedule for the next semester. In conjunction with this counseling, you may be asked to take some additional tests so that you can be placed at the proper course level.

External Degree Programs

If you have acquired a considerable amount of college-level knowledge through job experience, reading, or noncredit courses, if you have accumulated college credits at a variety of colleges over a period of years, or if you prefer studying on your own rather than in a classroom setting, you may want to investigate the possibility of enrolling in an external degree program. Connecticut, New Jersey, and New York offer external degree programs that allow you to earn a degree by passing examinations (including CLEP), transferring credit from other colleges, and demonstrating in other ways that you have satisfied certain educational requirements. No classroom attendance is required, and the programs are open to out-of-state candidates as well as residents. Thomas Edison State College in New Jersey and Charter Oak State College in Connecticut are fully accredited independent state colleges; the New York program is part of the state university system and is also fully accredited. If you are interested in exploring an external degree, you may contact:

Charter Oak State College
66 Cedar Street
Newington, CT 06111
(203) 666-4595

Regents College
7 Columbia Circle
Albany, New York 12203-5159
(518) 464-8500

Thomas Edison State College
101 West State Street
Trenton, New Jersey 08608-1176
(609) 984-1150

Many other colleges also have external degree or weekend programs. While they often require that a number of courses be taken on campus, the external degree programs tend to be more flexible in transferring credit, granting credit-by-examination, and allowing independent study than other traditional programs. When applying to a college, you may wish to ask whether it offers these kinds of programs.

Questions to Ask about a College's CLEP Policy

Before taking CLEP examinations for the purpose of earning college credit, try to find the answers to these questions:

1. *Which CLEP examinations are accepted by this college?*

A college may accept some CLEP examinations for credit and not others — possibly not the one you are considering. For this reason, it is important that you know the specific CLEP exams for which you can receive credit.

2. *Does the college require the optional free-response (essay) section for Subject Examinations in Composition and Literature as well as the multiple-choice portion of the CLEP examination you are considering? Will you be required to pass a departmental test such as an essay, laboratory, or oral examination in addition to the CLEP multiple-choice examination?*

Knowing the answers to these questions ahead of time will permit you to schedule the optional free-response or departmental examination when you register to take your CLEP examination.

3. *Is credit granted for specific courses at the college? If so, which ones?*

You are likely to find that credit is granted for specific courses and that the course titles are designated in the college's CLEP policy. It is not necessary, however, that credit be granted for a specific course for you to benefit from your CLEP credit. For instance, at many liberal arts colleges, all students must take certain types of courses; these courses may be labeled the core curriculum, general education requirements, distribution requirements, or liberal arts requirements. The requirements are often expressed in terms of credit hours. For example, all students may be required to take at least six hours of humanities, six hours of English, three hours of mathematics, six hours of natural science, and six hours of social science, with no particular courses in these disciplines specified. In these instances, CLEP credit may be given as "6 hrs. English Credit" or "3 hrs. Math Credit" without specifying for which English or mathematics courses credit has been awarded. To avoid possible disappointment, you should know before taking a CLEP examination what type of credit you can receive or whether you will be exempted from a required course but receive no credit.

4. *How much credit is granted for each examination you are considering, and does the college place a limit on the total amount of CLEP credit you can earn toward your degree?*

Not all colleges that grant CLEP credit award the same amount for individual tests. Furthermore, some colleges place a limit on the total amount of credit you can earn through CLEP or other examinations. Other colleges may grant you exemption but no credit toward your degree. Knowing several colleges' policies concerning these issues may help you decide which college to attend. If you think you are capable of passing a number of CLEP examinations, you may want to attend a college that will allow you to earn credit for all or most of them. For example, the state external degree programs grant credit for most CLEP examinations.

5. *What is the required score for earning CLEP credit for each exam you are considering?*

Most colleges publish the required scores or percentile ranks for earning CLEP credit in their general catalog or in a brochure. The required score may vary from exam to exam, so find out the required score for each exam you are considering.

6. *What is the college's policy regarding prior course work in the subject in which you are considering taking a CLEP examination?*

Some colleges will not grant credit for a CLEP exam if the student has already attempted a college-level course closely aligned with that exam. For example, if you successfully completed English 101 or a comparable course on another campus, you will probably not be permitted to also receive CLEP credit in that subject. Some colleges will not permit you to earn CLEP credit for a course that you failed.

7. *Does the college make additional stipulations before credit will be granted?*

It is common practice for colleges to award CLEP credit only to their enrolled students. There are other stipulations, however, that vary from college to college. For example, does the college require you to formally apply for or accept CLEP credit by completing and signing a form? Or does the college require you to "validate" your CLEP score by successfully completing a more advanced course in the subject? Getting answers to these and other questions will help to smooth the process of earning college credit through CLEP.

The preceding questions and the discussions that follow them indicate some of the ways in which CLEP policies can vary from college to college. Find out as much as possible about the CLEP policies at the colleges you are interested in so that you can choose a college with a policy that is compatible with your educational goals. Once you have selected the college you will attend, you can find out which CLEP examinations your college recognizes and its requirements for earning CLEP credit.

III. Deciding Which Examinations to Take

If You're Taking the Examinations for College Credit or Career Advancement . . .

Most people who take CLEP examinations want to earn credit for college courses. Others take the examinations to qualify for job promotions or for professional certification or licensing. Whatever the reason, it is vital to most candidates that they be well prepared for the exams so that they can advance as rapidly as possible toward their educational or career goals.

Those who have limited knowledge in the subjects covered by the exams they are considering are advised to enroll in the college courses in which that material is taught. Those who are uncertain about whether or not they know enough to do well on a particular CLEP exam will find the following guidelines helpful.

There is no way to predict whether you will pass a particular CLEP examination, but answering the questions that follow should give you some indication.

1. *Test Descriptions*

Read the description of the exam provided in this handbook. Are you familiar with most of the topics and terminology in the outline?

2. *Textbooks*

Examine the suggested textbooks and other resource materials following the exam descriptions in this handbook. Have you recently read one or more of these books, or have you read similar college-level books on this subject? If you have not, read through one or more of the textbooks listed, or study the textbook used for this course at your college. Are you familiar with most of the topics and terminology in the book?

3. *Sample Questions*

The sample questions are intended to be representative of the content and difficulty of the questions on the exam. Although they do not appear on the actual exam, the proportion of the sample questions you can answer correctly should be a rough estimate of the proportion of questions you will be able to answer correctly on the exam.

Following the instructions and suggestions in chapter 5, answer as many of the sample questions for the exam as you can. Check your answers against the correct answers in Appendix B. Did you answer more than half the questions correctly?

Because of variations in course content at different institutions, and because questions on CLEP exams vary in difficulty — with most being of moderate difficulty — the average student who passes a course in a subject can usually answer correctly about half the questions on the corresponding CLEP examination. Most colleges set their passing scores near this level, but some set them higher. If your college has set its required score above the level required by most colleges, you may need to answer a larger proportion of questions on the exam correctly.

4. *Previous Study*

Have you taken noncredit courses in this subject offered by an adult school or a private school, through correspondence, or in connection with your job? Did you do exceptionally well in this subject in high school, or did you take an honors course in this subject?

5. *Experience*

Have you learned or used the knowledge or skills included in this exam in your job or life experience? For example, if you lived in a Spanish-speaking country and spoke the language for a year or more, you might consider taking the College Spanish examination. Or, if you have worked at a job in which you used accounting and finance skills, Introductory Accounting would be a likely exam for you to take. Or, if you have read a considerable amount of literature and attended many art exhibits, concerts, and plays, you might expect to do well on the General Examination in Humanities.

6. *Other Examinations*

Have you done well on other standardized tests in subjects related to the one you want to take? For example, did you score well above average on a portion of a college entrance examination covering similar skills, or did you obtain an exceptionally high score on a high school equivalency test or a licensing examination in this subject? Although such tests do not cover exactly the same material as the CLEP examinations and may be easier, persons who do well on these tests often do well on CLEP examinations, too.

7. *Advice*

Has a college counselor, professor, or some other professional person familiar with your ability advised you to take a CLEP examination?

If you answered yes to several of the above questions, you probably have a good chance of passing the CLEP examination you are considering. It is unlikely that you would have acquired sufficient background from experience alone. Learning gained through reading and study is essential, and you will probably find some additional study helpful before taking a CLEP examination. Information on how to review for CLEP examinations can be found in chapter 4 and in the examination guides in chapter 7.

If You're Taking the Examinations to Prepare for College . . .

Many people entering college, particularly adults returning to college after several years away from formal education, are uncertain about their ability to compete with other college students. You may wonder whether you have sufficient background for college study, and if you've been away from formal study for some time, you may wonder whether you have forgotten how to study, how to take tests, and how to write papers. You may wish to improve your test-taking and study skills prior to enrolling in courses.

One way to assess your ability to perform at the college level and to improve your test-taking and study skills at the same time is to prepare for and take one or more CLEP examinations. You need not be enrolled in a college to take a CLEP examination. You may have your scores sent only to yourself and later request that a transcript be sent to a college if you then decide to apply for credit. By reviewing the exam descriptions and sample questions in this handbook, you may find one or several subject areas in which you think you have substantial knowledge. Select one examination, or more if you like, and carefully read at least one of the textbooks listed in the Study Resources section following the sample questions. (As indicated in the examination guides, it may be necessary to study more than one textbook to cover the entire scope of material covered by the exam.) By doing this, you will get a better idea of how much you know of what is usually taught in a college-level course in that subject. Study as much material as you can, until you think you have a good grasp of the subject matter. Then take the exam at a college in your area. It may be two to three weeks before you receive your score report, and you may wish to begin reviewing for another exam in the meantime.

To find out whether you are eligible for credit based on your CLEP score, you must compare your score with the one required by the college you plan to attend. If you are not yet sure which college you will attend, or whether you will enroll in college at all, you should begin to follow the steps outlined in chapter 2. It is best that you do this before taking a CLEP exam, but if you are taking the exam only for the experience and to familiarize yourself with college-level material and requirements, you might take the exam before you approach a college. Even if the college you decide to attend does not accept the exam you took, the experience of taking such an exam will give you more confidence about pursuing your college-level studies.

You will find information about how to interpret your scores in *What Your CLEP Score Means*, a pamphlet you will receive with your score report. Many colleges follow the recommendations of the American Council on Education (ACE) for setting their required scores, so you can use this information as a guide in determining how well you did. The ACE recommendations are included in the pamphlet.

If you do not do well enough on the exam to earn college credit, don't be discouraged. The fact that you did not get credit for your score means that you should probably enroll in a college course to learn the material. However, if your score was close to the required score, or if you feel you could do better on a second try or after some additional study, you may retake the test after six months. Do not take it sooner or your score will not be reported and your fee will be forfeited.

If you do earn the score required to earn credit, you will have demonstrated that you already have some college-level knowledge. You will also have a better idea of whether you should take additional CLEP examinations.

IV. Preparing to Take CLEP Examinations

Having made the decision to take one or more CLEP examinations, most people then want to know how to prepare for them — how much, how long, when, and how should they go about it? The precise answers to these questions vary greatly from individual to individual. However, most candidates find that some type of test preparation is helpful.

Most people who take CLEP examinations do so to show that they have already learned the key material taught in a college course. Many of them need only a quick review to assure themselves that they have not forgotten what they once studied, and to fill in some of the gaps in their knowledge of the subject. Others feel that they need a thorough review and spend several weeks studying for an exam. Some people take a CLEP examination as a kind of "final examination" for independent study of a subject. This last group requires significantly more study than those who only need to review, and they may need some guidance from professors of the subjects they are studying.

The key to how you prepare for CLEP examinations often lies in locating those skills and areas of prior learning in which you are strong and deciding where to focus your energies. Some people may know a great deal about a certain subject area but may not test well. These individuals would probably be just as concerned about strengthening their test-taking skills as they would about studying for a specific test. Many mental and physical skills are used in preparing for a test. It is important not only to review or study for the examinations but to make certain that you are alert, relatively free of anxiety, and aware of how to approach standardized tests. Suggestions on developing test-taking skills and preparing psychologically and physically for a test are given in this chapter. The following section suggests ways of assessing your knowledge of the content of an exam and then reviewing and studying the material.

Using the Examination Guides

In chapter 7, you will find a guide for each CLEP examination. Each examination guide includes an outline of the knowledge and skills covered by the test, sample questions similar to those that appear on the examination, and a list of textbooks and other study resources that would be helpful in preparing for it.

As an alternative to the textbooks listed in the Study Resources section at the end of each exam description, check with a college in your area offering a course comparable to the CLEP exam you want

to take and use the textbook required for that course to help you prepare. To get this information, check the college's catalog for a list of courses offered. Then call the admission office, explain what subject you're interested in, and ask who in that academic department you can contact for specific information on textbooks and other study resources to use. Be sure that the college you're interested in gives credit for the CLEP exam for which you're preparing.

Begin by carefully reading the test description and outline of knowledge and skills required for the examination in the examination guide. As you read through the topics listed, ask yourself how much you know about each one. Also note the terms, names, and symbols that are mentioned, and ask yourself whether you are familiar with them. This will give you a quick overview of how much you know about the subject. If you are familiar with nearly all the material, you will probably need a minimum of review; however, if less than half of it is familiar, you will probably require substantial study to do well on the exam.

If, after reviewing the test description provided in the examination guide, you find that you need extensive review, delay answering the sample questions until you have done some reading in the subject. If you complete them before reviewing the material, you will probably look for the answers as you study, and they will not be a good assessment of your ability at a later date. Do not refer to the sample questions as you prepare for the exam. None of them appears on the CLEP examination, so concentrating on them without broader study of the subject won't help you.

If you think you are familiar with most of the test material, try to answer the sample questions. (You may use a copy of the sample answer sheet in Appendix A or the answer spaces provided next to each sample question.) Use the test-taking strategies described in chapter 5.

Check your answers against the answer key in Appendix B. If you could answer nearly all the questions correctly, you probably do not need to study the subject extensively. If you got about half the questions correct, you ought to review at least one textbook or other suggested material on the subject. If you could answer fewer than half the questions correctly, you will probably benefit from more extensive reading in the subject and thorough study of one or more textbooks. **The textbooks listed in each examination guide are used at many colleges, but they are not the only good texts. You will find helpful almost any standard textbook available to you, such as the one used at your college, or other recent editions of textbooks listed in the examination guide.**

Assessing Your Readiness
for a CLEP Examination

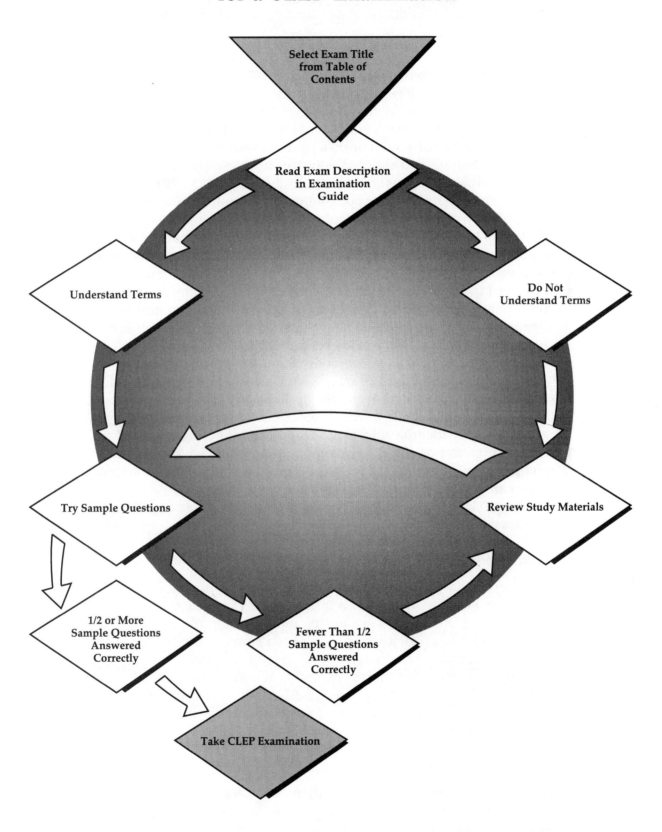

Suggestions for Studying

The following suggestions have been gathered from people who have prepared for CLEP examinations or other college-level tests.

1. *Define your goals and locate study materials.*

First, determine your study goals. Set aside a block of time to review the examination guides provided in this book, and then decide which exam(s) you will take. Using the suggestions in the examination guide(s), locate suitable resource materials. If a preparation course is offered by an adult school or college in your area, you might find it helpful to enroll. (You should be aware, however, that such courses are not authorized or sponsored by the College Board. Neither the College Board nor ETS has any responsibility for the content of these courses; nor are they responsible for books on preparing for CLEP examinations that have been published by other organizations.) If you know others who have taken CLEP examinations, ask them how they prepared.

If you have a good foundation of knowledge in a particular subject but need to brush up on one or two specific areas, you may wish to refer to an encyclopedia. American Encyclopedia, Encyclopedia Britannica, and World Book Encyclopedia are three possible options. Encyclopedias can also provide references to other scholarly works that could be of help as you prepare for CLEP examinations.

Also check with your librarian about locating other study aids to supplement those listed in the Study Resources section at the end of each examination guide in this handbook. These supplementary materials may include videotapes from National Geographic, Nova, and other education-oriented companies; audio language tapes; and computer software. And don't forget that what you do with your leisure time can be very educational, whether it's watching a PBS series, reading a financial newsletter, attending a play, or viewing a film, for instance.

2. *Find a good place to study.*

To determine what kind of place you need for studying, ask yourself questions such as, Do I need a quiet place? Does the telephone distract me? Do objects I see in this place remind me of things I should do? Is it too warm? Is it well lit? Am I too comfortable here? Do I have space to spread out my materials? You may find the library more conducive to studying than your home. If you decide to study at home, you might prevent interruptions by other household members by putting a sign on the door of your study room to indicate when you will be available.

3. *Schedule time to study.*

To help you determine where studying best fits into your schedule, try this exercise: Make a list of your daily activities (for example, sleeping, working, and eating) and estimate how many hours per day you spend on each activity. Now, rate all the activities on your list in order of their importance and evaluate your use of time. Often people are astonished at how an average day appears from this perspective. They may discover that they were unaware how large portions of time are spent, or they learn their time can be scheduled in alternative ways. For example, they can remove the least important activities from their day and devote that time to studying or another important activity.

4. *Establish a study routine and a set of goals.*

To study effectively, you should establish specific goals and a schedule for accomplishing them. Some people find it helpful to write out a weekly schedule and cross out each study period when it is completed. Others maintain their concentration better by writing down the time when they expect to complete a study task. Most people find short periods of intense study more productive than long stretches of time. For example, they may follow a regular schedule of several 20- or 30-minute study periods with short breaks between them. Some people like to allow themselves rewards as they complete each study goal. It is not essential that you accomplish every goal exactly within your schedule; the point is to be committed to your task.

5. *Learn how to take an active role in studying.*

If you have not done much studying for some time, you may find it difficult to concentrate at first. Try a method of studying, such as the one outlined below, that will help you concentrate on and remember what you read.

a. First, read the chapter summary and the introduction. Then you will know what to look for in your reading.

b. Next, convert the section or paragraph headlines into questions. For example, if you are reading a section entitled "The Causes of the American Revolution," ask yourself, "What were the causes of the American Revolution?" Compose the answer as you read the paragraph. Reading and answering questions aloud will help you understand and remember the material.

c. Take notes on key ideas or concepts as you read. Writing will also help you fix concepts more firmly in your mind. Underlining key ideas or writing notes in your book can be helpful and will be useful for review. Underline only important points. If you underline more than a third of each paragraph, you are probably underlining too much.

d. If there are questions or problems at the end of a chapter, answer or solve them on paper as if you were asked to do them for homework. Mathematics textbooks (and some other books) sometimes include answers to some or all of the exercises. If you have such a book, write your answers before looking at the ones given. When problem-solving is involved, work enough problems to master the required methods and concepts. If you have difficulty with problems, review any sample problems or explanations in the chapter.

e. To retain knowledge, most people have to review the material periodically. If you are preparing for an exam over an extended period of time, review key concepts and notes each week or so. Do not wait for weeks to review the material or you will need to relearn much of it.

Psychological and Physical Preparation

Most people feel at least some nervousness before taking a test. Adults who are returning to college may not have taken a test in many years or they may have had little experience with standardized tests. Some younger students, as well, are uncomfortable with testing situations. People who received their education in countries outside the United States may find that many tests given in this country are quite different from the ones they are accustomed to taking.

Not only might candidates find the types of tests and questions unfamiliar, but other aspects of the testing environment may be strange as well. The physical and mental stress that results from meeting this new experience can hinder a candidate's ability to demonstrate his or her true degree of knowledge in the subject area being tested. For this reason, it is important to go to the test center well prepared, both mentally and physically, for taking the test. You may find the following suggestions helpful.

1. Familiarize yourself as much as possible with the test and the test situation before the day of the examination. It will be helpful for you to know ahead of time:

   a. How much time will be allowed for the test and whether there are timed subsections. (This information is included in the examination guides in chapter 7.)

   b. What types of questions and directions appear on the examination. (See the examination guides.)

   c. How your test score will be computed. (See chapter 6 for a brief explanation.)

   d. Whether you will record your answers on an answer sheet or on a microcomputer.

   e. How to complete the answer sheet. (See suggestion 4d, below; a sample answer sheet is provided in Appendix A.)

   f. How a microcomputer looks and operates, if you will be using one. (Simple instructions will be given on the day of the test, and you will be given ample time to use the computer in answering practice questions before you begin the actual test.)

g. In which building and room the examination will be administered. If you don't know where the building is, get directions ahead of time.

h. The time of the test administration. You might wish to confirm this information a day or two before the examination and find out what time the building and room will be open so that you can plan to arrive early.

i. Where to park your car or, if you will be taking public transportation, which bus or train to take and the location of the nearest stop.

j. Whether smoking will be permitted during the test.

k. Whether there will be a break between examinations (if you will be taking more than one on the same day), and whether there is a place nearby where you can get something to eat or drink.

2. Be relaxed and alert during the test. To prepare:

a. Get a good night's sleep. Last minute cramming, particularly late the night before, is usually counterproductive.

b. Eat normally. It is usually not wise to skip breakfast or lunch on the day of the test or to eat a big meal just before the test.

c. Avoid tranquilizers and stimulants. If you follow the other directions in this book, you won't need artificial aids. It's better to be a little tense than to be drowsy, but stimulants such as coffee and cola can make you nervous and interfere with your concentration.

d. Don't drink a lot of liquids before the test. Leaving to use the rest room during the test will disturb your concentration and take valuable time away from the test.

e. If you are inclined to be nervous or tense, learn some relaxation exercises and use them to prepare for the test.

3. Arrive for the test early and prepared. Be sure to:

a. Arrive early enough so that you can find a parking place, locate the test center, and get settled comfortably before testing begins. Allow some extra time in case you are delayed unexpectedly.

b. Take the following with you:

- Your completed Admission Form, which will have been validated in advance by the test administrator. You will need to refer to this form to record on your answer sheet the code number of the college to which you want your scores sent.

- Personal identification that includes your photograph and signature. You will be asked to show such identification to be admitted.

- Two or more soft-lead (No. 2) pencils with good erasers.

- An unprogrammed hand calculator if you wish to use one for the College Algebra, Introductory Accounting, or General Chemistry examinations. Check with the test center in advance for any change in this policy. All calculator memories must be cleared of programs and data, and no peripheral devices such as magnetic cards or tapes will be allowed. Candidates are not permitted to share calculators or other supplies.

- A watch so that you can time your progress.

- Your glasses if you need them for reading or seeing the chalkboard or wall clock.

c. Leave all books, papers, and notes outside the test center. You will not be permitted to use your own scratch paper, but there will be adequate space for notes and calculations on the pages of your test book.

d. Be able to adjust to an uncomfortable temperature in the testing room. Wear layers of clothing that can be removed if the room is too hot but that will keep you warm if it is too cold.

4. When you enter the test room:

a. Although you will be assigned to a seat, the test center administrator can usually accommodate special needs. For example, if you are left-handed, ask to be assigned to a seat with a left-handed writing board, if possible. Be sure to communicate your needs *before* the test begins.

b. Read directions carefully and listen to all instructions given by the test administrator. If you don't understand the directions, ask for help before test timing begins. If you must ask a question after the test has begun, raise your hand and a proctor will assist you. The proctor can answer certain kinds of questions but cannot help you with the test.

c. Know your rights as a test taker. You can expect to be given the full working time allowed for the test(s) and a reasonably quiet and comfortable place in which to work. If a poor test situation is preventing you from doing your best, ask if the situation can be remedied. If bad test conditions cannot be remedied, ask the person in charge to report the problem in the Irregularity Report that will be sent to ETS with the answer sheets. You may also wish to immediately write a letter to CLEP, P.O. Box 6601, Princeton, NJ 08541-6601. Describe the exact circumstances as completely as you can. Be sure to include the name of the test center, the test date, and the name(s) of the test(s) you took. ETS will investigate the problem to make sure it does not happen again, and, if the problem is serious enough, may arrange for you to retake the test without charge.

d. If you will be using an answer sheet as opposed to a microcomputer, complete it correctly. CLEP answer sheets are scored by an electronic optical scanner that reads the marks you make on your answer sheet. Therefore, it is important that all the marks you put on your answer sheet are dark enough, that you put them in the right places, and that you erase completely all marks you do not want the scanner to read. Use a soft-lead (No. 2) pencil when completing your answer sheet.

A sample CLEP answer sheet is shown in Appendix A. The second and third page have been completed for a fictional candidate, Nancy B. Baker. Familiarize yourself with this completed sample answer sheet before taking your examination so that you are able to complete your answer sheet properly when you take the test. Filling out your answer sheet incorrectly or incompletely will delay your score report.

If you will be entering your answers on a microcomputer, complete instructions will be provided on the day of the test. You will be given ample time to practice answering sample questions on the microcomputer before you begin the actual test.

Arrangements for Students with Disabilities

If you have a learning or physical disability that would prevent you from taking a CLEP examination under standard conditions, you may request special accommodations and arrangements to take it on either a regularly scheduled test date or at a specially scheduled administration. For details, please contact the CLEP test administrator at the college where you plan to take the test.

V. Taking the Examinations

A person may know a great deal about the subject being tested but not be able to demonstrate it on the test. Knowing how to approach a test is an important part of the testing process. While a command of test-taking skills cannot substitute for knowledge of the subject matter, it can be a significant factor in successful testing.

Test-taking skills enable a person to use all available information to earn a score that truly reflects her or his ability. There are different strategies for approaching different kinds of test questions. For example, free-response questions require a very different approach than do multiple-choice questions. Other factors, such as how the test will be graded, may also influence your approach to the test and your use of test time. Thus, your preparation for a test should include finding out all you can about the test so that you can use the most effective test-taking strategies.

Before taking a test, you should know approximately how many questions are on the test, how much time you will be allowed, how the test will be scored or graded, whether there is a penalty for wrong answers, what types of questions and directions are on the test, and how you will be required to record your answers. All this information for CLEP examinations is discussed in the preceding pages or in the individual examination guides in chapter 7. The following sections summarize some of the strategies that you may use in taking multiple-choice and free-response tests.

Taking Multiple-Choice Tests

1. Listen carefully to the instructions given by the test administrator and read carefully all directions in the test book before you begin to answer the questions.

2. Note the time that the test administrator starts timing the test. As you proceed, make sure that you are not working too slowly. You should have answered at least half the questions in a section when half the time for that section has passed. If you have not reached that point in the section, speed up your pace on the remaining questions.

3. Before answering a question, read the entire question, including all the answer choices. Don't think that because the first or second answer choice looks good to you, it isn't necessary to read the remaining options. Instructions usually tell you to select the "best" answer. Sometimes one answer choice is partially correct but

another option is better; therefore, it is usually a good idea to read all the answers before you choose one.

4. Read and consider every question. Questions that look complicated at first glance may not actually be so difficult once you have read them carefully.

5. Do not puzzle too long over any one question. If you don't know the answer after you've considered it briefly, go on to the next question. Mark that question in your test book and go back to it later, if you have time.

6. Make sure you record your response on the answer sheet or microcomputer screen beside the same number as the number of the question in the test book. If you skip a question, be sure you also skip a space on the answer sheet or microcomputer screen. If you have not answered all the questions in a section when you are told to go on to the next section, be sure to skip the spaces for those questions on your answer sheet. If you discover that you have been marking your answers in the wrong spaces, tell the test supervisor. The test supervisor will note this in the Irregularity Report that will be returned to ETS with the answer sheets, and your answer sheet will be hand-scored.

7. Certain foreign language and mathematics tests have only four answer options to choose from, "A" through "D," even though the answer sheet has five lettered answer spaces for each question. Be careful not to mark answers you intend as "D" in the "E" spaces; "E" answers will not be counted toward your score.

8. Don't hesitate to write notes or to do your calculations in your test book. The test books will not be used again, nor will anything you write in the test book affect your score. Do not, however, make any unnecessary marks on your answer sheet, and be sure you erase all stray marks completely.

9. In trying to determine the correct answer, you may find it helpful to cross out those options that you know are incorrect, and to make marks next to those you think might be correct. If you decide to skip the question and come back to it later, you will save yourself the time of reconsidering all the options.

10. Watch for the following key words in test questions:

all	generally	never	perhaps
always	however	none	rarely
but	may	not	seldom
except	must	often	sometimes
every	necessary	only	usually

When a question or answer option contains words such as "always," "every," "only," "never," and "none," there can be no exceptions to the answer you choose. Use of words such as "often," "rarely," "sometimes," and "generally" indicates that there may be some exceptions to the answer.

11. Do not guess wildly or randomly fill in answers to questions you do not have time to read, because there is a penalty for incorrect answers on CLEP examinations. (An explanation of the procedures used for scoring CLEP examinations is given in chapter 6.) It is improbable that mere guessing will improve your score significantly; it may even lower your score, and it does take time. If, however, you are not sure of the correct answer but have some knowledge of the question and are able to eliminate one or more of the answer choices as wrong, your chance of getting the right answer is improved and, on the average, it will be to your benefit to answer such a question.

12. Do not waste your time looking for clues to right answers based on flaws in question wording or patterns in correct answers. Professionals at the College Board and ETS put a great deal of effort into developing valid, reliable, fair tests. CLEP test development committees are composed of college faculty who are experts in the subject covered by the test and are appointed by the College Board to write test questions and to scrutinize each question that is included on a CLEP test. Committee members make every effort to ensure that the questions are not ambiguous, that they have only one correct answer, and that they cover college-level topics. These committees do not intentionally include "trick" questions. If you think a question is flawed, ask the test administrator to report it, or write immediately to College Board Test Development, P.O. Box 6656, Princeton, NJ 08541-6656. Include the name of the test and test center, the test date, and the number of the test question. All such inquiries are investigated by the ETS test development staff.

Taking Free-Response or Essay Tests

If your college requires the optional free-response or essay portion of any of the four CLEP Subject Examinations in Composition and Literature or the General Examination in English Composition with Essay, you should do some additional preparation for your CLEP test. Taking an essay or a problem-solving test is very different from taking a multiple-choice test, so you will need to use some other strategies.

The essay written as part of the General Examination in English Composition is graded by English professors from a variety of colleges and universities. A process called holistic scoring is used to rate your writing ability. This process is explained in the examination guide for the General Examination in English Composition in chapter 7. The handbook also includes graded sample essays and essay questions.

The optional free-response portions of the Subject Examinations in Composition and Literature, on the other hand, are graded by the faculty of the college you designate as a score recipient. Guidelines and criteria for grading essays are not specified by the College Board or ETS. You may find it helpful, therefore, to talk with someone at your college to find out what criteria will be used to determine whether you will get credit. Ask how much emphasis will be placed on your writing ability and your ability to organize your thoughts as opposed to your knowledge of the subject matter. Find out how much weight will be given to your multiple-choice test score in comparison with your free-response grade in determining whether you will get credit. This will give you an idea of where you should expend the greatest effort in preparing for and taking the test.

Here are some strategies you will find useful in taking any essay test:

1. Before you begin to write, read all the questions carefully and take a few minutes to jot down some ideas you might include in each answer.

2. If you are given a choice of questions to answer, choose the questions that you think you can answer most clearly and knowledgeably.

3. Determine in what order you will answer the questions. Answer those you find the easiest first so that any extra time can be spent on the more difficult questions.

4. When you know which questions you will answer and in what order, determine how much testing time remains and estimate how many minutes you will devote to each question. Unless suggested times are given for the questions or one question appears to require more or less time than the others, allot an equal amount of time to each question.

5. Before answering each question, indicate the number of the question as it is given in the test book. You need not copy the entire question from the question sheet, but it will be helpful to you and to the person grading your test if you indicate briefly the topic you are addressing — particularly if you are not answering the questions in the order in which they appear on the test.

6. Before answering each question, read it again carefully to make sure you are interpreting it correctly. Underline key words, such as those listed below, that often appear in free-response questions. Be sure you know the exact meaning of these words before taking the test.

analyze	demonstrate	enumerate	list
apply	derive	explain	outline
assess	describe	generalize	prove
compare	determine	illustrate	rank
contrast	discuss	interpret	show
define	distinguish	justify	summarize

If a question asks you to "outline," "define," or "summarize," do not write a detailed explanation; if a question asks you to "analyze," "explain," "illustrate," "interpret," or "show," you must do more than briefly describe the topic.

VI. Interpreting Your Scores

College score requirements for awarding credit vary from institution to institution. The College Board, however, recommends that colleges refer to the standards set by the American Council on Education (ACE). All ACE recommendations are the result of careful and periodic review by evaluation teams made up of faculty who are subject-matter experts and technical experts in testing and measurement. To determine whether you are eligible for credit for your CLEP scores, you should refer to the policy of the college you will be attending. The policy will state either the score or the percentile that is required to earn credit at that institution. Many colleges award credit at the score levels recommended by ACE. Many others use the 50th percentile. Some require scores that are higher or lower than these.

The pamphlet *What Your CLEP Score Means,* which you will receive with your score report, gives detailed information about interpreting your scores. A copy of the pamphlet is in Appendix D. A brief explanation appears below.

How CLEP Scores Are Computed

Your score report will show the total score for each CLEP examination you take. For the General Examinations, total scores fall between 200 and 800, and for the Subject Examinations between 20 and 80. For Subject Examinations, percentile ranks for scaled scores will be shown on the score report. For foreign language examinations, subscores are reported.

When your scores are computed, you receive one point for each correct answer. A percentage of the number of your incorrect answers is subtracted from this total to discourage random guessing. As a penalty for guessing, one-fourth of a point is subtracted for each five-choice question you answer incorrectly; one-third of a point is deducted for each incorrect answer to a four-choice question. There is no deduction for a question you do not answer. The resulting figure, called the formula score, is converted to a scaled score between 200 and 800 or between 20 and 80. This conversion makes scores earned on different forms and editions of the same CLEP examination comparable to one another.

How Free-Response Answers and Essays Are Graded

The College Board arranges for college English professors to grade the essays written for the General Examination in English Composition. These carefully selected college faculty consultants represent the current curriculums being taught at two- and four-year institutions nationwide. The faculty consultants receive extensive training and thoroughly review the College Board scoring policies and procedures before grading the essays. Each essay is read and graded by two professors, the sum of the two grades is combined with the multiple-choice score, and the result is reported as a scaled score between 200 and 800. CLEP does not report separate scores for the multiple-choice and essay sections of the General Examination in English Composition because a 45-minute test is not considered extensive enough to assess reliably a candidate's writing skills for college credit. Although the format of the two sections is very different, both measure skills required for expository writing. Knowledge of formal grammar is necessary for the multiple-choice section, but the emphasis in the free-response section is on writing skills rather than grammar.

Composition and Literature Subject Examination essays are evaluated and graded by the colleges that require them, rather than by ETS or the College Board. If you take an optional essay, it will be sent with a copy of your score report (which includes only the results of your multiple-choice test) to the institution you designate on your answer sheet.

You may opt not to have your score sent to a college until after you have seen it. In this case, your essay can still be sent to the college of your choice as long as you request a transcript within 90 days after you take the test. Copies of essays are not held by ETS beyond 90 days or after they have been sent to an institution.

VII. Examination Guides

English Composition (Revised)

Description of the Examination

The General Examination in English Composition (Revised) measures the skills required in most first-year college composition courses. It measures the writing skills needed for college assignments and, in particular, for writing that explains, interprets, analyzes, presents, or supports a point of view. The examination does not cover some topics included in first-year college writing courses, such as research skills or literary analysis. Nor does it require knowledge of grammatical terms as such. However, the student will need to apply the principles and conventions expected of academic written discourse.

The title of the exam reflects significant changes to content specifications made in 1993.

Two versions of the exam are offered. The all-multiple-choice version contains approximately 100 multiple-choice questions to be answered in two separately timed 45-minute sections. The version with essay has a 45-minute multiple-choice section with approximately 55 questions and another section with one essay question to be responded to in 45 minutes.

The essay is evaluated by college teachers of writing who meet at a central location to do the scoring. Each essay is read and assigned a rating by two scorers; the sum of the two ratings is weighted and then combined with the candidate's multiple-choice score. The resulting combined score is reported as a scaled score between 200 and 800. Separate scores are not reported for the multiple-choice and essay sections.

College policies differ with regard to their acceptance of the two versions of the English Composition examination. Some grant credit only for the version with essay; others grant credit only for the all-multiple-choice version; still others grant credit for either of the two versions. Many colleges grant six semester hours (or the equivalent) of credit toward satisfying a liberal arts or distribution requirement in English; others grant six hours of course credit for a specific first-year composition or English course that emphasizes expository writing.

Candidates who are taking the examination to gain credit at a particular college should call or write to the admission office or the counseling and testing office at that college. They should ask for the following information:

- Whether credit is given for the all-multiple-choice version of the CLEP General Examination or for the version with essay, or for the CLEP Subject Examination in Freshman College Composition

- How much credit will be given and for which requirements or courses

- What minimum score is required to receive credit

On the day of the test, candidates should check the title on the cover of the test book to make sure they are taking the appropriate examination.

Knowledge and Skills Required

The multiple-choice questions of the examination measure students' writing skills both at the sentence level and within the context of passages. The current General Examination in English Composition does, in fact, reflect a greater emphasis on revising work in progress than did previous forms of the test. The examination is designed so that average students who have completed the general education requirement in English composition can usually answer about half of the multiple-choice questions correctly.

Skills at the Sentence Level

The examination measures the candidate's awareness of a variety of logical, structural, and grammatical relationships within sentences (these skills are tested by approximately 55 percent of the all-multiple-choice version and 30 percent of the multiple-choice questions in the version with essay). Questions test recognition of acceptable usage relating to:

Sentence boundaries

Economy and clarity of expression

Concord/Agreement: subject-verb; verb tense; pronoun reference, shift, number

Active/passive voice

Diction and idiom

Syntax: parallelism, coordination, subordination, dangling modifiers

Sentence variety

Several kinds of question formats throughout the test are intended to measure these sentence-level skills:

Identifying Sentence Errors — This type of question appears in Section I of both versions and in Section II of the all-multiple-choice version. It requires the candidate to identify wording that violates the standard conventions of written discourse.

Improving Sentences — This type of question appears only in Section I of both versions. It requires the candidate to choose the phrase, clause, or sentence that best conveys the intended meaning of a sentence.

Restructuring Sentences — This type of question appears only in Section II of the all-multiple-choice version. The candidate is given a sentence to reword in order to change emphasis or improve clarity. He or she then must choose from five options the phrase that will likely appear in the new sentence.

Skills in Context

Questions in approximately 45 percent of the all-multiple-choice version and 20 percent of the version with essay measure recognition of the following in the context of works in progress or of published prose.

Main idea, thesis

Organization of ideas in the paragraph or essay

Relevance of evidence, sufficiency of detail, levels of specificity

Audience and purpose (effect on style, tone, language, or argument)

Logic of argument (inductive, deductive reasoning)

Coherence within and between paragraphs

Rhetorical emphasis, effect

Sustaining tense or point of view

Sentence joining, sentence variety

The following kinds of questions measure writing skills in context:

Revising Work in Progress — This type of question appears in Section I of both versions and in Section II of the all-multiple-choice version. The candidate identifies ways to improve an early draft of an essay.

Analyzing Writing — Two prose passages written in very different modes appear only in Section II of the all-multiple-choice version. The candidate answers questions about each passage and about the strategies used by the author of each passage.

The Essay

This section comprises 50 percent of the version with essay. The student is expected to present a point of view in response to a topic and to support it with a logical argument and appropriate evidence.

Scoring the Essays

Shortly after each administration of the CLEP English Composition Test with Essay, college English faculty from throughout the country assemble to score the essays. Each essay is scored independently by two different readers, and the two scores are then combined. This score is weighted approximately equally with the score from the multiple-choice section, then combined with it to yield the reported score for the test.

Each reader awards an essay a score on a scale of 2 to 8; when the two independent scores are summed, the scale for the essay ranges from 4 to 16. In addition, a score of zero, which can be awarded only by the Chief Reader (a faculty member), is given to off-topic essays and blank papers.

The college English teachers who score the essays expect that the writer has a command of English grammar and sentence structure and can use words precisely; they also expect that the essay will be organized, the ideas will be presented logically, and the examples will be pertinent. These are basic requirements for the score of 5, which is the score in the middle of the scoring scale. If the essay writer fails in any of these important aspects of a good essay, then the essay is given a score below 5; if the essay does any of these very well or displays additional qualities of good writing, particularly a strong development of the argument, then the essay receives a score above 5.

Each writing assignment, however, sets unique requirements for the writer. One assignment might require the writer to describe and defend an opinion; another, to describe and argue for a particular solution to a problem. These demands upon the writer can be fulfilled in many different ways, but fairness requires that the scoring take into account what the writers can actually do in the time allotted; they are not expected to produce a polished essay. Thus, the basic standards for scoring are set in terms of what the group of test takers actually writes in response to a given topic.

To provide standards that are specific to each topic, the Chief Reader, Assistant Chief Reader (both faculty members), and members of ETS test development staff convene before the first scoring of the topic and read hundreds of essays written in response to the assignment. From these actual responses, they select those papers that will be used in training the scorers. Such papers represent every point on the scoring scale, present various approaches to fulfilling the assignment well, vary in length, and show examples of particular difficulties in scoring that readers may encounter.

Every essay written in response to a topic is unique. To allow for this uniqueness, scorers derive an idea of the scoring standards from scoring the training samples. No prescribed analytical guides are imposed.

As part of the initial reader training, the Chief Reader explains holistic scoring, which relies on the total impression that a paper creates on the reader. Every aspect of the writing — from spelling to style — is taken into account in this method; however, a single spelling error or a misused comma may not carry the weight that it would in another scoring system, for those minor flaws might be outweighed by good organization and effective use of language. Readers for the CLEP English Composition Test with Essay are chosen because they have experience with student writing and because they know what to expect of a student writer who has only 45 minutes to complete a response to a writing assignment that she or he has never seen before. In addition, scorers who read holistically are encouraged to do three things:

- Understand the requirements of the assignment and the situation for the test taker.

- Read supportively. Look particularly for what has been done well rather than what has been done poorly.

- Compare responses. Compare the quality of each paper to the quality of the papers scored during training.

After the Chief Reader explains the scoring system, including the way in which papers will be distributed to readers and scores will be recorded, the Chief Reader and the readers go over the writing assignment together, discussing the specific requirements of the topic and pertinent specific criteria for scoring. Then readers score the training papers, discussing these also so that the basis for awarding particular scores to individual sample papers becomes clear. When the readers agree on the scoring standards, as demonstrated by their scoring of the samples, they begin scoring the actual papers. At that time, the Chief Reader, Assistant Chief Reader, and table leaders begin the quality-control procedures that will be maintained throughout the readings. Scored papers are rescored at random by the table leader, an experienced reader who is in charge of maintaining standards in a group of about six other readers. Some of these papers are then rescored by the Chief Reader and the Assistant Chief Reader. In order to reinforce the criteria, new samples are scored by the entire group periodically.

Despite these quality controls, some essays will receive discrepant scores, or scores more than two points apart on the 7-point scale. Such papers will be given to the Chief Reader, Assistant Chief Reader, or designated table leaders for a third independent scoring. As a result of this third scoring, one of the two original scores will be eliminated; the third reader's score will be used instead, along with the original score identical to or closest to the third reader's score.

Sample Questions

The 50 sample questions that follow are similar to questions on the all-multiple-choice version of the General Examination in English Composition; however, they do not appear on the actual test.

Before attempting to answer the sample questions, read all the information about the English Composition examination on the preceding pages. Additional suggestions for preparing for CLEP examinations are provided in chapter 4.

Try to answer correctly as many questions as possible. Even if you are taking the version with essay, you will find it helpful to attempt the sample questions for both sections. The correct answers are given in Appendix B.

Sample essay questions and sample essays follow the multiple-choice questions.

SECTION I

(These are samples of questions that appear in Section I of both the all-multiple-choice version and the version with essay.)

Identifying Sentence Errors

Directions: The following sentences test your knowledge of grammar, usage, diction (choice of words), and idiom.

Some sentences are correct.
No sentence contains more than one error.

You will find that the error, if there is one, is underlined and lettered. Assume that elements of the sentence that are not underlined are correct and cannot be changed. In choosing answers, follow the requirements of standard written English.

If there is an error, select the one underlined part that must be changed to make the sentence correct and fill in the corresponding oval on your answer sheet.

If there is no error, select answer (E).

Example:

Sample Answer
Ⓐ ● Ⓒ Ⓓ Ⓔ

The other delegates and
    A
him immediately accepted
  B   C
the resolution drafted by
                D
the neutral states. No error
              E

1. Hydroelectric dams work <u>on a simple</u> principle: <u>the greater the</u>
    A B
   distance that the water has <u>to fall</u>, the more the power that
    C
   <u>was generated.</u> <u>No error</u>
    D E

   Ⓐ Ⓑ Ⓒ Ⓓ Ⓔ

2. Alexis <u>has discovered</u> that she can express her creativity more freely
    A
   <u>through</u> her <u>sketches</u> <u>and not in</u> her photography. <u>No error</u>
    B C D E

   Ⓐ Ⓑ Ⓒ Ⓓ Ⓔ

3. Ms. Marco found that it was easier for her <u>teaching</u> children
    A
   arithmetic <u>once</u> <u>they became</u> <u>familiar with</u> the idea of a set. <u>No error</u>
    B C D E

   Ⓐ Ⓑ Ⓒ Ⓓ Ⓔ

4. Many readers <u>still think</u> of Sinclair Lewis, whose strength
    A
   <u>was supposedly</u> his <u>ability to tell</u> a story, <u>as one of</u> America's best
    B C D
   social critics. <u>No error</u>
    E

   Ⓐ Ⓑ Ⓒ Ⓓ Ⓔ

5. <u>Although</u> a lottery may seem a <u>relatively easy</u> way for a state
    A B
   <u>to increase</u> revenues, <u>they</u> may encourage some individuals to gamble
    C D
   excessively. <u>No error</u>
    E

   Ⓐ Ⓑ Ⓒ Ⓓ Ⓔ

6. <u>Even when using</u> a calculator, you must have a basic <u>understanding</u>
    A B
   of mathematics if <u>one expects</u> to solve complex problems <u>correctly</u>.
    C D
   <u>No error</u>
    E

   Ⓐ Ⓑ Ⓒ Ⓓ Ⓔ

7. Although science offers the hope <u>of preventing</u> serious genetic
                                   A
   diseases, <u>there is</u> difficult ethical questions <u>raised by</u> the <u>possibility</u>
             B   C   D
   of altering human heredity. <u>No error</u>
                                    E

   Ⓐ Ⓑ Ⓒ Ⓓ Ⓔ

8. If they <u>would have</u> <u>known</u> how capricious the winds on Lake
           A   B
   Winasteke were, the boys would have sailed in the <u>larger</u> <u>of their</u> two
                                                     C   D
   boats. <u>No error</u>
              E

   Ⓐ Ⓑ Ⓒ Ⓓ Ⓔ

9. Even the careful listener <u>could scarcely</u> tell liberal <u>from</u> conservative
                            A   B
   among the speakers, for the issue had become <u>a highly</u> emotional
                                                C
   <u>one</u>. <u>No error</u>
    D   E

   Ⓐ Ⓑ Ⓒ Ⓓ Ⓔ

10. <u>To learn more</u> about Hispanic culture, we invited a <u>lecturer who</u> had
              A   B
    spoken frequently <u>with regard to</u> <u>the life of</u> early settlers in Santa Fe.
                      C   D
    <u>No error</u>
        E

    Ⓐ Ⓑ Ⓒ Ⓓ Ⓔ

Improving Sentences

Directions: The following sentences test correctness and
effectiveness of expression. In choosing answers, follow the
requirements of standard written English: that is, pay attention to
grammar, diction (choice of words), sentence construction, and
punctuation.

In each of the following sentences, part of the sentence or the entire
sentence is underlined. Beneath each sentence you will find five
versions of the underlined part. Choice A repeats the original; the
other four are different.

Choose the answer that best expresses the meaning of the original sentence. If you think the original is better than any of the alternatives, choose it; otherwise choose one of the others. Your choice should produce the most effective sentence — one that is clear and precise, without awkwardness or ambiguity.

Example   **Sample Answer**

Laura Ingalls Wilder published her first book <u>and she was sixty-five years old then.</u>

(A) and she was sixty-five years old then
(B) when she was sixty-five
(C) being age sixty-five years old
(D) upon the reaching of sixty-five years
(E) at the time when she was sixty-five

11. Because the eleven women functioned as a <u>team is why they had a successful season.</u>

    (A) team is why they had a successful season
    (B) team, they had a success this season
    (C) team, they had a successful season
    (D) team, success was theirs this season
    (E) team is why their season was a success

    Ⓐ Ⓑ Ⓒ Ⓓ Ⓔ

12. <u>In 1827 *Freedom's Journal* was the first Black American newspaper in the United States, it was published in New York City.</u>

    (A) In 1827 *Freedom's Journal* was the first Black American newspaper in the United States, it was published in New York City.
    (B) In 1827 the first Black American newspaper in the United States, *Freedom's Journal*, was published in New York City.
    (C) In New York City in 1827 *Freedom's Journal*, the first Black American newspaper in the United States, was published there.
    (D) With publication in New York City in 1827, it was the first Black American newspaper in the United States, *Freedom's Journal*.
    (E) The first Black American newspaper published in the United States was when there was *Freedom's Journal* in New York City in 1827.

    Ⓐ Ⓑ Ⓒ Ⓓ Ⓔ

13. Astronomers have developed extremely sophisticated instruments which is helpful for measuring the properties of objects in space.

    (A) instruments, which is helpful for measuring the properties of objects in space
    (B) instruments to help measure the properties of objects in space
    (C) instruments, which are helpful for measurement of space objects' properties
    (D) instruments helpful to measure the properties of objects in space
    (E) instruments, a help for measuring the properties of objects in space

    Ⓐ Ⓑ Ⓒ Ⓓ Ⓔ

14. Foreign correspondents are like birds of passage, resting for a few weeks, then flying off again to a new place.

    (A) then flying off again
    (B) after which again they fly off
    (C) then they fly off again
    (D) when once again they fly off
    (E) but soon they are flying off again

    Ⓐ Ⓑ Ⓒ Ⓓ Ⓔ

15. Reducing individual taxes while eliminating as much waste as possible are traditional methods for increasing a nation's economy.

    (A) are traditional methods for increasing
    (B) is a traditional method for increasing
    (C) is a traditional method of stimulating
    (D) traditionally are methods for increasing
    (E) are traditional methods of stimulating

    Ⓐ Ⓑ Ⓒ Ⓓ Ⓔ

16. Arguably the most distinctive regional cuisine in the United States, the South is noted for such specialties as Brunswick stew and hush puppies.

    (A) the South is noted for such specialties as
    (B) the South has such specialties of note as
    (C) the South includes among its noteworthy specialties
    (D) southern cooking includes such noteworthy specialties as
    (E) southern cooking is including such specialties of note as

    Ⓐ Ⓑ Ⓒ Ⓓ Ⓔ

17. The complex trajectories of the knuckleball providing one of baseball's greatest challenges to physicists.

    (A) The complex trajectories of the knuckleball providing
    (B) The knuckleball with its complex trajectories having provided
    (C) Providing that the complex trajectories of the knuckleball is
    (D) It is the complex trajectories of the knuckleball providing
    (E) The complex trajectories of the knuckleball provide

    Ⓐ Ⓑ Ⓒ Ⓓ Ⓔ

18. After the Civil Rights Act of 1964, most inequalities in public accommodations were essentially eliminated, but less progress was made in school desegregation.

    (A) but less progress was made in school desegregation
    (B) with school desegregation being the lesser of the two in terms of progress
    (C) school desegregation having lesser progress
    (D) for lesser progress was to be seen in school desegregation
    (E) and school desegregation showed less progress

    Ⓐ Ⓑ Ⓒ Ⓓ Ⓔ

19. Home computers themselves are no longer expensive, but video display terminals, printers, and links to other computers cause the total financial cost of a computer system to rise up greatly.

    (A) cause the total financial cost of a computer system to rise up greatly
    (B) greatly increase thte total cost of a computer system
    (C) highly inflate the cost totals of a computer system
    (D) drive up the expense of a computer system totally
    (E) totally add to the expense of a computer system

    Ⓐ Ⓑ Ⓒ Ⓓ Ⓔ

20. Today's fashion designers must consider both how much a fabric costs and its wearability.

    (A) its wearability
    (B) is it going to wear well
    (C) if it has wearability
    (D) how well it wears
    (E) the fabric's ability to wear well

    Ⓐ Ⓑ Ⓒ Ⓓ Ⓔ

Revising Work in Progress

Directions: Each of the following selections is an early draft of a student essay in which the sentences have been numbered for easy reference. Some parts of the selections need to be changed.

Read each selection and then answer the questions that follow. Some questions are about particular sentences or parts of sentences and ask you to improve sentence structure and diction (word choice). In making these decisions, follow the conventions of standard written English. Other questions refer to the entire essay or parts of the essay and ask you to consider organization, development, and effectiveness of language in relation to purpose and audience. After you choose each answer, fill in the corresponding oval on your answer sheet.

Questions 21-25 are based on the following draft of a student essay.

(1) *I used to be convinced that people didn't actually win radio contests; I thought that the excited winners I heard were only actors.* (2) *Sure, people could win T-shirts.* (3) *They couldn't win anything of real value.*

(4) *I've always loved sports.* (5) *Unlike my friends, who fall asleep to "Top 40 Radio," I listen to "Sports Night with Dave Sims."* (6) *His show is hardly usual fare for a young woman.* (7) *One night I heard Dave Sims announce a sports trivia contest with cash prizes of two thousand dollars.* (8) *I jump at the chance to combine my talk-show knowledge with everything my father had taught me about sports.* (9) *I sent in my self-addressed stamped envelope.* (10) *I forgot about the whole matter.* (11) *Then the questionnaire appeared in my mailbox ten days later.* (12) *Its arrival gave me a rude surprise.* (13) *Instead of sitting down and whipping through it, I trudged to libraries and spent hours digging for answers to such obscure questions as "Which NHL goalie holds the record for most career shutouts?"*

(14) *Finally, after days of double-checking answers, I mailed off my answer sheet, certain I would hear no more about the matter.* (15) *Certain, until two weeks later, I ripped open the envelope with the NBC peacock and read "Congratulations..."* (16) *I was a winner, a winner of more than a T-shirt.*

21. Which of the following is the best way to revise the underlined portions of sentences 2 and 3 (reproduced below) so that the two sentences are combined into one?

    Sure, people could win T-shirts. They couldn't win anything of real value.

    (A) T-shirts, and they couldn't win
    (B) T-shirts, but they couldn't win
    (C) T-shirts, but not being able to win
    (D) T-shirts, so they do not win
    (E) T-shirts, while there was no winning   Ⓐ Ⓑ Ⓒ Ⓓ Ⓔ

22. Which of the following sentences, if added after sentence 3, would best link the first paragraph with the rest of the essay?

    (A) I have held this opinion about contests for a long time.
    (B) The prizes offered did not inspire me to enter the contests.
    (C) However, I recently changed my opinion about these contests.
    (D) Usually the questions on these contests are really easy to answer.
    (E) Sometimes my friends try to convince me to enter such contests.   Ⓐ Ⓑ Ⓒ Ⓓ Ⓔ

23. In the context of the second paragraph, which of the following is the best version of the underlined portion of sentence 8 (reproduced below)?

    I jump at the chance to combine my talk-show knowledge with everything my father had taught me about sports.

    (A) (As it is now)
    (B) I jumped at the chance to combine
    (C) Having jumped at the chance to combine
    (D) Jumping at the chance and combining
    (E) Jumping at the chance by combining   Ⓐ Ⓑ Ⓒ Ⓓ Ⓔ

24. Which of the following is the best way to revise and combine sentences 9 and 10 (reproduced below)?

    I sent in my self-addressed stamped envelope. I forgot about the whole matter.

    (A) Having sent in my self-addressed stamped envelope, the whole matter was forgotten.
    (B) After sending in my self-addressed stamped envelope, the matter was wholly forgotten.
    (C) After my self-addressed stamped envelope was sent in, it was then that I forgot the whole matter.
    (D) After sending in my self-addressed stamped envelope, I forgot about the whole matter.
    (E) Forgetting about the whole matter after sending in my self-addressed stamped envelope.

    Ⓐ Ⓑ Ⓒ Ⓓ Ⓔ

25. All of the following strategies are used by the writer of the passage EXCEPT

    (A) selecting specific examples
    (B) telling a story to develop a point
    (C) criticizing those whose opinions differ from hers
    (D) building suspense with references to the passage of time
    (E) disproving the assumption stated in the first sentence of the passage

    Ⓐ Ⓑ Ⓒ Ⓓ Ⓔ

<u>Questions 26-30</u> are based on the following early draft of a letter to the editor of a local newspaper.

(1) *Our community needs more parks and play areas.* (2) *Living in a world where concrete surrounds us, it is important that we create places that are green and natural so that children can run and play.*

(3) *It is possible to do much with little expense to the city.* (4) *An abandoned lot can become a big patch of green grass ideal for running games.* (5) *And buying expensive playground equipment and strange pieces of modern art for children to climb on is unnecessary.* (6) *Children will climb on anything if one lets them.* (7) *A large concrete pipe or an old truck with its wheels and doors removed makes an imaginative plaything.* (8) *Simply remove any part that may be breakable or unsafe, then paint the equipment with bright colors.* (9) *Bury the truck or pipe a foot or two deep so that it is stable.* (10) *Great opportunities for fun!* (11) *Children can play for hours, crawling through a secret tunnel or navigating to a distant planet.* (12) *Neighborhood committees could contribute other discards.*

(13) *We should do these things because children need oases in this concrete desert we live in.* (14) *This may take time, but if people get together and contribute both ideas and labor, much can be completed successfully.*

26. Which of the following is the best way to revise the underlined portion of sentence 2 (reproduced below)?

    Living in a world where concrete surrounds us, it is important that we create places that are green and natural so that children can run and play.

    (A) Living in a world where concrete surrounds us, the important thing is to
    (B) We live in a world where concrete surrounds us, it is important that we
    (C) Being surrounded by a world of concrete, it is important to
    (D) Surrounding us with a world of concrete, we need to
    (E) Surrounded by a world of concrete, we need to

    Ⓐ Ⓑ Ⓒ Ⓓ Ⓔ

27. Which of the following would best replace "And" at the beginning of sentence 5?

    (A) Furthermore,
    (B) Instead,
    (C) Despite this,
    (D) Nevertheless,
    (E) Excepting this,

    Ⓐ Ⓑ Ⓒ Ⓓ Ⓔ

28. The writer of the passage could best improve sentence 12 by

    (A) acknowledging drawbacks to suggestions
    (B) providing specific examples
    (C) including personal opinions
    (D) discussing other community problems
    (E) defining the idea of a neighborhood

    Ⓐ Ⓑ Ⓒ Ⓓ Ⓔ

29. In context, the best phrase to replace *"do these things"* in sentence 13 is

    (A) accomplish our intentions
    (B) help these children
    (C) consider other options
    (D) build these play areas
    (E) have new ideas

    Ⓐ Ⓑ Ⓒ Ⓓ Ⓔ

30. Which is the best version of the underlined portion of sentence 14 (reproduced below)?

    This may take time, but if people get together and contribute both ideas and labor, much can be completed successfully.

    (A) (as it is now)
    (B) and if people get together and they contribute
    (C) but if people will get together and they will also contribute
    (D) but if people get together and they would have contributed
    (E) however, if people get together, also contributing

    Ⓐ Ⓑ Ⓒ Ⓓ Ⓔ

SECTION II

(The following types of questions appear only in the all-multiple-choice version, not in the version with essay. Section II of the all-multiple-choice version also includes more of the "Identifying Sentence Errors" and "Revising Work in Progress" questions described previously.)

Restructuring Sentences

Directions: Effective revision requires choosing among the many options available to a writer. The following questions test your ability to use these options effectively.

Revise each of the sentences below according to the directions that follow it. Some directions require you to change only part of the original sentence; others require you to change the entire sentence. You may need to omit or add certain words in constructing an acceptable revision, but you should keep the meaning of your revised sentence as close to the meaning of the original sentence as the directions permit. Your new sentence should follow the conventions of standard written English and should be clear and concise.

Look through answer choices A-E under each question for the exact word or phrase that is included in your revised sentence and fill in the corresponding space on your answer sheet. If you have thought of a revision that does not include any of the words or phrases listed, try to revise the sentence again so that it does include the wording in one of the answer choices.

You may make notes in your test book, but be sure to mark your answers on the separate answer sheet.

Examples:

I. **Sentence:** Owing to her political skill, Ms. French had many supporters.

Directions: Begin with Many people supported.

(A) so
(B) while
(C) although
(D) because
(E) and

Sample Answer

Your rephrased sentence will probably read: "Many people supported Ms. French because she was politically skillful." This new sentence contains the correct answer: (D), "because." None of the other choices will fit into an effective, grammatically correct sentence that retains the original meaning.

II. **Sentence:** Coming to the city as a young man, he found a job as a newspaper reporter.

Directions: Change Coming to He came.

(A) and so he found
(B) and found
(C) and there he had found
(D) and then finding
(E) and had found

Sample Answer

Your rephrased sentence will probably read: "He came to the city as a young man and found a job as a newspaper reporter." This new sentence contains the correct answer: (B), "and found."

31. Should Antarctica's average temperature ever rise ten degrees, the oceans of the world would drown out all low-lying coastal regions.

Begin with If Antarctica's average temperature rises.

(A) should drown
(B) will drown
(C) will have drowned
(D) will result in the drowning
(E) drowning would be

Ⓐ Ⓑ Ⓒ Ⓓ Ⓔ

32. Ms. Perry claimed that, because of special promotions by the airline industry, air travel has become "as American as apple pie."

    Change that, because to that special.

    (A) industry, making
    (B) industry, which has made
    (C) industry had made
    (D) industry have made
    (E) industry, and they have made

    Ⓐ Ⓑ Ⓒ Ⓓ Ⓔ

33. Luther Burbank's development of an edible pitless plum was accomplished by crossing a pitless plum tree many times with standard varieties of plum trees.

    Begin with Luther Burbank.

    (A) by many crossings
    (B) frequent crossings
    (C) by repeatedly crossing
    (D) plum was crossed many times
    (E) it was by repeated crossings

    Ⓐ Ⓑ Ⓒ Ⓓ Ⓔ

34. Most people who run in marathons have little expectation of being among the first to finish.

    Begin with Few people.

    (A) lack expectation
    (B) expect to be
    (C) expect their being
    (D) have no expectation
    (E) have much to expect

    Ⓐ Ⓑ Ⓒ Ⓓ Ⓔ

35. The new ideas that influenced several American painters were brought to the United States in the 1940's by artists who left Europe during the war.

    Begin with The artists.

    (A) and brought
    (B) ideas have been brought
    (C) war have brought
    (D) thus bringing
    (E) war brought

    Ⓐ Ⓑ Ⓒ Ⓓ Ⓔ

36. Posters, buttons, and balloons were considered by many volunteers to be the most effective vote-getting devices.

    Change were considered to considered.

    (A) balloons in the light of
    (B) balloons would be
    (C) balloons that
    (D) balloons the
    (E) balloons as most

    Ⓐ Ⓑ Ⓒ Ⓓ Ⓔ

37. "My production of *Hamlet* will have only a shadow of the Ghost on stage, with a recorded tape and no actor," the director announced.

    Begin with The director announced that.

    (A) my *Hamlet* will have
    (B) her production of *Hamlet* had
    (C) her production of *Hamlet* would have
    (D) her production of *Hamlet* was
    (E) *Hamlet* were to have

    Ⓐ Ⓑ Ⓒ Ⓓ Ⓔ

38. Madeline's seemingly innocuous announcement caused considerable consternation among her students.

    Change caused to but it caused.

    (A) announcement, and it seemed
    (B) announcement seemed
    (C) announcement which seemed
    (D) announcement, seemingly
    (E) announcement, despite seeming

    Ⓐ Ⓑ Ⓒ Ⓓ Ⓔ

39. When we consider how technology encroaches on our daily life, we can understand why many works of modern art are strident and fragmented.

    Change we can understand to explains.

    Your new sentence will begin with which of the following?

    (A) Technology encroaching
    (B) On account of technology's encroaching
    (C) The fact of technology's encroachment
    (D) Due to the encroachment of technology
    (E) The encroachment of technology

    Ⓐ Ⓑ Ⓒ Ⓓ Ⓔ

Analyzing Writing

Directions: Each of the following passages consists of numbered sentences. Because the passages are part of longer writing samples, they do not necessarily constitute a complete discussion of the issues presented.

Read each passage carefully and answer the questions that follow it. The questions test your awareness of a writer's purpose and of characteristics of prose that are important to good writing.

Questions 40-45 refer to the following paragraph.

(1) In Lovedu society, the individual was held to be inviolate. (2) The exercise of force of any kind, except in dealing with the very young infant, was never approved. (3) Even the courts of law refrained from executing their decisions, on the principle that to do so would be to coerce, and coercion should be avoided. (4) The parties involved in a case were expected to work out matters between them, aiming at a conciliatory solution and implementing the court decision through mutual agreement. (5) The culprit, if there was one, was left to pay restitution at his or her own pace. (6) Preferably, disputes were settled before they came to the point where they had to be submitted for a court decision. (7) If an individual wronged another, either deliberately or accidentally, it was the usual practice to send a conciliator to express regret and to offer a goat as a gesture of reconciliation. (8) This procedure was urged first of all, as the preferred solution, even when disagreements were brought to court. (9) Explicit condemnation was avoided as violating the individual, and as not leading to rehabilitation; punishment was seen as bad because it meant vengeful retribution.

40. Which of the following best describes the relationship of sentence 1 to the rest of the paragraph?

    (A) It establishes the organization for the paragraph as a whole.
    (B) It establishes the basis for comparisons later in the paragraph between one kind of society and another.
    (C) It demonstrates the writer's authority on the subject to be discussed in the paragraph.
    (D) It presents the principle on which the behavior described in the rest of the paragraph is based.
    (E) It describes the idea that will be refuted in the rest of the paragraph.

    Ⓐ Ⓑ Ⓒ Ⓓ Ⓔ

41. Which of the following best describes the function of sentence 4?

    (A) It indicates the procedure by which the court's decisions were carried out.
    (B) It demonstrates the laxness of the court in not executing its own decisions.
    (C) It gives an example of what can happen when the courts do not exercise common sense.
    (D) It alludes to the disorder that resulted from the court's decision.
    (E) It forces the reader to make an independent judgment about the issues in the case.

    Ⓐ Ⓑ Ⓒ Ⓓ Ⓔ

42. In sentence 5, the effect of using the expression "if there was one" is to

    (A) reveal the writer's uncertainty about the details of the sequence of events
    (B) emphasize the court decision mentioned in sentence 4 by referring back to it
    (C) reinforce the idea that assigning blame was not always important in the view of justice under discussion
    (D) suggest the carelessness inherent in this method of dealing with injustices
    (E) prepare the reader for the statement about court decisions in sentence 6

    Ⓐ Ⓑ Ⓒ Ⓓ Ⓔ

43. The function of sentence 7 is primarily to

    (A) illustrate the ineffectiveness of informal methods of dealing with conflict
    (B) present a specific incident that symbolizes the issues discussed in the paragraph
    (C) give an example to support the generalization in sentence 5
    (D) indicate the method by which the ideal described in sentence 6 would be realized
    (E) prepare for the suggestion in sentence 8 that most disputes eventually ended up in court

    Ⓐ Ⓑ Ⓒ Ⓓ Ⓔ

44. Which treatment of sentence 6 is most needed?

   (A) Leave it as it is.
   (B) It should be placed after sentence 7.
   (C) It should be omitted.
   (D) "Preferably" should be changed to "In any event".
   (E) "Preferably, disputes were settled" should be changed to "Disputes were thus settled".

   Ⓐ Ⓑ Ⓒ Ⓓ Ⓔ

45. The purpose of the paragraph is primarily to

   (A) tell the story of a society that is not well known
   (B) demonstrate the extremes of behavior arising from a specific idea
   (C) describe a particular system of social interactions
   (D) analyze the effects on society of dogmatic ideas
   (E) propose a change in methods of administering justice

   Ⓐ Ⓑ Ⓒ Ⓓ Ⓔ

Questions 46-50 refer to the following passage.

(1) Michael Goldman wrote in a poem, "When the Muse comes She doesn't tell you to write;/She says get up for a minute, I've something to show you, stand here." (2) What made me look up at that roadside tree?

(3) The road to Grundy, Virginia, is, as you might expect, a narrow scrawl scribbled all over the most improbably peaked and hunched mountains you ever saw. (4) The few people who live along the road also seem peaked and hunched. (5) But what on earth...? (6) It was hot, sunny summer. (7) The road was just bending off sharply to the right. (8) I hadn't seen a house in miles, and none was in sight. (9) At the apogee of the road's curve grew an enormous oak, a massive bur oak 200 years old, 150 feet high, an oak whose lowest limb was beyond the span of the highest ladder. (10) I looked up; there were clothes spread all over the tree. (11) Red shirts, blue trousers, black pants, little baby smocks — they weren't hung from branches. (12) They were outside, carefully spread, splayed as if to dry, on the outer leaves of the great oak's crown. (13) Were there pillowcases, blankets? (14) I can't remember. (15) There was a gay assortment of cotton underwear, yellow dresses, children's green sweaters, plaid skirts.... (16) You know roads. (17) A bend comes and you take it, thoughtlessly, moving on. (18) I looked behind me for another split second, astonished; both sides of the tree's canopy, clear to the top, bore clothes.

46. Which of the following best describes the relationship between the two paragraphs in this passage?

   (A) The second paragraph answers the question at the end of the first.
   (B) The second paragraph offers a concrete illustration of the quotation in the first.
   (C) The second paragraph takes an opposite point of view from the first.
   (D) The second paragraph generalizes about the quotation in the first.
   (E) The second paragraph is an elaborate contradiction of the thesis in the first.

   Ⓐ Ⓑ Ⓒ Ⓓ Ⓔ

47. Which of the following most accurately describes what happens in the second paragraph?

   (A) The speaker has a poetic vision symbolizing cleansing renewal.
   (B) The speaker has a hallucination brought on by the heat.
   (C) The speaker tries to explain how what was seen is possible.
   (D) The speaker sees a tree full of flowers and imagines they are someone's washing.
   (E) The speaker sees a large tree inexplicably covered with clothes spread to dry.

   Ⓐ Ⓑ Ⓒ Ⓓ Ⓔ

48. The descriptive details in sentences 9-15 provide a

   (A) precise visual image
   (B) picture of something unearthly
   (C) representation of a blur of color
   (D) view from a child's perspective
   (E) distorted sense of motion

   Ⓐ Ⓑ Ⓒ Ⓓ Ⓔ

49. Which of the following pairs of words best describes the speaker's reaction to the experience?

   (A) Ecstasy and fear
   (B) Dismay and wonder
   (C) Delight and fear
   (D) Disgust and disbelief
   (E) Wonder and delight

   Ⓐ Ⓑ Ⓒ Ⓓ Ⓔ

50. The main implication of the passage is that

   (A) you never know what you will see on country roads
   (B) people are resourceful in finding ways to rise above domestic tasks
   (C) inspiration or vision is often a matter of chance or caprice
   (D) the poet sees more intensely than other people
   (E) the Muse encourages only the eccentric to write

Ⓐ Ⓑ Ⓒ Ⓓ Ⓔ

Sample Essays and Essay Topics

The section that follows includes directions as they appear in the test book, as well as a sample essay topic and three essays that were written in response to the topic. Although the papers written by candidates are actually rated on a scale from 8 to 2, the three essays presented here have been assigned one of only three ratings — high, middle, or low — to illustrate the scoring process in simplified form. Rating these three papers can give you a sense of the general quality of the papers and of the scoring process. You should read the essays and use the criteria described earlier to assign a rating (high, middle, or low) to each one. Then compare these ratings with those given at the end of the essays.

Following the three sample essays are two additional essay topics that may be used to practice writing essays.

Directions: You will have 45 minutes to plan and write an essay on the topic specified. Read the topic carefully. You are expected to spend a few moments considering the topic and organizing your thoughts before you begin writing. *Do not write on a topic other than the one specified. An essay on a topic of your own choice is not acceptable.*

The essay is intended to give you an opportunity to demonstrate your ability to write effectively. Take care to express your thoughts on the topic clearly and to make them of interest to the reader. Be specific, using supporting examples whenever appropriate. Remember that how well you write is much more important than how much you write.

Sample Topic 1:

In describing the times of the French Revolution, Charles Dickens wrote: "It was the best of times, it was the worst of times." Think about how Dickens' description might apply to today's times. Write an essay in which you use specific examples to explain how today could be described as *both* the best of times and the worst of times.

Essay A

"It was the best of times, it was the worst of times." Charles Dickens wrote this phrase to describe the times of the French revolution. This concept not only applies to historic times, but also to the present.

It is true that we live in both the best and the worst of times even though there might possibly be a small number of people taking sides. People present arguments stating that we are in the best of times, better off than we have ever been. But again, there are those people on the opposite side saying we are not making any progress at all. What these people don't realize is that they are both correct in their opinions. Perhaps we are better off than two-hundred years ago but aren't making any progress to prove that point.

With each new day we discover more things and make more technological advances. These advances include such things as more powerful rockets, better agricultural methods, and cures for diseases once considered terminal. One very important improvement that these advances has caused is the increase in the number of opportunities open to both men and women. You can look all around and see the endless number of things women can and will accomplish in today's society. The advances in our technology have also resulted in better wages for workers, not to mention better jobs, and, also, safety and efficiency in the many commodities of our everyday lives.

The times of today can also be termed the worst of times because of the many problems we face. We have heard so often of a shortage of one thing or another. We seem to be running out of the things that are vital to our existence. A major problem today is unemployment. Technology has introduced us to the robot age; thus, putting many laborers out of work. Many old people who grew up in "the olden days" often remark on the morals of today's young people. Our parents and grandparents believe that children grew up properly when they were young because they had more discipline. This resulted not only in higher personal morals but also closer family bonds.

Today we live in a society where things are more efficient, safer, and much more convenient for our ease and comfort. In this aspect we exist in "the best of times"; but, perhaps, our struggle for improvement has also caused us to suffer the consequences. "It was the best of times, it was the worst of times."

Essay B

The media and other attitude-shapers would have us believe that disaster is at our doorstep, the youth of this country have little faith that they will reach middle age, and millions of people all over the world are sick and starving. The general social mood today is one of pessimism, and yet is this really the worst of times? As Dickens so wisely observed, hope and despair can co-exist: the close of the twentieth century, just like the close of the eighteenth century, can as easily be called "the best of times" as "the worst of times."

Clearly, the future of the U.S. looks bleak in comparison to its prosperous past. Most Americans lack faith in the very institutions that once formed the backbone of the nation: the family, the public school and government. While our tax dollars are funnelled into preparations for the most gruesome and permanent destruction ever conceived, millions of the world's people are suffering for lack of food and medicine. Moreso than in any other period in history, the disrepancy between the standards of living of the rich and poor are staggering, and each day the gap grows wider. The impending doom of nuclear war, and the more immediate threat of poverty and starvation for millions all over the world in order to fuel the vision of destruction, create an impression that this is the worst of all possible worlds.

However, the prospects for curing today's social ills are bright indeed, and the outcome of our collective nightmare may well be a united world dedicated to the health of the planet. In the breakdown of our institutions lies a change for a new order, and the types of organizations that replace the old in our lifetimes are likely to bring humanity to a greater achievement of our social values than have ever before been realized. The very technology that is currently being used for spoiling the rich and planning world disaster could just as easily serve all the world's people, to meet the basic human needs of health, food, and shelter for all. Our era is one of revolution and immense progress in science and technology: this is a promise that if used wisely and with humanity, technology may help to bring about "the best of times."

The creative solution to today's world-wide problems lies not just in technology, but in the shared responsibility for the future of our race and our planet. To make these "the best of times," it is our challenge to reverse the trends that threaten to destroy us. Increased participation by people united with this one purpose, all over the world, is a positive trend. The "best of times" are those in which all mankind sees the world as one, and every person becomes an active world citizen: creating "the best of times" is the greatest challenge of all times.

Essay C

Revolution means change and it can be in the best of time when it brings out the changes it needs.

In order to make a country great, the government must look to the social and economic upliftment of the people. Many people nowadays need jobs in order to get the necessary things in their life. If there will be a decrease in the percentage of unemployment, less problems will arise.

It is the best of time when everyone has a job, the elderly are taken care of, there is equal opportunity for every one, desegregation in school, no long lines in the social services, no big companies are closed and people are well-secured in their jobs.

Today could be the worst of time if many people could not have jobs. If the situation is like this, many people will have great problems. It is like in the French revolution when many people revolted against the government because they were discontented. They were discontented because they saw that only the upper class or the elite had the nice things in life.

Ratings by Evaluators:

Essay A — middle rating
Essay B — high rating
Essay C — low rating

Sample Topic 2:

The school board has proposed to alleviate a serious budget problem for next year by eliminating certain extracurricular activities. The board has so far proposed eliminating the marching band and football trips outside the immediate vicinity. Next year, in the event of continued tight budgets, the board will eliminate student newspapers and courses in drama, music, and art.

As a thoughtful and concerned citizen, write an essay setting forth your ideas on this subject. You may either support these budget cuts or oppose them. Draw upon your own educational experiences or those of your children, if you wish to do so. You need not know the details of school finance. For purposes of your essay you may invent some statistics and situations related to the school system that are appropriate to your argument.

Sample Topic 3:

Some people feel that studying "traditional" subjects such as history, sciences, and literature does not have much importance today. They believe that education should be directed toward a career and that the most significant studies in college are those that will help one earn a living in today's society. As examples, they point to accounting courses, secretarial studies, electronics courses, and data processing courses.

Write an essay in which you support or refute this argument for career-oriented education. Be sure to give reasons for your opinion and to support those reasons with specific examples from your reading or experience.

Study Resources

The books listed here can help you improve your ability to express your ideas clearly in writing. They will help you become aware of the processes and the principles involved in presenting your ideas logically and expressing them clearly and effectively. They also describe the standard conventions of language used for written discourse. (Contact your local college to see whether it recommends additional textbooks to help you prepare for this examination.)

In addition to reading these books and engaging in the exercises they suggest, you should also practice writing. Ideally, you should try writing on a variety of subjects and issues, starting with those you know best and care about most. Ask someone you know and respect to respond to what you write and to help you discover which parts of your writing communicate effectively and which parts need revision to make the meaning clear. You should also try to read the works of published writers in a wide range of subjects, paying particular attention to the ways in which they use language to express their meaning.

Many libraries do not carry textbooks as a policy. If you can't find any of the following textbooks at the library, see whether the college bookstore has a used copy. If you can't locate the most recent edition, an edition that is one or two years older will suffice for most subject areas. As a final option, purchase a new copy of the suggested textbook as an investment in your education.

TEXTBOOKS

These books are mostly about the kinds of writing done in college classrooms. They discuss ways of planning and organizing a paper, expressing ideas effectively, rewriting and revising, and writing for particular audiences and purposes.

Axelrod, Rise B. and Charles R. Cooper, *The St. Martin's Guide to Writing,* 3rd ed. New York: St. Martin's Press, 1991.

Barnet, Sylvan and Marcia Stubbs, *Barnet & Stubbs's Practical Guide to Writing,* 6th ed. with additional readings. Glenview, IL: Scott-Foresman/Little-Brown, 1990.

Behrens, Laurence and Leonard J. Rosen, *Writing and Reading Across the Curriculum,* 4th ed. New York: HarperCollins, 1992.

Buscemi, Santi and Charlotte Smith, eds., *75 Readings: An Anthology,* 3rd ed. New York: McGraw-Hill, 1991.

Colombo, Gary et al., *Rereading America: Cultural Contexts for Critical Thinking and Writing,* 2nd ed. Boston: Bedford Books of St. Martin's Press, 1992.

Cooley, Thomas, *The Norton Sampler: Short Essays for Composition,* 3rd ed. New York: W. W. Norton, 1985.

Decker, Randall E. and Robert A. Schwegler, *Decker's Patterns of Exposition 12.* Glenview, IL: Scott-Foresman/Little-Brown, 1990.

Hunt, Douglas, *The Riverside Guide to Writing.* Boston: Houghton Mifflin, 1991.

Reid, Stephen, *The Prentice Hall Guide for College Writers,* 2nd ed. Englewood Cliffs, NJ: Prentice Hall, 1992.

Rottenberg, Annette T., *Elements of Argument: A Text and Reader,* 3rd ed. Boston: Bedford Books of St. Martin's Press, 1991.

Trimmer, Joseph F., *Writing With A Purpose,* 10th ed. Boston: Houghton Mifflin, 1992.

HANDBOOKS

Handbooks are reference books about the conventions of writing. They discuss topics such as paragraphing and writing complete and correct sentences; they also discuss points of grammar and usage. Many of them include drills and exercises that you can use to learn the conventions of standard written English that are measured in the examination.

Most major textbook publishers put out at least one handbook. Nearly all of them are worth looking at for reference, including the following:

Beene, Lynn and William Vande Kopple, *The Riverside Handbook.* Boston: Houghton Mifflin, 1992.

Crews, Frederick C. and Sandra Schor, *The Borzoi Handbook for Writers,* 2nd ed. New York: Knopf, 1989.

Elbow, Peter and Pat Belanoff, *A Community of Writers: A Workshop Course in Writing,* 1st ed. New York: Random House, 1989.

Fowler, H. Ramsey and Jane E. Aaron, *The Little, Brown Handbook,* 5th ed. New York: HarperCollins, 1992.

Hacker, Diana, *A Writer's Reference,* 2nd ed. Boston: Bedford Books of St. Martin's Press, 1992.

Hodges, John C. et al., *Harbrace College Handbook,* 11th ed. San Diego: Harcourt Brace Jovanovich, 1990.

Langan, John, *College Writing Skills,* 3rd ed. New York: McGraw-Hill, 1992.

Troyka, Lynn Quitman et al., *Simon and Schuster Handbook for Writers,* 2nd ed. Englewood Cliffs, NJ: Prentice Hall, 1990.

Humanities

Description of the Examination

The General Examination in Humanities tests general knowledge of literature, art, and music. It is broad in its coverage, with questions on all periods from classical to contemporary and in many different fields: poetry, prose, philosophy, history of art, music, dance, and theater. The examination requires candidates to demonstrate their understanding of the humanities through recollection of specific information, comprehension and application of concepts, and analysis and interpretation of various works of art.

Because the examination is very broad in its coverage, it is unlikely that any one person will be well informed about all the fields it covers. The examination is 90 minutes long and includes approximately 150 multiple-choice questions to be answered in two separately timed 45-minute sections.

For candidates with satisfactory scores on the Humanities examination, colleges may grant up to six semester hours (or the equivalent) of credit toward fulfillment of a distribution requirement. Some may grant credit for a particular course that matches the examination in content. Although subscores are reported for Fine Arts and Literature to indicate areas of strength and weakness, the subscores are not intended for use in awarding credit for specific courses in these areas. Subscores are computed independently of the total score; thus, an individual's total score cannot be determined by combining the two subscores. Although subscores are not designed to be used to grant course credit, colleges may require that the Fine Arts and Literature subscores be above a certain level to ensure that credit is not awarded to a student who is deficient in either of these areas.

Knowledge and Skills Required

Questions on the test require candidates to demonstrate one or more of the following abilities.

- Knowledge of factual information (names, works, etc.) (about 50 percent of the examination)

- Recognition of techniques such as rhyme scheme, medium, and matters of style, and ability to identify them as characteristic of certain writers, artists, schools, or periods (about 30 percent of the examination)

- Understanding and interpretation of literary passages and art works (provided in reproductions) that most candidates probably will not have seen before (about 20 percent of the examination)

The subject matter of the General Examination in Humanities is drawn from the following topics.

➡	Approximate Percent of Examination

Fine Arts (50%)

25%	Visual arts (painting, sculpture, etc.)
15%	Music
5%	Performing arts (film, dance, etc.)
5%	Architecture

Literature (50%)

5-10%	Drama
15-20%	Poetry
10-15%	Fiction
5-10%	Nonfiction
5%	Philosophy

The test questions, drawn from the entire history of Western art and culture, are fairly evenly divided among the following periods: Classical, Medieval and Renaissance, seventeenth and eighteenth centuries, nineteenth century, and twentieth century. In addition, there are questions that draw on non-Western cultures, such as those of Africa and Asia. Some of the questions cross disciplines and/or chronological periods, and a substantial number test knowledge of terminology, genre, and style.

Sample Questions

The 25 sample questions that follow are similar to questions on the Humanities examination, but they do not appear on the actual examination. Four examples (followed by answers and explanations) are provided first to give you an idea of the types of questions that appear on the Humanities examination.

Before attempting to answer the sample questions, read all the information about the Humanities examination on the preceding pages. Additional suggestions for preparing for CLEP examinations are provided in chapter 4.

EXAMPLE 1

The following lines are from a poem by Elizabeth Barrett Browning that you would not be expected to have read before. In fact, it was chosen because it is not likely to be familiar to you already. The questions that accompany such a passage are designed to examine your ability to analyze and interpret.

> I tell you, hopeless grief is passionless;
> That only men incredulous of despair,
> Half-taught in anguish, through the midnight air
> Beat upward to God's throne in loud access
> Of shrieking and reproach.

In the context of the lines quoted above, "passionless" (line 1) means

(A) reasonable   (B) practical and efficient
    (C) numb and still   (D) uncaring and untouched
        (E) able to find release

Ⓐ Ⓑ Ⓒ Ⓓ Ⓔ

Explanation and Answer

This question concerns the basic point of the passage. It focuses on the word *passionless*, which is central to the meaning of the lines. Normally, one describes grief as a state of extreme emotion; the point Browning makes is that hopeless grief has gone beyond despair. It is without passion; the emotions are frozen. The correct answer, therefore, is (C) *numb and still.*

The hasty reader may choose (A) *reasonable* because of the familiar contrast between reason and emotion (passion), or (B) *practical and efficient* because these descriptions are typical contrasts with the word *passionate.* In both instances, the reader would be somewhat careless; he or she would not be considering the special meaning Browning chose for the word in the context of the lines. Without careful examination, *passionless* might suggest that the person who grieves is simply without emotion, *uncaring and untouched,* and that (D) is then the answer. Or, the reader might assume that, if passionless, a person is (E) *able to find release.* Again, both (D) and (E) miss the central point and are not logical in terms of the rest of the passage.

In this question, you are asked to deal with an idea about grief that is somewhat unusual. If you read inattentively or have a preconception about poetry that leads you to expect all poems to be optimistic or soothing, you may be misled. Answering the question correctly, however, demonstrates your ability to deal with poetic language.

EXAMPLES 2 AND 3

Test questions on passages may also deal with such matters as rhyme scheme, poetic devices, and matters of style. If the style or ideas expressed are particularly distinctive and representative, you may be asked to identify the author. The questions below ask you to apply what you know to two lines of poetry.

> Nature and Nature's laws lay hid in night;
> God said, Let Newton be! and all was light.

The lines above were written by

(A) Geoffrey Chaucer   (B) Alexander Pope
  (C) William Blake   (D) Robert Frost
    (E) Emily Dickinson

Ⓐ Ⓑ Ⓒ Ⓓ Ⓔ

Which of the following describes the lines above?

(A) Blank verse   (B) Free verse   (C) A triolet
  (D) A couplet   (E) A quatrain

Ⓐ Ⓑ Ⓒ Ⓓ Ⓔ

Explanation and Answers

The quotation is a typical example of its period, and you should be able to use both form and content in answering the first question. [The correct answer is (B).] For the second question, you must apply your knowledge of poetic forms. [The correct answer is (D).] In the same way, you may be asked to identify the style of a building or a painting or to recognize or interpret its subject matter.

EXAMPLE 4

Another type of test question asks you to relate the content of one work of art to another work of art. In the following question, for example, you are asked about the style and subject of a work by the twentieth-century painter Lois Mailou Jones.

The National Museum of American Art,
Smithsonian Institution, Purchase
made possible by Mrs. N.H. Green, Dr.
R. Harlan, and Francis Musgrave.

The painting above has been influenced most strongly by which of the following?

(A) Japanese prints   (B) Native American blankets
    (C) Assyrian sculpture   (D) Gothic gargoyles
        (E) African masks

Ⓐ Ⓑ Ⓒ Ⓓ Ⓔ

Explanation and Answer

To answer this question correctly, you must look at the picture carefully, note the principal features of its style, and connect that style to another kind of art. The painting features a mask-like shape in which the elements of the human face are highly abstracted to almost purely geometric forms.

Japanese prints, choice (A), use abstraction but not in the way seen in the face here. Some Japanese prints of the eighteenth century, for example, use bold lines and decorative patterns to create a tension between the representation of space and the use of two-dimensional patterns. Native American blankets, choice (B), such as some from the Pacific Northwest made by the Tlingit people, sometimes feature abstract portrayals of faces. However, these faces are often represented in a two-dimensional manner, again focusing on line rather than on three-dimensional shapes. Assyrian sculpture, choice (C), often uses monumental sculpted figures of human heads with animal bodies, a combination not seen in this mask-like representation. Gothic gargoyles, choice (D), are grotesque, sculpted, animal-like figures that were incorporated in the architecture of Gothic cathedrals. In contrast to the work shown here, they did not depict human figures. African masks, choice (E), the correct choice, are often similar to the mask-like image seen in this painting. Masks from the Dan people of Liberia, for example, frequently emphasize abstraction of human features, as well as symmetry of design and sharpness of carving. African art exerted a strong influence on Cubist art of the early twentieth century. In this work of 1938, an African American artist interprets an African tradition.

Now, try to answer correctly as many of the following questions as possible. Then compare your answers with the correct answers, in Appendix B.

Directions: Each of the questions or incomplete statements below is followed by five suggested answers or completions. Select the one that is best in each case.

1. Often read as a children's classic, it is in reality a scathing indictment of human meanness and greed. In its four books, the Lilliputians are deranged, the Yahoos obscene.

   The passage above discusses

   (A) *Tom Jones*
   (B) *David Copperfield*
   (C) *The Pilgrim's Progress*
   (D) *Gulliver's Travels*
   (E) *Alice in Wonderland*   Ⓐ Ⓑ Ⓒ Ⓓ Ⓔ

2. Which of the following deals with the bigotry an anguished Black family faces when it attempts to move into an all-White suburb?

   (A) O'Neill's *Desire Under the Elms*
   (B) Miller's *Death of a Salesman*
   (C) Baraka's *Dutchman*
   (D) Albee's *Who's Afraid of Virginia Woolf?*
   (E) Hansberry's *A Raisin in the Sun*   Ⓐ Ⓑ Ⓒ Ⓓ Ⓔ

3. Which of the following has as its central theme the idea that wars are mass insanity and that armies are madhouses?

   (A) *Song of Solomon*
   (B) *Portnoy's Complaint*
   (C) *Catch-22*
   (D) *Heart of Darkness*
   (E) *The Woman Warrior*

   Ⓐ Ⓑ Ⓒ Ⓓ Ⓔ

4. Which of the following is often a symbol of new life arising from death?

   (A) A gorgon
   (B) The minotaur
   (C) A unicorn
   (D) A griffin
   (E) The phoenix

   Ⓐ Ⓑ Ⓒ Ⓓ Ⓔ

5. The lute is most similar to the modern

   (A) guitar
   (B) piano
   (C) violin
   (D) accordion
   (E) flute

   Ⓐ Ⓑ Ⓒ Ⓓ Ⓔ

6. The troubadours of the Middle Ages are best described as

   (A) poet-musicians
   (B) moralistic orators
   (C) free-lance illustrators
   (D) character actors
   (E) religious philosophers

   Ⓐ Ⓑ Ⓒ Ⓓ Ⓔ

Questions 7-9 refer to illustrations (A) through (E).

(A)

(B)

(C)

(D)

(E)

The Metropolitan Museum of Art, gift of Thomas F. Ryan, 1910.

7. Which is a bas-relief? Ⓐ Ⓑ Ⓒ Ⓓ Ⓔ

8. Which is by Rodin? Ⓐ Ⓑ Ⓒ Ⓓ Ⓔ

9. Which is Mayan? Ⓐ Ⓑ Ⓒ Ⓓ Ⓔ

Questions 10-12 refer to the following lines.

(A) "Where the bee sucks there suck I:
   In a cowslip's bell I lie . . ."

(B) "Exult O shores, and ring O bells!
   But I with mournful tread,
   Walk the deck my Captain lies,
   Fallen cold and dead."

(C) "Ring out, wild bells, to the wild sky."

(D) "Oh, what a noble mind is here o'erthrown!
   . . . I now see that noble and most sovereign reason,
   Like sweet bells jangled, out of tune and harsh, . . . "

(E) "Oh, the bells, bells, bells!
   What a tale their terror tells
      Of Despair!
   . . . Yet the ear, it fully knows.
      By the twanging,
      And the clanging, . . .
      In the jangling,
      And the wrangling . . ."

10. Which excerpt contains several
    examples of onomatopoeia?   Ⓐ Ⓑ Ⓒ Ⓓ Ⓔ

11. Which is from *Hamlet*?   Ⓐ Ⓑ Ⓒ Ⓓ Ⓔ

12. Which alludes to Abraham Lincoln's death? Ⓐ Ⓑ Ⓒ Ⓓ Ⓔ

Questions 13-15 refer to the following.

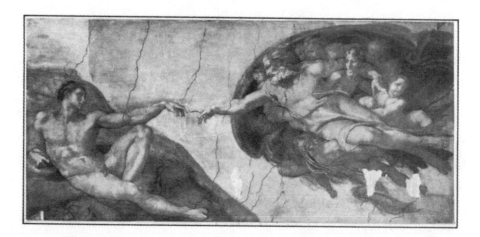

13. The work pictured above is

    (A) a fresco
    (B) a stabile
    (C) a woodcut
    (D) an illumination
    (E) an etching   Ⓐ Ⓑ Ⓒ Ⓓ Ⓔ

14. The theme of the work is the

    (A) sacrifice of Isaac
    (B) expulsion from Eden
    (C) reincarnation of Vishnu
    (D) creation of Adam
    (E) flight of Icarus   Ⓐ Ⓑ Ⓒ Ⓓ Ⓔ

15. The work is located in the

    (A) Alhambra
    (B) Sistine Chapel
    (C) Parthenon
    (D) palace at Versailles
    (E) Cathedral of Notre Dame   Ⓐ Ⓑ Ⓒ Ⓓ Ⓔ

Questions 16-17 refer to the following descriptions of the stage settings of plays.

    (A) The exterior of a two-story corner building on a street in New Orleans which is named Elysian Fields and runs between the L & N tracks and the river

    (B) The living room of Mr. Vandergelder's house, over his hay, feed, and provision store in Yonkers, fifteen miles north of New York City

    (C) In, and immediately outside of, the Cabot farmhouse in New England, in the year 1850

    (D) The stage of a theater; daytime

    (E) A room that is still called the nursery. . . . It is May, the cherry trees are in blossom, but in the orchard it is cold, with a morning frost.

16. Which is for a play by Tennessee Williams?   Ⓐ Ⓑ Ⓒ Ⓓ Ⓔ

17. Which is for a play by Anton Chekhov?   Ⓐ Ⓑ Ⓒ Ⓓ Ⓔ

Questions 18-20 refer to the following groups of people.

    (A) George Balanchine, Agnes de Mille, Martha Graham

    (B) John Cage, Aaron Copland, Paul Hindemith

    (C) Spike Lee, Ingmar Bergman, Federico Fellini

    (D) Allen Ginsberg, Gwendolyn Brooks, Sylvia Plath

    (E) I. M. Pei, Henry Richardson, Frank Lloyd Wright

18. Which is a group of architects?   Ⓐ Ⓑ Ⓒ Ⓓ Ⓔ

19. Which is a group of choreographers?   Ⓐ Ⓑ Ⓒ Ⓓ Ⓔ

20. Which is a group of twentieth-century poets?   Ⓐ Ⓑ Ⓒ Ⓓ Ⓔ

21. He believed that tragedy effects the proper purgation of those emotions of pity and fear that it has aroused.

    The author and concept referred to in the sentence above are

    (A) Plato..*hubris*　(B) Leibniz..monad
    　(C) Aristotle..catharsis　(D) Locke..*tabula rasa*
    　　(E) Kant..the categorical imperative

    Ⓐ Ⓑ Ⓒ Ⓓ Ⓔ

22. Which of the following composers was Picasso's closest musical contemporary?

    (A) Monteverdi　(B) Josquin des Prez　(C) Chopin
    　(D) Stravinsky　(E) Beethoven

    Ⓐ Ⓑ Ⓒ Ⓓ Ⓔ

23. Which of the following satirizes the eighteenth-century doctrine "whatever is, is right" in this "best of all possible worlds"?

    (A) Brontë's *Wuthering Heights*
    (B) Voltaire's *Candide*
    (C) Defoe's *Moll Flanders*
    (D) Hugo's *Les Misérables*
    (E) Hawthorne's *The Scarlet Letter*

    Ⓐ Ⓑ Ⓒ Ⓓ Ⓔ

24. Haiku is a form of Japanese

    (A) drama　(B) poetry　(C) pottery
    　(D) sculpture　(E) architecture

    Ⓐ Ⓑ Ⓒ Ⓓ Ⓔ

25. The terms "pas de deux," "plié," "tendu," and "glissade" are primarily associated with

    (A) ballet　(B) string quartets　(C) painting
    　(D) theater　(E) opera

    Ⓐ Ⓑ Ⓒ Ⓓ Ⓔ

Study Resources

To do well on the Humanities examination, you should know something about each of the forms of literature and fine arts from the various periods and cultures listed earlier, in the paragraph following the examination percentages. No single book covers all these areas, so it will be necessary for you to refer to several different books to find study material on all the topics. The books listed here cover the full range of topics included on the test, but they are only examples of the many books available. These books are generally used as textbooks, supplementary reading, or references for introductory courses in literature and fine arts at the college level.

No reading list alone can prepare you for the examination, however. A lively interest in the arts — going to museums and concerts, attending plays, seeing motion pictures, watching public television programs such as "Great Performances" and "Masterpiece Theatre," listening to radio stations that play classical music and feature discussions of the arts, and, of course, reading widely — constitutes excellent preparation.

Additional suggestions for preparing for CLEP examinations are provided in chapter 4.

Many libraries do not carry textbooks as a policy. If you can't find any of the following textbooks at the library, see whether the college bookstore has a used copy. If you can't locate the most recent edition, an edition that is one or two years older will suffice for most subject areas. As a final option, purchase a new copy of the suggested textbook as an investment in your education.

LITERATURE

Abrams, M. H., *A Glossary of Literary Terms,* 5th ed. New York: Holt, Rinehart & Winston, 1988.

Abrams, M. H. et al., eds., *The Norton Anthology of English Literature,* 2 vols., 5th ed. New York: W. W. Norton, 1988.

Baker, Nancy L., *A Research Guide for Undergraduate Students: English and American Literature,* 3rd ed. New York: Modern Language Association of America, 1989.

Baym, Nina et al., eds., *The Norton Anthology of American Literature,* 2 vols., 3rd ed. New York: W. W. Norton, 1989.

Brower, Reuben A., *The Fields of Light: An Experiment in Critical Reading.* 1951. Reprint. Westport, CT: Greenwood Press, 1980.

Gilbert, Sandra M. and Susan Gubar, eds., *The Norton Anthology of Literature by Women: The Tradition in English.* New York: W. W. Norton, 1985.

Hall, Donald, *To Read Literature: Fiction, Poetry, Drama,* 2nd ed. New York: Holt, Rinehart & Winston, 1987.

Holman, C. Hugh, *A Handbook to Literature,* 6th ed. New York: Macmillan, 1992.

Kennedy, X. J., *Literature: An Introduction to Fiction, Poetry, and Drama,* 5th ed. Hudson, NH: HarperCollins, 1991.

Long, Richard A. and Eugenia W. Collier, eds., *Afro-American Writing: An Anthology of Prose and Poetry,* 2nd and enl. ed. University Park: Pennsylvania State University Press, 1985.

Mack, Maynard, ed., *Norton Anthology of World Masterpieces*, 2 vols., 6th ed. New York: W. W. Norton, 1992.

Shakespeare, William, *The Riverside Shakespeare*, G. Blakemore Evans et al., eds. Boston: Houghton Mifflin, 1974.

Simpson, Louis, ed., *An Introduction to Poetry*, 3rd ed. New York: St. Martin's Press, 1986.

FINE ARTS

Clark, Kenneth, *Civilisation: A Personal View*. New York: HarperPerennial, 1990.

De la Croix, Horst et al., *Gardner's Art Through the Ages*, 9th ed. San Diego: Harcourt Brace Jovanovich, 1991, and *Study Guide for Gardner's Art Through the Ages*, Kathleen Cohen and Horst de la Croix. San Diego: Harcourt Brace Jovanovich.

Fleming, William, *Arts and Ideas*, 8th ed. Fort Worth: Holt, Rinehart & Winston, 1991.

Grant, Michael, *Myths of the Greeks and Romans*. New York: New American Library, 1986.

Grout, Donald Jay and Claude V. Palisca, *A History of Western Music*, 4th ed. New York: W. W. Norton, 1988.

Hartt, Frederick, *Art: A History of Painting, Sculpture, Architecture*, 3rd ed. New York: H. N. Abrams, 1989.

Janson, H. W. and Anthony Janson, *History of Art*, 4th ed. New York: H. N. Abrams, 1991, and *Study Guide*, Evelyn Phillips. Englewood Cliffs, NJ: Prentice Hall.

Kerman, Joseph and Vivian Kerman, *Listen*, 3rd ed. New York: Worth, 1980.

Levy, Kenneth, *Music: A Listener's Introduction*. New York: Harper & Row, 1983.

Randel, Don Michael, ed., *The New Harvard Dictionary of Music*. Cambridge, MA: Harvard University Press, 1986.

Mathematics

Description of the Examination

The General Examination in Mathematics covers material that is generally taught in a college course for non-mathematics majors and majors in other fields not requiring a knowledge of advanced mathematics. The examination consists of two sections. Section I tests facility in arithmetic, algebra, geometry, and data interpretation — skills that are generally taught in high school and assumed at the college level. This part of the test has approximately 40 questions to be answered in 30 minutes. A subscore, Basic Skills and Concepts, is reported for Section I, and one-third of a candidate's total score is based on performance on this section.

Section II covers material that is studied at the college level. Material includes logic and sets, the real number system, functions, and probability and statistics. This part of the test has approximately 50 questions to be answered in 60 minutes. A second subscore, Content, is reported for this section, and two-thirds of a candidate's total score is based on Section II performance. Subscores are computed independently of the total score; thus, an individual's total score cannot be determined by combining the two subscores.

Colleges generally grant students credit or exemption based on their total score on this test, and not on their subscores. However, colleges may require a minimum score for both parts of the test to assure that students are not awarded credit if they are deficient in either area. Some colleges grant credit for, or exemption from, a specific required mathematics course that covers material similar to what is contained in this test; others grant three or six semester hours (or the equivalent) of general credit to satisfy a liberal arts or distribution requirement in mathematics.

The examination places little emphasis on arithmetic calculations. Familiarity with certain symbolism and notation as illustrated by the sample questions is assumed. The test was not designed for use with calculators; therefore, the use of calculators and other computing devices is not permitted during the examination.

Knowledge and Skills Required

Section I of the Mathematics examination focuses on basic mathematical skills that are frequently used in courses other than mathematics. The following outline indicates the proportions of questions in Section I that relate to each of the four skill areas.

	Approximate Percent of Section I
30%	Arithmetic
35%	Algebra
15-20%	Geometry
15-20%	Data Interpretation (graphs and charts)

Section II of the examination requires an understanding of the following topics.

	Approximate Percent of Section II

10%   Sets
        Union and intersection
        Subsets
        Venn diagrams
        Cartesian product

10%   Logic
        Truth tables
        Conjunctions and disjunctions
        Negations
        Conditional statements
        Necessary and sufficient conditions
        Converse, inverse, and contrapositive
        Implications, conclusions, and counterexamples

30%   Real Number System
        Prime and composite numbers
        Odd and even numbers
        Factors and divisibility
        Rational and irrational numbers
        Absolute value and order

20%   Functions and Their Graphs
       Domain and range
       Linear, polynomial, composite, and inverse functions

15%   Probability and Statistics
       Counting problems, including permutations and
         combinations
       Computation of probabilities of simple and compound
         events
       Simple conditional probability
       The mean and median

15%   Miscellaneous Topics
       Complex numbers
       Number bases
       Logarithms and exponentials
       Newly defined binary operations
       Identity and inverse elements

Sample Questions

The 25 sample questions that follow are similar to questions on the Mathematics examination, but they do not appear on the actual examination.

Before attempting to answer the sample questions, read all the information about the Mathematics examination on the preceding pages. Additional suggestions for preparing for CLEP examinations are provided in chapter 4.

The questions on this examination contain only four answer choices, but your answer sheet will have five answer spaces. Be sure not to make any marks in column E on your answer sheet.

Special directions are required for some of the questions in Section I. These directions are given on the next page along with three examples and explanations. These directions and examples are also included in the actual test book.

Directions: Questions E1-E3 each consist of two quantities, one in Column A and one in Column B. You are to compare the two quantities and on the answer sheet fill in space

A   if the quantity in Column A is greater;
B   if the quantity in Column B is greater;
C   if the two quantities are equal;
D   if the relationship cannot be determined from the information given.

Notes:

1. In certain questions, information concerning one or both of the quantities to be compared is centered above the two columns.
2. A symbol that appears in both columns represents the same thing in Column A as it does in Column B.
3. Letters such as x, n, and k stand for real numbers.

EXAMPLES:			
	Column A	Column B	Answers
E1.	2×6	$2 + 6$	● Ⓑ Ⓒ Ⓓ
	$x°$	$y°$	
E2.	$180 - x$	y	Ⓐ Ⓑ ● Ⓓ
E3.	$p - q$	$q - p$	Ⓐ Ⓑ Ⓒ ●

Explanation of Examples:

E1. The answer is A because 12 is greater than 8.
E2. The answer is C because $x° + y° = 180°$ and, therefore, $y = 180 - x$.
E3. The answer is D because nothing is known about p and q.

Four examples of the types of questions in Section II of the Mathematics examination are provided on the next two pages along with the answers and their explanations.

EXAMPLE 1:

If R = {x:x > 0} and S = {x:x < 3}, what is the number of integers in R ∩ S?

(A) None   (B) Two   (C) Three   (D) Four

Explanation and Answer:

This question requires knowledge of sets and set notation. Set R is the set of all real numbers greater than zero and set S is the set of all real numbers less than three. Because 1 and 2 are the only integers in both R and S, the number of integers in R ∩ S is two. The correct answer choice is (B).

EXAMPLE 2:

The conditional statement r → s, that is "if r, then s," is false whenever

(A) r is false   (B) r is false or s is true
(C) r is true and s is false   (D) r and s are false

Explanation and Answer:

This question requires knowledge of the principles of logic. The conditional statement r → s is considered to be false only if r is true and s is false. The correct answer choice is (C).

EXAMPLE 3:

If $f(x) = 4x^2 + 5$ and $g(x) = 2^x$, then $f(g(-1)) =$

(A) $\frac{1}{2}$ (B) 6   (C) 9   (D) 21

Explanation and Answer:

This question requires the recognition of the conventional meaning of $f(g(x))$ as the composite of two functions. Since $g(-1) = 2^{-1} = \frac{1}{2}$, $f(g(-1)) = f\left(\frac{1}{2}\right) = 4\left(\frac{1}{2}\right)^2 + 5 = 6$. The correct answer choice is (B).

EXAMPLE 4:

A drawer contains exactly 5 red, 4 blue, and 3 green pencils. If two pencils are selected at random one after the other without replacing the first, what is the probability that the first one is red and the second one is green?

(A) $\frac{5}{44}$ (B) $\frac{5}{48}$ (C) $\frac{91}{132}$ (D) $\frac{2}{3}$

Explanation and Answer:

One way to solve this problem is to determine the ratio of the number of ways favorable to obtaining "first red, second green" to the total number of possible outcomes. Because there are 5 red and 3 green pencils, there are 5×3 ways of obtaining first red and second green. The total number of possible outcomes is 12×11, since there are 12 ways to select the first pencil and 11 remaining pencils from which the second pencil is to be chosen. The required probability is the ratio $\dfrac{5 \times 3}{12 \times 11} = \dfrac{5}{44}$.

A second solution method is to determine the probability that the first pencil is red and then find the probability that the second pencil is green. The probability that the first pencil is red is $\dfrac{5}{12}$. Given that a red pencil was drawn first, 11 pencils remain, 3 of which are green. Thus, the probability of a green on the second draw, given a red on the first, is $\dfrac{3}{11}$. The probability that both of these events occur in the order stated is $\dfrac{5}{12} \times \dfrac{3}{11} = \dfrac{5}{44}$. The correct answer choice is (A).

Now try to answer as many of the following sample questions as possible. Then compare your answers with the correct answers, given in Appendix B.

Section I: Basic Skills and Concepts

Directions: Questions 1-8 each consist of two quantities, one in Column A and one in Column B. You are to compare the two quantities and on the answer sheet fill in space

- A   if the quantity in Column A is greater;
- B   if the quantity in Column B is greater;
- C   if the two quantities are equal;
- D   if the relationship cannot be determined from the information given.

Notes:

1. In certain questions, information concerning one or both of the quantities to be compared is centered above the two columns.
2. A symbol that appears in both columns represents the same thing in Column A as it does in Column B.
3. Letters such as x, n, and k stand for real numbers.

EXAMPLES:

	Column A	Column B	Answers
E1.	2 × 6	2 + 6	● Ⓑ Ⓒ Ⓓ

E2.	180 − x	y	Ⓐ Ⓑ ● Ⓓ
E3.	p − q	q − p	Ⓐ Ⓑ Ⓒ ●

Choose:

A if the quantity in Column A is greater;
B if the quantity in Column B is greater;
C if the two quantities are equal;
D if the relationship cannot be determined from the information given.

	Column A	Column B	
1.	10 × 11 × 12	11 × 11 × 11	Ⓐ Ⓑ Ⓒ Ⓓ
2.	$\sqrt[3]{8}$	2	Ⓐ Ⓑ Ⓒ Ⓓ

A customer paid $54 for a radio that had been marked down 10 percent.

3.	Original price of the radio	$59.40	Ⓐ Ⓑ Ⓒ Ⓓ
4.	$\|-3 + (-6)\|$	$\|-3 + 6\|$	Ⓐ Ⓑ Ⓒ Ⓓ

Questions 5-6 refer to the following table and are based on the assumption that the statistics are constant for the entire year.

**PUBLIC ELEMENTARY AND SECONDARY EDUCATION
IN TEN STATES — 1970**

State	Fall 1970 Enrollment	School Districts' Expenditure per Pupil		Number of Pupils per Teacher	1968-1969 Personal Income per Capita
		High	Low		
Alabama	806,000	$ 581	$344	24.4	$2,365
California	4,633,000	2,414	569	24.0	4,010
Idaho	182,000	1,763	474	22.7	2,660
Illinois	2,357,000	2,295	391	21.1	3,989
Kansas	512,000	1,831	454	19.8	3,283
Michigan	2,181,000	1,364	491	23.4	3,715
New Mexico	282,000	1,183	477	24.2	2,666
New York	3,477,000	1,889	669	19.6	4,141
Texas	2,840,000	5,334	264	21.9	3,019
Virginia	1,078,000	1,126	441	22.5	3,074

Column A	**Column B**

5. Number of pupils per teacher in Kansas

    Number of pupils per teacher in Virginia

    Ⓐ Ⓑ Ⓒ Ⓓ

6. The average (arithmetic mean) number of teachers per 1,000 pupils in 1970 in the state with the lowest personal income per capita in 1968-1969

    30

    Ⓐ Ⓑ Ⓒ Ⓓ

Column A	Column B

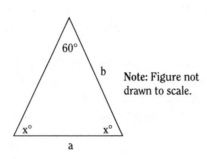

Note: Figure not drawn to scale.

7. a   b

Ⓐ Ⓑ Ⓒ Ⓓ

$$\frac{a}{b} = \frac{c}{d}$$

8. ab   cd

Ⓐ Ⓑ Ⓒ Ⓓ

Directions: For problems 9-12, indicate the correct answer in the appropriate space on the answer sheet.

9. If $7x - 4 = 5x + 8$, then $x =$

(A) $\frac{1}{3}$ (B) 1   (C) 2   (D) 6

Ⓐ Ⓑ Ⓒ Ⓓ

10. What is the perimeter of a square that has area 81?

(A) 9   (B) 18   (C) 24   (D) 36

Ⓐ Ⓑ Ⓒ Ⓓ

11. For $x \neq 0$, $\dfrac{6x^2 + 2x}{2x} =$

(A) $3x + 1$ (B) $3x$ (C) $6x^2 + 1$ (D) $6x^2$

Ⓐ Ⓑ Ⓒ Ⓓ

12. A phonograph record rotating at a rate of 45 revolutions per minute turns how many degrees per second?

(A) 180°   (B) 270°   (C) 360°   (D) 450°

Ⓐ Ⓑ Ⓒ Ⓓ

Section II: Content

Directions: For each of the following problems, indicate the correct answer in the appropriate space on the answer sheet.

Note: Figures that accompany problems in this part are intended to provide information useful in solving the problems. They are drawn as accurately as possible EXCEPT when it is stated in a specific problem that the figure is not drawn to scale. All figures lie in a plane unless otherwise indicated.

13. If $g(x) = x^3 - 1$, then $g(-2) =$

    (A) 5   (B) -3 (C) -7 (D) -9 Ⓐ Ⓑ Ⓒ Ⓓ

14. Which of the following is a Venn diagram of $A \cap (B \cup C)$?

    Ⓐ Ⓑ Ⓒ Ⓓ

    (A) 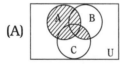   (B)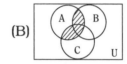

    (C) 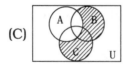   (D)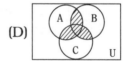

15. A student asserted that $n^2 \geq n$ for all real numbers. Of the following, which is a value of n that provides a counterexample to the student's claim?

    (A) $-\dfrac{1}{2}$ (B) 0   (C) $\dfrac{1}{2}$ (D) 2   Ⓐ Ⓑ Ⓒ Ⓓ

16. If m is an odd integer, which of the following is an even integer?

    (A) $2m - 1$ (B) $2m + 1$
    (C) $m^2 - m$ (D) $m^2 + m + 1$ Ⓐ Ⓑ Ⓒ Ⓓ

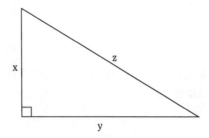

Figure not drawn to scale.

17. For the right triangle above, z is irrational if (x, y) =

    (A) (1,2)   (B) (3,4)   (C) (5,12)   (D) (6,8)   Ⓐ Ⓑ Ⓒ Ⓓ

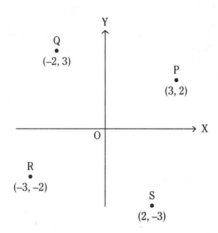

18. In the figure above, which pair of points is on the line 3x + 2y = 0 ?

    (A) P and Q   (B) Q and R
    (C) Q and S   (D) R and S   Ⓐ Ⓑ Ⓒ Ⓓ

19. If x and y are nonzero integers, which of the following is necessarily an integer?

    (A) $x + \dfrac{y}{x}$ (B) $\dfrac{x + y^2}{x}$

    (C) $\dfrac{x^2 + xy}{x}$ (D) $\dfrac{x^2 + y^2}{x}$ Ⓐ Ⓑ Ⓒ Ⓓ

20. If the operation ∘ is defined for all integers by x ∘ y = xy + x − y, then 2 ∘ (3 ∘ 4) =

    (A) 13   (B) 21   (C) 24   (D) 31   Ⓐ Ⓑ Ⓒ Ⓓ

21. If $i = \sqrt{-1}$, then $i + i^2 + i^3 + i^4 =$

    (A) $-i$ (B) i (C) -1 (D) 0

    Ⓐ Ⓑ Ⓒ Ⓓ

22. A fair coin is tossed and a fair die is rolled. What is the probability that the coin will fall heads up and the top face of the die will show 3 or 5?

    (A) $\dfrac{1}{12}$ (B) $\dfrac{1}{6}$ (C) $\dfrac{1}{3}$ (D) $\dfrac{5}{6}$

    Ⓐ Ⓑ Ⓒ Ⓓ

23. The difference between the mean and the median of the numbers 27, 27, 29, 32, and 35 is

    (A) 0   (B) 1   (C) 3   (D) 8

    Ⓐ Ⓑ Ⓒ Ⓓ

24. In base two, the next whole number greater than 10101 is

    (A) 101011   (B) 10110
    (C) 10111   (D) 10102

    Ⓐ Ⓑ Ⓒ Ⓓ

25. If $\log_b x = 6$ and $\log_b y = 2$, then $\log_b\left(\dfrac{x^2}{y}\right) =$

    (A) 4   (B) 8   (C) 10   (D) 18

    Ⓐ Ⓑ Ⓒ Ⓓ

Study Resources

The textbooks listed here are examples of those used in introductory mathematics courses at the college level. The topics covered are not exactly the same in all the books, but all the books include something on most of the topics and skill areas listed under "Knowledge and Skills Required." Elementary algebra textbooks also cover many of the topics on the Mathematics examination. See the Study Resources section of the College Algebra examination for a list of commonly used college algebra textbooks.

Additional suggestions for preparing for CLEP examinations are provided in chapter 4.

Many libraries do not carry textbooks as a policy. If you can't find any of the following textbooks at the library, see whether the college bookstore has a used copy. If you can't locate the most recent edition, an edition that is one or two years older will suffice for most subject areas. As a final option, purchase a new copy of the suggested textbook as an investment in your education.

TEXTBOOKS

Baley, John and Martin Holstege, *Understanding Algebra*, rev. ed. New York: McGraw-Hill, 1991.

Baley, John and Martin Holstege, *Algebra: A First Course*, 3rd ed. Belmont, CA: Wadsworth, 1990.

Meserve, Bruce E. et al., *Introduction to Mathematics*, 6th ed. Englewood Cliffs, NJ: Prentice Hall, 1989.

Setek, William M., Jr., *Fundamentals of Mathematics*, 6th ed. New York: Macmillan, 1992.

Stein, Sherman K., *Mathematics, the Man-Made Universe: An Introduction to the Spirit of Mathematics*, 3rd ed. San Francisco: W. H. Freeman, 1976.

Natural Sciences

Description of the Examination

The General Examination in Natural Sciences covers a wide range of topics frequently taught in introductory college courses surveying both biological and physical sciences at the first- or second-year level. Such courses generally satisfy a distribution or general education requirement in science but usually are neither required of nor taken by science majors. The Natural Sciences examination is not intended for those specializing in science but is intended to test the understanding of scientific concepts that should be attained by an adult who has had the benefit of a liberal arts education. The examination does not stress the retention of factual details; rather, it emphasizes the knowledge and application of the basic principles and concepts of science, the comprehension of scientific information, and the understanding of issues of science in contemporary society.

The primary objective of the examination is to give candidates the opportunity to demonstrate that they possess the level of knowledge and understanding expected of college students meeting a distribution or general education requirement in the natural sciences. Many colleges grant three or six semester hours (or the equivalent) for a satisfactory CLEP score to satisfy such a requirement. Some may grant specific course credit, on the basis of the total score, for a two-semester survey course covering both biological and physical sciences.

Although Biological Science and Physical Science subscores are reported, they are not intended for use in granting credit for typical two-semester courses in biology, chemistry, or other more specialized sciences. Such courses treat these topics in greater depth than does the Natural Sciences examination. Therefore, success on the examination should not be considered an appropriate prerequisite for more advanced study in these specific areas. The Subject Examinations in General Biology and General Chemistry may be more appropriate for awarding credit for such courses.

The examination consists of 115 to 120 multiple-choice questions in two separately timed 45-minute sections, one covering biological science, the other covering physical science. The two subscores are computed independently of the total score; thus, an individual's total score cannot be determined by combining the two subscores.

Knowledge and Skills Required

Questions on the exam require candidates to demonstrate one or more of the following abilities.

- Knowledge of fundamental facts, concepts, and principles (about 40 percent of the examination)

- Interpretation of information presented in the form of graphs, diagrams, tables, equations, or verbal passages (about 20 percent of the examination)

- Qualitative and quantitative application of scientific principles (about 40 percent of the examination), including applications based on material presented in the form of graphs, diagrams, tables, equations, or verbal passages. More emphasis is given to qualitative than quantitative applications.

The content of the Natural Sciences examination is drawn from the following topics:

➡	*Approximate Percent of Examination*
	Biological Science (50%)
10%	Origin and evolution of life, classification of organisms
10%	Cell organization, cell division, chemical nature of the gene, bioenergetics, biosynthesis
20%	Structure, function, and development in organisms; patterns of heredity
10%	Concepts of population biology with emphasis on ecology
	Physical Science (50%)
7%	Atomic structure and properties, elementary particles, nuclear reactions
10%	Chemical elements, compounds, and reactions; molecular structure and bonding
12%	Heat, thermodynamics, and states of matter; classical mechanics; relativity
4%	Electricity and magnetism, waves, light and sound
7%	The universe: galaxies, stars, the solar system
10%	The Earth: atmosphere, hydrosphere, structure, properties, surface features, geological processes, history

The examination includes some questions that are interdisciplinary and cannot be uniquely classified in one of the above categories. About 15 percent of the questions on the examination cover topics that overlap among those listed above and also draw on areas such as the history and philosophy of science, scientific methods, science applications and technology, and the relationship of science to contemporary problems of society, such as environmental pollution and depletion of energy supplies. Some questions on the exam are laboratory oriented.

Sample Questions

The 25 sample questions that follow are similar to questions on the Natural Sciences examination, but they do not appear on the actual examination.

Before attempting to answer the sample questions, read all the information about the Natural Sciences examination on the preceding pages. Additional suggestions for preparing for CLEP examinations are provided in chapter 4.

Try to answer correctly as many questions as possible. Then compare your answers with the correct answers, given in Appendix B.

Directions: Each group of questions below consists of five lettered choices followed by a list of numbered phrases or sentences. For each numbered phrase or sentence select the one choice that is most closely related to it. Each choice may be used once, more than once, or not at all in each group.

Questions 1-2

    (A) Cell wall
    (B) Cell membrane
    (C) Nucleus
    (D) Mitochondrion
    (E) Ribosome

1. The chief site of energy production in the cell

    Ⓐ Ⓑ Ⓒ Ⓓ Ⓔ

2. The site of protein synthesis in the cell

    Ⓐ Ⓑ Ⓒ Ⓓ Ⓔ

Questions 3-5

(A) 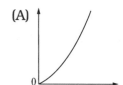   (B)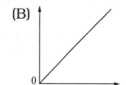

(C) 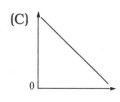   (D)

(E)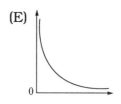

3. A sample of gas remains at constant temperature.

   Vertical axis: Volume of the sample

   Horizontal axis: Pressure on the sample   Ⓐ Ⓑ Ⓒ Ⓓ Ⓔ

4. An object moves at constant speed.

   Vertical axis: Distance traveled since time t = 0

   Horizontal axis: Time   Ⓐ Ⓑ Ⓒ Ⓓ Ⓔ

5. A constant unbalanced force acts on an object.

   Vertical axis: Acceleration of the object

   Horizontal axis: Time   Ⓐ Ⓑ Ⓒ Ⓓ Ⓔ

Directions: Each of the questions or incomplete statements below is followed by five suggested answers or completions. Select the one that is best in each case.

6. As a result of photosynthesis, energy is stored in molecules of

   (A) RNA   (B) DNA   (C) glucose
       (D) O_2 (E) CO_2 Ⓐ Ⓑ Ⓒ Ⓓ Ⓔ

7. A person whose gallbladder has been removed has a decreased ability to store bile and therefore may have a reduced ability to digest

    (A) fats   (B) starches   (C) sugars
    (D) proteins   (E) vitamins

    Ⓐ Ⓑ Ⓒ Ⓓ Ⓔ

Questions 8-9

In fruit flies, the trait for straight wings (S) is dominant over the trait for curly wings (s), and the trait for gray body color (G) is dominant over the trait for black body color (g). A straight-winged female with gray body color was mated with a straight-winged male with black body color and the following ratios of offspring resulted. Experimental conditions were kept at 25°C.

Ratio	Phenotype
$\frac{3}{8}$	straight-winged; gray body color
$\frac{3}{8}$	straight-winged; black body color
$\frac{1}{8}$	curly-winged; gray body color
$\frac{1}{8}$	curly-winged; black body color

8. It can be inferred from the data above that the genotype of the male parent is

    (A) SsGg   (B) SSGg   (C) ssgg
    (D) Ssgg   (E) ssGg

    Ⓐ Ⓑ Ⓒ Ⓓ Ⓔ

9. It can be inferred from the data above that the genotype of the offspring with curly wings and black body color is

    (A) SsGg   (B) SSGg   (C) ssgg
    (D) Ssgg   (E) ssGg

    Ⓐ Ⓑ Ⓒ Ⓓ Ⓔ

10. The characteristics used to classify an animal or plant to the genus level are more general than those used for which of the following levels?

    (A) A class   (B) An order   (C) A species
    (D) A family   (E) A phylum

    Ⓐ Ⓑ Ⓒ Ⓓ Ⓔ

11. Which of the following adaptations is more likely to be found in the leaves of desert plants than in those of plants that grow in moist regions?

    (A) Stomata mostly on upper leaf surface
    (B) A thin, transparent cuticle
    (C) A smooth leaf surface free of hairs
    (D) A thickened epidermis and cuticle
    (E) A loosely packed mesophyll layer

    Ⓐ Ⓑ Ⓒ Ⓓ Ⓔ

Questions 12-14

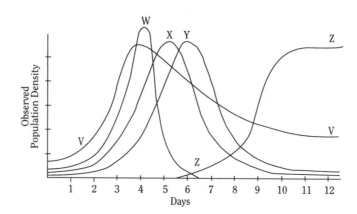

Each curve in the diagram above represents the observed population of a different microorganism in a jar of pond water and dried grass.

12. The organism that reached its maximum population at the climax of the succession is

    (A) V   (B) W   (C) X   (D) Y   (E) Z

    Ⓐ Ⓑ Ⓒ Ⓓ Ⓔ

13. On the basis of the diagram, one could most logically infer which of the following to be a food chain within the culture?

    (A) Y→X→W→Z
    (B) Z→Y→X→W
    (C) W→X→Y→V
    (D) V→W→X→Y
    (E) X→Y→V→Z

    Ⓐ Ⓑ Ⓒ Ⓓ Ⓔ

14. The fact that X and Y had similar population histories during the 12-day period could be explained by all of the following EXCEPT:

   (A) Both have similar pH requirements.
   (B) Both have similar food requirements.
   (C) The survival of Y depends on the presence of X.
   (D) The survival of both depends on the population density of W.
   (E) Both are influenced adversely by the appearance of V.

   Ⓐ Ⓑ Ⓒ Ⓓ Ⓔ

15. A theory fails to meet the criteria of scientific methodology if

   (A) it is unpopular
   (B) it contradicts certain parts of other theories
   (C) it has not been conclusively proved
   (D) it has not been stated in mathematical terms
   (E) no experiments can be designed to test it

   Ⓐ Ⓑ Ⓒ Ⓓ Ⓔ

16. Dark lines in the Sun's spectrum are explained as resulting from the

   (A) radiation of certain frequencies from the Sun's atmosphere
   (B) absorption of energy by atoms in the outer layers of the Sun
   (C) radiation of ultraviolet light from sunspots
   (D) continuous radiation from the corona
   (E) x-radiation from the Sun's atmosphere

   Ⓐ Ⓑ Ⓒ Ⓓ Ⓔ

17. Which of the following best describes the principal way in which the Earth's atmosphere is heated?

   (A) Heat flows from the center of the Earth and is conducted through the ground to the air.
   (B) The atmosphere absorbs short-wave radiation from the Sun as the Sun's rays pass through it.
   (C) The Earth absorbs short-wave radiation from the Sun and reradiates long-wave radiation which is absorbed by the atmosphere.
   (D) The air absorbs short-wave radiation from the Sun after it has been reflected by the clouds.
   (E) Warm air rises and cold air sinks and, as it sinks, it is warmed by compression.

   Ⓐ Ⓑ Ⓒ Ⓓ Ⓔ

Questions 18-20

$$CuO + H_2 \rightarrow Cu + H_2O$$

The drawing below depicts an apparatus for reducing copper (II) oxide to the metal by the reaction above.

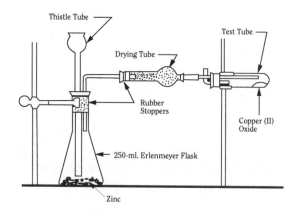

18. To produce a stream of hydrogen gas for this reaction, one should add which of the following through the thistle tube?

    (A) Water
    (B) Dilute hydrochloric acid
    (C) Dilute copper (II) sulfate solution
    (D) Hydrogen peroxide
    (E) Dilute ammonia solution   Ⓐ Ⓑ Ⓒ Ⓓ Ⓔ

19. After the production of hydrogen gas starts, withdrawing the thistle tube would result in which of the following?

    (A) Water would back up into the flask.
    (B) The evolution of hydrogen gas would stop.
    (C) Much hydrogen gas would escape without coming in contact with the copper oxide.
    (D) Air would enter the flask faster than hydrogen gas would be evolved.
    (E) The rate of production of hydrogen gas would increase.

        Ⓐ Ⓑ Ⓒ Ⓓ Ⓔ

20. To reduce the copper (II) oxide effectively with hydrogen gas, the test tube must be

    (A) heated
    (B) cooled
    (C) put under reduced pressure
    (D) filled with dilute HCl solution
    (E) filled with dilute NaOH solution
    Ⓐ Ⓑ Ⓒ Ⓓ Ⓔ

21. Which of the following natural resources is NOT a fossil fuel?

    (A) Uranium   (B) Lignite   (C) Petroleum
        (D) Anthracite   (E) Bituminous coal
    Ⓐ Ⓑ Ⓒ Ⓓ Ⓔ

22. The half-life of $^{14}_{6}C$ is 5,600 years. Which of the following statements about a 10-gram sample of $^{14}_{6}C$ is correct?

    (A) The radioactive decay of the sample will be complete after 5,600 years.

    (B) The $^{14}_{6}C$ sample will start radioactive decay after 5,600 years.

    (C) A time of 5,600 years has been required to produce this sample of $^{14}_{6}C$ in nature.

    (D) After 5,600 years the sample will contain only 5 grams of $^{14}_{6}C$.

    (E) After 11,200 years the sample will not contain any $^{14}_{6}C$.

    Ⓐ Ⓑ Ⓒ Ⓓ Ⓔ

23. Of the planets that are best known and that can be seen with the naked eye (Venus, Mars, Jupiter, Saturn), only Venus has an orbit smaller than that of the Earth. This means that Venus

    (A) is seen only in the morning or the evening sky
    (B) can be seen in the sky near midnight more often than at other times
    (C) can rarely be seen at all
    (D) has an orbit that is more elliptical than that of the Earth
    (E) has a longer year than the Earth
    Ⓐ Ⓑ Ⓒ Ⓓ Ⓔ

24. Which of the following would be most likely to deposit an unsorted mixture of clay, boulders, sand, and silt?

(A) Glacial ice
(B) Subsurface water
(C) Streams
(D) Waves
(E) Wind

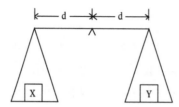

25. The balance shown above is in equilibrium in a laboratory at the Earth's surface, and the two arms have the same length d. Thus the two objects, X and Y (not necessarily drawn to scale), must have identical

(A) densities   (B) masses   (C) shapes
    (D) specific gravities   (E) volumes

Study Resources

The textbooks listed here are examples of those used in introductory science courses at the college level. Students are advised to study from more than one textbook to cover the subject matter included on the Natural Sciences examination. Select at least one biological science and one physical science textbook.

If students maintain an interest in scientific issues, read science articles in newspapers and magazines, watch public television programs such as "Nova," or work in fields that require a knowledge of certain areas of science such as nursing and laboratory work, they will probably be knowledgeable about many of the topics included on the Natural Sciences examination.

Additional suggestions for preparing for CLEP examinations are provided in chapter 4.

Many libraries do not carry textbooks as a policy. If you can't find any of the following textbooks at the library, see whether the college bookstore has a used copy. If you can't locate the most recent edition, an edition that is one or two years older will suffice for most subject areas. As a final option, purchase a new copy of the suggested textbook as an investment in your education.

TEXTBOOKS

Campbell, Neil A., *Biology*, 2nd ed. Redwood City, CA: Benjamin/
Cummings, 1990.

Curtis, Helena and N. Sue Barnes, *Invitation to Biology*, 5th ed. New York:
Worth, 1989.

Hill, John W., *Chemistry for Changing Times*, 6th ed. New York:
Macmillan, 1992.

Keeton, William T. and Carol H. McFadden, *Elements of Biological Science*,
3rd ed. New York: W. W. Norton, 1983.

Krauskopf, Konrad B. and Arthur Beiser, *The Physical Universe*, 6th ed.
New York: McGraw-Hill, 1991.

Merken, Melvin, *Physical Science with Modern Applications*, 4th ed.
Philadelphia: Saunders, 1989.

Social Sciences and History

Description of the Examination

The General Examination in Social Sciences and History covers a wide range of topics from the social sciences and history areas. While the examination is based on no specific course, its content is drawn from introductory college courses that cover United States history, Western Civilization, World Civilization, government/political science, economics, sociology, anthropology, psychology, and geography.

The primary objective of the examination is to give candidates the opportunity to demonstrate that they possess the level of knowledge and understanding expected of college students meeting a distribution or general education requirement in the social science-history area. Many colleges will award three or six semester hours (or the equivalent) for a satisfactory CLEP score toward such a requirement. Some may grant specific course credit for a survey course that discusses social science and history topics and that closely matches the examination.

This examination, however, is not intended for use in granting course credit for specific social science or history courses. The CLEP Subject Examinations in Principles of Microeconomics, Principles of Macroeconomics, Introductory Sociology, American History I and II, Western Civilization I and II, and American Government cover more completely the material taught in these courses.

The Social Sciences and History examination includes approximately 125 multiple-choice questions to be answered in two separately timed 45-minute sections.

Knowledge and Skills Required

Questions on the examination require candidates to demonstrate one or more of the following abilities.

- Familiarity with terminology, facts, conventions, methodology, concepts, principles, generalizations, and theories

- Ability to understand, interpret, and analyze graphic, pictorial, or written material

- Ability to apply abstractions to particulars, and to apply hypotheses, concepts, theories, or principles to given data

107

The content of the Social Sciences and History examination is drawn from the following topics.

→ *Approximate Percent of Examination*

History (40%)

17%   United States history

Requires a general understanding of historical issues associated with the following periods in United States history: colonial, revolutionary, late eighteenth and early nineteenth centuries, Civil War and Reconstruction, and late nineteenth and twentieth centuries

15%   Western Civilization

Requires familiarity with three broad historical periods: ancient, medieval, and modern

8%   World Civilization

Requires general knowledge of important historical topics in six broad chronological periods:

Prehistory

Ancient history to 500 B.C.E.

500 B.C.E. to 500 C.E.

500 C.E. to 1500 C.E.

1500 C.E. to 1900 C.E.

The twentieth century in Africa, Asia, Europe, and Latin America

Social Sciences (60%)

13%   Government/Political Science, including topics such as

Methods

Constitutional government

Voting and political behavior

International relations

Comparative government

←	*Approximate Percent of Examination*

11%   Sociology, including topics such as
- Methods
- Demography
- Ecology
- Social stratification
- Deviance
- Social organization
- Interaction
- Social change

10%   Economics, with emphasis on topics such as
- Opportunity cost
- Comparative advantage
- Competitive markets
- Monetary and fiscal policy
- International trade
- Measurement concepts

10%   Psychology, including topics such as
- Aggression
- Socialization
- Conformity
- Methodology
- Group formation
- Performance

10%   Geography, including topics such as
- Weather and climate
- Cultural geography
- Ecology

6%   Anthropology, including topics such as
- Cultural anthropology
- Physical anthropology
- Demography
- Family
- Methods

Sample Questions

The 40 sample questions that follow are similar to questions on the Social Sciences and History examination, but they do not actually appear on it.

Before attempting to answer the sample questions, read all the information above about the Social Sciences and History examination. Additional suggestions for preparing for CLEP examinations are provided in chapter 4.

Try to answer correctly as many questions as possible. Then compare your answers with the correct answers, given in Appendix B.

Directions: Each of the questions or incomplete statements below is followed by five suggested answers or completions. Select the one that is best in each case.

1. Prior to the campaign of 1828, most candidates for President of the United States were nominated by

    (A) state legislatures
    (B) the electoral college
    (C) national party conventions
    (D) state primary elections
    (E) party leaders in Congress   Ⓐ Ⓑ Ⓒ Ⓓ Ⓔ

2. Which of the following best describes the impact of Spanish colonization on the Indians of Central and South America in the sixteenth and early seventeenth centuries?

    (A) Their economic well-being was improved by the wealth they produced at the direction of the Spanish rulers.
    (B) The Indians maintained a separate society and culture that coexisted with that of the Spanish colonial system.
    (C) Their high level of artistic and scientific development put them at the top of the colonial class system.
    (D) Their system of religious beliefs and practices was unaffected.
    (E) Their populations decreased dramatically as a result of contact with the Spanish.
    Ⓐ Ⓑ Ⓒ Ⓓ Ⓔ

3. An individual who believes that "government is best which governs not at all" favors

    (A) anarchy   (B) tyranny   (C) monarchy
    (D) oligarchy   (E) democracy   Ⓐ Ⓑ Ⓒ Ⓓ Ⓔ

4. Which of the following statements concerning the process of socialization is true?

(A) In the upbringing of a child, the agencies of socialization tend to function together harmoniously.
(B) In a modern society, the individual is subjected to many diverse socializing influences.
(C) In a traditional society, socializing influences are likely to be in conflict.
(D) In a traditional society, there are no socializing agencies.
(E) In modern society, the media has little impact on the socialization of children.

Ⓐ Ⓑ Ⓒ Ⓓ Ⓔ

CONFIDENCE IN AMERICAN INSTITUTIONS, 1973-1986
(Percentage saying "a great deal or quite a lot")

ORGANIZATION	1973	1977	1981	1986
Military	NA*	57%	50%	63%
Church-organized religion	66%	64%	64%	57%
U.S. Supreme Court	44%	46%	46%	53%
Public Schools	58%	54%	42%	49%
Congress	42%	40%	29%	41%
Organized labor	30%	39%	28%	29%
Big Business	28%	26%	33%	20%

*Not asked   The Gallup Poll News Service

5. Which of the following can be inferred about American public opinion from the table above?

(A) In the 1980's public schools functioned to the satisfaction of American citizens.
(B) Big business generally enjoys more confidence than organized labor.
(C) Confidence in the military has remained constant over time.
(D) During the Reagan presidency, esteem for the Supreme Court increased.
(E) Support for Congress depends on the popularity of individual members of Congress.

Ⓐ Ⓑ Ⓒ Ⓓ Ⓔ

6. Which of the following statements about the concept of charisma is correct?

   (A) It is possible only in the absence of legitimate authority.
   (B) It involves a basically political appeal.
   (C) It rests on devotion of followers to the exceptional qualities of an individual.
   (D) It is an inherited personality trait.
   (E) It is a prerequisite for high office in traditional societies.

   Ⓐ Ⓑ Ⓒ Ⓓ Ⓔ

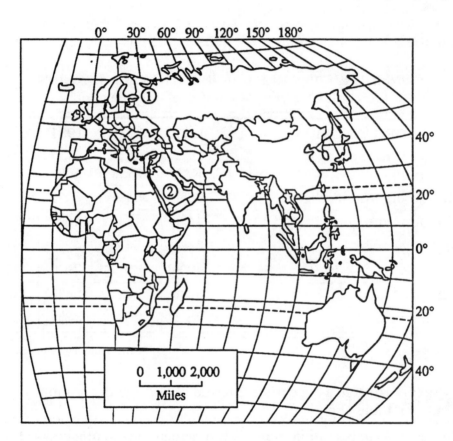

7. A traveler going from Nation 1 to Nation 2, shown on the map above, would experience a climatic change from

   (A) humid cold to desert
   (B) humid subtropical to Mediterranean
   (C) desert to tropical rain forest
   (D) tropical wet and humid to Mediterranean
   (E) Mediterranean to humid cold

   Ⓐ Ⓑ Ⓒ Ⓓ Ⓔ

8. In most cultures where a belief in ancestral spirits exists, these beings are generally seen as

   (A) being primarily malevolent
   (B) being responsible for natural disasters
   (C) having no authority over the living
   (D) being beyond the spiritual reach of the living
   (E) retaining an active membership in the society

   Ⓐ Ⓑ Ⓒ Ⓓ Ⓔ

9. "To industry and frugality I owe the early easiness of my circumstances and the acquisition of my fortune with all that knowledge that has enabled me to be a useful citizen."

   The statement above is most characteristic of which of the following?

   (A) Franklin   (B) Emerson   (C) Thoreau
       (D) Vanderbilt   (E) Jefferson

   Ⓐ Ⓑ Ⓒ Ⓓ Ⓔ

10. One of the fundamental changes taking place in the twentieth century is the gradual

    (A) decline in nationalistic feelings among peoples of the Eastern Hemisphere
    (B) decline in the economic self-sufficiency of individuals
    (C) decline in world trade
    (D) decrease in the pressure of world population on economic resources
    (E) decrease in services, as opposed to manufacturing, in developed nations

    Ⓐ Ⓑ Ⓒ Ⓓ Ⓔ

11. A person who lived in the 1790's in the United States and who believed in a strong central government, broad construction of the Constitution, and funding of the public debt would most probably have been

    (A) a socialist   (B) an anti-Federalist   (C) a Federalist
        (D) a believer in monarchy   (E) a Jeffersonian Republican

    Ⓐ Ⓑ Ⓒ Ⓓ Ⓔ

12. Among the several social science methods of research, the one used for conducting public opinion polls can best be described as

    (A) laboratory experimentation
    (B) participant observation
    (C) field experimentation
    (D) survey research
    (E) computer simulation

    (A) (B) (C) (D) (E)

13. Which of the following policies is likely to result in the greatest reduction in aggregate demand?

    (A) A $5 billion increase in personal income taxes
    (B) A $5 billion decrease in government transfer payments
    (C) A $5 billion decrease in government purchases of goods and services
    (D) A $5 billion decrease in government purchases accompanied by a $5 billion increase in personal income taxes
    (E) A $5 billion decrease in government purchases accompanied by a $5 billion decrease in personal income taxes

    (A) (B) (C) (D) (E)

14. Which of the following statements about the control group in a well-designed experiment is correct?

    (A) It differs from the experimental group in the way in which subjects are sampled.
    (B) It is like the experimental group except for differences in exposure to the dependent variable.
    (C) It is like the experimental group and receives the same experimental treatment.
    (D) It is like the experimental group except for differences in exposure to the independent variable.
    (E) It must contain the same number of individuals as the experimental group.

    (A) (B) (C) (D) (E)

15. The area of the African continent is approximately

    (A) half the area of Western Europe
    (B) the same as the area of the United States east of the Mississippi River
    (C) three times the area of the continental United States
    (D) two times the area of California
    (E) four times the area of South America

    (A) (B) (C) (D) (E)

114

16. Chinese culture and influence were most significant in shaping the institutions of which of the following countries?

    (A) Bangladesh, Burma, and Pakistan
    (B) India, Japan, and Korea
    (C) Indonesia, the Philippines, and Thailand
    (D) Japan, Korea, and Vietnam
    (E) Korea, Nepal, and the Philippines

    Ⓐ Ⓑ Ⓒ Ⓓ Ⓔ

17. The most immediate consequence of abolitionism in the United States in the 1830's and 1840's was

    (A) widespread support for the abolition of slavery
    (B) intensified resentment toward the movement by slaveholders
    (C) better treatment of freed African Americans in the North
    (D) greater sympathy for popular sovereignty
    (E) increased interest in African colonization

    Ⓐ Ⓑ Ⓒ Ⓓ Ⓔ

18. "We know so little about how to live in this life that there is no point in worrying about what may happen to us after death. First let us learn to live in the right way with other men and then let whatever happens next take care of itself."

    The above quotation best expresses the philosophy of

    (A) Jesus
    (B) Muhammad
    (C) Confucius
    (D) Marx
    (E) Aquinas

    Ⓐ Ⓑ Ⓒ Ⓓ Ⓔ

19. Major political revolutions in the twentieth century have most often occurred in countries with

    (A) comparatively low unemployment
    (B) high levels of industrialization
    (C) small industrial and large agricultural sectors
    (D) representative governments
    (E) small populations

    Ⓐ Ⓑ Ⓒ Ⓓ Ⓔ

20. The tendency for an individual's rank on one status dimension to be positively correlated with his or her rank on other status dimensions is known as

    (A) structural balance
    (B) rank ordering
    (C) status polarization
    (D) status congruence
    (E) status stability

    Ⓐ Ⓑ Ⓒ Ⓓ Ⓔ

21. To reduce inflationary pressure in the economy, the Federal Reserve would most likely

    (A) sell government securities on the open market
    (B) reduce margin requirements
    (C) lower legal reserve requirements
    (D) decrease the discount rate
    (E) encourage member banks to increase their loans

    Ⓐ Ⓑ Ⓒ Ⓓ Ⓔ

22. Participant satisfaction will increase in those groups that

    (A) have competing subgroups in interaction
    (B) are low in cohesion among group members
    (C) identify clear goals and supportive roles
    (D) have incompatible directions
    (E) fail to coordinate member interaction

    Ⓐ Ⓑ Ⓒ Ⓓ Ⓔ

23. The construction of the Panama Canal shortened the sailing time between New York and

    (A) London
    (B) Port-au-Prince
    (C) Rio de Janeiro
    (D) New Orleans
    (E) San Francisco

    Ⓐ Ⓑ Ⓒ Ⓓ Ⓔ

24. Of the following, which is the earliest human innovation?

    (A) Development of complex urban societies
    (B) Extensive use of written language
    (C) Use and control of fire
    (D) Domestication of animals
    (E) Dependence on agriculture for the major source of food

    Ⓐ Ⓑ Ⓒ Ⓓ Ⓔ

25. Which of the following prompted African Americans to move to cities in the North during the first quarter of the twentieth century?

    I. The impact of the boll weevil plague
   II. The availability of industrial opportunities in the North
  III. The impact of segregation legislation in the South

(A) II only   (B) I and II only   (C) I and III only
  (D) II and III only   (E) I, II, and III

Ⓐ Ⓑ Ⓒ Ⓓ Ⓔ

26. Abolition of the transatlantic slave trade was difficult to achieve in the early 1800's because

(A) the British were strongly in favor of slavery
(B) slave labor was needed in Europe
(C) the profits from slavery were high
(D) most countries in Europe had extensive African colonies
(E) slavery was widespread in all parts of the New World

Ⓐ Ⓑ Ⓒ Ⓓ Ⓔ

27. Public opinion polls in the United States commonly make use of

(A) sampling theory
(B) population trends
(C) intelligence tests
(D) clinical interviews
(E) Rorschach tests

Ⓐ Ⓑ Ⓒ Ⓓ Ⓔ

28. A population that is aging necessarily has

(A) more people over 40 than under 40
(B) more males than females
(C) a decreasing death rate
(D) an increasing mean age
(E) an increasing birthrate

Ⓐ Ⓑ Ⓒ Ⓓ Ⓔ

UNITED STATES MARKET FOR APPLES

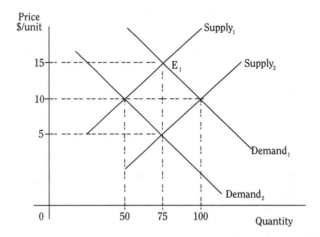

29. The United States market for apples is in equilibrium at E, where 75 units are sold for $15 each. If consumers' per capita disposable income decreases, the equilibrium price and quantity of apples sold will be which of the following?

	PRICE	QUANTITY
(A)	$15	75
(B)	$10	50
(C)	$10	100
(D)	$ 5	75
(E)	$ 5	100

Ⓐ Ⓑ Ⓒ Ⓓ Ⓔ

30. In psychology, the biosocial approach seeks to explain behavior in terms of

(A) environmental influences
(B) genetic factors
(C) unconscious motivations
(D) an integration of cultural and biological factors
(E) genetic drifts within population groups

Ⓐ Ⓑ Ⓒ Ⓓ Ⓔ

31. In the late twentieth century Islamic fundamentalism has been a significant influence in all of the following countries EXCEPT

(A) Algeria
(B) China
(C) Egypt
(D) India
(E) Indonesia

Ⓐ Ⓑ Ⓒ Ⓓ Ⓔ

32. In which of the following types of societies do women typically have as much power as men?

    (A) Hunting-gathering
    (B) Pastoral
    (C) Horticultural
    (D) Agricultural
    (E) Industrial   Ⓐ Ⓑ Ⓒ Ⓓ Ⓔ

33. Which of the following is true of the First Amendment to the United States Constitution?

    (A) It established presidential control over the budget.
    (B) It created the Supreme Court.
    (C) It declared all people to be equal.
    (D) It outlined the basic pattern of church-state relations.
    (E) It guaranteed citizens the right to bear arms.   Ⓐ Ⓑ Ⓒ Ⓓ Ⓔ

34. The Peloponnesian Wars were primarily the result of

    (A) Athenian imperialism
    (B) Spartan militarism
    (C) the invasion of Greece by Hammurabi's army
    (D) the conquests of Alexander the Great
    (E) the spread of Athenian democracy   Ⓐ Ⓑ Ⓒ Ⓓ Ⓔ

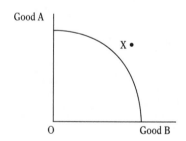

35. In the production-possibility curve for a closed economy illustrated above, X indicates a point at which

    (A) intended saving is greater than investment
    (B) the economy cannot achieve its existing productive potential
    (C) the factors of production are not fully employed
    (D) the production level cannot be maintained in the long run
    (E) income is unequally distributed to the factors of production

       Ⓐ Ⓑ Ⓒ Ⓓ Ⓔ

36. Which of the following philosophers asserted that all human beings possess the natural rights of life, liberty, and property?

    (A) Thomas Hobbes   (B) John Locke   (C) Thomas Aquinas
    (D) Karl Marx   (E) Socrates

    Ⓐ Ⓑ Ⓒ Ⓓ Ⓔ

37. Which of the following is NOT compatible with the traditional conception of bureaucracy?

    (A) Salaried remuneration
    (B) Recruitment of personnel by examination
    (C) A hierarchical structure
    (D) A decentralization of authority
    (E) A formal allocation of obligation and duties

    Ⓐ Ⓑ Ⓒ Ⓓ Ⓔ

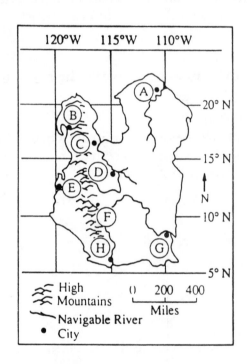

38. According to the map above, which of the following land formations would most likely be found near city A?

    (A) A plateau
    (B) A volcano
    (C) A delta
    (D) A peninsula
    (E) A mountain

    Ⓐ Ⓑ Ⓒ Ⓓ Ⓔ

39. On the basis of empirical evidence gathered during the Second World War, which of the following was most successful in motivating United States soldiers to perform well under overseas combat conditions?

  (A) Emphasizing to them that the civilian population is dependent on them
  (B) Developing their dedication to dominant political and ethical values
  (C) Instilling in the soldiers loyalty to national leaders
  (D) Developing in the soldiers a satisfactory self-image of their individual abilities
  (E) Emphasizing positive relationships among members of small combat units

  Ⓐ Ⓑ Ⓒ Ⓓ Ⓔ

40. Of the following, which first opened up lines of trade with East Africa and the upper Niger Valley?

  (A) Portuguese navigators sailing around Africa on their way to India
  (B) English merchants seeking slaves for the American colonies
  (C) Arab traders extending their trade routes to include both the Persian Gulf and northern Africa
  (D) Spanish nobles seeking sources of gold in Africa
  (E) French explorers crossing the Mediterranean and penetrating through the Sahara

  Ⓐ Ⓑ Ⓒ Ⓓ Ⓔ

Study Resources

The following list contains several textbooks that are typical of those used in social science survey courses and history courses at the college level. To prepare for the Social Sciences and History examination, you will need to consult several textbooks because there are none that cover all the major topics on the exam.

The textbooks suggested for preparing for other CLEP examinations would also be helpful. Study resources for the Subject Examinations in American Government, American History I and II, Principles of Macroeconomics and Principles of Microeconomics, Introductory Sociology, and Western Civilization I and II would be particularly relevant, and they can be found in the Study Resources section for these examinations. Additional suggestions for preparing for CLEP examinations are provided in chapter 4.

Many libraries do not carry textbooks as a policy. If you can't find any of the following textbooks at the library, see whether the college bookstore has a used copy. If you can't locate the most recent edition, an edition that is one or two years older will suffice for most subject areas. As a final option, purchase a new copy of the suggested textbook as an investment in your education.

SOCIAL SCIENCE TEXTBOOKS

Hunt, Elgin F. and David C. Colander, *Social Science: An Introduction to the Study of Society*, 7th ed. New York: Macmillan, 1990.

Mendoza, Manuel G. and Vince Napoli, *Systems of Society: An Introduction to Social Science*, 5th ed. Lexington, MA: D. C. Heath, 1990.

Perry, John A. and Erna K. Perry, *Contemporary Society: An Introduction to Social Science*. New York: Harper & Row, 1991.

HISTORY TEXTBOOKS

Bailey, Thomas A. and David M. Kennedy, *The American Pageant: A History of the Republic*, 2 vols. 9th ed. Lexington, MA: D. C. Heath, 1991.

Blum, John M. et al., *The National Experience: A History of the United States*, 7th ed. San Diego: Harcourt Brace Jovanovich, 1989.

Chambers, Mortimer et al., *The Western Experience*, Vols. I & II, 5th ed. New York: McGraw-Hill, 1991.

American Literature

Description of the Examination

The Subject Examination in American Literature covers the material that is usually taught in a two-semester survey course (or the equivalent) at the college level. It deals with prose and poetry written in the United States from colonial times to the present. It is primarily a test of knowledge about literary works — their content, backgrounds, and authors — but also requires familiarity with the terminology used by literary critics and historians. The examination emphasizes fiction and poetry, and deals to a lesser degree with the essay, drama, and autobiography.

In both coverage and approach, the examination resembles the chronologically organized survey of American literature offered by many colleges. It assumes that the candidate has read widely and developed an appreciation of American literature, knows the basic literary periods, and has a sense of the historical development of American literature.

The test contains approximately 100 multiple-choice questions to be answered in two separately timed 45-minute sections.

Knowledge and Skills Required

Questions on the test require candidates to demonstrate one or more of the following abilities.

- Knowledge of the content of particular literary works — their characters, plots, settings, themes, etc. (about 50-60 percent of the examination)

- Ability to understand and interpret short poems or excerpts from long poems and prose works presented in the test book (about 25-35 percent of the examination)

- Knowledge of the historical and social settings of specific works, their authors and influences on them, and their relations to other literary works and to literary traditions (about 10 percent of the examination)

- Understanding of the critical theories of American writers, and of critical terms, verse forms, and literary devices (about 5 percent of the examination)

The American Literature examination requires a knowledge and understanding of the works and writers of the following periods. The column at the left indicates the percentage of questions devoted to each of the five periods.

Approximate Percent of Examination

10-15%	Colonial and Early National (1620-1830)
30%	Romantic (1830-1870)
25%	Realistic and Early Naturalistic (1870-1910)
25%	Modern (1910-1945)
5-10%	Contemporary (1945-present)

Sample Questions

The 25 sample questions that follow are similar to questions on the American Literature examination, but they do not actually appear on it.

Before attempting to answer the sample questions, read all the information about the American Literature examination on the preceding pages. Additional suggestions for preparing for CLEP examinations are provided in chapter 4.

Try to answer correctly as many questions as possible. Then compare your answers with the correct answers, given in Appendix B.

Directions: Each of the questions or incomplete statements below is followed by five suggested answers or completions. Select the one that is best in each case.

1. Which of the following first recognized Walt Whitman as the great poet of the democratic spirit of America?

    (A) Nathaniel Hawthorne   (B) Ralph Waldo Emerson
      (C) Herman Melville   (D) Edgar Allan Poe
        (E) Henry David Thoreau

    Ⓐ Ⓑ Ⓒ Ⓓ Ⓔ

2. The "unpardonable sin" committed by Ethan Brand is

    (A) allowing one's intellectual curiosity to violate the privacy of others
    (B) any mortal transgression not followed by repentance
    (C) the attempt to improve upon God's handiwork
    (D) loss of faith in God
    (E) ambition deteriorating into a lust for power

    Ⓐ Ⓑ Ⓒ Ⓓ Ⓔ

Questions 3-4

> Thou ill-formed offspring of my feeble brain,
> Who after birth didst by my side remain,
> Till snatched from thence by friends, less wise than true,
> Who thee abroad, exposed to public view,
> (5) Made thee in rags, halting to th' press to trudge
> Where errors were not lessened (all may judge).
> At thy return my blushing was not small,
> My rambling brat (in print) should mother call,
> I cast thee by as one unfit for light,
> Thy visage was so irksome in my sight . . . .

3. In line 1, "offspring" most probably refers to the author's

   (A) philosophy   (B) book of poems
     (C) unwanted child   (D) despair
       (E) intelligence   Ⓐ Ⓑ Ⓒ Ⓓ Ⓔ

4. "My rambling brat" (line 8) is an example of

   (A) epigram
   (B) symbolism
   (C) simile
   (D) metaphor
   (E) hyperbole   Ⓐ Ⓑ Ⓒ Ⓓ Ⓔ

---

5. In his *Autobiography,* Benjamin Franklin claims that success can best be achieved by

   (A) hard work and moral self-perfecting
   (B) religious study and ascetic denial of worldly goods
   (C) study of the classics and of several languages
   (D) extensive investment of capital and strict attention to business
   (E) inducing scholars to participate in business ventures

   Ⓐ Ⓑ Ⓒ Ⓓ Ⓔ

6. Characters with the last names of Snopes, Compson, and Sartoris figure prominently in the fiction of

   (A) Eudora Welty   (B) Flannery O'Connor
     (C) Thomas Wolfe   (D) William Faulkner
       (E) Ernest Hemingway   Ⓐ Ⓑ Ⓒ Ⓓ Ⓔ

125

Questions 7-8

The mass of men lead lives of quiet desperation.

To be a philosopher is not merely to have subtle thoughts, nor even to found a school, but so to love wisdom as to live according to its dictates a life of simplicity, independence, magnanimity, and trust.

(5) I had three pieces of limestone on my desk, but I was terrified to find that they required to be dusted daily, when the furniture of my mind was all undusted still, and I threw them out the window in disgust.

7. The sentences above are taken from the opening pages of

(A) *The House of the Seven Gables,* Hawthorne
(B) *Nature,* Emerson
(C) *Bartleby the Scrivener,* Melville
(D) *Democratic Vistas,* Whitman
(E) *Walden,* Thoreau

Ⓐ Ⓑ Ⓒ Ⓓ Ⓔ

8. The phrase "the furniture of my mind was all undusted still" can best be paraphrased by which of the following?

(A) I had become morose and antisocial.
(B) I had not examined my ideas and beliefs.
(C) I needed a change of scene.
(D) I was intellectually and emotionally exhausted.
(E) I had become so lazy that I could not work.

Ⓐ Ⓑ Ⓒ Ⓓ Ⓔ

---

9. Which of the following poets derived the title, the plan, and much of the symbolism of one of his or her major poems from Jessie Weston's *From Ritual to Romance?*

(A) Wallace Stevens　　(B) T. S. Eliot
　(C) Robert Frost　　(D) Marianne Moore
　　(E) Langston Hughes

Ⓐ Ⓑ Ⓒ Ⓓ Ⓔ

10. Of which of the following works did Ernest Hemingway say, "It's the best book we've had. All American writing comes from that"?

(A) *The Last of the Mohicans*
(B) *Moby-Dick*
(C) *The Scarlet Letter*
(D) *Walden*
(E) *Adventures of Huckleberry Finn*

Ⓐ Ⓑ Ⓒ Ⓓ Ⓔ

11. Which of the following writers was particularly important in the development of the short story as a literary form?

   (A) James Fenimore Cooper   (B) Harriet Beecher Stowe
    (C) Frederick Douglass   (D) Edgar Allan Poe
    (E) Edith Wharton   Ⓐ Ⓑ Ⓒ Ⓓ Ⓔ

     Make me, O Lord, thy Spining Wheele compleate,
     Thy Holy Worde my Distaff make for mee.
     Make mine Affections thy Swift Flyers neate
     And make my Soule thy holy Spoole to bee.
(5)   My Conversation make to be thy Reele
     And reele the yarn thereon spun of thy Wheele.

12. The passage above is notable chiefly for

   (A) irony of statement   (B) pathetic fallacy
    (C) a literary conceit   (D) a paradox
    (E) a simile   Ⓐ Ⓑ Ⓒ Ⓓ Ⓔ

13. Which of the following best states the theme of Stephen Crane's "The Open Boat"?

   (A) The fate of humanity is largely in our own hands.
   (B) By acts of courage, people may overcome inherent weaknesses.
   (C) Nature, though seemingly hostile, is indifferent to human beings.
   (D) Through perseverance, a world of peace and harmony will
        ultimately be achieved.
   (E) In any struggle, the strongest are fated to survive.

                         Ⓐ Ⓑ Ⓒ Ⓓ Ⓔ

14. The last part of *Native Son* is about

   (A) the main character's trial
   (B) the wedding of two characters
   (C) the main character's journey to a new home
   (D) a resolution of the racial conflicts in the book
   (E) the main character's later years

                         Ⓐ Ⓑ Ⓒ Ⓓ Ⓔ

15. Mark Twain and William Dean Howells are commonly described by literary critics as

   (A) transcendentalists   (B) symbolists
    (C) realists   (D) romantics   (E) naturalists
                         Ⓐ Ⓑ Ⓒ Ⓓ Ⓔ

16. All of the following were written by Toni Morrison EXCEPT

    (A) *Song of Solomon*   (B) *Tar Baby*
     (C) *The Bluest Eye*   (D) *Sula*
      (E) *The Color Purple*   Ⓐ Ⓑ Ⓒ Ⓓ Ⓔ

Questions 17-18

     Tree at my window, window tree,
     My sash is lowered when night comes on;
     But let there never be curtain drawn
     Between you and me.

(5)   Vague dream-head lifted out of the ground,
     And thing next most diffuse to cloud,
     Not all your light tongues talking aloud
     Could be profound.

     But, tree, I have seen you taken and tossed,
(10) And if you have seen me when I slept,
     You have seen me when I was taken and swept
     And all but lost.

     That day she put our heads together,
     Fate had her imagination about her,
(15) Your head so much concerned with outer,
     Mine with inner, weather.

From *The Poetry of Robert Frost* edited by Edward Connery Lathem. Copyright 1928, © 1969 by Holt, Rinehart and Winston. Copyright © 1956 by Robert Frost. Reprinted by permission of Henry Holt and Company, Inc.

17. The "light tongues" (line 7) are a metaphorical reference to the tree's

    (A) frivolous thoughts   (B) inquisitiveness   (C) large branches
     (D) imagination (E) leaves
                          Ⓐ Ⓑ Ⓒ Ⓓ Ⓔ

18. When the tree is "taken and tossed" (line 9), the speaker sees the tree as an image of

    (A) the ruthlessness of nature
    (B) his own troubled mind
    (C) the uncertainty of Fate herself
    (D) a lack of seriousness in nature
    (E) shaken but unbowed human will   Ⓐ Ⓑ Ⓒ Ⓓ Ⓔ

19. Which of the following novels has as its main concern the life of Black people in the United States?

    (A) *All the King's Men*   (B) *The Age of Innocence*
      (C) *Henderson the Rain King*   (D) *Invisible Man*
        (E) *The Catcher in the Rye*   Ⓐ Ⓑ Ⓒ Ⓓ Ⓔ

20. All of the following are familiar images from the poems of Emily Dickinson EXCEPT a

    (A) fly in a still room making an "uncertain stumbling buzz"
    (B) slanted ray of late afternoon winter sunlight
    (C) rain-filled red wheelbarrow "beside the white chickens"
    (D) train metaphorically described in terms of a horse
    (E) saddened person who "never lost as much but twice"

    Ⓐ Ⓑ Ⓒ Ⓓ Ⓔ

Questions 21-22

Let me tell you about the very rich. They are different from you and me. They possess and enjoy early, and it does something to
(5) them, makes them soft where we are hard, and cynical where we are trustful, in a way that, unless you were born rich, it is very difficult to understand. They think, deep in their hearts, that they are better than we are because we had to discover the compensations and refuges of life for ourselves. Even when they enter deep into our world or sink below us, they still think that they are better than we are. They are different.

21. In the passage, which of the following best describes the speaker's attitude toward the very rich?

    (A) He finds their cynicism alarming and unwarranted.
    (B) He believes that, because of their advantages and experience, the rich know more than we do.
    (C) He is envious of their power and position.
    (D) He thinks that he understands their psychology even though he has not shared their advantages.
    (E) He finds them so different from the rest of us as to be practically unknowable.   Ⓐ Ⓑ Ⓒ Ⓓ Ⓔ

22. The passage can be attributed to

    (A) F. Scott Fitzgerald   (B) Willa Cather   (C) John Steinbeck
      (D) Sinclair Lewis   (E) Theodore Dreiser
        Ⓐ Ⓑ Ⓒ Ⓓ Ⓔ

23. At the end of Kate Chopin's *The Awakening*, the heroine does which of the following?

    (A) Travels to a new home.
    (B) Walks into the sea.
    (C) Makes a speech.
    (D) Has a child.
    (E) Marries for the second time.

Ⓐ Ⓑ Ⓒ Ⓓ Ⓔ

24. John Steinbeck's *The Grapes of Wrath* depicts

    (A) the plight of dispossessed farmers who migrate to California
    (B) prison conditions in turn-of-the-century America
    (C) a wounded soldier who tries in vain to escape the effects of war
    (D) racial problems in a small farming town in Oklahoma
    (E) a drifter and his friend who dream hopelessly of better lives

Ⓐ Ⓑ Ⓒ Ⓓ Ⓔ

25. All of the following were first published in the 1850's EXCEPT

    (A) Thoreau's *Walden*
    (B) Emerson's *Nature*
    (C) Whitman's *Leaves of Grass*
    (D) Melville's *Moby-Dick*
    (E) Hawthorne's *The Scarlet Letter*

Ⓐ Ⓑ Ⓒ Ⓓ Ⓔ

Optional Free-Response Section

If your college requires that the optional free-response section be taken in addition to the multiple-choice examination, you should review the following information.

The optional free-response section of the American Literature examination draws from the same general content as does the multiple-choice test. Its purpose is to test the candidate's ability to write about American literature in an informed and organized manner. While good writing skills and knowledge of grammar will enhance the candidate's ability to respond to the questions, the optional section is not intended to be a test of these abilities.

Candidates are required to answer two of three essay questions within a 90-minute period. The first question, which is required, asks candidates to apply to American authors a critical generalization stated in the test book. They must support their statements with examples from the works of a list of American authors. For the second essay, candidates may choose to discuss either a prose passage or a poem printed in the test book. Instructions for each selection indicate what should be included in the discussion, and some thought-provoking comments and questions are provided as guides in organizing the essay.

For additional information, read the sections on "Taking Free-Response or Essay Tests," in chapter 5, and "How Free-Response Answers and Essays Are Graded," in chapter 6.

Study Resources

The list that follows contains textbooks typically used in American literature courses at the college level. To prepare for the American Literature examination, you should read critically the contents of at least one anthology. Most textbook anthologies contain a representative sample of readings as well as discussions of historical background, literary styles and devices characteristic of various authors and periods, and other material relevant to the test. The anthologies do vary somewhat in their content, approach, and emphasis; you are advised to consult more than one or to consult some specialized books on major authors, periods, and literary forms and terminology. You should also read some of the major novels that are mentioned or excerpted in the anthologies, such as Nathaniel Hawthorne's *The Scarlet Letter*, Mark Twain's *Adventures of Huckleberry Finn*, and Kate Chopin's *The Awakening*. Other novelists whose major works you should be familiar with include Melville, Crane, Wharton, Cather, Fitzgerald, Hemingway, Faulkner, Ellison, and Wright. You can probably obtain an extensive reading list of American literature from a college English department, library, or bookstore.

Additional suggestions for preparing for CLEP examinations are given in chapter 4.

Many libraries do not carry textbooks as a policy. If you can't find any of the following textbooks at the library, see whether the college bookstore has a used copy. If you can't locate the most recent edition, an edition that is one or two years older will suffice for most subject areas. As a final option, purchase a new copy of the suggested textbook as an investment in your education.

SUGGESTED TEXTBOOKS

Barksdale, Richard and Keneth Kinnamon, eds. *Black Writers of America: A Comprehensive Anthology*. New York: Macmillan, 1972.

Baym, Nina et al., eds., *The Norton Anthology of American Literature*, 2 vols., 3rd ed. New York: W. W. Norton, 1989.

Lauter, Paul et al., eds., *The Heath Anthology of American Literature*, 2 vols. Lexington, MA: D.C. Heath, 1990.

McMichael, George et al., eds., *Anthology of American Literature*, 2 vols., 4th ed. New York: Macmillan, 1989.

Perkins, George et al., eds., *The American Tradition in Literature*, 2 vols., 7th ed. New York: McGraw-Hill, 1990.

Analysis and Interpretation of Literature

Description of the Examination

The Subject Examination in Analysis and Interpretation of Literature covers material that is usually taught in a general two-semester undergraduate course in literature. Although it does not require familiarity with specific works, it does assume that the student has read widely and perceptively in poetry, drama, fiction, and nonfiction. The questions are based on passages supplied in the test. These passages have been selected so that no previous experience with them is required to answer the questions. The passages are taken primarily from American and British literature.

The test includes approximately 90 multiple-choice questions to be answered in two separately timed 45-minute sections.

Knowledge and Skills Required

Questions on the Analysis and Interpretation of Literature examination require candidates to demonstrate the following abilities.

- Ability to read prose, poetry, and drama with understanding

- Ability to analyze the elements of a literary passage and to respond to nuances of meaning, tone, imagery, and style

- Ability to interpret metaphors, to recognize rhetorical and stylistic devices, to perceive relationships between parts and wholes, and to grasp a speaker's or author's attitudes

- Knowledge of the means by which literary effects are achieved

- Familiarity with the basic terminology used to discuss literary texts

The examination emphasizes comprehension, interpretation, and analysis of literary works. Only a minimum of specific factual knowledge is required; however, a broad knowledge of literature gained through reading widely is assumed, as is a familiarity with basic literary terminology. The following outline indicates the relative emphasis given to the various types of literature and the periods from which the passages are taken.

	Approximate Percent of Examination
35-45%	Poetry
35-45%	Prose (fiction and nonfiction)
15-25%	Drama
50-65%	British literature
30-45%	American literature
5-15%	Works in translation
3-7%	Classical and pre-Renaissance
20-30%	Renaissance and 17th century
35-45%	18th and 19th centuries
25-35%	20th century

Sample Questions

The 25 sample questions that follow are similar to questions on the Analysis and Interpretation of Literature examination, but they do not actually appear on it.

Before attempting to answer the sample questions, read all the information about the Analysis and Interpretation of Literature examination on the preceding pages. Additional suggestions for preparing for CLEP examinations are provided in chapter 4.

Try to answer correctly as many questions as possible. Then compare your answers with the correct answers, given in Appendix B.

Directions: The samples below consist of selections from literary works and questions on their content, form, and style. After reading a passage, choose the best answer to each question.

Questions 1-10

    "A clear fire, a clean hearth, and the rigor of the game." This was the celebrated wish of old Sarah Battle (now with God) who, next to her devotions, loved a good game at whist. She was none of your lukewarm gamesters, your half-and-half players, who have no

(5)   objection to take a hand, if you want one to make up a rubber; who affirm that they have no pleasure in winning; that they like to win one game, and lose another; that they can while away an hour very agreeably at a card table, but are indifferent whether they play or no; and will desire an adversary, who has slipt a wrong card, to take

(10)   it up and play another. These insufferable triflers are the curse of a table. One of these flies will spoil a whole pot. Of such it may be said, that they do not play at cards, but only play at playing at them.

    Sarah Battle was none of that breed. She detested them, as I do,

(15)   from her heart and soul; and would not, save upon a striking emergency, willingly seat herself at the same table with them. She loved a thorough-paced partner, a determined enemy. She took, and gave, no concessions. She hated favors. She never made a revoke, nor ever passed it over in her adversary without exacting the utmost

(20)   forfeiture. She fought a good fight: cut and thrust. She held not her sword (her cards) "like a dancer." She sate bolt upright; and neither showed you her cards, nor desired to see yours. All people have their blind side — their superstitions; and I have heard her declare, under the rose,* that Hearts was her favorite suit.

---

*under the rose: *sub rosa*, in confidence

1. The phrase "now with God" (line 2) reveals that Sarah Battle

    (A) was a religious person
    (B) had an unexpected religious experience
    (C) placed devotion to God ahead of whist
    (D) had decided to give up cards
    (E) is no longer alive

    Ⓐ Ⓑ Ⓒ Ⓓ Ⓔ

2. In line 2, "next to" is best paraphrased as

    (A) second only to   (B) alongside   (C) before
    (D) in addition to   (E) even more than

    Ⓐ Ⓑ Ⓒ Ⓓ Ⓔ

3. To Sarah Battle, the most significant characteristic of the "triflers" described in lines 4-13 is their

    (A) amiable sociability
    (B) generosity toward their opponents
    (C) nonchalant attitude toward whist
    (D) tendency to play unfairly
    (E) dislike of all games   Ⓐ Ⓑ Ⓒ Ⓓ Ⓔ

4. In context, the phrases "insufferable triflers" (line 10) and "striking emergency" (lines 15-16) exemplify which of the following?

    (A) Metaphor   (B) Alliteration   (C) Paradox
      (D) Hyperbole   (E) Personification
                                              Ⓐ Ⓑ Ⓒ Ⓓ Ⓔ

5. It can be inferred from the description of Sarah Battle's behavior at the whist table that she

    (A) would respect a superior opponent
    (B) did not care whether she won or lost
    (C) would cheat to win
    (D) did not enjoy the game of whist
    (E) was a beginning player   Ⓐ Ⓑ Ⓒ Ⓓ Ⓔ

6. In context, "exacting the utmost forfeiture" (lines 19-20) means

    (A) measuring the final payment
    (B) requiring the total penalty
    (C) plotting full retribution
    (D) estimating her opponents' losses
    (E) demanding the greatest sacrifice   Ⓐ Ⓑ Ⓒ Ⓓ Ⓔ

7. The basic metaphor underlying much of this character sketch is drawn from

    (A) nature   (B) religion   (C) finance
      (D) swordplay   (E) running   Ⓐ Ⓑ Ⓒ Ⓓ Ⓔ

8. The attitude of the narrator toward Sarah Battle is chiefly one of

    (A) sarcastic anger
    (B) affectionate respect
    (C) tolerant understanding
    (D) arrogant condescension
    (E) fearful regard   Ⓐ Ⓑ Ⓒ Ⓓ Ⓔ

9. From the passage we learn all of the following about the narrator EXCEPT that the narrator

    (A) has a sense of humor
    (B) has spent time in Sarah Battle's presence
    (C) is an excellent whist player
    (D) scorns casual whist players
    (E) sees Sarah Battle's weakness

    Ⓐ Ⓑ Ⓒ Ⓓ Ⓔ

10. Which of the following best summarizes the structure of the passage?

    (A) The first paragraph concentrates on Sarah Battle's serious side, the second on her fun-loving side.
    (B) The first paragraph defines Sarah Battle by what she is not, the second by what she is.
    (C) The passage interprets, in turn, what Sarah Battle would regard as "A clear fire, a clean hearth, and the rigor of the game" (line 1).
    (D) The passage moves from a discussion of the refinements of whist to an explanation of what makes Sarah Battle like the game.
    (E) The first paragraph describes Sarah Battle as a gambler, the second as a soldier of reform.

    Ⓐ Ⓑ Ⓒ Ⓓ Ⓔ

Questions 11-16

How many thousand of my poorest subjects
Are at this hour asleep! O sleep! O gentle sleep!
Nature's soft nurse, how have I frighted thee,
That thou no more wilt weigh my eyelids down,
(5)   And steep my senses in forgetfulness?
Why rather, sleep, liest thou in smoky cribs,
Upon uneasy pallets stretching thee,
And hush'd with buzzing night-flies to thy slumber,
Than in the perfum'd chambers of the great,
(10) Under the canopies of costly state,
And lull'd with sound of sweetest melody?
O thou dull god, why li'st thou with the vile
In loathsome beds, and leavest the kingly couch
A watch-case or a common 'larum-bell?
(15) Wilt thou upon the high and giddy mast
Seal up the ship-boy's eyes, and rock his brains
In cradle of the rude imperious surge,
And in the visitation of the winds,
Who take the ruffian billows by the top,

(20)   Curling their monstrous heads and hanging them
        With deafening clamor in the slippery clouds,
        That with the hurly death itself awakes?
        Canst thou, O partial sleep, give then repose
        To the wet sea-boy in an hour so rude,
(25)   And in the calmest and most stillest night,
        With all appliances and means to boot,
        Deny it to a king? Then happy low, lie down!
        Uneasy lies the head that wears a crown.

11. The dramatic situation suggested by the speech is that of a king

    (A) cast down from high estate
    (B) concerned about the poverty of his subjects
    (C) setting forth on a dangerous journey
    (D) fearful of death
    (E) restless with cares   Ⓐ Ⓑ Ⓒ Ⓓ Ⓔ

12. In lines 23-27, the speaker asks about the

    (A) discrepancy between the appearance and the actuality of death
    (B) brevity of time when considered from the perspective of a king
    (C) reasons why the common people take their duties so lightly
    (D) problem of succession when a king dies suddenly
    (E) reason why sleep is allotted to the king's subjects but not to the
          king himself
        Ⓐ Ⓑ Ⓒ Ⓓ Ⓔ

13. In the context of the passage, "partial" (line 23) means

    (A) biased   (B) unrequited   (C) half-waking
      (D) two-faced   (E) favorite   Ⓐ Ⓑ Ⓒ Ⓓ Ⓔ

14. In line 27, "low" refers to

    (A) "my poorest subjects" (line 1)
    (B) "sweetest melody" (line 11)
    (C) "rude imperious surge" (line 17)
    (D) "O partial sleep" (line 23)
    (E) "a king" (line 27)   Ⓐ Ⓑ Ⓒ Ⓓ Ⓔ

15. The speaker's tone in addressing sleep changes from

    (A) confident to insecure
    (B) bitter to victorious
    (C) pleading to reproachful
    (D) outraged to sarcastic
    (E) angry to bewildered   Ⓐ Ⓑ Ⓒ Ⓓ Ⓔ

16. With minor variations, the passage is written in

(A) elegy form   (B) blank verse   (C) free verse
(D) heroic couplets   (E) the form of an ode

Ⓐ Ⓑ Ⓒ Ⓓ Ⓔ

Questions 17-20

The Palace Hotel at Fort Romper was painted a light blue, a shade
that is on the legs of a kind of heron, causing the bird to declare its
position against any background. The Palace Hotel, then, was
always screaming and howling in a way that made the dazzling
(5)   winter landscape of Nebraska seem only a gray swampish hush. It
stood alone on the prairie, and when the snow was falling the town
two hundred yards away was not visible. But when the traveller
alighted at the railway station he was obliged to pass the Palace
Hotel before he could come upon the company of low clapboard
(10) houses which composed Fort Romper, and it was not to be thought
that any traveller could pass the Palace Hotel without looking at it.
Pat Scully, the proprietor, had proved himself a master of strategy
when he chose his paints. It is true that on clear days, when the
great transcontinental expresses, long lines of swaying Pullmans,
(15) swept through Fort Romper, passengers were overcome at the sight,
and the cult that knows the brown-reds and the subdivisions of the
dark greens of the East expressed shame, pity, horror, in a laugh.
But to the citizens of this prairie town and to the people who would
naturally stop there, Pat Scully had performed a feat. With this
(20) opulence and splendor, these creeds, classes, egotisms, that
streamed through Romper on the rails day after day, they had no
color in common.
   As if the displayed delights of such a blue hotel were not
sufficiently enticing, it was Scully's habit to go every morning and
(25) evening to meet the leisurely trains that stopped at Romper and
work his seductions upon any man that he might see wavering,
gripsack in hand.

17. The second sentence (lines 3-5) suggests that, like the heron, the
    hotel

(A) is standing in a swamp
(B) is hard to discern against its background
(C) is part of a larger group
(D) is often a raucous place
(E) stands out against its surroundings

Ⓐ Ⓑ Ⓒ Ⓓ Ⓔ

18. The word "company" (line 9) suggests that the houses are

    (A) comforting to a lonely traveller
    (B) close together
    (C) pretentious residences
    (D) filled with military personnel
    (E) owned by a corporation

    (A) (B) (C) (D) (E)

19. Lines 19-22 imply that Pat Scully's efforts have given the citizens of Romper a

    (A) complex and rich history
    (B) greater love of the past
    (C) reinvigorated economy
    (D) sense of local distinction
    (E) reputation for poor taste

    (A) (B) (C) (D) (E)

20. Scully's dominant trait as presented in the passage is

    (A) ingenuity   (B) laziness   (C) timidity
       (D) lust   (E) friendliness

    (A) (B) (C) (D) (E)

Questions 21-25

In My Craft or Sullen Art

        In my craft or sullen art
        Exercised in the still night
        When only the moon rages
        And the lovers lie abed
   (5) With all their griefs in their arms,
        I labour by singing light
        Not for ambition or bread
        Or the strut and trade of charms
        On the ivory stages
  (10) But for the common wages
        Of their most secret heart.

        Not for the proud man apart
        From the raging moon I write
        On these spindrift* pages
  (15) Nor for the towering dead
        With their nightingales and psalms
        But for the lovers, their arms
        Round the griefs of the ages,
        Who pay no praise or wages
  (20) Nor heed my craft or art.

          *spindrift: wind-blown sea spray

21. The negative constructions "Not . . . But" (lines 7 and 10) and "Not . . . Nor . . . But" (lines 12, 15, and 17) emphasize a contrast between the

   (A) typical motivations of most people and the motivation of the speaker
   (B) speaker's self-image and the speaker's view of the lovers
   (C) lovers embracing their own griefs and embracing the griefs of the ages
   (D) attitude of the speaker toward the lovers and their attitude toward the speaker
   (E) common craft of writing light verse and the sublime art of writing poetry

   Ⓐ Ⓑ Ⓒ Ⓓ Ⓔ

22. Which of the following is the antecedent of "their" (line 11)?

   (A) "lovers" (line 4)
   (B) "griefs" (line 5)
   (C) "strut and trade of charms" (line 8)
   (D) "ivory stages" (line 9)
   (E) "wages" (line 10)

   Ⓐ Ⓑ Ⓒ Ⓓ Ⓔ

23. The fact that the speaker writes "spindrift pages" (line 14) while "the moon rages" (line 3) allows the reader to infer that "the proud man apart/From the raging moon" (lines 12-13) is

   (A) a poet who overestimates his own talent
   (B) a poet who has condemned the work of the speaker
   (C) someone who is unmoved by the passion of nature
   (D) someone who believes that nature is more beautiful than art
   (E) someone who seeks fame through an avenue other than art

   Ⓐ Ⓑ Ⓒ Ⓓ Ⓔ

24. The phrase "the towering dead/With their nightingales and psalms" (lines 15-16) alludes to the

   (A) fear of death and longing for immortality
   (B) poet's physical and spiritual future
   (C) interplay of nature and the supernatural
   (D) artificiality and futility of human institutions
   (E) great poets and poetry of the past

   Ⓐ Ⓑ Ⓒ Ⓓ Ⓔ

25. How does the speaker feel about the response of the lovers to his efforts?

    (A) The speaker wishes to get vengeance by revealing the secrets of the lovers.
    (B) The speaker will stop writing out of resentment for their indifference.
    (C) The speaker will seek a new audience and relegate the lovers to the position of the proud man.
    (D) The speaker will continue to write for the lovers regardless of their response.
    (E) The speaker really writes only for himself and does not desire an audience.

    Ⓐ Ⓑ Ⓒ Ⓓ Ⓔ

Optional Free-Response Section

If your college requires that the optional free-response section be taken in addition to the multiple-choice examination, you should review the following information.

The optional free-response section of the Analysis and Interpretation of Literature examination requires candidates to demonstrate their ability to write well-organized critical essays. Candidates are asked to write two essays within a 90-minute time period. In the first essay, they are asked to discuss a poem printed in the test book; in the second essay, the candidates read a general literary statement and then apply it to a work of recognized literary merit which they choose and with which they are familiar. In responding to the questions, candidates are expected to avoid vague generalities, irrelevant philosophizing, and unnecessary plot summaries. They should pay particular attention to the quality of their writing (organization, sentence structure, diction and clarity, the relevance of their illustrations to the questions asked, and the critical perceptiveness of their answers).

For additional information, read the sections on "Taking Free-Response or Essay Tests," in chapter 5, and "How Free-Response Answers and Essays Are Graded," in chapter 6.

Study Resources

The most relevant preparation that you can do for the Analysis and Interpretation of Literature examination is attentive and reflective reading of the various literary genres of poetry, drama, and prose. There are several ways to prepare for the test:

1. Read a variety of poetry, drama, fiction, and nonfiction.
2. Read critical analyses of various literary works.
3. Write your own analysis and interpretation of the works you read.
4. Discuss with others the meaning of the literature you read.

Textbooks used in college courses in analysis and interpretation of literature contain a sampling of literary works in a variety of genres. They also contain material that can help you to comprehend the sense and intent of literary works and to recognize the devices used by writers to convey that sense and intent. The following list contains several textbooks that are typical of those used in such courses. To prepare for the examination, you should study the contents of at least one textbook. You would do well to consult two or three texts because they do vary somewhat in content, approach, and emphasis. For example, Perrine is a basic introduction to reading literature; Roberts emphasizes literary analysis; both Barnet and Perrine include glossaries of literary terms.

Additional suggestions for preparing for CLEP examinations are given in chapter 4.

Many libraries do not carry textbooks as a policy. If you can't find any of the following textbooks at the library, see whether the college bookstore has a used copy. If you can't locate the most recent edition, an edition that is one or two years older will suffice for most subject areas. As a final option, purchase a new copy of the suggested textbook as an investment in your education.

TEXTBOOKS

Bain, Carl E. et al., *The Norton Introduction to Literature*, 5th ed. New York: W. W. Norton, 1991.

Barnet, Sylvan et al., *An Introduction to Literature: Fiction, Poetry, Drama*, 9th ed. Glenview, IL: Scott Foresman, 1989.

Kennedy, X. J., ed., *Literature: An Introduction to Fiction, Poetry, and Drama*, 5th ed. Hudson, NH: HarperCollins, 1991.

Perrine, Laurence and Thomas R. Arp, eds., *Literature: Structure, Sound, and Sense*, 5th ed. San Diego: Harcourt Brace Jovanovich, 1988.

Pickering, James H. and Jeffery D. Hoeper, comps., *Literature*, 3rd ed. New York: Macmillan, 1990.

Roberts, Edgar V. and Henry E. Jacobs, eds., *Literature: An Introduction to Reading and Writing*, 3rd ed. Englewood Cliffs, NJ: Prentice-Hall, 1991.

Scholes, Robert et al., *Elements of Literature: Essay, Fiction, Poetry, Drama, Film*, 4th ed. New York: Oxford University Press, 1991.

English Literature

Description of the Examination

The Subject Examination in English Literature covers the material that is usually taught in a two-semester course (or the equivalent) at the college level. The test is primarily concerned with major authors and literary works, but it also includes questions on some minor writers. Candidates are expected to be acquainted with common literary themes, common literary terms, such as metaphor and personification, and basic literary forms, such as the sonnet and ballad.

In both coverage and approach, the examination resembles the historically organized survey of English literature offered by many colleges that deals with literature from Beowulf to the present. It assumes that the candidate has read widely and developed an appreciation of English literature, knows the basic literary periods, has a sense of the historical development of English literature, and is able to identify the author of a representative quotation or to recognize the period in which an excerpt was written.

The examination consists of approximately 105 multiple-choice questions to be answered in two separately timed 45-minute sections.

Knowledge and Skills Required

The English Literature examination requires the following knowledge and abilities. The percentages at the left show the relative emphasis given to knowledge and ability, but most questions draw on both.

♦   *Approximate Percent of Examination*

45%   Knowledge of information related to:

        Literary background

        Identification of authors

        Metrical patterns

        Literary references

➡ *Approximate Percent of Examination*

55%   Ability to:
    Analyze the elements of form in a literary passage
    Perceive meanings
    Identify tone and mood
    Follow patterns of imagery
    Identify characteristics of style

Sample Questions

The 25 sample questions that follow are similar to questions on the English Literature examination, but they do not actually appear on it.

Before attempting to answer the sample questions, read all the information about the English Literature examination on the preceding pages. Additional suggestions for preparing for CLEP examinations are provided in chapter 4.

Try to answer correctly as many questions as possible. Then compare your answers with the correct answers, given in Appendix B.

Directions: Each of the questions or incomplete statements below is followed by five suggested answers or completions. Select the one that is best in each case.

In a pungent critique of humanity addressed to the mature imagination, the author comments on human nature by examining the life of the Lilliputians, Yahoos, and Houyhnhnms.

1. The book described above is

    (A) *The Way of All Flesh*
    (B) *Through the Looking Glass*
    (C) *Gulliver's Travels*
    (D) *The Pilgrim's Progress*
    (E) *Robinson Crusoe*   Ⓐ Ⓑ Ⓒ Ⓓ Ⓔ

One of the great triumphs of the play is Shakespeare's addition of the character of the Fool, who attempts to comfort his old master and is distressed and puzzled by his madness, but who also ironically emphasizes the folly and the tragedy of the old man.

2. The play referred to above is

    (A) *Macbeth*   (B) *Julius Caesar*   (C) *King Lear*
      (D) *Othello*   (E) *Hamlet*
                                              Ⓐ Ⓑ Ⓒ Ⓓ Ⓔ

Questions 3-4

> For I have learned
> To look on nature, not as in the hour
> Of thoughtless youth; but hearing oftentimes
> The still, sad music of humanity,
> Nor harsh nor grating, though of ample power
> To chasten and subdue. And I have felt
> A presence that disturbs me with the joy
> Of elevated thoughts; a sense sublime
> Of something far more deeply interfused,
> Whose dwelling is the light of setting suns,
> And the round ocean and the living air,
> And the blue sky, and in the mind of man.

3. The lines above are written in

   (A) heroic couplets   (B) terza rima   (C) ballad meter
   (D) blank verse   (E) iambic tetrameter

   Ⓐ Ⓑ Ⓒ Ⓓ Ⓔ

4. The language and ideas in these lines are most characteristic of which of the following literary periods?

   (A) Medieval   (B) Restoration   (C) Augustan
   (D) Romantic   (E) Early twentieth century

   Ⓐ Ⓑ Ⓒ Ⓓ Ⓔ

---

5. Samuel Richardson, Henry Fielding, and Tobias Smollett are best known as eighteenth-century

   (A) novelists   (B) dramatists   (C) essayists
   (D) poets   (E) critics

   Ⓐ Ⓑ Ⓒ Ⓓ Ⓔ

A man may be in as just possession of Truth as of City, and yet be forced to surrender; 'tis therefore far better to enjoy her with peace, than to hazard her on a battle.

6. Which of the following is the best summary of the lines above?

   (A) One must continually seek Truth, no matter what the cost.
   (B) One who knows Truth cannot always defend Truth, and so should avoid battle.
   (C) One can never be harmed by Truth, if one enjoys Truth in peace.
   (D) Truth painfully won is rarely forgotten by those who defend Truth.
   (E) Truth can decay, even though one possesses Truth justly.

   Ⓐ Ⓑ Ⓒ Ⓓ Ⓔ

7. An anonymous narrative poem focusing on the climax of a particularly dramatic event and employing frequent repetition, conventional figures of speech, and sometimes a refrain — altered and transmitted orally in a musical setting — is called a

    (A) popular ballad   (B) pastoral elegy
    (C) courtly lyric   (D) villanelle
    (E) chivalric romance

Ⓐ Ⓑ Ⓒ Ⓓ Ⓔ

Questions 8-10

They, looking back, all the eastern side beheld
Of Paradise, so late their happy seat,
Waved over by that flaming brand, the gate
With dreadful faces thronged and fiery arms.
(5) Some natural tears they dropped, but wiped them soon;
The world was all before them, where to choose
Their place of rest, and Providence their guide:
They hand in hand, with wandering steps and slow
Through Eden took their solitary way.

8. These lines were written by

    (A) John Donne   (B) Edmund Spenser   (C) Christopher Marlowe
    (D) William Shakespeare   (E) John Milton

Ⓐ Ⓑ Ⓒ Ⓓ Ⓔ

9. In line 2, "late" is best interpreted to mean

    (A) recently   (B) tardily   (C) unfortunately
    (D) long   (E) soon

Ⓐ Ⓑ Ⓒ Ⓓ Ⓔ

10. The people referred to as "they" in the passage were probably experiencing all the following emotions EXCEPT

    (A) awe   (B) doubt   (C) suspicion
    (D) regret   (E) sorrow

Ⓐ Ⓑ Ⓒ Ⓓ Ⓔ

Whan that Aprill with his shoures soote
The droghte of March hath perced to the roote

11. The lines above were written by

    (A) Geoffrey Chaucer   (B) William Shakespeare
    (C) Alexander Pope   (D) William Wordsworth
    (E) Robert Browning

Ⓐ Ⓑ Ⓒ Ⓓ Ⓔ

12. Alfred Tennyson's "Ulysses" and T. S. Eliot's "The Love Song of J. Alfred Prufrock" are both

    (A) pastoral elegies
    (B) literary ballads
    (C) mock epics
    (D) dramatic monologues
    (E) irregular odes   Ⓐ Ⓑ Ⓒ Ⓓ Ⓔ

Questions 13-14

> Our two souls therefore, which are one,
>   Though I must go, endure not yet
> A breach, but an expansion,
>   Like gold to airy thinness beat.

13. The passage contains an example of

    (A) an epic simile
    (B) a metaphysical conceit
    (C) an epic catalog
    (D) an alexandrine
    (E) sprung rhythm   Ⓐ Ⓑ Ⓒ Ⓓ Ⓔ

14. The passage is from a poem by

    (A) Alexander Pope
    (B) Robert Herrick
    (C) Samuel Taylor Coleridge
    (D) Samuel Johnson
    (E) John Donne   Ⓐ Ⓑ Ⓒ Ⓓ Ⓔ

Questions 15-17

> . . . He's here in double trust:
> First, as I am his kinsman and his subject,
> Strong both against the deed; then, as his host,
> Who should against his murtherer shut the door,
> (5) Not bear the knife myself. Besides, this Duncan
> Hath borne his faculties so meek, hath been
> So clear in his great office, that his virtues
> Will plead like angels, trumpet-tongu'd, against
> The deep damnation of his taking-off;
> (10) And pity, like a naked new-born babe,
> Striding the blast, or heaven's cherubin, hors'd
> Upon the sightless couriers of the air,
> Shall blow the horrid deed in every eye.
> That tears shall drown the wind.

15. The speaker of these lines might best be described as a

    (A) coward
    (B) man badly treated by Duncan
    (C) man seeking revenge
    (D) man concerned only with his own safety
    (E) man troubled by moral law   Ⓐ Ⓑ Ⓒ Ⓓ Ⓔ

16. The "horrid deed" (line 13) is compared metaphorically to

    (A) a cinder or speck irritating the eye
    (B) a naked newborn babe
    (C) an assassination
    (D) the wind
    (E) the consequences of the murder of Duncan   Ⓐ Ⓑ Ⓒ Ⓓ Ⓔ

17. These lines are spoken by

    (A) Hamlet   (B) Cassius   (C) Macbeth
    (D) Iago   (E) Richard III   Ⓐ Ⓑ Ⓒ Ⓓ Ⓔ

---

18. Which of the following is the first line of a poem by John Keats?

    (A) "What dire offence from amorous causes springs"
    (B) "They flee from me that sometime did me seek"
    (C) "Thou still unravished bride of quietness"
    (D) "I weep for Adonais — he is dead"
    (E) "Not, I'll not, carrion comfort, Despair, not feast on thee"

                                                    Ⓐ Ⓑ Ⓒ Ⓓ Ⓔ

Questions 19-20

> O threats of Hell and Hopes of Paradise!
> One thing at least is certain — *This* life flies;
>   One thing is certain and the rest is Lies:
> The Flower that once has blown for ever dies.

19. In the fourth line, "blown" means

    (A) blown up   (B) blown away   (C) bloomed
       (D) died   (E) been planted

    Ⓐ Ⓑ Ⓒ Ⓓ Ⓔ

20. Which of the following is the best summary of the four lines?

    (A) Do not ignore the serious aspects of life; earnest dedication is
         necessary for success.
    (B) Do not rely on a theoretical afterlife; you can be sure only that the
         present moment will pass.
    (C) Life is like a flower with roots in both good and evil.
    (D) Religious belief is essential to a happy life.
    (E) The only safe course in life is to ignore outside events and
         cultivate one's own garden.

    Ⓐ Ⓑ Ⓒ Ⓓ Ⓔ

---

21. Which of the following was written earliest?

    (A) *The Waste Land*
    (B) *The Rime of the Ancient Mariner*
    (C) *Songs of Innocence*
    (D) *The Faerie Queene*
    (E) *The Rape of the Lock*

    Ⓐ Ⓑ Ⓒ Ⓓ Ⓔ

Questions 22-23

She was alone and still, gazing out to sea; and when she felt his presence and the worship of his eyes turned to him in quiet suffrance of his gaze, without shame or wantonness. Long, long she suffered his gaze and then quietly withdrew her eyes from his and bent them towards the stream, gently stirring the water with her foot hither and thither. The first faint noise of gently moving water broke the silence, low and faint and whispering, faint as the bells of sleep; hither and thither, hither and thither: and a faint flame trembled on her cheek.

—Heavenly God! cried Stephen's soul, in an outburst of profane joy.

22. The passage above appears in which of the following novels?

  (A) *Victory*
  (B) *A Portrait of the Artist as a Young Man*
  (C) *Tess of the D'Urbervilles*
  (D) *The Egoist*
  (E) *Sons and Lovers*

  Ⓐ Ⓑ Ⓒ Ⓓ Ⓔ

23. The passage presents an example of what its author would have termed

  (A) synecdoche
  (B) pathetic fallacy
  (C) stream of consciousness
  (D) an eclogue
  (E) an epiphany

  Ⓐ Ⓑ Ⓒ Ⓓ Ⓔ

---

24. Jane Austen is the author of

  (A) *Jane Eyre* and *Wuthering Heights*
  (B) *Daisy Miller* and *The Golden Bowl*
  (C) *Martin Chuzzlewit* and *Dombey and Son*
  (D) *Emma* and *Pride and Prejudice*
  (E) *The Mill on the Floss* and *Middlemarch*

  Ⓐ Ⓑ Ⓒ Ⓓ Ⓔ

25. The "Age of Johnson" in English literature was dominated by which of the following styles?

  (A) Romanticism
  (B) Neoclassicism
  (C) Expressionism
  (D) Naturalism
  (E) Abstractionism

  Ⓐ Ⓑ Ⓒ Ⓓ Ⓔ

Optional Free-Response Section

If your college requires that the optional free-response section be taken in addition to the multiple-choice examination, you may wish to review the following information.

The optional free-response section of the English Literature examination requires the candidate to write two essays. The first essay should be a well-organized critical essay on an excerpt from a literary work provided in the test book. For the second essay, candidates must discuss one of two given general statements, drawing from their reading for pertinent examples and supportive evidence.

For additional information, read the sections on "Taking Free-Response or Essay Tests," in chapter 5, and "How Free-Response Answers and Essays Are Graded," in chapter 6.

Study Resources

The list below contains several anthologies typically used as textbooks in English literature courses at the college level. To prepare for the English Literature examination, you should read critically the contents of at least one such anthology.

Most textbook anthologies contain a representative sample of readings as well as discussions of historical background, literary styles and devices characteristic of various authors and periods, and other material relevant to the test. The anthologies do vary somewhat in content, approach, and emphasis, and you are therefore advised to consult more than one anthology or some specialized books on major authors, periods, and literary forms and terminology. You should also read some of the major novels that are mentioned or excerpted in the anthologies. You can probably obtain an extensive reading list of English literature from a college English department, library, or bookstore.

Additional suggestions for preparing for CLEP examinations are provided in chapter 4.

Many libraries do not carry textbooks as a policy. If you can't find any of the following textbooks at the library, see whether the college bookstore has a used copy. If you can't locate the most recent edition, an edition that is one or two years older will suffice for most subject areas. As a final option, purchase a new copy of the suggested textbook as an investment in your education.

ANTHOLOGIES

Abrams, M. H. et al., eds., *The Norton Anthology of English Literature*, 2 vols., 5th ed. New York: W. W. Norton, 1988.

Baugh, Albert C., ed., *A Literary History of England*, 2nd ed. New York: Appleton-Century-Crofts, 1967.

Kermode, Frank et al., *Oxford Anthology of English Literature*. New York: Oxford University Press, 1973.

EXAMPLES OF BOOKS ON SPECIALIZED TOPICS

Abrams, M. H., A *Glossary of Literary Terms*, 5th ed. New York: Holt, Rinehart & Winston, 1988.

Beckson, Karl and Arthur Ganz, *Literary Terms: A Dictionary*, 3rd ed. New York: Noonday Press, 1989.

Drabble, Margaret, ed., *Oxford Companion to English Literature*, 2 vols., 5th ed. New York: Oxford University Press, 1985.

Shakespeare, William, *The Riverside Shakespeare*, ed. G. Blakemore Evans et al., 2 vols. Boston: Houghton Mifflin, 1974.

Freshman College Composition

Description of the Examination

The Subject Examination in Freshman College Composition measures the skills required in most first-year English courses. It is a test that addresses elements of language and grammar; various types of writing, both formal and informal; and limited analysis and interpretation of short passages of prose and poetry. The examination assumes that the candidate knows the fundamental principles of rhetoric and can apply the principles of standard written English. In addition, the test requires familiarity with research papers and reference skills.

The test has approximately 100 multiple-choice questions to be answered in two separately timed 45-minute sections.

There is also an optional free-response (essay) section that can be taken in addition to the multiple-choice test. The free-response section is graded by the institution that requests it.

Knowledge and Skills Required

The multiple-choice questions of the examination measure students' writing skills both at the sentence level and within the context of passages. Elements of language, grammar, different styles of writing, and limited literary analysis of short prose and poetry selections are tested. The examination is designed so that average students who have completed the first-year English requirement in composition can usually answer about half of the multiple-choice questions correctly.

Ability to Recognize and Use Standard Written English — The examination measures the candidate's awareness of a variety of logical, structural, and grammatical relationships within sentences. These skills are tested by approximately 20 percent of the multiple-choice questions in the examination. Questions test recognition of acceptable usage relating to:

Syntax: parrallelism, coordination, subordination, dangling modifiers

Sentence boundaries (comma-splice, run-ons, sentence fragments)

Recognition of correct sentences

Sentence variety

Concord/Agreement: subject-verb; verb tense; pronoun reference, shift, number

Correct idiom

Active/passive voice

Logical comparison

Test of punctuation

Several kinds of question formats throughout the test are intended to measure the above skills:

- *Identifying Sentence Errors* — This type of question appears in Section I of the examination. It requires the candidate to identify wording that violates the standard conventions of written discourse.

- *Improving Sentences* — This type of question appears only in Section I of the examination. It requires the candidate to choose the version of a phrase, clause, or sentence that best conveys the intended meaning of a sentence.

Ability to Recognize Logical Development — Questions in approximately 65 percent of the examination measure recognition of the following in the context of works in progress (student drafts) or of published prose.

Organization

Evaluation of evidence

Awareness of audience, tone, and purpose

Level of detail

Consistency of topic focus (sustaining coherence between paragraphs)

Sentence variety

Paragraph coherence

Main idea, thesis

Rhetorical effects and emphasis

Use of language

Evaluation of author's authority and appeal

Evaluation of reasoning

Shift in point of view

The following kinds of multiple-choice questions measure writing skills in context.

- *Revising Work in Progress* — This type of question appears in Section I of the examination. The candidate identifies ways to improve an early draft of an essay.

- *Analyzing Writing* — Two prose passages written in very different modes and a poetry selection appear in Section II of the examination. The candidate answers questions about each passage and poem and about the strategies used by the author of each selection.

- *Analyzing and Evaluating Writers' Choices* — This type of question appears in Section II of the examination. The candidate answers questions about tone, attitude, ambiguity, and clarity within short prompts.

Ability to Use Resource Materials — Approximately 15 percent of the questions in Section I of the examination test the candidate's familiarity with the following basic reference skills. Skills are tested both in context and in individual questions.

Evaluating sources

Integrating resource material into the research paper

Manuscript format and documentation

Reference skills

Use of reference books

Sample Questions

The 50 sample questions that follow are similar to questions on the Freshman College Composition examination, but they do not appear on the actual test.

Before attempting to answer the sample questions, read all the information about the Freshman College Composition examination on the preceding pages. Additional suggestions for preparing for CLEP examinations are provided in chapter 4.

Try to answer correctly as many questions as possible. Then compare your answers with the correct answers, given in Appendix B.

SECTION I

IDENTIFYING SENTENCE ERRORS

Directions: The following sentences test your knowledge of grammar, usage, diction (choice of words), and idiom.

Some sentences are correct.
No sentence contains more than one error.

You will find that the error, if there is one, is underlined and lettered. Assume that elements of the sentence that are not underlined are correct and cannot be changed. In choosing answers, follow the requirements of standard written English.

If there is an error, select the one underlined part that must be changed to make the sentence correct and fill in the corresponding oval on your answer sheet.

If there is no error, fill in answer oval E

EXAMPLE: **SAMPLE ANSWER**

The other delegates and him immediately   Ⓐ ● Ⓒ Ⓓ Ⓔ
‾‾‾‾‾‾‾‾‾   ‾‾‾ ‾‾‾‾‾‾‾‾‾‾‾
    A   B   C
accepted the resolution drafted by the
                        ‾‾‾‾‾‾‾‾‾‾
                             D
neutral states. No error
                 ‾‾‾‾‾‾‾‾
                    E

1. Hydroelectric dams work on a simple principle: the greater the
                            ‾‾‾‾‾‾‾‾‾‾‾   ‾‾‾‾‾‾‾‾‾‾‾
                                 A   B
   distance that the water has to fall, the more the power that
                                ‾‾‾‾‾‾
                                  C
   was generated. No error   Ⓐ Ⓑ Ⓒ Ⓓ Ⓔ
   ‾‾‾‾‾‾‾‾‾‾‾‾‾ ‾‾‾‾‾‾‾‾
        D   E

2. Alexis has discovered that she can express her creativity more freely
         ‾‾‾‾‾‾‾‾‾‾‾‾‾
              A
   through her sketches and not in her photography. No error
   ‾‾‾‾‾‾‾   ‾‾‾‾‾‾‾‾ ‾‾‾‾‾‾   ‾‾‾‾‾‾‾‾
      B   C   D   E

                                                    Ⓐ Ⓑ Ⓒ Ⓓ Ⓔ

3. To learn <u>more</u> about Hispanic culture, we invited a <u>lecturer who</u> had
   ⎯⎯⎯⎯⎯   ⎯⎯⎯⎯⎯⎯⎯⎯⎯⎯⎯
      A   B

   spoken frequently <u>with regard to</u> <u>the life of</u> early settlers in Santa Fe.
                     ⎯⎯⎯⎯⎯⎯⎯⎯⎯⎯⎯⎯ ⎯⎯⎯⎯⎯⎯⎯⎯
                           C   D

   <u>No error</u>
      E

   Ⓐ Ⓑ Ⓒ Ⓓ Ⓔ

4. Many readers <u>still think</u> of Sinclair Lewis, whose strength
                ⎯⎯⎯⎯⎯⎯⎯⎯⎯
                    A

   <u>was allegedly</u> his <u>ability to tell</u> a story, <u>as one of</u> America's best
   ⎯⎯⎯⎯⎯⎯⎯⎯⎯⎯⎯   ⎯⎯⎯⎯⎯⎯⎯⎯⎯⎯⎯⎯   ⎯⎯⎯⎯⎯⎯⎯⎯⎯
        B   C   D

   social critics. <u>No error</u>
                       E

   Ⓐ Ⓑ Ⓒ Ⓓ Ⓔ

5. <u>Although</u> a lottery may seem a <u>relatively easy</u> way for a state
   ⎯⎯⎯⎯⎯⎯⎯   ⎯⎯⎯⎯⎯⎯⎯⎯⎯⎯⎯⎯⎯
      A   B

   <u>to increase</u> revenues, <u>they</u> may encourage some individuals to gamble
   ⎯⎯⎯⎯⎯⎯⎯⎯⎯⎯   ⎯⎯⎯⎯
        C   D

   excessively. <u>No error</u>
                    E

   Ⓐ Ⓑ Ⓒ Ⓓ Ⓔ

6. Even when <u>using</u> a calculator, you must have a basic <u>understanding of</u>
             ⎯⎯⎯⎯⎯   ⎯⎯⎯⎯⎯⎯⎯⎯⎯⎯⎯⎯⎯⎯⎯
               A   B

   mathematics if <u>one expects</u> to solve complex problems <u>correctly.</u>
                  ⎯⎯⎯⎯⎯⎯⎯⎯⎯⎯   ⎯⎯⎯⎯⎯⎯⎯⎯⎯
                       C   D

   <u>No error</u>
      E

   Ⓐ Ⓑ Ⓒ Ⓓ Ⓔ

7. Gwendolyn Brooks is <u>widely known</u> and highly praised for her <u>poetry,</u>
                       ⎯⎯⎯⎯⎯⎯⎯⎯⎯⎯⎯⎯   ⎯⎯⎯⎯⎯⎯⎯
                             A   B

   fewer people <u>realize that</u> she has <u>also</u> published a novel. <u>No error</u>
                ⎯⎯⎯⎯⎯⎯⎯⎯⎯⎯   ⎯⎯⎯⎯   ⎯⎯⎯⎯⎯⎯⎯
                     C   D   E

   Ⓐ Ⓑ Ⓒ Ⓓ Ⓔ

8. Although science offers the hope <u>of preventing</u> serious genetic
   A

   diseases, <u>there is</u> difficult ethical questions <u>raised by</u> the <u>possibility of</u>
   B   C   D

   altering human heredity. <u>No error</u>
   E

   Ⓐ Ⓑ Ⓒ Ⓓ Ⓔ

9. If they <u>would have</u> known how capricious the winds on Lake
   A

   Winasteke <u>are</u>, the boys would have sailed in the <u>larger</u> <u>of their</u> two
   B   C   D

   boats. <u>No error</u>
   E

   Ⓐ Ⓑ Ⓒ Ⓓ Ⓔ

10. Faulkner <u>had published</u> <u>only</u> a few novels when critics <u>seriously began</u>
    A   B   C

    to compare his work to <u>Hemingway</u>. <u>No error</u>
    D   E

    Ⓐ Ⓑ Ⓒ Ⓓ Ⓔ

IMPROVING SENTENCES

Directions: The following sentences test correctness and effectiveness of expression. In choosing answers, follow the requirements of standard written English: that is, pay attention to grammar, diction (choice of words), sentence construction, and punctuation.

In each of the following sentences, part of the sentence or the entire sentence is underlined. Beneath each sentence you will find five versions of the underlined part. Choice A repeats the original; the other four are different.

Choose the answer that best expresses the meaning of the original sentence. If you think the original is better than any of the alternatives, choose it; otherwise choose one of the others. Your choice should produce the most effective sentence — one that is clear and precise, without awkwardness or ambiguity.

Example   **Sample Answer**

Ⓐ ● Ⓒ Ⓓ Ⓔ

Laura Ingalls Wilder published her first book <u>and she was</u>
<u>sixty-five years old then.</u>

    (A)   and she was sixty-five years old then
    (B)   when she was sixty-five
    (C)   being age sixty-five years old
    (D)   upon the reaching of sixty-five years
    (E)   at the time when she was sixty-five

---

11. <u>In 1827 *Freedom's Journal* was the first Black American newspaper</u>
<u>in the United States, it was published in New York City.</u>

    (A) In 1827 *Freedom's Journal* was the first Black American
         newspaper in the United States, it was published in New York
         City.
    (B) In 1827 the first Black American newspaper in the United States,
         Freedom's Journal, was published in New York City.
    (C) In New York City in 1827 *Freedom's Journal*, the first Black
         American newspaper in the United States, was published there.
    (D) With publication in New York City in 1827, it was the first Black
         American newspaper in the United States, *Freedom's Journal*.
    (E) The first Black American newspaper published in the United
         States was when there was *Freedom's Journal* in New York City
         in 1827.

Ⓐ Ⓑ Ⓒ Ⓓ Ⓔ

12. Astronomers have developed extremely sophisticated <u>instruments,</u>
<u>which is helpful for measuring the properties of objects in space.</u>

    (A) instruments, which is helpful for measuring the properties of
         objects in space
    (B) instruments to help measure the properties of objects in space
    (C) instruments, which are helpful for measurement of space objects'
         properties
    (D) instruments helpful to measure the properties of objects in space
    (E) instruments, a help for measuring the properties of objects in
         space

Ⓐ Ⓑ Ⓒ Ⓓ Ⓔ

13. Foreign correspondents are like birds of passage, resting for a few weeks, <u>then flying off</u> again to a new place.

    (A) then flying off again
    (B) after which again they fly off
    (C) then they fly off again
    (D) when once again they fly off
    (E) but soon they are flying off again

    Ⓐ Ⓑ Ⓒ Ⓓ Ⓔ

14. Reducing individual taxes while eliminating as much waste as possible <u>are traditional methods for increasing</u> a nation's economy.

    (A) are traditional methods for increasing
    (B) is a traditional method for increasing
    (C) is a traditional method of stimulating
    (D) traditionally are methods for increasing
    (E) are traditional methods of stimulating

    Ⓐ Ⓑ Ⓒ Ⓓ Ⓔ

15. Arguably the most distinctive regional cuisine in the United States, <u>the South is noted for such specialties as</u> Brunswick stew and hush puppies.

    (A) the South is noted for such specialties as
    (B) the South has such specialties of note as
    (C) the South includes among its noteworthy specialties
    (D) southern cooking includes such noteworthy specialties as
    (E) southern cooking is including such specialties of note as

    Ⓐ Ⓑ Ⓒ Ⓓ Ⓔ

16. Today's fashion designers must consider both how much a fabric costs and <u>its wearability</u>.

    (A) its wearability
    (B) is it going to wear well
    (C) if it has wearability
    (D) how well it wears
    (E) the fabric's ability to wear well

    Ⓐ Ⓑ Ⓒ Ⓓ Ⓔ

17. Because the eleven women functioned as a <u>team is why they had a successful season</u>.

    (A) team is why they had a successful season
    (B) team, they had a success this season
    (C) team, they had a successful season
    (D) team, success was theirs this season
    (E) team is why their season was a success

    Ⓐ Ⓑ Ⓒ Ⓓ Ⓔ

18. Home computers themselves are no longer expensive, but video display terminals, printers, and links to other computers <u>cause the total financial cost of a computer system to rise up greatly.</u>

    (A) cause the total financial cost of a computer system to rise up greatly
    (B) greatly increase the total cost of a computer system
    (C) highly inflate the cost totals of a computer system
    (D) drive up the expense of a computer system totally
    (E) totally add to the expense of a computer system

    Ⓐ Ⓑ Ⓒ Ⓓ Ⓔ

REVISING WORK IN PROGRESS

Directions: Each of the following selections is an early draft of a student essay in which the sentences have been numbered for easy reference. Some parts of the selections need to be changed.

Read each selection and then answer the questions that follow. Some questions are about particular sentences or parts of sentences and ask you to improve sentence structure and diction (word choice). In making these decisions, follow the conventions of standard written English. Other questions refer to the entire essay or parts of the essay and ask you to consider organization, development, and effectiveness of language in relation to purpose and audience. After you choose each answer, fill in the corresponding oval on your answer sheet.

Questions 19-23 are based on the following draft of a student essay.

(1) *I used to be convinced that people didn't actually win radio contests; I thought that the excited winners I heard were only actors.* (2) *Sure, people could win T-shirts.* (3) *They couldn't win anything of real value.*

(4) *I've always loved sports.* (5) *Unlike my friends, who fall asleep to "Top 40 Radio," I listen to "Sports Night with Dave Sims."* (6) *His show is hardly usual fare for a young woman.* (7) *One night I heard Dave Sims announce a sports trivia contest with cash prizes of two thousand dollars.* (8) *I jump at the chance to combine my talk-show knowledge with everything my parents had taught me about sports.* (9) *I sent in my self-addressed stamped envelope.* (10) *I forgot about the whole matter.* (11) *Then the questionnaire appeared in my mailbox ten days later.* (12) *Its arrival gave me a rude surprise.* (13) *Instead of sitting down and whipping through it, I trudged to libraries and spent hours digging for answers to such obscure questions as "Which National Hockey League goalie holds the record for most career shutouts?"*

(14) *Finally, after days of double-checking answers, I mailed off my answer sheet, certain I would hear no more about the matter.* (15) *Certain, until two weeks later, I ripped open the envelope with the NBC peacock and read "Congratulations..."* (16) *I was a winner, a winner of more than a T-shirt.*

19. Which of the following is the best way to revise the underlined portions of sentences 2 and 3 (reproduced below) so that the two sentences are combined into one?

    Sure, people could win <u>T-shirts. They couldn't win</u> anything of real value.

    (A) T-shirts, and they couldn't win
    (B) T-shirts, but they couldn't win
    (C) T-shirts, but not being able to win
    (D) T-shirts, so they do win
    (E) T-shirts, while there was no winning

    Ⓐ Ⓑ Ⓒ Ⓓ Ⓔ

20. Which of the following sentences, if added after sentence 3, would best link the first paragraph with the rest of the essay?

    (A) I have held this opinion about contests for a long time.
    (B) The prizes offered did not inspire me to enter the contests.
    (C) However, I recently changed my opinion about these contests.
    (D) Usually the questions on these contests are really easy to answer.
    (E) Sometimes my friends try to convince me to enter such contests.

    Ⓐ Ⓑ Ⓒ Ⓓ Ⓔ

21. In the context of the second paragraph, which of the following is the best version of the underlined portion of sentence 8 (reproduced below)?

    I jump at the chance to combine my talk-show knowledge with everything my parents had taught me about sports.

    (A) (As it is now)
    (B) I jumped at the chance to combine
    (C) Having jumped at the chance to combine
    (D) Jumping at the chance and combining
    (E) Jumping at the chance by combining

    Ⓐ Ⓑ Ⓒ Ⓓ Ⓔ

22. Which of the following is the best way to revise and combine sentences 9 and 10 (reproduced below)?

    I sent in my self-addressed stamped envelope. I forgot about the whole matter.

    (A) Having sent in my self-addressed stamped envelope, the whole matter was forgotten.
    (B) After sending in my self-addressed stamped envelope, the matter was wholly forgotten.
    (C) After my self-addressed stamped envelope was sent in, it was then that I forgot the whole matter.
    (D) After sending in my self-addressed stamped envelope, I forgot about the whole matter.
    (E) Forgetting about the whole matter after sending in my self-addressed stamped envelope.

    Ⓐ Ⓑ Ⓒ Ⓓ Ⓔ

23. All of the following strategies are used by the writer of the passage EXCEPT

    (A) selecting specific examples
    (B) telling a story to develop a point
    (C) criticizing those whose opinions differ from hers
    (D) building suspense with references to the passage of time
    (E) disproving the assumption stated in the first sentence of the passage

    Ⓐ Ⓑ Ⓒ Ⓓ Ⓔ

Questions 24-28 are based on the following early draft of a letter to the editor of a local newspaper.

(1) *Our community needs more parks and play areas.* (2) *Living in a world where concrete surrounds us, it is important that we create places that are green and natural so that children can run and play.*

(3) *It is possible to do much with little expense to the city.* (4) *An abandoned lot can become a big patch of green grass ideal for running games.* (5) *And buying expensive playground equipment and strange pieces of modern art for children to climb on is unnecessary.* (6) *Children will climb on anything if one lets them.* (7) *A large concrete pipe or an old truck with its wheels and doors removed makes an imaginative plaything.* (8) *Simply remove any part that may be breakable or unsafe, then paint the equipment with bright colors.* (9) *Bury the truck or pipe a foot or two deep so that it is stable.* (10) *Great opportunities for fun!* (11) *Children can play for hours, crawling through a secret tunnel or navigating to a distant planet.* (12) *Neighborhood committees could contribute other discards.*

(13) *We should do these things because children need oases in this concrete desert we live in.* (14) *This may take time, but if people get together and contribute both ideas and labor, much can be completed successfully.*

24. Which of the following is the best way to revise the underlined portion of sentence 2 (reproduced below)?

    Living in a world where concrete surrounds us, it is important that we create places that are green and natural so that children can run and play.

    (A) Living in a world where concrete surrounds us, the important thing is to
    (B) We live in a world where concrete surrounds us, it is important that we
    (C) Being surrounded by a world of concrete, it is important to
    (D) Surrounding us with a world of concrete, we need to
    (E) Surrounded by a world of concrete, we need to

    Ⓐ Ⓑ Ⓒ Ⓓ Ⓔ

25. Which of the following would best replace "*And*" at the beginning of sentence 5?

    (A) Furthermore,
    (B) Instead,
    (C) Despite this,
    (D) Nevertheless,
    (E) Excepting this,

    Ⓐ Ⓑ Ⓒ Ⓓ Ⓔ

26. The writer of the passage could best improve sentence 12 by

    (A) acknowledging drawbacks to suggestions
    (B) providing specific examples
    (C) including personal opinions
    (D) discussing other community problems
    (E) defining the idea of a neighborhood

    Ⓐ Ⓑ Ⓒ Ⓓ Ⓔ

27. In context, the best phrase to replace *"do these things"* in sentence 13 is

    (A) accomplish our intentions
    (B) help these children
    (C) consider other options
    (D) build these play areas
    (E) have new ideas

    Ⓐ Ⓑ Ⓒ Ⓓ Ⓔ

28. Which is the best version of the underlined portion of sentence 14 (reproduced below)?

    This may take time, but if people get together and contribute both ideas and labor, much can be completed successfully.

    (A) (as it is now)
    (B) and if people get together and they contribute
    (C) but if people will get together and they will also contribute
    (D) but if people get together and they would have contributed
    (E) however, if people get together, also contributing

    Ⓐ Ⓑ Ⓒ Ⓓ Ⓔ

RECOGNIZING AND APPLYING WRITING SKILLS

Directions: For each question below, choose the best answer and fill in the corresponding oval on the answer sheet.

29. In a student's research paper, the place at which a footnote is introduced should be marked with an Arabic numeral that is

    (A) elevated slightly above the line
    (B) followed by a quotation mark
    (C) enclosed in brackets
    (D) followed by a period
    (E) preceded by a slash and followed by a period

    Ⓐ Ⓑ Ⓒ Ⓓ Ⓔ

30. The best way to find current sources of information for a library research paper on the overprescribing of medication for elderly patients is to

    (A) consult a medical textbook
    (B) look in indexes to journals and periodicals
    (C) go through recent issues of newspapers and magazines
    (D) locate the section of the library containing science books
    (E) check in a recent almanac

    Ⓐ Ⓑ Ⓒ Ⓓ Ⓔ

31. Siegfried Sassoon, "The Old Huntsman," *The Revised College Omnibus,* ed. James D. McCallum (New York: Harcourt, Brace and Company, 1939), p. 87.

    The footnote given above shows that

    (A) the author of *The Revised College Omnibus* is James D. McCallum
    (B) *The Revised College Omnibus* is a periodical
    (C) "The Old Huntsman" is technically termed a subtitle
    (D) "The Old Huntsman" is the name of a book
    (E) Siegfried Sassoon wrote a work that appears in *The Revised College Omnibus*

    Ⓐ Ⓑ Ⓒ Ⓓ Ⓔ

32. When you consult a glossary in a book, you can expect to find

    (A) a list of other books the author has written
    (B) a biographical sketch of the author
    (C) a description of characters who appear in the book
    (D) a list of the books the author consulted
    (E) definitions of technical or unfamiliar words in the book

    Ⓐ Ⓑ Ⓒ Ⓓ Ⓔ

SECTION II
ANALYZING WRITING

> **Directions:** Each of the following passages consists of numbered sentences. Because the passages are part of longer writing samples, they do not necessarily constitute a complete discussion of the issues presented.
>
> Read each passage carefully and answer the questions that follow it. The questions test your awareness of a writer's purpose and of characteristics of prose that are important to good writing.

Questions 33-36 refer to the following passage.

(1) The place called the Great Plains spreads southward from the upper Saskatchewan River down to the Rio Grande — a high country, a big country of vast reaches, tremendous streams, and stories of death on the ridges, derring-do in the valleys, and the sweetness and heartbreak of springtime on the prairies.

(2) Half of this geographical area was the old Nebraska Territory that lay like a golden hackberry leaf in the sun, a giant curling, tilted leaf. (3) The veins of it were the long streams rising out near the mountains and flowing eastward to the Big Muddy, the wild Missouri. (4) The largest that cut through the center of the Plains was the broad, flat-watered Platte, usually pleasant and easygoing as an October day, and below it the Republican, deceptively limpid but roaring into sudden gullywashers that flooded all the wide valley and could sweep away even the most powerful of the wilderness herds.

33. The language, style, and subject of this passage suggest that it can best be classified as

    (A) a narrative episode
    (B) an expository statement
    (C) a descriptive piece
    (D) an exclamatory tribute
    (E) a rational argument

                Ⓐ Ⓑ Ⓒ Ⓓ Ⓔ

34. The effect of the second paragraph depends most heavily on the use of

    (A) personification
    (B) understatement
    (C) reasoned argument
    (D) metaphor and simile
    (E) dramatic exaggeration

                Ⓐ Ⓑ Ⓒ Ⓓ Ⓔ

35. As used in the last sentence, "limpid," most nearly means

    (A) calm
    (B) cool
    (C) troublesome
    (D) destructive
    (E) beautiful

    Ⓐ Ⓑ Ⓒ Ⓓ Ⓔ

36. In the second paragraph, the image of the leaf suggests the

    (A) barrenness of the dry land
    (B) topography of the territory
    (C) rich forest of the river valleys
    (D) changes caused by the seasons
    (E) vigor of life throughout the land

    Ⓐ Ⓑ Ⓒ Ⓓ Ⓔ

Questions 37-41 refer to the following passage.

(1) Michael Goldman wrote in a poem, "When the Muse comes She doesn't tell you to write;/She says get up for a minute, I've something to show you, stand here." (2) What made me look up at that roadside tree?

(3) The road to Grundy, Virginia, is, as you might expect, a narrow scrawl scribbled all over the most improbably peaked and hunched mountains you ever saw. (4) The few people who live along the road also seem peaked and hunched. (5) But what on earth...? (6) It was hot, sunny summer. (7) The road was just bending off sharply to the right. (8) I hadn't seen a house in miles, and none was in sight. (9) At the apogee of the road's curve grew an enormous oak, a massive bur oak 200 years old, 150 feet high, an oak whose lowest limb was beyond the span of the highest ladder. (10) I looked up; there were clothes spread all over the tree. (11) Red shirts, blue trousers, black pants, little baby smocks — they weren't hung from branches. (12) They were outside, carefully spread, splayed as if to dry, on the outer leaves of the great oak's crown. (13) Were there pillowcases, blankets? (14) I can't remember. (15) There was a gay assortment of cotton underwear, yellow dresses, children's green sweaters, plaid skirts.... (16) You know roads. (17) A bend comes and you take it, thoughtlessly, moving on. (18) I looked behind me for another split second, astonished; both sides of the tree's canopy, clear to the top, bore clothes.

37. Which of the following best describes the relationship between the two paragraphs in this passage?

    (A) The second paragraph answers the question at the end of the first.
    (B) The second paragraph offers a concrete illustration of the quotation in the first.
    (C) The second paragraph takes an opposite point of view from the first.
    (D) The second paragraph generalizes about the quotation in the first.
    (E) The second paragraph is an elaborate contradiction of the thesis in the first.

    Ⓐ Ⓑ Ⓒ Ⓓ Ⓔ

38. Which of the following most accurately describes what happens in the second paragraph?

    (A) The speaker has a poetic vision symbolizing cleansing renewal.
    (B) The speaker has a hallucination brought on by the heat.
    (C) The speaker tries to explain how the phenomenon was accomplished.
    (D) The speaker sees a tree full of flowers and imagines they are someone's washing.
    (E) The speaker sees a large tree inexplicably covered with clothes spread to dry.

    Ⓐ Ⓑ Ⓒ Ⓓ Ⓔ

39. The descriptive details in sentences 9-15 provide a

    (A) precise visual image
    (B) picture of something unearthly
    (C) representation of a blur of color
    (D) view from a child's perspective
    (E) distorted sense of motion

    Ⓐ Ⓑ Ⓒ Ⓓ Ⓔ

40. Which of the following pairs of words best describes the speaker's reaction to the experience?

    (A) Ecstasy and fear
    (B) Dismay and wonder
    (C) Delight and fear
    (D) Disgust and disbelief
    (E) Wonder and delight

    Ⓐ Ⓑ Ⓒ Ⓓ Ⓔ

41. The main implication of the passage is that

    (A) people should be more observant as they travel country roads
    (B) people are resourceful in finding ways to rise above domestic tasks
    (C) inspiration or vision is often a matter of chance or caprice
    (D) the poet sees more intensely than other people
    (E) the Muse encourages only the eccentric to write

    Ⓐ Ⓑ Ⓒ Ⓓ Ⓔ

Questions 42-43 refer to the following poem.

> From the road looking to the hill I saw
> One hollow house hunched in the shoulder.
> Windows blinded in a level sun
> Stared with not random malice,
> Though I had not been in that place.

42. To the speaker, the house is

    (A) foreboding
    (B) quaint
    (C) majestic
    (D) cheerful
    (E) tranquil

    Ⓐ Ⓑ Ⓒ Ⓓ Ⓔ

43. That the house's windows are "blinded in a level sun" indicates that the

    (A) windows in the abandoned house are broken
    (B) setting for the poem is about noontime
    (C) sun is low on the horizon
    (D) speaker feels the warmth of the sun
    (E) word "sun" plays on the word "son"

    Ⓐ Ⓑ Ⓒ Ⓓ Ⓔ

ANALYZING AND EVALUATING WRITERS' CHOICES

Directions: For each question below, choose the best answer and fill in the corresponding oval on the answer sheet.

44. The controversy was a bitter one, but reasonable compromise <u>alleviated</u> some of the ill will.

    Which of the following best captures the meaning of the underlined word above?

    (A) Spared
    (B) Delayed
    (C) Eased
    (D) Made obvious
    (E) Militated against

    Ⓐ Ⓑ Ⓒ Ⓓ Ⓔ

45. Anita <u>pays attention</u> to details.

    Which of the following substitutions for the underlined words presents most emphatically a negative picture of Anita?

    (A) is finicky about
    (B) focuses only on
    (C) handles
    (D) likes to deal with
    (E) is very exact

    Ⓐ Ⓑ Ⓒ Ⓓ Ⓔ

46. He told Henry that his package would arrive tomorrow.

    Which of the following is a correct revision of the ambiguous sentence above?

    (A) That "his" package would arrive tomorrow is what Henry told him.
    (B) He told Henry that it was his package which would arrive tomorrow.
    (C) He said to Henry "that your package will arrive tomorrow."
    (D) "Henry, your package will arrive tomorrow," he said.
    (E) "Henry," he said, "tomorrow will be arriving the package."

    Ⓐ Ⓑ Ⓒ Ⓓ Ⓔ

Questions 47-48 refer to the following excerpts.

(A) When will it all end? The idiocy and the tension, the dying of young people, the destruction of homes, of cities, starvation, exhaustion, disease, children parentless and lost, the endless pounding of the battle line.

(B) Yet let us begin today as though the millennium were tomorrow, and start "Village Improvement Parade" down Main Street, and turn the corner east toward the rising sun to a land of clear picture and young hearts.

(C) Beyond the gate and above the wall, one sees a littered cobbled street, an old gas street lamp, and, beyond that again, the blue expanse of the bay, with Fort Sumter showing on the horizon.

(D) Prohibition of the production and sale of alcoholic drinks was a social experiment that had behind it more than a century of agitation and local legislation.

(E) Still, whatever the plans for repairing the damage wrought on the land, chances are that the genius for destruction will not be daunted by pious vows and mammoth budgets. Free enterprise will prevail.

47. In which excerpt does the speaker's tone convey a profound urgency?

Ⓐ Ⓑ Ⓒ Ⓓ Ⓔ

48. In which excerpt is the tone sarcastic?

Ⓐ Ⓑ Ⓒ Ⓓ Ⓔ

Questions 49-50 refer to the following excerpt.

The two speech writers were amused by the contrast between the two speakers. The press-club president had edited her speech heavily, changing the phrases "in a nutshell" to "to summarize" and "a man needing no introduction" to "someone well known to this audience." The governor, in turn, had delivered a major policy speech without even reviewing the speech writer's text. "That was a bit of a risk," said the first speech writer. "That was bungee jumping!" said the second.

49. The two changes that the press-club president made were in an effort to avoid

(A) irony
(B) cliches
(C) sexist language
(D) metaphor
(E) jargon

Ⓐ Ⓑ Ⓒ Ⓓ Ⓔ

50. To create emphasis, the second speech writer uses all of the following EXCEPT

(A) metaphor
(B) exclamatory tone
(C) structure parallel to that of the first speech writer
(D) hyperbole
(E) speculation

Ⓐ Ⓑ Ⓒ Ⓓ Ⓔ

Optional Free-Response Section

If your college requires that the optional free-response section be taken in addition to the multiple-choice examination, you may wish to review the following information.

The optional free-response section of the Freshman College Composition examination requires candidates to demonstrate their ability to write clearly and effectively on two essays. Three topics are given in the test book. An essay on the first topic is required, and candidates are advised to spend 35-40 minutes on this essay. For the second essay, candidates choose one of two topics and may spend the remainder of the 90-minute period on this essay. Local faculty assumes essay-grading responsibility. Below are examples of possible essay topics. The topic in which the candidate writes a letter is required.

Sample Topic 1:

Suppose that you injure your shoulder while exercising. You are immediately rushed to a hospital emergency room and wait to be seen by the physician on duty. After your shoulder is X-rayed, the physician on duty reports that you have a separated shoulder; she then instructs a nurse to wrap your arm and place it in a sling. You are told to see your physician for follow-up treatment.

Two weeks later, your doctor examines you and your hospital X-rays and says that your shoulder was not separated but only sprained. You are relieved, yet surprised that your injury had been misdiagnosed.

Eventually, you receive several medical bills, one of which is from a Dr. Robin Smith, a specialist in orthopedic surgery, for "Consultation in the emergency room." The bill is for $80.00. When you call Dr. Smith's office, you learn that Dr. Smith consulted the attending physician about the diagnosis; however, you do not remember ever having met Dr. Smith.

Write the first two paragraphs of a letter to Dr. Smith explaining why you will recommend that your insurance company refuse payment. Refer to an enclosed copy of your doctor's diagnosis. (Spend approximately 35-40 minutes on essay.)

Sample Topic 2:

In describing the times of the French Revolution, Charles Dickens wrote: "It was the best of times, it was the worst of times." Think about how Dickens' description might apply to today's times. Write an essay in which you use specific examples to explain how today could be described as both the best of times and the worst of times.

For additional information, read the sections on "Taking Free-Response or Essay Tests," in chapter 5, and "How Free-Response Answers and Essays Are Graded," in chapter 6.

Study Resources

The list below contains several books that are typically used as textbooks or reference books for first-year English Composition and Rhetoric courses. You will find these and similar books useful in preparing for the Freshman College Composition examination. The books in the first group are valuable primarily as reference books; they include handbooks of grammar and manuals for writing papers and research papers. They offer guidance on the various elements of writing (sentences, paragraphs, essays) as well as examples illustrating acceptable usage, punctuation, etc. As you attempt to develop and refine your writing skills, it is helpful to consult at least one book of this type.

The books in the second group are aids to improvement in reading comprehension and guides to different kinds of writing. They suggest ways to make your own writing interesting, effective, and suitable to a particular purpose, and they can help heighten your awareness about your writing.

The suggestions and resources for preparing for the General Examination in English Composition will also be helpful in preparing for the Freshman College Composition examination.

HANDBOOKS

Dornan, Edward A. and Charles W. Dawe, *The Brief English Handbook,* 3rd ed. Glenview, IL: Scott, Foresman/Little-Brown, 1990.

Gibaldi, Joseph and Walter S. Achtert, *MLA Handbook for Writers of Research Papers,* 3rd ed. New York: Modern Language Association of America, 1988.

Hacker, Diana, *The Bedford Handbook For Writers,* 3rd ed. Boston: Bedford Books of St. Martin's Press, 1991.

Hubbuch, Susan M., *Writing Research Papers Across the Curriculum,* 3rd ed. Fort Worth: Harcourt Brace Jovanovich, 1992.

Kirszner, Laurie G. and Stephen R. Mandell, *Patterns for College Writing: A Rhetorical Reader and Guide,* 4th ed. New York: St. Martin's Press, 1989.

Lauer, Janice M. et al., *Four Worlds of Writing,* 3rd ed. New York: Harper Collins Publishers, 1991.

Lester, James D., *Writing Research Papers: A Complete Guide*, 6th ed. Glenview, IL: Scott, Foresman, 1990.

Lunsford, Andrea A. and Robert Connors, *The St. Martin's Handbook*, 2nd ed. New York: St. Martin's Press, 1991.

Skwire, David et al., *Student's Book of College English: Rhetoric, Readings, Handbook*, 5th ed. New York: Macmillan Pub. Co., 1990.

Winkler, Anthony and Jo Ray McCuen, *Writing the Research Paper: A Handbook with Both the MLA and APA Documentation Styles*, 3rd ed. San Diego: Harcourt Brace Jovanovich, 1989.

RHETORIC READERS

Baker, Sheridan Warner, *The Practical Stylist with Readings*, 7th ed. New York: Harper Collins Publishers, 1991.

Barnet, Sylvan et al., *Literature for Composition: Essays, Fiction, Poetry, and Drama*, 3rd ed. New York: Harper Collins Publishers, 1992.

Hunt, Douglas, *The Dolphin Reader*, 2nd ed. Boston: Houghton Mifflin, 1990.

Jacobus, Lee A., *A World of Ideas: Essential Readings for College Writers*, 2nd ed. New York: St. Martin's Press, 1986.

Kennedy, X. J., *Literature: An Introduction to Fiction, Poetry and Drama*, 5th ed. Hudson, NH: Harper Collins, 1991.

McCuen, Jo Ray, and Anthony C. Winkler, *Readings for Writers*, 6th ed. San Diego: Harcourt Brace Jovanovich, 1989.

McCuen, Jo Ray, and Anthony C. Winkler, *Rewriting Writing: A Rhetoric Reader and Handbook*, 2nd ed. San Diego: Harcourt Brace Jovanovich, 1990.

Nadell, Judith and John Langan, *The Macmillan Reader*, 2nd ed. New York: Macmillan, 1990.

Perrine, Laurence and Thomas R. Arp., *Literature: Structure, Sound, and Sense*, 5th ed. San Diego: Harcourt Brace Jovanovich, 1988.

Rico, Barbara Roche and Sandra Mano, *American Mosaic: Multicultural Reading in Context*. Boston: Houghton Mifflin Co., 1991.

College French — Levels 1 and 2

Description of the Examination

The Subject Examination in College French is designed to measure knowledge and ability equivalent to that of students who have completed from two to four semesters of college language study. The "Levels 1 and 2" designation indicates that the examination focuses on skills typically achieved from the end of the first year through the second year of college study; material taught during both years is incorporated into a single examination.

The examination is 90 minutes long and is administered in two separately timed sections: a 60-minute Reading section of approximately 90 questions, and a 30-minute Listening section of approximately 55 questions presented orally on a tape. The two sections are weighted so that they contribute equally to the total score. Subscores are reported for the two sections, but they are computed independently of the total score; thus, an individual's total score is not necessarily the average of the two subscores.

Most colleges that award credit for the College French examination award either two or four semesters of credit, depending on how high the student scores on the exam. The subscores are not intended to be used to award credit separately for Reading and Listening, but colleges may require that both scores be above a certain level to insure that credit is not awarded to a student who is deficient in either of these essential skills.

Knowledge and Skills Required

Questions on the College French examination require candidates to demonstrate the abilities listed below. Some questions may require more than one of the abilities; for example, while some questions are identified as vocabulary questions, vocabulary mastery is tested implicitly throughout the exam.

➡	Approximate Percent of Examination
	Reading (62%)*
17%	Vocabulary mastery: meaning of words and idiomatic expressions in context of printed sentences or situations
28%	Grammatical control: ability to identify usage that is structurally correct and appropriate
17%	Reading comprehension: ability to read passages representative of various styles and levels of difficulty

---

Approximate Percent of Examination

Listening (38%)*

7%   Recognition of sounds in single sentences by means of picture identification

17%   Listening comprehension through short dialogues based on everyday situations

14%   Ability to understand the language as spoken by native speakers in longer dialogues and narratives

---

*Although there are unequal numbers of questions in the two sections of the test, each section (Reading and Listening) is weighted so as to contribute 50 percent to the candidate's total score.

Sample Questions

The 25 sample questions that follow are similar to questions on the College French examination, but they do not actually appear on the examination. The questions on this examination contain only four answer choices, but your answer sheet will have five answer spaces. Be sure not to make any marks in column E on your answer sheet.

Before attempting to answer the sample questions, read all the information about the College French examination given above. Additional suggestions for preparing for CLEP examinations are provided in chapter 4.

Try to answer correctly as many questions as possible. Then compare your answers with the correct answers, given in Appendix B.

Section I: Reading

Directions: This part (questions 1-4) consists of a number of incomplete statements, each having four suggested completions. Select the most appropriate completion.

Example:

Elle habite dans . . . tranquille près d'un parc.

(A) un quartier
(B) un quart
(C) une section
(D) une partie

Answer

●

---

1. Je ne peux pas conduire sans mes . . . de soleil.

   (A) spectacles   (B) rayons
      (C) lunettes   (D) pare-brise   Ⓐ Ⓑ Ⓒ Ⓓ

2. Il avait . . . de déjeuner au petit restaurant du coin.

   (A) l'habit   (B) le costume
      (C) l'habitude   (D) l'usage   Ⓐ Ⓑ Ⓒ Ⓓ

3. C'était tellement drôle que tout le monde a . . . de rire.

   (A) éclaté   (B) cessé   (C) refusé   (D) craint   Ⓐ Ⓑ Ⓒ Ⓓ

4. Le livre que je viens de . . . est intéressant.

   (A) craindre   (B) donner
      (C) parler   (D) lire   Ⓐ Ⓑ Ⓒ Ⓓ

Directions: Each of the following sentences (questions 5-8) contains one or more underlined words. From the choices given, select the one which, when substituted for the underlined word or words, fits grammatically into the original sentence.

Example:

Il conduit très bien.

(A) vite
(B) rapide
(C) lent   **Answer**
(D) mauvais   ● Ⓑ Ⓒ Ⓓ

---

5. Voilà mes crayons; les vôtres sont là-bas.

   (A) les tiens   (B) les tiennes
      (C) le tien   (D) la tienne   Ⓐ Ⓑ Ⓒ Ⓓ

6. Je m'étonne qu'il parle si bien l'anglais.

   (A) comprend   (B) sait   (C) lit   (D) écrive   Ⓐ Ⓑ Ⓒ Ⓓ

7. J'ai mangé <u>moins</u> que vous.

   (A) avant   (B) aussi   (C) de plus   (D) autant   Ⓐ Ⓑ Ⓒ Ⓓ

8. Vous <u>habituez</u>-vous à ses procédés?

   (A) étonnez   (B) souvenez
     (C) intéressez   (D) moquez   Ⓐ Ⓑ Ⓒ Ⓓ

Directions: The following paragraph contains blank spaces (questions 9-12) indicating omissions in the text. Below each blank are four choices. Select the choice that is grammatically correct in the context. There is no example for this part.

Les renseignements que ---- amie Jeanne a demandés

         9. (A) mon
           (B) ma
           (C) mienne
           (D) mien   Ⓐ Ⓑ Ⓒ Ⓓ

pour son voyage de ---- hiver ne lui ont pas encore

       10. (A) ces
          (B) ce
          (C) cet
          (D) cette   Ⓐ Ⓑ Ⓒ Ⓓ

---- envoyés. Elle aimerait bien qu'on ---- fasse

11. (A) été   12. (A) les y
   (B) étaient   (B) y en
   (C) était   (C) le lui
   (D) eu   Ⓐ Ⓑ Ⓒ Ⓓ   (D) les lui   Ⓐ Ⓑ Ⓒ Ⓓ

parvenir le plus tôt possible.

Directions: Read the following passage carefully for comprehension. The passage is followed by a number of questions or incomplete statements. For each question or statement, select the answer or completion that is best according to the passage. There is no example for this part.

Cette année-là, il y avait donc pour la première fois une grève des paysans, qui protestaient contre les conditions économiques en barrant les routes vers les grandes villes pour en empêcher le ravitaillement. De nombreux incidents semblables se sont produits depuis lors. Tandis que la population de la France maintient une courbe de croissance régulière, celle de la campagne diminue, car les jeunes préfèrent l'usine et la vie en ville, où il est plus facile de trouver du travail bien payé et des amusements. Le dépeuplement crée des problèmes sérieux. En 1911, quarante-cinq pour cent de la population laborieuse travaillait dans l'agriculture; aujourd'hui, ce chiffre est tombé à vingt-cinq pour cent, et la main d'oeuvre commence à manquer. Le gouvernement cherche à améliorer la situation du paysan. Il lui offre les bénéfices de la sécurité sociale; il y a des allocations pour la vieillesse, pour les familles nombreuses, et pour les mères qui restent au foyer au lieu d'aller travailler à l'extérieur.

13. Les chiffres cités dans ce passage indiquent que

  (A) la population de la France diminue
  (B) la campagne se dépeuple
  (C) l'industrie manque d'ouvriers
  (D) les paysans ne se révoltent pas souvent   Ⓐ Ⓑ Ⓒ Ⓓ

14. Qu'est-ce qui s'est passé cette année-là?

  (A) Les paysans ont refusé la sécurité sociale.
  (B) Les femmes ont refusé de travailler.
  (C) Des villes ont été attaquées.
  (D) Des camions de vivres ont été arrêtés.   Ⓐ Ⓑ Ⓒ Ⓓ

15. Quelle catégorie sociale lutte pour l'amélioration de sa condition?

  (A) Les habitants des grandes villes
  (B) Les agriculteurs
  (C) Les employés du gouvernement
  (D) Les mères de familles nombreuses   Ⓐ Ⓑ Ⓒ Ⓓ

Section II: Listening

All the italicized material in Section II represents what you would hear on an actual test recording. This material does not appear in the actual test book.

Directions: For each question in this part (questions 16 and 17) you will hear a single sentence. In the 10-second pause following each sentence, choose from the four pictures the one that corresponds to the spoken sentence.

Example:

You hear:

(Man) *Le garçon sourit.*

Now look at the four pictures printed in your test book.

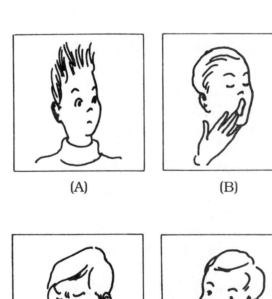

(A)   (B)

(C)   (D)

The correct answer is picture (D), so you would mark the letter (D) on your answer sheet.

16. (Man) *Le poisson est sur la table.*

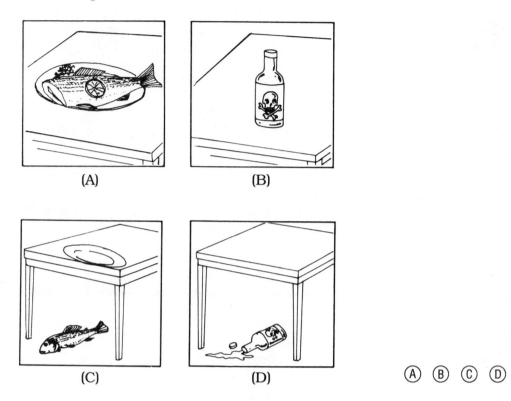

(A)   (B)

(C)   (D)   Ⓐ Ⓑ Ⓒ Ⓓ

17. (Woman) *Elle achète des boissons.*

(A)   (B)

(C)   (D)   Ⓐ Ⓑ Ⓒ Ⓓ

Directions: For each question in this part (questions 18-20) you will hear a short conversation between two people and you will read a question about the conversation. In the 12-second pause following each conversation, choose the most appropriate response to the printed question.

Example:

You hear:

(Male Voice)   *Hélène, écrivez au tableau les phrases de la leçon d'aujourd'hui.*

(Female Voice)   *Je regrette, monsieur, hier soir je ne me sentais pas bien, et je n'ai pas fait mon devoir.*

Now read the question and the four choices printed in your test book.

Qui parle?

(A) Un professeur et son élève.
(B) Un homme d'affaires et sa secrétaire.
(C) Un médecin et une malade.
(D) Un garçon de café et une cliente.

Of the four choices, (A) is the most appropriate response to the question, so you would mark the letter (A) on your answer sheet.

---

18. (Male Voice A) *Je fais le plein, Monsieur?*
    (Male Voice B) *Oui, s'il vous plaît, et vérifiez l'huile et les pneus.*

    Où se trouve-t-on?

    (A) Au restaurant.
    (B) Chez l'épicier.
    (C) A la station-service.
    (D) Chez le pharmacien.   Ⓐ Ⓑ Ⓒ Ⓓ

19. (Female Voice) *Selon la carte, nous devons prendre la première route à droite.*
    (Male Voice)   *Est-ce celle-là qui doit nous mener au premier village?*

    Que font ces gens?

    (A) Ils se promènent en ville.
    (B) Ils regardent des cartes chez eux.
    (C) Ils voyagent dans une région inconnue.
    (D) Ils rentrent chez eux.   Ⓐ Ⓑ Ⓒ Ⓓ

20. (Female Voice) *Etes-vous allé voir la dernière pièce de notre ami?*
    (Male Voice) *Non, car je refuse de faire la queue pendant des heures!*
    (Female Voice) *Mais, vous pouvez louer vos places d'avance!*
    (Male Voice) *J'ai bien essayé, mais il y avait un monde fou.*

De quoi s'agit-il?

(A) De la location d'une chambre.
(B) D'une représentation théâtrale.
(C) D'un projet de voyage.
(D) D'une vente dans un magasin.   Ⓐ Ⓑ Ⓒ Ⓓ

Directions: In this part (questions 21-25) you will hear two spoken selections, each followed by a series of spoken questions. In the 12-second pause following each question, you are to choose the most appropriate answer from the four printed choices. There is no example for this part.

First Selection:

(Female Voice) *Et bien voilà, Monsieur l'agent. Je faisais tranquillement les vitrines lorsqu'un inconnu s'est approché de moi.*
(Male Voice) *Bon. Et après, Madame, dites-moi ce qui s'est passé.*
(Female Voice) *Alors l'homme m'a bousculée et puis il s'est sauvé. C'est à ce moment-là que je me suis rendu compte que ma montre avait disparu.*
(Male Voice) *Asseyez-vous là, Madame, et signez votre déposition.*

21. (Female Voice) *Qui parle?*

(A) Un policier et une femme.
(B) Un homme et sa femme.
(C) Un assureur et sa cliente.
(D) Un étranger et une vendeuse.   Ⓐ Ⓑ Ⓒ Ⓓ

22. (Female Voice) *Où cette conversation a-t-elle lieu?*

(A) Dans la rue.   (B) Devant un magasin.
   (C) Au poste de police.   (D) Chez la femme.   Ⓐ Ⓑ Ⓒ Ⓓ

23. (Female Voice) *De quoi s'agit-il?*

(A) D'un achat.   (B) D'un vol.
   (C) D'une interview.   (D) D'un accident.   Ⓐ Ⓑ Ⓒ Ⓓ

Second Selection:

(Female Voice) *Le ministre de l'Education Nationale, accompagné de son épouse, est arrivé ce matin dans notre ville où il assistera à l'inauguration du nouveau lycée de filles. Il a été accueilli à sa descente d'avion par monsieur le maire ainsi que par un groupe d'enfants des écoles qui ont remis à la femme du ministre un beau bouquet de fleurs.*

24. (Male Voice) *Avec qui le ministre est-il arrivé?*

    (A) Avec le maire. (B) Avec ses filles.
    (C) Avec des enfants. (D) Avec sa femme. Ⓐ Ⓑ Ⓒ Ⓓ

25. (Male Voice) *Pourquoi le ministre est-il venu?*

    (A) Pour passer ses vacances.
    (B) Pour un concours d'aviation.
    (C) Pour une exposition de fleurs.
    (D) Pour inaugurer un lycée. Ⓐ Ⓑ Ⓒ Ⓓ

Study Resources

Following is a list of textbooks that are widely used in courses in the first two years of college French. Familiarize yourself thoroughly with the contents of at least one of these or other French textbooks. Besides studying basic vocabulary, you should understand and be able to apply the grammatical principles that make up the language. The review grammars listed below will help you do this. To improve your reading comprehension, use the passages in the textbooks and readers listed below and other reading material of your choice. To improve your listening comprehension, seek opportunities to hear the language spoken by native speakers and to converse with native speakers. All the textbooks listed below include tape programs; these and other French records and tapes are available in many libraries. Take advantage of opportunities to join organizations with French-speaking members, to attend French movies, or to hear French-language radio broadcasts.

Additional suggestions for preparing for CLEP examinations are provided in chapter 4.

Many libraries do not carry textbooks as a policy. If you can't find any of the following textbooks at the library, see whether the college bookstore has a used copy. If you can't locate the most recent edition, an edition that is one or two years older will suffice for most subject areas. As a final option, purchase a new copy of the suggested textbook as an investment in your education.

TEXTBOOKS

Bragger, Jeannette D. and Donald B. Rice, *Allons-y!: Le Français par étapes,* 3rd ed. Boston: Heinle & Heinle, 1992.

Brown, Thomas H., *Pas à Pas — French: Listening, Speaking, Reading, Writing.* New York: Wiley, 1991.

Dinneen, David A. and Madeleine Kernen. *Chapeau!: First-Year French.* New York: Wiley, 1989.

Harris, Julian, André Lévêque, and Constance Knop, *Basic Conversational French,* 8th ed. New York: Holt, Rinehart & Winston, 1987.

Heilenman, L. Kathy, Isabelle Kaplan, and Claude Toussaint Tournier, *Voila!: An Introduction to French,* 2nd ed. Boston: Heinle & Heinle, 1992.

Jian, Gérard and Ralph Hester, *Découverte et Création: Les Bases du Français Moderne,* 5th ed. Boston: Houghton Mifflin, 1990.

Lenard, Yvone, *Parole et Pensée: Introduction au français d'aujourd'hui,* 5th ed. New York: Harper & Row, 1987.

Rassias, John A. and Jacqueline de la Chapelle-Skubly. *Le Français: Départ-Arrivée.* Boston: Heinle & Heinle, 1992.

Valette, J. and R. Valette, *Contacts: Langue et Culture Françaises,* 4th ed. Boston: Houghton Mifflin, 1989.

French language reading materials and information can be obtained from American distributors such as:

- Adler's Foreign Books, Inc., 915 Foster Street, Evanston, IL 60201
- European Book Company, 925 Larkin Street, San Francisco, CA 94109
- Gérard Hamon, Inc., P.O. Box 758, 721 West Boston Post Road, Mamaroneck, NY 10543
- Midwest European Publications, 915 Foster Street, Evanston, IL 60201
- Schoenhof's Foreign Books, 76A Mount Auburn Street, Cambridge, MA 02138

College German — Levels 1 and 2

Description of the Examination

The Subject Examination in College German is designed to measure knowledge and ability equivalent to that of students who have completed from two to four semesters of college language study. The "Levels 1 and 2" designation indicates that the examination focuses on skills typically achieved from the end of the first year through the second year of college study; material taught during both years is incorporated into a single examination.

The examination is 90 minutes long and is administered in two separately timed sections: a 60-minute Reading section of approximately 80 questions, and a 30-minute Listening section of approximately 55 questions presented orally on a tape. The two sections are weighted so that they contribute equally to the total score. Subscores are reported for the two sections, but they are computed independently of the total score; thus, an individual's total score is not necessarily the average of the two subscores.

Most colleges that award credit for the College German examination award either two or four semesters of credit, depending on how high the student scores on the exam. The subscores are not intended to be used to award credit separately for Reading and Listening, but colleges may require that both scores be above a certain level to insure that credit is not awarded to a student who is deficient in either of these essential skills.

Knowledge and Skills Required

Questions on the College German examination require candidates to demonstrate the abilities listed below. Some questions may require more than one of the abilities; for example, while some questions are identified as vocabulary questions, vocabulary mastery is tested implicitly throughout the exam.

◆	*Approximate Percent of Examination*
	Reading (59%)*
15%	Vocabulary mastery: meaning of words and idiomatic expressions in context of printed sentences or situations
25%	Grammatical control: ability to identify usage that is structurally correct and appropriate

---

Approximate Percent of Examination

19%	Reading comprehension: ability to read passages representative of various styles and levels of difficulty

Listening (41%)*

10%	Phonemic discrimination in single sentences by means of picture identification
10%	Listening comprehension through short dialogues based on everyday situations
21%	Ability to understand the language as spoken by native speakers in longer dialogues and narratives

---

*Although there are unequal numbers of questions in the two sections of the test, each section (Reading and Listening) is weighted so as to contribute 50 percent to the candidate's total score.

Sample Questions

The 26 sample questions that follow are similar to questions on the College German examination, but they do not actually appear on the examination.

The questions on this examination contain only four answer choices, but your answer sheet will have five answer spaces. Be sure not to make any marks in column E on your answer sheet.

Before attempting to answer the sample questions, read all the information about the College German examination given above. Additional suggestions for preparing for CLEP examinations are provided in chapter 4.

Try to answer correctly as many questions as possible. Then compare your answers with the correct answers, given in Appendix B.

Section I: Reading

Directions: This part (questions 1-11) consists of a number of incomplete statements, each having four suggested completions. Select the most appropriate completion for each sentence.

Example:

Ich weiß nicht, . . . das eine gute Idee ist.

(A) wenn   (B) als   (C) ob   (D) wann

Answer

Ⓐ Ⓑ ● Ⓓ

---

1. Wie geht es . . . ?

   (A) dich
   (B) dein
   (C) du
   (D) dir

   Ⓐ Ⓑ Ⓒ Ⓓ

2. Ich sage dir doch, Angelika wußte nichts . . . !

   (A) davor
   (B) wovon
   (C) davon
   (D) wovor

   Ⓐ Ⓑ Ⓒ Ⓓ

3. Wenn ich soviel Geld hätte, . . . ich dir gern aushelfen.

   (A) wollte
   (B) würde
   (C) möchte
   (D) sollte

   Ⓐ Ⓑ Ⓒ Ⓓ

4. Es klingelt. Das wird wohl Karin. . . .

   (A) ist
   (B) sein
   (C) gewesen
   (D) war

   Ⓐ Ⓑ Ⓒ Ⓓ

5. Das Haus steht am Rande eines . . . Waldes.

   (A) großes
   (B) großem
   (C) großen
   (D) große

   Ⓐ Ⓑ Ⓒ Ⓓ

6. Weißt du, . . . diese Brieftasche gehört?

   (A) wer
   (B) wessen
   (C) wem
   (D) wen

   Ⓐ Ⓑ Ⓒ Ⓓ

7. Hatten Sie etwas Besonderes an dem Fremden . . . ?

   (A) bemerkt
   (B) bekannt
   (C) bedenkt
   (D) gedacht

   Ⓐ Ⓑ Ⓒ Ⓓ

8. Ruh' dich doch ein wenig aus. Von dieser Anstrengung mußt
du ja . . . sein.

   (A) gar nicht müde
   (B) ganz erschöpft
   (C) ganz begeistert
   (D) gar nicht böse   Ⓐ Ⓑ Ⓒ Ⓓ

9. In Tübingen sind die . . . für Wohnungen sehr hoch.

   (A) Renten
   (B) Mieten
   (C) Geldstücke
   (D) Pensionen   Ⓐ Ⓑ Ⓒ Ⓓ

10. Ich kann es einfach nicht . . . , daß so etwas passieren konnte!

    (A) denken
    (B) kennen
    (C) halten
    (D) glauben   Ⓐ Ⓑ Ⓒ Ⓓ

11. Die Teller kann man leider nicht . . . kaufen; man muß das ganze
Service nehmen.

    (A) einsam
    (B) einmalig
    (C) einzig
    (D) einzeln   Ⓐ Ⓑ Ⓒ Ⓓ

Directions: Read the following passage carefully for comprehension. The
passage is followed by a number of questions or incomplete statements
(questions 12-15). Select the answer or completion in each case that is
best according to the passage.

   Mehrere Häuser, in denen der deutsche Dichter Theodor Storm in
Husum, „der grauen Stadt am Meer", gewohnt hat, stehen noch in fast
unveränderter Form. Nur ein Haus befindet sich im Besitz der Stadt. Es
ist das Bürgerhaus an der Wasserreihe 31, nicht weit entfernt vom Hafen.
Dort hat der Dichter von 1866 bis 1880 gelebt und 23 seiner Novellen
und Erzählungen geschrieben. Dieses Haus ist völlig restauriert und
steht als Storm-Gedächtnisstätte dem Publikum offen.

Heutzutage ist die Wasserreihe eine belebte Straße. Im Stormhaus sind die Räume wieder genau so hergestellt, wie Storm sie einst benutzt hat. Träger dieses Unternehmens war die Storm-Gesellschaft, die mit 800 Mitgliedern zu den größten literarischen Gesellschaften Deutschlands zählt. Die Storm-Gesellschaft in Husum verfügt heute über die größte Storm-Bibliothek der Welt. Diese Bibliothek ist eine begehrte Studienquelle für Literaturhistoriker und Sprachwissenschaftler aus allen Ländern.

12. Was erfahren wir über die Häuser, in denen Storm gewohnt hat?

    (A) Sie befinden sich jetzt alle im Besitz der Stadt.
    (B) Sie haben sich kaum verändert.
    (C) Sie sind alle der Öffentlichkeit zugänglich.
    (D) Sie gehören der Storm-Gesellschaft.   Ⓐ Ⓑ Ⓒ Ⓓ

13. Was hat der Dichter in dem Haus an der Wasserreihe gemacht?

    (A) Er hat die Räume umgebaut.
    (B) Er hat eine Bibliothek eingerichtet.
    (C) Er hat hier viele seiner Werke geschrieben.
    (D) Er hat eine Gesellschaft gegründet.   Ⓐ Ⓑ Ⓒ Ⓓ

14. Das Haus an der Wasserreihe ist so hergerichtet, daß es

    (A) wie zur Lebenszeit des Dichters aussieht
    (B) die Wasserreihe zur belebten Straße macht
    (C) Räume hat, die man benutzen kann
    (D) über eine Bibliothek verfügt   Ⓐ Ⓑ Ⓒ Ⓓ

15. Welche Rolle spielte die Storm-Gesellschaft bei der Einrichtung einer Storm-Gedächtnisstätte?

    (A) Sie zählte ihre Mitglieder.
    (B) Sie wurde zu einer der größten literarischen Gesellschaften Deutschlands.
    (C) Sie unterstützte das ganze Unternehmen.
    (D) Sie schlug die Gründung einer Bibliothek vor.   Ⓐ Ⓑ Ⓒ Ⓓ

Directions: The paragraph below contains blank spaces (questions 16-19) indicating omissions in the text. Below each blank are four choices. Select the choice that is grammatically correct in the context. Be sure to read the entire paragraph first.

Deine Freundin Gerda hat gerade ----. Sie wollte wissen, ---- du

16. (A) angerufen   17. (A) wenn
    (B) anrufen   (B) da
    (C) anzurufen   (C) weil
    (D) rief an   (D) ob

Ⓐ Ⓑ Ⓒ Ⓓ   Ⓐ Ⓑ Ⓒ Ⓓ

mit ihr ins Kino gehen ----. Du hättest es schon seit ---- versprochen.

18. (A) möchten   19. (A) lange
    (B) möchte   (B) langem
    (C) möchtest   (C) lang
    (D) mochten   (D) langen

Ⓐ Ⓑ Ⓒ Ⓓ   Ⓐ Ⓑ Ⓒ Ⓓ

Section II: Listening

All the italicized material in Section II represents what you would hear on an actual test recording. This material does not appear in the actual test book.

Directions: For each question in this part (question 20) you will hear a single sentence. In the 10-second pause following each sentence, choose from the four pictures the one that corresponds to the spoken sentence.

Example:

You hear:

(Man) *Hier wird gebaut.*

Now look at the four pictures printed in your test book.

(A)

(B)

(C)

(D)

The correct answer is picture (D), so you would mark the letter (D) on your answer sheet.

20. (Woman) *Vom Flugzeug aus sehen die Berge ganz anders aus.*

(A)　　　　　　　　　(B)

(C)　　　　　　　　　(D)

Directions: For each question in this part (question 21) you will hear a short conversation between two people. In the 12-second pause following each conversation, choose the most appropriate remark that the first speaker could make in response to the second speaker.

Example:

You hear:

(Woman)　*Könnten Sie mir bitte einen Hundertmarkschein wechseln?*
(Man)　　*Leider nicht, aber direkt nebenan ist eine Bank.*

Now read the four choices printed in your test book.

(A) Hoffentlich ist sie noch offen.
(B) Aber ich bin ja gar nicht müde.
(C) Leider habe ich kein Geld bei mir.
(D) Ist das sehr weit von hier?

The most appropriate remark the first speaker could make is (A), so you would mark the letter (A) on your answer sheet.

---

21. (Woman) *Mein Sohn hat übermorgen Geburtstag, und ich weiß einfach nicht, was ich ihm schenken soll.*

    (Man) *Wie wäre es denn mit einer Armbanduhr?*

    (A) So spät ist es noch nicht.
    (B) Er hat schon eine.
    (C) Er wird schon achtgeben.
    (D) Die könnte ich gut gebrauchen.

    Ⓐ Ⓑ Ⓒ Ⓓ

Directions: In this part (questions 22-26) you will hear a conversation, followed by a series of spoken questions. In the 12-second pause following each question, you are to choose the most appropriate answer from the four printed choices. There is no example for this part.

(Man) *Herr Jahn, der berühmte Jurist, wird im Fernsehen interviewt.*

(Woman) *Herr Jahn, Sie feiern heute ein großes Jubiläum. Eintausend gewonnene Prozesse — das ist eine Leistung, die nur ganz wenige erreichen. Unsere allerbesten Glückwünsche! Dürfte ich Sie bitten, mir einige Fragen zu beantworten, für die sich unsere Hörer interessieren? Da wären vor allen Dingen die wichtigsten Stationen in Ihrer Karriere. Wollen Sie mir dazu etwas sagen?*

(Man) *Gerne.*

(Woman) *Punkt eins: Weshalb wurden Sie Rechtsanwalt?*

(Man) *Ganz einfach. Im Leben gibt es viele Konflikte und Streitereien. Wer da sein eigener Anwalt ist, hat es einfacher und spart viel Geld.*

(Woman) *Das ist klar. Punkt zwei: Gab es eine spezielle Schwierigkeit in ihrer Laufbahn?*

(Man) *O ja! Diese Schwierigkeit war mein Onkel. Er finanzierte mein Studium, aber (Pause) er wollte, daß ich Theologe werde. Als er endlich merkte, daß ich statt Theologie Rechtswissenschaft studiert hatte, war es schon zu spät. Ich hatte mein Examen schon hinter mir.*

(Woman) *Fabelhaft! Punkt drei: Haben Sie Ihren ersten Prozeß gewonnen oder verloren?*

(Man) *Gewonnen! Und das war eine harte Nuß!*

(Woman) *Okay! Punkt vier: Gegen wen führten Sie Ihren ersten Prozeß und worum ging es?*

(Man) *Ich führte ihn gegen meinen Onkel. Er wollte das Geld für mein Studium zurückhaben!*

22. (Man) *Warum ist heute ein besonderer Tag für Herrn Jahn?*

    (A) Er hat heute Geburtstag.
    (B) Er feiert heute ein Jubiläum.
    (C) Er hat seinen ersten Prozess gewonnen.
    (D) Er feiert den Gewinn seines Onkels.

    Ⓐ Ⓑ Ⓒ Ⓓ

23. (Man) *Warum kann Herr Jahn stolz auf seine Karriere sein?*

    (A) Weil wenige Anwälte so viele Prozesse gewinnen.
    (B) Weil er im Radio interviewt wird.
    (C) Weil er seinem Onkel geholfen hat.
    (D) Weil er so lange studiert hat. Ⓐ Ⓑ Ⓒ Ⓓ

24. (Man) *Warum is Herr Jahn Rechtsanwalt geworden?*

    (A) Er wollte anderen Anwälten helfen.
    (B) Er konnte nicht Theologie studieren.
    (C) Er hatte kein Interesse an Geld.
    (D) Er wollte sich selbst verteidigen können. Ⓐ Ⓑ Ⓒ Ⓓ

25. (Man) *Gegen wen hat der Rechtsanwalt seinen ersten Prozess geführt?*

    (A) Gegen einen Anwalt.
    (B) Gegen einen Pfarrer.
    (C) Gegen seinen Onkel.
    (D) Gegen eine Familie. Ⓐ Ⓑ Ⓒ Ⓓ

26. (Man) *Warum wollte der Onkel sein Geld zurückhaben?*

    (A) Der Onkel konnte das Studium nicht bezahlen.
    (B) Herr Jahn hatte seinen ersten Prozeß verloren.
    (C) Herr Jahn hatte dem Onkel nicht gehorcht.
    (D) Der Onkel brauchte das Geld für sein Studium. Ⓐ Ⓑ Ⓒ Ⓓ

Study Resources

Following is a list of textbooks that are widely used in courses in the first two years of college German. Familiarize yourself thoroughly with the contents of at least one of these or other German textbooks. Besides studying basic vocabulary, you should understand and be able to apply the grammatical principles that make up the language. The review grammars listed will help you do this. To improve your reading comprehension, use the passages in the textbooks and readers listed in this section and other reading material of your choice. To improve your listening comprehension, seek opportunities to hear the language spoken by native speakers and to converse with native speakers. Most of the textbooks listed include tape programs; these and other German records and tapes are available in many libraries. If you have opportunities to join organizations with German-speaking members, to attend German movies, or to listen to German-language radio broadcasts, take advantage of them.

Additional suggestions for preparing for CLEP examinations are provided in chapter 4.

Many libraries do not carry textbooks as a policy. If you can't find any of the following textbooks at the library, see whether the college bookstore has a used copy. If you can't locate the most recent edition, an edition that is one or two years older will suffice for most subject areas. As a final option, purchase a new copy of the suggested textbook as an investment in your education.

TEXTBOOKS

Crean, John E., Marilyn Scott, Claude Hill, and Jeanine Briggs, *Deutsche Sprache und Landeskunde,* 3rd ed. New York: Random House, 1989.

Dollenmayer, David B. and Thomas S. Hansen, *Neue Horizonte: A First Course in German Language and Culture,* 2nd ed. Lexington, MA: D.C. Heath, 1988.

Lohnes, Walter F., F. W. Strothmann, and William E. Petig, *German: A Structural Approach,* 4th ed. New York: W. W. Norton, 1989.

Moeller, Jack and Helmut Liedloff, *Deutsch Heute: Grundstufe,* 4th ed. Boston: Houghton Mifflin, 1988.

Moeller, Jack et al., *Kaleidoskop: Kulture, Literatur und Grammatik,* 3rd ed. Boston: Houghton Mifflin, 1991.

REVIEW GRAMMARS

Dippmann, Gerda, *A Practical Review of German Grammar.* New York: Macmillan, 1987.

Sparks, Kimberly and Van Horn Vail, *German in Review,* 2nd ed. San Diego: Harcourt Brace Jovanovich, 1986.

READERS

Clausing, Gerhard and Katharina von Hammerstein, *Interaktion: A Text-based Intermediate German Course.* Boston: Houghton Mifflin, 1990.

Isaak, Gudrun and Susan Ray, *Prosa der Gegenwart: A Collection of Contemporary German Prose.* New York: Langenscheidt, 1985.

Konrad, Rosalinde and Kim Vivian, *Deutsche Literatur,* 2nd ed. New York: Random House, 1986.

Ryder, F. G. and E. A. McCormick, *Lebendige Literatur: Deutsches Lesebuch für Anfänger,* 3rd ed. Boston: Houghton Mifflin, 1986.

Vail, Van Horn and Kimberly Sparks, *Der Weg zum Lesen,* 3rd ed. New York: Harcourt Brace Jovanovich, 1986.

Additional German language reading material can be obtained from American distributors such as:

- Adler's Foreign Books, Inc., 915 Foster Street, Evanston, IL 60201
- European Book Co., 925 Larkin Street, San Francisco, CA 94109
- Gessler Publishing Co., Inc., 55 W. 13th St., New York, NY 10011
- Mary S. Rosenberg, Foreign Books, 1841 Broadway, New York, NY 10023
- Midwest European Publications, 915 Foster St., Evanston, IL 60201-3199
- National Textbook Co., 4255 W. Touhy Ave., Lincolnwood, IL 60646
- Schoenhof's Foreign Books, Inc., 76A Mt. Auburn St., Cambridge, MA 02138

College Spanish — Levels 1 and 2

Description of the Examination

The Subject Examination in College Spanish is designed to measure knowledge and ability equivalent to that of students who have completed from two to four semesters of college language study. The "Levels 1 and 2" designation indicates that the examination focuses on skills typically achieved from the end of the first year through the second year of college study; material taught during both years is incorporated into a single examination.

The examination is 90 minutes long and is administered in two separately timed sections: a 45-minute Reading section of about 70 questions read from a test book, and a 45-minute Listening section of about 70 questions presented orally on a tape. The two sections are weighted so that they contribute equally to the total score. Subscores are reported for the two sections, but they are computed independently of the total score; thus, an individual's total score is not necessarily the average of the two subscores.

Most colleges that award credit for the College Spanish examination award either two or four semesters of credit, depending on how high the student scores on the exam. The subscores are not intended to be used to award credit separately for Reading and Listening, but colleges may require that both scores be above a certain level to insure that credit is not awarded to a student who is deficient in either of these essential skills.

Knowledge and Skills Required

Candidates must demonstrate their ability to comprehend written and spoken Spanish by answering various types of questions. The following components of reading and listening skills are tested in the examination.

✦	*Approximate Percent of Examination*

Reading (50%)

10%	Vocabulary mastery: meaning of words and idiomatic expressions in context of printed sentences
20%	Grammatical control: ability to identify usage that is structurally correct and appropriate
20%	Reading comprehension: ability to read passages representative of various styles and levels of difficulty

---

→ *Approximate Percent of Examination*

Listening (50%)

10%   Phonemic discrimination in single sentences by means of picture identification

7%   Listening comprehension through short dialogues based on everyday situations

20%   Ability to understand the language as spoken by native speakers in longer dialogues and narratives

13%   Vocabulary mastery: meaning of words and idiomatic expressions in context of spoken sentences or situations

Sample Questions

The 25 sample questions that follow are similar to questions on the College Spanish examination, but they do not appear on the actual examination.

The questions on this examination contain only four answer choices, while your answer sheet will have five answer spaces. Be sure not to make any marks in column E on your answer sheet.

Before attempting to answer the sample questions, read all the information about the College Spanish examination given above. Additional suggestions for preparing for CLEP examinations are provided in chapter 4.

Try to answer correctly as many questions as possible. Then compare your answers with the correct answers, given in Appendix B.

Section I: Reading

Directions: This part (questions 1-3) consists of a number of incomplete statements, each having four suggested completions. Select the most appropriate completion.

Example:

No me levanto temprano porque la oficina está . . . hoy.

(A) cerrada
(B) rota
(C) fuera
(D) cerca

Answer

 ⒷⒸⒹ

---

1. Como llevaba tres horas caminando, le dolían . . .

   (A) los dientes   (B) las manos   (C) los ojos   (D) los pies

   Ⓐ Ⓑ Ⓒ Ⓓ

2. Para cortar la carne necesitas . . .

   (A) una cuchara   (B) un mantel   (C) una botella   (D) un cuchillo

   Ⓐ Ⓑ Ⓒ Ⓓ

3. Lola se manchó el vestido, pero después lo . . .

   (A) abrió   (B) lavó   (C) midió   (D) levantó

   Ⓐ Ⓑ Ⓒ Ⓓ

Directions: In this part (questions 4-7) you are to select the word or phrase that makes the sentence grammatically correct.

Example:

---- que ir mañana.

(A) Debo
(B) Tengo
(C) Insisto
(D) Pregunto

Answer

Ⓐ ● Ⓒ Ⓓ

---

4. En esta clase ---- presta atención.

   (A) algo   (B) ningún   (C) algún   (D) nadie

   Ⓐ Ⓑ Ⓒ Ⓓ

5. El se enfadó y yo no ---- dije nada.

   (A) se   (B) le   (C) lo   (D) la

   Ⓐ Ⓑ Ⓒ Ⓓ

6. Paco ---- estudiar.

   (A) necesita   (B) aprende   (C) trata   (D) va

   Ⓐ Ⓑ Ⓒ Ⓓ

7. Dudo que ---- terminar el capítulo.

   (A) pudo   (B) puedo   (C) podia   (D) pueda

   Ⓐ Ⓑ Ⓒ Ⓓ

Directions: Read the following passage carefully for comprehension. The passage is followed by a number of questions or incomplete statements (questions 8-12). Select the answer or completion that is best according to the passage. There is no example for this part.

Benicarló, 24 de agosto. — "Día sin sol, día perdido," parecen pensar los turistas que visitan las playas españolas, a juzgar por su paciente exposición al sol todas las horas en que es posible. Un avispado hotelero, dueño de una serie de apartamentos en la zona de playa que va desde Benicarló a Peñíscola, ha decidido hacer de esta frase su lema. Por ello ha hecho colocar grandes anuncios declarando que está dispuesto a bajar el precio a sus inquilinos por cada día sin sol. Hasta ahora, y como es tradicional en la zona, el sol no le ha hecho perder dinero porque ha lucido a más y mejor. A pesar de todo, el lema no deja de hacer efecto en los turistas que llenan sus apartamentos, tostándose muy a gusto en las playas cercanas.

8. La frase "Día sin sol, día perdido" sirvió

    (A) para confirmar el pésimo clima de la región
    (B) como lema de la campaña propagandista del hotelero
    (C) para desilusionar a los más fuertes tradicionalistas
    (D) como serio obstáculo a todo plan de desarrollo económico

        Ⓐ Ⓑ Ⓒ Ⓓ

9. Benicarló y Peñíscola deben ser dos

    (A) turistas
    (B) hoteleros
    (C) pueblos de la costa
    (D) casas de apartamentos   Ⓐ Ⓑ Ⓒ Ⓓ

10. Los turistas frecuentan aquella zona de España para

    (A) lucirse
    (B) alquilar apartamentos en la sierra
    (C) enriquecerse
    (D) aprovechar el sol y la playa   Ⓐ Ⓑ Ⓒ Ⓓ

11. ¿Qué les pasaría a los clientes del hotelero los días sin sol?

    (A) Podrían pintar dentro del hotel.
    (B) Dejarían el apartamento.
    (C) Le pagarían menos al hotelero.
    (D) No le pagarían nada al hotelero.   Ⓐ Ⓑ Ⓒ Ⓓ

12. El dueño de los apartamentos quedó satisfecho con su plan porque

    (A) los inquilinos se resignaron a pagar la cuota extraordinaria
    (B) el sol salió a lucir como nunca en la zona
    (C) a los turistas les gustó pasar todo el tiempo fuera de la zona
    (D) habría muchos inquilinos los días sin sol

                                               Ⓐ Ⓑ Ⓒ Ⓓ

Section II: Listening

The italicized material in Section II represents what you would hear on a test recording. This material does not appear in the test book.

Directions: For each question in this part (questions 13-15) you will hear a single sentence. In the 10-second pause following each sentence, you are to choose the picture that corresponds to the spoken sentence.

Example:

You hear:

(Woman) *El muchacho va a correr.*

Now look at the four pictures in your test book.

The correct answer is picture (D), so you would mark the letter (D) on your answer sheet.

13. (Man) *El correo siempre llega por la mañana.*

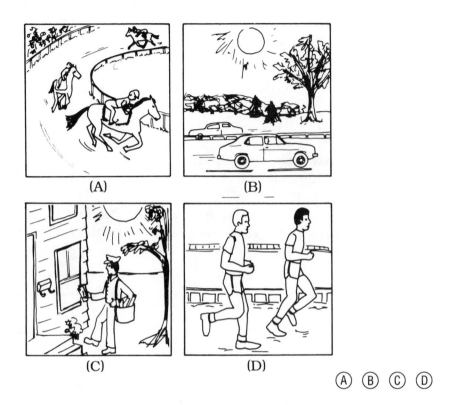

(A) (B)

(C) (D)

Ⓐ Ⓑ Ⓒ Ⓓ

14. (Woman) *A los muchachos les gusta el jugo.*

(A) (B)

(C) (D)

Ⓐ Ⓑ Ⓒ Ⓓ

15. (Man) *Está comiendo un plátano.*

(A)   (B)

(C)   (D)

Ⓐ Ⓑ Ⓒ Ⓓ

Directions: For each question in this part (questions 16-19) you will hear a short conversation between two people and you will read a question about the conversation. In the 10-second pause following each conversation, choose the appropriate response to the printed question.

Example:

You hear:

(Man)   *Ya llegamos. ¿Quiere Ud. bajar, señora?*
(Woman) *Sí, por favor. ¿Cuánto le debo?*

Now read the question and the four choices printed in your test book.

¿Dónde tiene lugar esta conversación?

(A) En un taxi.
(B) En un tren.
(C) En un ascensor.
(D) En un avión.

Of the four choices, (A) is the most appropriate response, so you would mark the letter (A) on your answer sheet.

---

16. (Man A) *¿Qué tal, José? ¿Cómo sigues?*
    (Man B) *Me siento mejor, pero el médico dice que tengo que quedarme
    cinco o seis días más en esta institución.*

    ¿Dónde tiene lugar esta conversación?

    (A) En la calle.
    (B) En el club deportivo.
    (C) En un sanatorio.
    (D) En una casa de huéspedes. Ⓐ Ⓑ Ⓒ Ⓓ

17. (Woman) *Vamos, hijo, que ya es hora.*
    (Man)   *Un poco más, mamá.*
    (Woman) *Sonó el reloj hace cinco minutos.*
    (Man)   *Estoy cansado.*
    (Woman) *Llegarás tarde si no te apuras.*

    ¿Qué debe hacer el muchacho?

    (A) Levantarse.
    (B) Esperar cinco minutos.
    (C) Hablar del tiempo.
    (D) Poner el reloj en hora. Ⓐ Ⓑ Ⓒ Ⓓ

18. (Man)   *Señorita, ¿ya salió el vuelo 45 para Quito?*
    (Woman) *Sí, señor, acaba de salir.*
    (Man)   *¡Qué lástima! ¿Y cuándo es el próximo vuelo? Tengo
    necesidad de llegar a Quito esta noche.*
    (Woman) *Lo siento mucho, señor, pero no hay vuelos a Quito de noche.
    El próximo sale a las siete de la mañana y llega a Quito a las
    nueve.*

    ¿Cuándo llegará el señor a Quito?

    (A) Esa noche.
    (B) Dentro de dos horas.
    (C) Al día siguiente.
    (D) La semana próxima. Ⓐ Ⓑ Ⓒ Ⓓ

19. (Man)   *Sra. Andújar, déle a Sultán una pastilla al día.*
    (Woman) *El pobrecito no ladra desde el lunes.*
    (Man)   *Y no lo deje comer huesos hasta la semana entrante.*

    ¿Quién es Sultán?

    (A) El esposo de la señora.
    (B) Un perro.
    (C) Un gato.
    (D) Un ladrón.   Ⓐ Ⓑ Ⓒ Ⓓ

Directions: In this part (questions 20-22) you will hear a spoken selection, followed by a series of spoken questions. In the 10-second pause following each question, you are to choose the most appropriate answer from the four printed choices. There is no example for this part.

(Woman) *Tú conoces a Pedro. Pero, ¿sabes que es el hombre más testarudo y bruto del mundo? Se enloquece por el fútbol e insiste en que le acompañe al partido del domingo y lo hago, a pesar de que el espectáculo me aburre. Prefiero que nos quedemos en casa o que demos un paseo. Así ahorramos dinero y podemos estar solos. Figúrate, le echo de menos tanto cuando estamos separados. El fin de semana me es muy importante y lo echamos a perder en el estadio metropolitano. Pero, ¿qué se puede hacer?*

20. (Man) *¿De qué se queja la señora?*

    (A) De que el marido nunca sale.
    (B) Del resultado del partido de fútbol.
    (C) De lo difícil que es su marido.
    (D) De la necesidad de permanecer en casa.   Ⓐ Ⓑ Ⓒ Ⓓ

21. (Man) *¿Por qué no quiere la señora asistir al fútbol?*

    (A) Porque prefiere otro equipo.
    (B) Porque no le gusta el deporte.
    (C) Porque no se lo permiten sus padres.
    (D) Porque le falta dinero.   Ⓐ Ⓑ Ⓒ Ⓓ

22. (Man) *¿Por qué le da la señora tanta importancia al fin de semana?*

    (A) Porque quiere estar con Pedro.
    (B) Porque no hay partidos.
    (C) Porque va al estadio.
    (D) Porque se queda sola el domingo.   Ⓐ Ⓑ Ⓒ Ⓓ

Note: Directions for the next part of the exam will be given only on the recording.

Directions: Each question that you will hear in this part (questions 23-25) will be followed immediately by four suggested answer choices. You will need to listen carefully to all four answers before choosing the most appropriate response to the question in the 5-second period that follows each one.

Example:

You hear:

(Man)   *Perdone, ¿dónde está la biblioteca?*
(Woman) (A) *A las seis y media.*   (B) *Tengo prisa.*
        (C) *Voy mañana.*   (D) *En la calle Mayor.*

The correct response is (D), "En la calle Mayor"; therefore you would mark the letter (D) on your answer sheet.

---

23. (Woman A) *¿Cómo está Ud., Señora Gómez?*
    (Woman B) (A) *Hace frío.*   (B) *Mañana a las ocho.*
          (C) *Bastante bien, gracias.*
          (D) *Sí, por favor.*   Ⓐ Ⓑ Ⓒ Ⓓ

24. (Man)   *¿Cómo vino Julio?*
    (Woman) (A) *Yo como con vino.*   (B) *El vino no está bueno.*
        (C) *Vino en coche.*   (D) *Vino en julio.*

                          Ⓐ Ⓑ Ⓒ Ⓓ

25. (Man)   *¿Quién llamó anoche?*
    (Woman) (A) *No sé quién va.*   (B) *Yo llamo después.*
        (C) *Viene esta noche.*   (D) *Fue mi primo Luis.*

                          Ⓐ Ⓑ Ⓒ Ⓓ

Study Resources

Following is a list of textbooks that are widely used in courses during the first two years of college Spanish. Familiarize yourself thoroughly with the contents of at least one of these or with other Spanish textbooks. Besides studying basic vocabulary, you should understand and be able to apply the grammatical principles that make up the language. To improve your reading comprehension, use the passages in the textbooks, the readers listed, and other reading material of your choice. To improve your listening comprehension, seek opportunities to hear the language spoken by native speakers and to converse with native speakers.

Most of the textbooks listed include tape programs; these and other Spanish records and tapes are available in many libraries. If you have opportunities to join organizations with Spanish-speaking members, to attend Spanish movies, or to listen to Spanish-language television or radio broadcasts, take advantage of them. Additional suggestions for preparing for CLEP examinations are provided in chapter 4.

Many libraries do not carry textbooks as a policy. If you can't find any of the following textbooks at the library, see whether the college bookstore has a used copy. If you can't locate the most recent edition, an edition that is one or two years older will suffice for most subject areas. As a final option, purchase a new copy of the suggested textbook as an investment in your education.

TEXTBOOKS

Brod, Evelyn F. and Carol J. Brady, *Viajemos 2001: Repaso y progreso.* New York: Macmillan, 1990.

Da Silva, Zenia Sacks, *A Concept Approach to Spanish,* 4th ed. New York: Harper & Row, 1987.

Da Silva, Zenia Sacks, *Experiencias: Lenguaje.* New York: Harper & Row, 1990.

Neale-Silva, Eduardo and Robert L. Nicholas, *¡En camino! A Cultural Approach to Beginning Spanish,* 4th ed. New York, McGraw-Hill, 1990.

Solé, Carlos and Yolanda Solé, *Español: Ampliación y repaso,* 2nd ed. New York: Macmillan, 1987.

Turk, Laurel, Carlos Solé, Jr. and Aurelio Espinosa, *Foundation Course in Spanish,* 7th ed. Lexington, MA: D.C. Heath, 1989.

Additional foreign language reading material can be obtained from American distributors such as:

- The French and Spanish Book Corp., 115 Fifth Ave., New York, NY 10003
- Midwest European Publications, 915 Foster St., Evanston, IL 60201
- Schoenhof's Foreign Books, 76A Mount Auburn St., Cambridge, MA 02138

American Government

Description of the Examination

The Subject Examination in American Government covers material that is usually taught in a one-semester introductory course in American government and politics at the college level. The scope and emphasis of the examination reflect what is most commonly taught in introductory American government courses that emphasize the national government. The examination covers topics such as the institutions and policy processes of the federal government, the federal courts and civil liberties, political parties and pressure groups, political beliefs and behavior, and the content and history of the Constitution.

The exam is 90 minutes long and includes approximately 100 multiple-choice questions to be answered in two separately timed 45-minute sections.

Knowledge and Skills Required

Questions on the exam require candidates to demonstrate one or more of the following abilities.

- Knowledge of American government and politics (about 55-60 percent of the examination)

- Understanding of typical patterns of political processes and behavior (including the components of the behavioral situation of a political actor), and the principles used to explain or justify various governmental structures and procedures (about 30-35 percent of the examination)

- Analysis and interpretation of simple data that are relevant to American government and politics (10-15 percent of the examination)

The subject matter of the American Government examination is drawn from the following topics.

←	*Approximate Percent of Examination*

30-35% Institutions and policy processes: Presidency, Bureaucracy, and Congress

    The major formal and informal institutional arrangements and powers

    Policy processes and outputs

    Relationships among these three institutions and links between them and political parties, interest groups, the media, and public opinion

15-20% Federal courts and civil liberties

    Structure and processes of the judicial system with emphasis on the role and influence of the Supreme Court

    The development of civil rights and civil liberties by judicial interpretation

    First Amendment freedoms

    The rights of the accused

    The meaning of equality

15-20% Political parties and pressure groups, whose mechanisms facilitate the communication of common interests and preferences by like-minded citizens

    Political parties (including their function, organization, historical development, and effects on the political process)

    Pressure groups (including the variety of activities they typically undertake and their effects on the political process)

    Elections (including the electoral process)

10-15% Political beliefs and behavior

    Processes by which citizens learn about politics

    The ways in which citizens vote and otherwise participate in political life

    Public opinion

    Beliefs that citizens hold about their government and its leaders

    The variety of factors that predispose citizens to differ from one another in terms of their political perceptions, values, attitudes, and activities

    The relationships between the general public and its political leaders

---

➤   *Approximate Percent of Examination*

15-20%   Constitutional underpinnings of American democracy

         The development of concepts such as:

                Federalism (with attention to intergovernmental relations)

                Separation of powers

                Majority rule

                Minority rights

         Considerations that influenced the formulation and adoption of the Constitution

Sample Questions

The 40 sample questions that follow are similar to questions on the American Government examination, but they do not appear on the actual examination.

Before attempting to answer the sample questions, read all the information above about the American Government examination. Additional suggestions for preparing for CLEP examinations are provided in chapter 4.

Try to answer correctly as many questions as possible. Then compare your answers with the correct answers, given in Appendix B.

Directions: Each of the questions or incomplete statements below is followed by five suggested answers or completions. Select the one that is best in each case.

1. Which of the following statements reflects a pluralist theory of American politics?

   (A) American politics is dominated by a small elite.

   (B) Public policies emerge from cooperation among elites in business, labor, and government.

   (C) Public policies emerge from compromises reached among competing groups.

   (D) American politics is dominated by cities at the expense of rural areas.

   (E) The American political arena is made up of isolated individuals who have few group affiliations outside the family.

                             Ⓐ Ⓑ Ⓒ Ⓓ Ⓔ

2. The most influential source of a citizen's attitudes about politics, political values, and public issues generally is which of the following?

(A) Religious affiliation
(B) Family
(C) Formal education
(D) Party platforms
(E) Peers

Ⓐ Ⓑ Ⓒ Ⓓ Ⓔ

3. A member of the House of Representatives who was <u>not</u> worried about reelection but wanted to increase his or her power and influence in Congress would be best advised to seek appointment to which of the following committees?

(A) Agriculture
(B) Ways and Means
(C) Veteran's Affairs
(D) Armed Services
(E) Education and Labor

Ⓐ Ⓑ Ⓒ Ⓓ Ⓔ

4. Which of the following statements about *Brown* v. *Board of Education of Topeka* is correct?

(A) It declared Bible reading in the public schools unconstitutional.
(B) It established the principle of one person, one vote.
(C) It required that citizens about to be arrested be read a statement concerning their right to remain silent.
(D) It declared segregation by race in the public schools unconstitutional.
(E) It declared segregation by race in places of public accommodation unconstitutional.

Ⓐ Ⓑ Ⓒ Ⓓ Ⓔ

5. "The Constitution limits the size of the District of Columbia to _____."
— State of Alabama literacy test, 1936

The question above and the literacy test from which it came were most likely designed to

(A) determine the literacy of potential voters
(B) prevent Black people from exercising their right to vote
(C) assess the general population's understanding of the Constitution
(D) promote opposition to statehood for the District of Columbia
(E) stop people from moving to the District of Columbia

Ⓐ Ⓑ Ⓒ Ⓓ Ⓔ

6. Presidents often have difficulty getting their legislative programs passed because of

   (A) differences in the viewpoints of elected officials in the national government and elected officials in state and local governments
   (B) the influence of regional, party, and special interests on congressional deliberations
   (C) the differences between House and Senate party leaders
   (D) constitutional provisions limiting the size of the White House staff
   (E) uncertain guidelines from the Supreme Court

   Ⓐ Ⓑ Ⓒ Ⓓ Ⓔ

7. Usually, the first political figure perceived by a young child is the

   (A) President of the United States
   (B) United States representative from the child's congressional district
   (C) governor of the state in which the child lives
   (D) city council representative from the child's district
   (E) mayor of the city in which the child lives

   Ⓐ Ⓑ Ⓒ Ⓓ Ⓔ

8. Which of the following principles protects a citizen from imprisonment without trial?

   (A) Representative government
   (B) Separation of powers
   (C) Due process
   (D) Checks and balances
   (E) Popular sovereignty

   Ⓐ Ⓑ Ⓒ Ⓓ Ⓔ

9. The fact that many bills passed by Congress are products of a system of mutual accommodation means that to some extent congressional behavior is based on

   (A) ideological divisions
   (B) regional alignments
   (C) the principle of reciprocity
   (D) the norm of deference
   (E) party loyalty

   Ⓐ Ⓑ Ⓒ Ⓓ Ⓔ

10. The President's veto power is accurately described by which of the following statements?

    I. A President sometimes threatens to veto a bill that is under discussion in order to influence congressional decision-making.
    II. A President typically vetoes about a third of the bills passed by Congress.
    III. Congress is usually unable to override a President's veto.

    (A) I only
    (B) III only
    (C) I and III only
    (D) II and III only
    (E) I, II, and III   Ⓐ Ⓑ Ⓒ Ⓓ Ⓔ

11. All of the following issues were decided at the Constitutional Convention of 1787 EXCEPT

    (A) representation in the legislature
    (B) voting qualifications of the electorate
    (C) method of electing the President
    (D) congressional power to override a presidential veto
    (E) qualifications for members of the House and Senate

                           Ⓐ Ⓑ Ⓒ Ⓓ Ⓔ

12. Which of the following statements about political action committees (PAC's) is true?

    (A) PAC's may give unlimited contributions to the election campaigns of individual candidates.
    (B) PAC spending has not kept pace with inflation.
    (C) PAC activity is limited to direct contributions to candidates.
    (D) Social-issue groups are the source of most PAC dollars.
    (E) PAC spending makes up a higher percentage of congressional campaign funds than of presidential campaign funds.

                           Ⓐ Ⓑ Ⓒ Ⓓ Ⓔ

13. The usefulness to the President of having cabinet members as political advisers is undermined by the fact that

    (A) the President has little latitude in choosing cabinet members
    (B) cabinet members have no political support independent of the President
    (C) cabinet members are usually drawn from Congress and retain loyalties to Congress
    (D) the loyalties of cabinet members are often divided between loyalty to the President and loyalty to their own executive departments
    (E) the cabinet operates as a collective unit and individual members have no access to the President

    Ⓐ Ⓑ Ⓒ Ⓓ Ⓔ

14. All of the following constitutional rights of the accused have been interpreted to apply to state criminal proceedings EXCEPT the right to

    (A) be represented by counsel
    (B) remain silent during questioning
    (C) be indicted by grand jury
    (D) be informed of the charges pending
    (E) receive a trial by jury in a criminal case

    Ⓐ Ⓑ Ⓒ Ⓓ Ⓔ

15. In the electoral history of the United States, third parties have been effective vehicles of protest when they

    (A) used political violence with tactical skill
    (B) presented innovative programs in Congress
    (C) dramatized issues and positions that were being ignored by the major parties
    (D) chose the President by depriving either of the major parties of an electoral college victory
    (E) supported a political agenda that appealed especially to women

    Ⓐ Ⓑ Ⓒ Ⓓ Ⓔ

16. Which of the following best defines the term "judicial activism"?

    (A) The demands on judges to hear large numbers of cases
    (B) The efforts of judges to lobby Congress for funds
    (C) The attempts by judges to influence election outcomes
    (D) The unwillingness of judges to remove themselves from cases in which they have a personal interest
    (E) The tendency of judges to interpret the Constitution according to their own views

    Ⓐ Ⓑ Ⓒ Ⓓ Ⓔ

17. High levels of political participation have been found to be positively associated with which of the following?

   I. A high level of interest in politics
  II. A belief in personal effectiveness
 III. A strong sense of civic duty

(A) III only
(B) I and II only
(C) I and III only
(D) II and III only
(E) I, II, and III

Ⓐ Ⓑ Ⓒ Ⓓ Ⓔ

18. In the last thirty years, the single most important variable in determining the outcome of an election for a member of the House of Representatives has been

(A) incumbency
(B) personal wealth
(C) previous political office held in the district
(D) membership in the political party of the President
(E) positions on key social issues

Ⓐ Ⓑ Ⓒ Ⓓ Ⓔ

19. The concept of federalism in the United States can best be described as a form of government in which

(A) powers are constitutionally divided between a central government and its constituent governments, with some powers being shared
(B) all governmental powers are constitutionally given to the central government, which may delegate authority to its constituent elements
(C) constituent governments join together and form a central government, which exists by approval of the constituent governments
(D) the central government creates constituent governments
(E) constituent governments are sovereign in all matters except foreign policy, which is reserved to the central government

Ⓐ Ⓑ Ⓒ Ⓓ Ⓔ

20. The power of the Rules Committee in the House of Representatives rests on its authority to

    (A) choose the chairs of other standing committees and issue rules for the selection of subcommittee chairs
    (B) initiate all spending legislation and hold budget hearings
    (C) place a bill on the legislative calendar, limit time for debate, and determine the type of amendments allowed
    (D) determine the procedures by which nominations by the President will be approved by the House
    (E) choose the President if no candidate wins a majority in the electoral college

    Ⓐ Ⓑ Ⓒ Ⓓ Ⓔ

21. All of the following are formal or informal sources of presidential power EXCEPT

    (A) presidential authority to raise revenue
    (B) presidential access to the media
    (C) precedents set during previous administrations
    (D) public support
    (E) the Constitution

    Ⓐ Ⓑ Ⓒ Ⓓ Ⓔ

22. A major difference between political parties and interest groups is that interest groups generally do NOT

    (A) suggest new legislation supportive of their interests
    (B) try to influence the outcome of legislation
    (C) try to place their members in political office
    (D) concern themselves with elections
    (E) have a national organization

    Ⓐ Ⓑ Ⓒ Ⓓ Ⓔ

23. An election is a "realigning" or "critical" election if

    (A) the minority party wins
    (B) voter turnout is higher than expected
    (C) it occurs during a major war
    (D) the voter coalitions that the parties mobilize change and last for a significant period of time
    (E) the same party controls both Congress and the presidency

    Ⓐ Ⓑ Ⓒ Ⓓ Ⓔ

24. Which of the following Supreme Court cases involved the principle of "one person, one vote"?

    (A) *Baker* v. *Carr*
    (B) *Roe* v. *Wade*
    (C) *Mapp* v. *Ohio*
    (D) *Korematsu* v. *United States*
    (E) *Gideon* v. *Wainwright*   Ⓐ Ⓑ Ⓒ Ⓓ Ⓔ

25. The passage of broad legislation that leaves the making of specific rules to the executive branch is an example of

    (A) shared powers
    (B) delegated authority
    (C) checks and balances
    (D) executive agreement
    (E) regulatory powers   Ⓐ Ⓑ Ⓒ Ⓓ Ⓔ

26. In the United States, the two-party system has had all of the following effects EXCEPT

    (A) lessening class and regional loyalties
    (B) promoting majority rule
    (C) increasing the need for runoff elections
    (D) fostering bargaining and compromise prior to general elections
    (E) helping voters to organize and interpret political information

    Ⓐ Ⓑ Ⓒ Ⓓ Ⓔ

27. The details of legislation are usually worked out in which of the following settings?

    (A) A party caucus
    (B) The majority leader's office
    (C) The floor of the House
    (D) Legislative hearings
    (E) A subcommittee   Ⓐ Ⓑ Ⓒ Ⓓ Ⓔ

28. A philosophical explanation of the operation of diverse interests in American politics is found in

    (A) the Virginia Plan
    (B) John Calhoun's *A Disquisition on Government*
    (C) *The Federalist* papers
    (D) the Declaration of Independence
    (E) John Locke's *The Second Treatise of Civil Government*

    Ⓐ Ⓑ Ⓒ Ⓓ Ⓔ

29. Which of the following best describes the jurisdiction that the Constitution gives to the Supreme Court?

(A) Much original jurisdiction and little appellate jurisdiction
(B) Much original jurisdiction and no appellate jurisdiction
(C) Little original jurisdiction and much appellate jurisdiction
(D) No original jurisdiction and much appellate jurisdiction
(E) No original jurisdiction and little appellate jurisdiction

Ⓐ Ⓑ Ⓒ Ⓓ Ⓔ

ISSUE VOTING, PARTY VOTING, ISSUE AND PARTY VOTING, 1956–1972

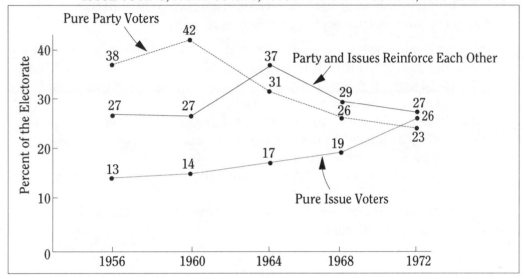

Copyright © 1976 by the President and Fellows of Harvard College

30. According to the information in the chart above, which of the following statements are true?

  I. The proportion of pure issue voters in the electorate increased continuously between 1956 and 1972.
 II. The proportion of pure party voters in the electorate decreased continuously between 1956 and 1972.
III. The net change in the proportion of the electorate for which party and issues reinforce each other was zero between 1956 and 1972.
IV. In 1956, compared to the number of pure issue voters, there were about twice as many voters for whom party and issues reinforced each other, and about three times as many pure party voters.

(A) I and II only
(B) III and IV only
(C) I, II, and III only
(D) I, III, and IV only
(E) I, II, III, and IV

Ⓐ Ⓑ Ⓒ Ⓓ Ⓔ

225

31. Which of the following activities of American labor unions is recognized by law?

    (A) Engaging in strikes
    (B) Denying the public access to a business
    (C) Refusing a subpoena to appear before an investigative committee of Congress
    (D) Disobeying a court injunction to return to work
    (E) Requiring members to make political contributions

    Ⓐ Ⓑ Ⓒ Ⓓ Ⓔ

32. Which of the following best describes the relationship between socioeconomic status and participation in politics?

    (A) The lower one's socioeconomic status, the more likely it is that one will run for public office.
    (B) The higher one's socioeconomic status, the greater the probability of active involvement in the political process.
    (C) Adults who are unemployed have a greater personal interest in policy and tend to participate more actively in politics than do employed adults.
    (D) People in the lower middle class are the most likely to participate in politics.
    (E) There is no relationship between socioeconomic status and political participation.

    Ⓐ Ⓑ Ⓒ Ⓓ Ⓔ

STUDENT PARTY IDENTIFICATION BY
PARENT PARTY IDENTIFICATION

Student Party Identification	Parent Party Identification		
	Democrat	Independent	Republican
Democrat	66%	29%	13%
Independent	27%	53%	36%
Republican	7%	18%	51%
Total	100%	100%	100%

M. Kent Jennings and Richard G. Niemi, *The Political Character of Adolescence: The Influence of Families and Schools.* Copyright © 1974 by Princeton University Press. Reprinted by permission of Princeton University Press.

33. According to the information in the table above, which of the following statements is correct?

(A) Students who identify themselves as independents are most likely to have parents who are Republicans.
(B) Of the three groups of parents, the Democrats are the most likely to pass on their party identification to their children.
(C) Students who identify with the Democratic party are more likely to have parents who are Republicans than parents who are independents.
(D) The children of Republicans are less likely to identify themselves as independents than are the children of Democrats.
(E) Parents who are independents are the least likely to have children who share their party identification.

Ⓐ Ⓑ Ⓒ Ⓓ Ⓔ

34. The creation of the Executive Office of the President (EOP) in 1939 and the accompanying executive order to move the Bureau of the Budget from the Treasury Department to the new EOP are considered to be important events in the process known as the institutionalization of the presidency. Which of the following would also be considered an example of this process?

(A) Creation of the National Security Council
(B) Creation of the Securities and Exchange Commission
(C) Impoundment by the President of funds appropriated by Congress
(D) Invocation of the principle of executive privilege in denying information to Congress
(E) Use of executive agreements rather than congressionally ratified treaties in the conduct of foreign policy

Ⓐ Ⓑ Ⓒ Ⓓ Ⓔ

35. All of the following statements correctly describe judicial appointments at the federal level EXCEPT:

    (A) The President, rather than Congress, has control over the creation of new federal judicial positions.
    (B) Federal judicial appointments are sent for evaluation to the American Bar Association's Committee on the Federal Judiciary.
    (C) If a senator is a member of the President's party, tradition may allow the senator to exercise an informal veto over an individual being considered from the senator's state.
    (D) Presidents seldom recommend for judicial appointment individuals from the opposition political party.
    (E) Federal judgeships are often considered by Presidents as patronage positions.

    Ⓐ Ⓑ Ⓒ Ⓓ Ⓔ

36. Which of the following agencies determines the domestic monetary policy of the United States?

    (A) The Council of Economic Advisors
    (B) The United States Department of the Treasury
    (C) The Office of Management and Budget
    (D) The Federal Reserve Board
    (E) The Export-Import Bank

    Ⓐ Ⓑ Ⓒ Ⓓ Ⓔ

37. Under which of the following conditions are interest groups most likely to influence policymaking?

    (A) When a problem has been dramatized by television network news
    (B) When the President has made a major address on the subject
    (C) When the parties in Congress have taken alternative positions on the issue
    (D) When presidential candidates have been disagreeing with one another on the subject
    (E) When the issue is a highly technical one requiring very detailed legislation

    Ⓐ Ⓑ Ⓒ Ⓓ Ⓔ

38. All of the following help to explain the President's difficulty in controlling cabinet-level agencies EXCEPT:

    (A) Agencies often have political support from interest groups.
    (B) Agency staff often have information and technical expertise that the President and presidential advisers lack.
    (C) The President can only fire appointees before they have been confirmed by the Senate.
    (D) Civil servants who remain in their jobs through changes of administration develop loyalties to their agencies.
    (E) Congress is a competitor for influence over the bureaucracy.

    Ⓐ Ⓑ Ⓒ Ⓓ Ⓔ

39. In the Constitution as originally ratified in 1788, the provisions regarding which of the following most closely approximate popular, majoritarian democracy?

    (A) Election of members of the House of Representatives
    (B) Election of members of the Senate
    (C) Election of the President
    (D) Ratification of treaties
    (E) Confirmation of presidential appointments

    Ⓐ Ⓑ Ⓒ Ⓓ Ⓔ

40. The most likely and often the most powerful policy coalition of interests would include a federal agency plus which of the following?

    (A) Other related agencies in the bureaucracy and a congressional committee chairperson
    (B) Congress and the President
    (C) A clientele interest group and the President
    (D) A clientele interest group and a congressional subcommittee
    (E) A clientele interest group and the majority party

    Ⓐ Ⓑ Ⓒ Ⓓ Ⓔ

Study Resources

Two types of materials that should be helpful to you in preparing for the American Government examination are listed here. Begin by reading an introductory textbook. A number of comprehensive textbooks are listed below. Because most texts are revised frequently, no editions or publication dates are included. Additional reading will enrich your understanding of American politics; examples of supplemental books are given at the end of this section.

Additional suggestions for preparing for CLEP examinations are provided in chapter 4.

Many libraries do not carry textbooks as a policy. If you can't find any of the following textbooks at the library, see whether the college bookstore has a used copy. If you can't locate the most recent edition, an edition that is one or two years older will suffice for most subject areas. As a final option, purchase a new copy of the suggested textbook as an investment in your education.

TEXTBOOKS

Johnson, Paul E., *American Government: People, Institutions, and Politics.* Boston: Houghton Mifflin.

Burns, James M. et al., *Government by the People.* Englewood Cliffs, NJ: Prentice Hall.

Dye, Thomas R. and L. Harmon Ziegler, *The Irony of Democracy.* Pacific Grove, CA: Brooks/Cole.

Greenberg, Edward S., *The American Political System: A Radical Approach.* Glenview, IL: Scott, Foresman.

Janda, Kenneth, et al., *The Challenge of Democracy: Government in America.* Boston: Houghton Mifflin.

Ladd, Everett C., Jr., *The American Polity: The People and Their Government.* New York: W.W. Norton.

Lineberry, Robert L. et al., *Government in America: People, Politics, and Policy.* New York: HarperCollins.

Patterson, Samuel C. et al., *A More Perfect Union: Introduction to American Government.* Pacific Grove, CA: Brooks/Cole.

Prewitt, Kenneth et al., *An Introduction to American Government.* New York: HarperCollins.

Stephenson, Donald G., Jr. et al., *American Government.* New York: HarperCollins.

Wilson, James Q., *American Government: Institutions and Policies.* Lexington, MA: D. C. Heath.

SUPPLEMENTAL BOOKS

Cigler, Allen and Burdett Loomis, *American Politics: Classic and Contemporary Readings.* Boston: Houghton Mifflin.

Gruberg, Martin et al., eds., *The Encyclopedic Dictionary of American Government.* Guilford, CT: Dushkin.

Nivola, Pietro and David H. Rosenbloom, eds., *Classic Readings in American Politics.* New York: St. Martin's Press.

Plano, Jack C. and Milton Greenberg, *The American Political Dictionary.* New York: Holt, Rinehart & Winston.

Stinebrickner, Bruce T., ed., *Annual Editions: American Government.* Guilford, CT: Dushkin.

Woll, Peter, *American Government: Readings and Cases.* Glenview, IL: Scott, Foresman.

American History I: Early Colonizations to 1877

Description of the Examination

The Subject Examination in American History I: Early Colonizations to 1877 covers material that is usually taught in the first semester of what is often a two-semester course in American history. The examination covers the period of American history from the Spanish and French colonizations to the end of Reconstruction, with the majority of questions on the period of nationhood. In the seventeenth and eighteenth centuries, emphasis is placed on the English colonies.

There are approximately 120 multiple-choice questions on the 90-minute exam, to be answered in two separately timed 45-minute sections.

Knowledge and Skills Required

Questions on the test require candidates to demonstrate one or more of the following abilities.

- Identification and description of historical phenomena (about 45 percent of the examination)

- Characterization and classification of historical phenomena (about 15 percent of the examination)

- Analysis and interpretation of historical phenomena (about 10 percent of the examination)

- Comparison and contrast of historical phenomena (about 10 percent of the examination)

- Explanation and evaluation of historical phenomena (about 20 percent of the examination)

The major topics covered by the examination are:

➡	*Approximate Percent of Examination*
50%	Political institutions and behavior and public policy
20%	Social and economic change
20%	Cultural and intellectual developments
10%	Diplomacy and international relations

About one-third of the questions deal with the period from 1500 to 1789, and about two-thirds are on the period from 1790 to 1877. Among the specific topics tested are the following:

The character of Colonial society

British relations with the Atlantic colonies in North America

The motivations and character of American expansionism

The content of the Constitution and its amendments, and their interpretation by the Supreme Court

The growth of political parties

The changing role of government in American life

The intellectual and political expressions of nationalism

Agrarianism, abolitionism, and other such movements

Long-term demographic trends

The process of economic growth and development

The origins and nature of Black slavery in America

Immigration and the history of racial and ethnic minorities

The causes and impacts of major wars in American history

Major movements and individual figures in the history of American arts and letters

Sample Questions

The 40 sample questions that follow are similar to questions on the American History I examination, but they do not appear on the actual examination.

Before attempting to answer the sample questions, read all the information about the American History I examination on the preceding pages. Additional suggestions for preparing for CLEP examinations are provided in chapter 4.

Try to answer correctly as many of the questions as possible. Then compare your answers with the correct answers, given in Appendix B.

Directions: Each of the questions or incomplete statements below is followed by five suggested answers or completions. Select the one that is best in each case.

1. In a sermon given aboard ship on the way to America, John Winthrop told the Puritans that their society would be regarded as "a city upon a hill" and that therefore they should be bonded together by love. But first he explained that there would always be inequalities of wealth and power, that some people would always be in positions of authority while others would be dependent. His statements best illustrate the Puritans'

   (A) reaction to unsuccessful socialist experiments in the Low Countries
   (B) acceptance of the traditional belief that order depended on a system of ranks
   (C) intention to vest political power exclusively in the ministers
   (D) desire to better themselves economically through means that included the institution of slavery
   (E) inability to take clear stands on social issues

   Ⓐ Ⓑ Ⓒ Ⓓ Ⓔ

2. The French and Indian War was a pivotal point in America's relationship to Great Britain because it led Great Britain to

   (A) encourage colonial manufactures
   (B) impose revenue taxes on the colonies
   (C) restrict emigration from England
   (D) ignore the colonies
   (E) grant increased colonial self-government

   Ⓐ Ⓑ Ⓒ Ⓓ Ⓔ

3. Under the Articles of Confederation, which of the following was true about the national government?

   (A) It had the power to conduct foreign affairs.
   (B) It had the power to regulate commerce.
   (C) It had the power to tax.
   (D) It included a President.
   (E) It included a federal judiciary.

   Ⓐ Ⓑ Ⓒ Ⓓ Ⓔ

4. Thomas Jefferson opposed some of Alexander Hamilton's programs because Jefferson believed that

   (A) the common bond of a substantial national debt would serve to unify the different states
   (B) the French alliance threatened to spread the violence of the French Revolution to America
   (C) the federal government should encourage manufacturing and industry
   (D) Hamilton's programs were weakening the military strength of the nation
   (E) Hamilton's programs favored wealthy financial interests

   Ⓐ Ⓑ Ⓒ Ⓓ Ⓔ

5. The Louisiana Purchase was significant because it

   (A) eliminated Spain from the North American continent
   (B) gave the United States control of the Mississippi River
   (C) eased tensions between Western settlers and Native Americans
   (D) forced the British to evacuate their posts in the Northwest
   (E) reduced sectional conflict over the slavery issue

   Ⓐ Ⓑ Ⓒ Ⓓ Ⓔ

6. The issue of constitutionality figured most prominently in the consideration of which of the following?

   (A) Tariff of 1789
   (B) First Bank of the United States
   (C) Funding of the national debt
   (D) Assumption of state debts
   (E) Excise tax on whiskey

   Ⓐ Ⓑ Ⓒ Ⓓ Ⓔ

7. The idea of Manifest Destiny included all of the following EXCEPT the belief that

   (A) commerce and industry would decline as the nation expended its agriculture base
   (B) the use of land for settled agriculture was preferable to its use for nomadic hunting
   (C) westward expansion was both inevitable and beneficial
   (D) God selected America as a chosen land populated by a chosen people
   (E) the ultimate extent of the American domain was to be from the tropics to the Arctic

   Ⓐ Ⓑ Ⓒ Ⓓ Ⓔ

8. Which of the following represents William Lloyd Garrison's attitude toward slavery?

   (A) Immediate emancipation and resettlement in Liberia
   (B) Immediate emancipation and resettlement in the Southwest
   (C) Immediate emancipation with compensation for owners
   (D) Gradual emancipation without compensation for owners
   (E) Immediate emancipation without compensation for owners

   Ⓐ Ⓑ Ⓒ Ⓓ Ⓔ

9. Which of the following was NOT an element of the Compromise of 1850 ?

   (A) A stronger fugitive slave law
   (B) Abolition of the slave trade in Washington, D.C.
   (C) Admittance of California as a free state
   (D) Organization of the Kansas Territory without slavery
   (E) Adjustment of the Texas-New Mexico boundary

   Ⓐ Ⓑ Ⓒ Ⓓ Ⓔ

10. At the end of the Civil War, the vast majority of freed slaves found work as

    (A) factory workers
    (B) railroad employees
    (C) independent craftsmen
    (D) tenant farmers
    (E) domestic servants

    Ⓐ Ⓑ Ⓒ Ⓓ Ⓔ

11. Prior to successfully colonizing the New World, England defeated a major rival; just prior to losing many of its New World colonies, England defeated another major rival. The rivals were first

    (A) France, then the United States
    (B) Spain, then France
    (C) France, then Holland
    (D) France, then Spain
    (E) Portugal, then Spain

    Ⓐ Ⓑ Ⓒ Ⓓ Ⓔ

12. Which of the following is a correct statement about the use of slave labor in colonial Virginia?

   (A) It was forced on reluctant White Virginians by profit-minded English merchants and the mercantilist officials of the Crown.
   (B) It was the first case in which Europeans enslaved Black people.
   (C) It fulfilled the original plans of the Virginia Company.
   (D) It first occurred after the invention of Eli Whitney's cotton gin, which greatly stimulated the demand for low-cost labor.
   (E) It spread rapidly in the late seventeenth century, as Black slaves displaced White indentured servants in the tobacco fields.

   Ⓐ Ⓑ Ⓒ Ⓓ Ⓔ

Questions 13-14 refer to the following statement.

   The present king of Great Britain . . . has combined with others to subject us to a jurisdiction foreign to our constitution, and unacknowledged by our laws.

13. The "constitution" referred to in the quotation above from the Declaration of Independence was

   (A) the principles common to all of the colonial charters
   (B) the Articles of Confederation
   (C) a constitution for the colonies written by Sir William Blackstone
   (D) the laws passed concurrently by the several colonial legislatures
   (E) the principles the colonists believed had traditionally regulated English government

   Ⓐ Ⓑ Ⓒ Ⓓ Ⓔ

14. The protest that the king had "combined with others to subject us to a jurisdiction foreign to our constitution" referred to George III's

   (A) alliance with the king of France
   (B) use of Hessian mercenaries
   (C) reliance on his representatives in the colonies
   (D) approval of parliamentary laws impinging on colonial self-government
   (E) intention to place a German prince on the throne of British America

   Ⓐ Ⓑ Ⓒ Ⓓ Ⓔ

15. All of the following conditions influenced the development of American agriculture during the first half of the nineteenth century EXCEPT

    (A) a government policy favoring rapid settlement of the public domain
    (B) a widespread interest in conserving soil and natural resources
    (C) the trend toward regional economic specialization
    (D) the enthusiasm for land speculation
    (E) improvements in transportation by water

    Ⓐ Ⓑ Ⓒ Ⓓ Ⓔ

Questions 16-17 refer to the following cartoon.

16. According to the cartoon, allowing the Southern states to leave the Union would cause

    (A) the North to be threatened by internal dissension
    (B) the Democratic party to collapse
    (C) the Southern states to be dominated by European powers
    (D) the Confederacy to expand into Latin America
    (E) President Buchanan to be impeached and removed

    Ⓐ Ⓑ Ⓒ Ⓓ Ⓔ

17. The best evidence to support the cartoonist's contention that Hickory (Jackson) would have acted to stop secession was Jackson's earlier reaction to the

    (A) election of John Quincy Adams to the presidency
    (B) Spanish and American Indian border attacks on Florida
    (C) South Carolina Nullification Ordinance
    (D) requests for annexation of Texas
    (E) Maysville Road Bill

18. A man who had visited the United States in the 1830's wrote, "Unmarried women in America were unusually emancipated." You would probably give the most credence to his judgment about American women if you also found that

    (A) modern social psychologists contend that America is a "feminine" culture
    (B) middle-class women in the 1830's were increasingly attracted to the "cult of true womanhood"
    (C) other travelers in the 1830's who came from many different nations had come to the same conclusion as the author
    (D) other travelers in the 1830's who came from the same nation as the author had come to the same conclusion
    (E) the first suffragist newspaper had been founded in the 1830's

    Ⓐ Ⓑ Ⓒ Ⓓ Ⓔ

19. The establishment of Brook Farm and the Oneida Community in the antebellum United States reflected

    (A) the influence of Social Darwinism on American thinkers
    (B) the continued impact of Calvinist ideas on American thought
    (C) the blossoming of perfectionist aspirations
    (D) attempts to foster racial integration
    (E) the implementation of all-female utopian communities

    Ⓐ Ⓑ Ⓒ Ⓓ Ⓔ

20. In the pre-Civil War era, the railroad's most important impact on the economy was the

    (A) creation of a huge new market for railway equipment
    (B) creation of the basis for greater cooperation between Southern planters and Northern textile manufacturers
    (C) generation of new employment opportunities for unskilled urban workers
    (D) participation of the federal government in the financing of a nationwide transportation network
    (E) accessibility to Eastern urban markets provided to Midwestern farmers

    Ⓐ Ⓑ Ⓒ Ⓓ Ⓔ

21. All of the following elements of the Radical Republican program were implemented during Reconstruction EXCEPT

    (A) provision of 40 acres to each freedman
    (B) enactment of the Fourteenth Amendment
    (C) military occupation of the South
    (D) punishment of the Confederate leaders
    (E) restrictions on the power of the President

    Ⓐ Ⓑ Ⓒ Ⓓ Ⓔ

VOLUME OF AMERICAN COLONIES' EXPORTS TO ENGLAND AND IMPORTS FROM ENGLAND (VALUE IN POUNDS STERLING)

Year	New England Exports	New England Imports	New York Exports	New York Imports	Pennsylvania Exports	Pennsylvania Imports	Virginia and Maryland Exports	Virginia and Maryland Imports	Carolina Exports	Carolina Imports
1743	63,185	172,461	15,067	135,487	9,596	79,340	557,821	328,195	235,136	111,499
1742	53,166	148,899	13,536	167,591	8,527	75,295	427,769	264,186	154,607	127,063
1741	60,052	198,147	21,142	140,430	17,158	91,010	577,109	248,582	236,830	204,770
1740	72,389	171,081	21,498	118,777	15,048	56,751	341,997	281,428	266,560	181,821

22. According to eighteenth-century theories of mercantilism, and in light of England's pattern of trade with America as shown in the chart above, England's most valuable colony or group of colonies was which of the following?

    (A) New England
    (B) New York
    (C) Pennsylvania
    (D) Virginia and Maryland
    (E) Carolina

    Ⓐ Ⓑ Ⓒ Ⓓ Ⓔ

241

23. By the time of the Revolution, the American colonists had generally come to believe that creation of a republic would solve the problems of monarchical rule because a republic would establish

   (A) a highly centralized government led by a social elite
   (B) a strong chief executive
   (C) a small, limited government responsible to the people
   (D) unlimited male suffrage
   (E) a society in which there were no differences of rank and status

   Ⓐ Ⓑ Ⓒ Ⓓ Ⓔ

24. The Ordinances of 1785 and 1787 were notable accomplishments because they

   (A) established the principal that western lands were the joint property of all the states
   (B) initiated a territorial policy that provided for the orderly creation of new states
   (C) made possible a policy of American Indian relations that enabled new western areas to be settled peacefully
   (D) put land into the hands of the actual settler rather than the speculator
   (E) were the basis for the future settlement of the dispute with Britain over the northwest posts

   Ⓐ Ⓑ Ⓒ Ⓓ Ⓔ

25. Deists of the late eighteenth and early nineteenth centuries believed that

   (A) natural laws, set by the Creator, govern the operation of the universe
   (B) prayer has the power to make significant changes in a person's life
   (C) the idea of God is merely the creation of people's minds
   (D) the universe was created by a natural, spontaneous combining of elements
   (E) intuition rather than reason leads human beings to an awareness of the divine

   Ⓐ Ⓑ Ⓒ Ⓓ Ⓔ

26. Which of the following provided sources of revenue for the federal government in the period from 1800 to 1860?

   I. Income tax
   II. Sales tax
   III. Customs duties
   IV. Land sales
   V. Real estate taxes

   (A) I and II only
   (B) I and III only
   (C) II and V only
   (D) III and IV only
   (E) III, IV, and V only   Ⓐ Ⓑ Ⓒ Ⓓ Ⓔ

27. Which of the following had the greatest impact on the institution of slavery in the United States in the first quarter of the nineteenth century?

   (A) Demands of Southern textile manufacturers for cotton
   (B) Introduction of crop rotation and fertilizers
   (C) Use of more stringent techniques for controlling the lives of slaves
   (D) Invention of the cotton gin
   (E) The "three-fifths" compromise   Ⓐ Ⓑ Ⓒ Ⓓ Ⓔ

28. The presidential election of 1840 is often considered the first "modern" election because

   (A) the slavery issue was first raised in this campaign
   (B) it was the first election in which women voted
   (C) voting patterns were similar to those later established in the 1890's
   (D) both parties for the first time widely campaigned among all the eligible voters
   (E) a second era of good feeling had just come to a close, marking a new departure in politics

   Ⓐ Ⓑ Ⓒ Ⓓ Ⓔ

29. The 1848 women's rights convention in Seneca Falls, New York, was a protest against

   (A) the use of women workers in textile factories
   (B) the abuse of female slaves on Southern plantations
   (C) the failure of the Democratic party to endorse a women's suffrage amendment
   (D) customs and laws that gave women a status inferior to that of men
   (E) state restrictions that prevented women from joining labor unions

   Ⓐ Ⓑ Ⓒ Ⓓ Ⓔ

30. Abraham Lincoln delayed making any commitment about emancipation of the slaves after his inauguration as President because he

    (A) basically had no sympathy with those who wanted to end slavery
    (B) was concerned that foreign governments might be critical of a proclamation freeing slaves
    (C) did not feel bound by the 1860 Republican party platform
    (D) did not feel he had the constitutional right to make such a commitment in regard to slavery in the territories
    (E) hoped to keep as many slave states as possible in the Union

    Ⓐ Ⓑ Ⓒ Ⓓ Ⓔ

31. Liberty of conscience was defended by Roger Williams on the ground that

    (A) all religions were equal in the eyes of God
    (B) the institutions of political democracy would be jeopardized without it
    (C) Puritan ideas about sin and salvation were outmoded
    (D) theological truths would emerge from the clash of ideas
    (E) the state was an improper and ineffectual agency in matters of the spirit

    Ⓐ Ⓑ Ⓒ Ⓓ Ⓔ

Questions 32-33 refer to the following historical problem.

It is popularly believed that Patrick Henry, in his speech against the Stamp Act of 1765, implied that George III would be assassinated, and then concluded with the phrase, "If this be treason, make the most of it." Four differing reports of this speech, two of which omit the concluding phrase, are found in the following sources: the diary of a Frenchman who was an eyewitness and described the event the same day; a letter printed in a London newspaper about six weeks later; a history of Virginia written in 1805; and a note written in 1817 by Thomas Jefferson, who also was an eyewitness.

32. The main issue raised for historians by the differing reports of Henry's speech is the

    (A) formation of hypotheses about historical causation
    (B) validity of historical metaphor
    (C) credibility of historical evidence
    (D) use of anachronisms
    (E) form of historical citation

    Ⓐ Ⓑ Ⓒ Ⓓ Ⓔ

33. Which of the following facts casts the greatest doubt on the accuracy of Jefferson's note confirming the concluding phrase in Henry's speech?

    (A) Jefferson and Henry had each served as governor of Virginia.
    (B) Jefferson was only twenty-two in 1765.
    (C) Jefferson's note was written to a man who was writing a biography of Henry.
    (D) Jefferson was not actually a member of the House of Burgesses in 1765.
    (E) Jefferson's note was written fifty-two years after the speech was delivered.

    Ⓐ Ⓑ Ⓒ Ⓓ Ⓔ

34. "There is an opinion that parties in free countries are useful checks upon the administration of the government and serve to keep alive the spirit of liberty. This within certain limits is probably true, and in governments of a monarchical cast patriotism may look with indulgence, if not with favor, upon the spirit of party. But in those of the popular character, in governments purely elective, it is a spirit not to be encouraged."

    Which of the following was most likely to have made these remarks while President?

    (A) George Washington
    (B) Thomas Jefferson
    (C) James Madison
    (D) Andrew Jackson
    (E) Abraham Lincoln

    Ⓐ Ⓑ Ⓒ Ⓓ Ⓔ

35. The Embargo Act of 1807 had which of the following effects on the United States?

    (A) It improved the balance of trade.
    (B) It enriched many cotton plantation owners.
    (C) It severely damaged American shipping.
    (D) It was ruinous to subsistence farmers.
    (E) It had little economic impact.

    Ⓐ Ⓑ Ⓒ Ⓓ Ⓔ

36. Of the following, the most important foreign affairs issue that faced the United States between the enunciation of the Monroe Doctrine (1823) and the Civil War (1861) was

    (A) securing access to Canadian fisheries
    (B) reopening the British West Indies to direct trade with the United States
    (C) securing international recognition
    (D) defining the nation's northern and southern boundaries
    (E) responding to Cuban independence

    Ⓐ Ⓑ Ⓒ Ⓓ Ⓔ

37. Henry Clay's "American System" was a plan to

    (A) compromise on the issue of extending slavery to new United States territories
    (B) foster the economic integration of the North, West, and South
    (C) export American political and economic values to oppressed peoples
    (D) maintain American noninvolvement in the internal affairs of Europe
    (E) assert the right of states to nullify decisions of the national government

    Ⓐ Ⓑ Ⓒ Ⓓ Ⓔ

38. The Great Awakening in the American colonies in the mid-eighteenth century had all of the following consequences EXCEPT

    (A) separatism and secession from established churches, due to the democratizing effect of more accessible forms of piety
    (B) the renewed persecution of people for witchcraft, because of the heightened interest in the supernatural
    (C) the growth of institutions of higher learning to fill the need for more ministers to spread the gospel
    (D) a flourishing of the missionary spirit as an outgrowth of more intensive religious devotion
    (E) the lessening of doctrinal rigor and a concomitant appreciation for the more direct experiences of faith

    Ⓐ Ⓑ Ⓒ Ⓓ Ⓔ

39. "Upon these considerations, it is the opinion of the court that the act of Congress which prohibited a citizen from holding and owning property of this kind in the territory of the United States north of the line therein mentioned, is not warranted by the Constitution, and is therefore void; and that neither the plaintiff himself, nor any of his family, were made free by being carried into this territory; even if they had been carried there by the owner, who intended to become a permanent resident."

The congressional act referred to in the passage was the

(A) Kansas-Nebraska Act
(B) Missouri Compromise
(C) Northwest Ordinance
(D) Compromise of 1850
(E) Fugitive Slave Act   Ⓐ Ⓑ Ⓒ Ⓓ Ⓔ

40. The 1850's have been called the "American Renaissance" because of the important literary works that appeared in that decade. Included among these works are all of the following EXCEPT

(A) Herman Melville's *Moby-Dick*
(B) Nathaniel Hawthorne's *The Scarlet Letter*
(C) Mark Twain's *Huckleberry Finn*
(D) Walt Whitman's *Leaves of Grass*
(E) Henry David Thoreau's *Walden*   Ⓐ Ⓑ Ⓒ Ⓓ Ⓔ

Study Resources

The following list contains representative examples of widely used college-level textbooks and readers in American History I and II. The standard comprehensive texts are typically published in two volumes, usually corresponding in coverage to the two CLEP examinations (Early Colonizations to 1877, and 1865 to the Present). To prepare for either of the American History examinations, read thoroughly the relevant material in one textbook. Because textbooks may differ in content, emphasis, and interpretation, consult a second or third textbook on some of the major topics. New editions of textbooks are published every three or four years. If you are purchasing a book, it is recommended that you specify the most recent edition.

Additional detail and differing interpretations can be gained by consulting readers and specialized historical studies. Pay attention to visual materials (pictures, maps, charts) as you study. A number of supplementary readings are included on the following list.

Additional suggestions for preparing for CLEP examinations are provided in chapter 4.

Many libraries do not carry textbooks as a policy. If you can't find any of the following textbooks at the library, see whether the college bookstore has a used copy. If you can't locate the most recent edition, an edition that is one or two years older will suffice for most subject areas. As a final option, purchase a new copy of the suggested textbook as an investment in your education.

COMPREHENSIVE TEXTBOOKS

Bailey, Thomas A. and David M. Kennedy, *The American Pageant: A History of the Republic*, 2 vols., 9th ed. Lexington, MA: D. C. Heath, 1991.

Bailyn, Bernard et al., *The Great Republic: A History of the American People*, 4th ed. Lexington, MA: D. C. Heath, 1992.

Blum, John M. et al., *The National Experience: A History of the United States*, 7th ed. San Diego: Harcourt Brace Jovanovich, 1989.

Brinkley, Alan et al., *American History: A Survey*, 8th ed. New York: McGraw-Hill, 1991.

Divine, Robert A. et al., *America: Past and Present*, 3rd ed. New York: HarperCollins, 1991.

Garraty, John and Robert A. McCaughey, *The American Nation: A History of the United States*, 2 vols., 7th ed. New York: HarperCollins, 1991.

Henretta, James A. et al., *America's History*. Chicago: Dorsey Press, 1987.

Nash, Gary B. et al., *The American People: Creating a Nation and a Society*, 2nd ed. New York: HarperCollins, 1990.

Norton, Mary Beth et al., *A People and a Nation: A History of the United States*, 3rd ed. Boston: Houghton Mifflin, 1990.

Tindall, George B., *America: A Narrative History*, 3rd ed. New York: W. W. Norton, 1992.

BOOKS OF READINGS

Most collections of readings are one of two basic types. Primary readers contain the texts of original documents such as speeches, government proclamations, and laws. Interpretive readers may contain portions of monographs, some scholarly articles, and original pieces prepared especially for the volume.

INTERPRETIVE READERS

Davidson, James West and Mark Lytle, *After the Fact: The Art of Historical Detection*, Vol. I & II, 3rd ed. McGraw-Hill, 1992.

Davis, Allen F. and Harold D. Woodman, *Conflict and Consensus in Early American History*, 8th ed. Lexington, MA: D. C. Heath, 1991.

Grob, Gerald N. and George A. Billias, *Interpretations of American History: Patterns and Perspectives*, 6th ed. New York: Free Press, 1992.

Nash, Gary B. and Cynthia J. Shelton, *The Private Side of American History: Readings in Everyday Life*, Vol. I & II, 4th ed. San Diego: Harcourt Brace Jovanovich, 1987.

Stoler, Mark A. and Marshall True, *Explorations in American History: A Skills Approach*, Vol. I & II. New York: Alfred A. Knopf, 1987.

There are also two widely used series of interpretive readings: the "Problems in American Civilization Series," edited by George R. Taylor and published by D. C. Heath, and the "American Problem Studies Series," edited by Oscar Handlin and published first by Holt, Rinehart & Winston and later by the Robert E. Krieger Publishing Company.

PRIMARY READERS

Boller, Paul F., Jr. and Ronald Story, *A More Perfect Union,* Vol. I & II, 2nd ed. Boston: Houghton Mifflin, 1987.

Commager, Henry Steele and Milton Cantor, *Documents of American History,* Vol. I & II, 10th ed. Englewood Cliffs, NJ: Prentice Hall, 1988.

Hofstadter, Richard and Beatrice Hofstadter, *Great Issues in American History,* Vol. I, II & III. New York: Vintage Books, 1982.

Wheeler, William and Susan Becker, *Discovering the American Past: A Look at the Evidence,* Vol. I & II, 2nd ed. Boston: Houghton Mifflin, 1990.

American History II: 1865 to the Present

Description of the Examination

The Subject Examination in American History II: 1865 to the Present covers material that is usually taught in the second semester of what is often a two-semester course in American history. The examination covers the period of American history from the end of the Civil War to the present, with the majority of questions on the twentieth century.

The examination is composed of approximately 120 multiple-choice questions to be answered in two separately timed 45-minute sections.

Knowledge and Skills Required

Questions on the test require candidates to demonstrate one or more of the following abilities.

- Identification and description of historical phenomena (about 45 percent of the examination)

- Characterization and classification of historical phenomena (about 15 percent of the examination)

- Analysis and interpretation of historical phenomena (about 10 percent of the examination)

- Comparison and contrast of historical phenomena (about 10 percent of the examination)

- Explanation and evaluation of historical phenomena (about 20 percent of the examination)

The major topics covered by the examination are:

←	*Approximate Percent of Examination*
50%	Political institutions and behavior and public policy
15%	Social and economical change
15%	Cultural and intellectual development
20%	Diplomacy and international relations

About one-third of the questions deal with the period from 1865 to 1914, and about two-thirds deal with the period from 1915 to the present. Among the specific topics tested are the following:

The motivations and character of American expansionism

The content of constitutional amendments and their interpretations by the Supreme Court

The development of American political parties

The emergence of regulatory and welfare-state legislation

The intellectual and political expressions of liberalism, conservatism, and other such movements

Long-term demographic trends

The process of economic growth and development

The changing occupational structure, nature of work, and labor organization

Immigration and the history of racial and ethnic minorities

Urbanization

The causes and impacts of major wars in American history

Major movements and individual figures in the history of American arts and letters

Sample Questions

The 40 sample questions that follow are similar to questions on the American History II examination, but they do not appear on the actual examination.

Before attempting to answer the sample questions, read all the information about the American History II examination on the preceding pages. Additional suggestions for preparing for CLEP examinations are provided in chapter 4.

Try to answer correctly as many of the questions as possible. Then compare your answers with the correct answers, given in Appendix B.

Directions: Each of the questions or incomplete statements below is followed by five suggested answers or completions. Select the one that is best in each case.

1. *Brown* v. *Board of Education of Topeka* was a Supreme Court decision that

   (A) was a forerunner of the Kansas-Nebraska Act
   (B) established free public colleges in the United States
   (C) declared racially segregated public schools inherently unequal
   (D) established free public elementary and secondary schools in the United States
   (E) provided for federal support of parochial schools

   Ⓐ Ⓑ Ⓒ Ⓓ Ⓔ

2. For which of the following was Franklin D. Roosevelt LEAST successful in securing congressional support?

   (A) Negotiation of tariff agreements by the executive department
   (B) Reduction of the gold content of the dollar
   (C) Removal of the restraints of the antitrust acts to permit voluntary trade associations
   (D) The levying of processing taxes on agricultural products
   (E) Reform of the judiciary to permit the enlargement of the Supreme Court

   Ⓐ Ⓑ Ⓒ Ⓓ Ⓔ

3. Which of the following is a correct statement about the United States at the close of the First World War?

   (A) It joined the League of Nations.
   (B) It emerged as the world's leading creditor nation.
   (C) It accorded diplomatic recognition to the Soviet Union.
   (D) It repealed the Prohibition amendment to the Constitution.
   (E) It received large reparations payments from Germany.

   Ⓐ Ⓑ Ⓒ Ⓓ Ⓔ

4. All of the following help to explain the presence of large numbers of expatriate American intellectuals in Europe during the 1920's EXCEPT the

   (A) repressive effects of Prohibition and the resurgence of conservatism in the United States
   (B) attraction of European cities, especially Paris, as centers of innovation and creativity
   (C) tradition among American writers of taking up temporary residence in Europe
   (D) claims of young American writers and critics that American culture was materialistic and hostile to the development of their art
   (E) European tradition of wealthy patrons supporting struggling American artists and writers

   Ⓐ Ⓑ Ⓒ Ⓓ Ⓔ

5. The American Federation of Labor under the leadership of Samuel Gompers organized

   (A) skilled workers in craft unions in order to achieve economic gains
   (B) all industrial and agricultural workers in "one big union"
   (C) unskilled workers along industrial lines
   (D) women into the Women's Trade Union League
   (E) workers into a fraternal organization to provide unemployment and retirement benefits

   Ⓐ Ⓑ Ⓒ Ⓓ Ⓔ

6. Between 1890 and 1914, most immigrants to the United States came from

   (A) Southern and Eastern Europe
   (B) Northern and Western Europe
   (C) Latin America
   (D) Southeast Asia
   (E) Canada

   Ⓐ Ⓑ Ⓒ Ⓓ Ⓔ

7. The Harlem Renaissance is accurately described by which of the following?

   I. It flourished during the 1920's.
   II. It was centered among Black Americans in the South.
   III. It consisted of a period of dramatic intellectual and artistic creativity among Black Americans.
   IV. It brought about significant gains in civil rights.

   (A) I only   (B) I and III only
     (C) II and IV only   (D) I, II, and IV only
       (E) I, III, and IV only

   Ⓐ Ⓑ Ⓒ Ⓓ Ⓔ

254

8. "In the summer of 1933, a nice old gentleman wearing a silk hat fell off the end of a pier. He was unable to swim. A friend ran down the pier, dived overboard, and pulled him out; but the silk hat floated off with the tide. After the old gentleman had been revived, he was effusive in his thanks. He praised his friend for saving his life. Today, three years later, the old gentleman is berating his friend because the silk hat was lost."

The "old gentleman" and the "friend" in this story told by Franklin D. Roosevelt to a Democratic party convention in 1936 were meant to refer, respectively, to

(A) farmers and crop acreage controls
(B) laborers and wage-hour controls
(C) businessmen and industrial regulations
(D) consumers and fixed prices
(E) the unemployed and relief-roll stipulations Ⓐ Ⓑ Ⓒ Ⓓ Ⓔ

9. Reform activity during the Progressive era was similar to that of the 1960's in all of the following ways EXCEPT:

(A) Civil rights for Black Americans were supported by the federal government.
(B) Reform activity was encouraged by strong and active Presidents.
(C) Many reformers advocated changes in the area of women's rights.
(D) Governmental reform initiatives were curtailed by war.
(E) Reform occurred despite the absence of severe economic depression.

Ⓐ Ⓑ Ⓒ Ⓓ Ⓔ

10. Which of the following was the LEAST important consideration in the United States decision to drop the atomic bombs on Japan in August 1945?

(A) Dropping the bombs would give a new and powerful argument to the Japanese government to cease fighting.
(B) Dropping the bombs would presumably shorten the war and therefore save the lives of American soldiers that would be lost in an invasion of the Japanese homeland.
(C) Scientists wished to demonstrate to Congress that the $2 billion spent, after long debate, on the six-year Manhattan Project had not been wasted.
(D) Scientists could propose no acceptable technical demonstration of the atomic bomb likely to convince Japan that further fighting was futile.
(E) The President and the State Department hoped to end the war in the Far East without Soviet assistance.

Ⓐ Ⓑ Ⓒ Ⓓ Ⓔ

11. All of the following were among Woodrow Wilson's Fourteen Points EXCEPT

    (A) a general association of nations
    (B) freedom to navigate the high seas in peace and war
    (C) an independent Poland
    (D) a partitioned Germany
    (E) abolition of secret diplomacy   Ⓐ Ⓑ Ⓒ Ⓓ Ⓔ

12. In his interpretation of the historical development of the United States, Frederick Jackson Turner focused on the importance of the

    (A) traditions of Western European culture
    (B) role of women in socializing children to become good citizens
    (C) historical consequences of the enslavement of Black people
    (D) conflict between capitalists and workers
    (E) frontier experience in fostering democracy   Ⓐ Ⓑ Ⓒ Ⓓ Ⓔ

13. The "rule of reason," handed down by the Supreme Court, held that the Sherman Antitrust Act forbade only unreasonable combinations or contracts in restraint of trade. This interpretation most closely parallels the ideas of

    (A) William McKinley
    (B) Robert M. LaFollette
    (C) Theodore Roosevelt
    (D) Woodrow Wilson
    (E) Louis D. Brandeis   Ⓐ Ⓑ Ⓒ Ⓓ Ⓔ

ORGIE MANIACLE

ALL FOR HONOR

ALL FOR DEMOCRACY

ALL FOR WORLD PEACE

ALL FOR JESUS

EDITOR   CAPITALIST   POLITICIAN   MINISTER

HAVING THEIR FLING

14. A socialist view of the First World War is reflected by all of the
following features of the cartoon above EXCEPT the

(A) expression of an antiwar viewpoint
(B) inclusion of a capitalist among the figures portrayed
(C) cynicism about the role of organized religion
(D) placement of the figures symbolically from left to right
(E) ridicule of Wilsonian rhetoric

Ⓐ Ⓑ Ⓒ Ⓓ Ⓔ

15. "The productive methods and facilities of modern industry have been completely transformed. . . . Skilled artisans make up only a small proportion of the workers. Obviously the bargaining strength of employees, under these conditions, no longer rests in organizations of skilled craftsmen. It is dependent upon a national union representing all employees — whether skilled or unskilled, or whether working by brain or brawn — in each basic industry."

The statement above best represents the views of

(A) Emma Goldman
(B) John L. Lewis
(C) William Green
(D) Bernard M. Baruch
(E) Jane Addams

Ⓐ Ⓑ Ⓒ Ⓓ Ⓔ

16. "The problem with hatred and violence is that they intensify the fears of the White majority, and leave them less ashamed of their prejudices toward Negroes. In the guilt and confusion confronting our society, violence only adds to chaos. It deepens the brutality of the oppressor and increases the bitterness of the oppressed. Violence is the antithesis of creativity and wholeness. It destroys community and makes brotherhood impossible."

During the 1960's all the following Black leaders would probably have supported the view above EXCEPT

(A) Roy Wilkins
(B) Martin Luther King, Jr.
(C) James Farmer
(D) Stokely Carmichael
(E) Whitney M. Young, Jr.

Ⓐ Ⓑ Ⓒ Ⓓ Ⓔ

17. Following the Second World War, President Truman was unable to expand significantly his predecessor's New Deal programs primarily because of

(A) the continuation of the Great Depression
(B) the need to maintain a large military force in Asia
(C) budget expenditures required to rebuild Europe
(D) controversy surrounding the Truman Doctrine
(E) the domination of Congress by Republicans and conservative Democrats

Ⓐ Ⓑ Ⓒ Ⓓ Ⓔ

18. Many Mexicans migrated to the United States during the First World War because

    (A) revolution in Mexico had caused social upheaval and dislocation
    (B) the United States offered special homestead rights to relatives of Mexican Americans serving in the armed forces
    (C) the war in Europe had disrupted the Mexican economy
    (D) American Progressives generally held liberal views on the issue of racial assimilation
    (E) the United States government recruited Mexican workers to accelerate the settlement of the Southwest

    Ⓐ Ⓑ Ⓒ Ⓓ Ⓔ

19. Which of the following was the greatest source of tension between the United States and the Soviet Union during the Second World War?

    (A) The Soviet refusal to fight Japan
    (B) The delay on the part of the United States in opening a second front in Europe
    (C) Lend-Lease allocations
    (D) The United States refusal to share atomic secrets
    (E) The Soviet massacre of Polish officers at Katyn Forest

    Ⓐ Ⓑ Ⓒ Ⓓ Ⓔ

The Cash Register Chorus

Fitzpatrick in the *St. Louis Post-Dispatch*

20. The political cartoonist who drew this picture probably believed that

    (A) European nations were pleased with aid given them by the
        Coolidge administration
    (B) governmental agencies were receiving too much financial support
        from the Coolidge administration
    (C) American industrial and commercial leaders approved of the
        Coolidge administration's business policies
    (D) consumers had benefited from the Federal Reserve Board's tight
        money policy from 1925 through 1928
    (E) Congress was pleased by President Coolidge's accommodating
        stance toward pork barrel legislation

Ⓐ Ⓑ Ⓒ Ⓓ Ⓔ

21. In the period 1890-1915, all of the following were generally true about Black Americans EXCEPT:

    (A) Voting rights previously gained were denied through changes in state laws and constitutions.
    (B) Back-to-Africa movements were widely popular among Black residents of cities.
    (C) Black leaders disagreed on the principal strategy for attaining equal rights.
    (D) Numerous physical attacks on Black individuals occurred in both the North and South.
    (E) Black people from the rural South migrated to both southern and northern cities.

    Ⓐ Ⓑ Ⓒ Ⓓ Ⓔ

22. Which of the following is true of the forced relocation of Japanese Americans from the West Coast during the Second World War?

    (A) President Roosevelt claimed that military necessity justified the action.
    (B) The Supreme Court declared the action unconstitutional.
    (C) The relocation was implemented according to congressional provisions for the internment of dissidents.
    (D) The Japanese Americans received the same treatment as that accorded German Americans and Italian Americans.
    (E) Few of those relocated were actually United States citizens.

    Ⓐ Ⓑ Ⓒ Ⓓ Ⓔ

23. A number of changes took place in the intellectual life of college-educated Americans between about 1880 and 1930. Which of the following changes is LEAST characteristic of this group in this period?

    (A) Expanded popularity of nonrational explanations for human behavior
    (B) Rise of pluralistic and relativistic world views
    (C) Accelerated professionalization of intellectual roles
    (D) Growth in influence of religious fundamentalism
    (E) Increased attention to the methods and outlook of the sciences

    Ⓐ Ⓑ Ⓒ Ⓓ Ⓔ

24. Reformers of the Progressive era proposed all of the following changes in city government and politics at the turn of the century EXCEPT

(A) a large city council elected by wards
(B) civil service
(C) home rule for cities
(D) city manager and commission governments
(E) nonpartisan elections

(A) (B) (C) (D) (E)

25. "I believe that it must be the policy of the United States to support free peoples who are resisting attempted subjugation by armed minorities or by outside pressures. I believe that we must assist free peoples to work out their own destinies in their own way. I believe that our help should be primarily through economic and financial aid which is essential to economic stability and orderly political processes."

The statement above is taken from

(A) Woodrow Wilson's request for a declaration of war against Germany (1917)
(B) Herbert Hoover's statement on Japanese aggression in China (1931)
(C) Franklin D. Roosevelt's request for a declaration of war against Japan (1941)
(D) Harry S Truman's request for funds to support Greece and Turkey against communism (1947)
(E) an address by Jeane Kirkpatrick to the United Nations (1983)

(A) (B) (C) (D) (E)

26. Which of the following constitutes a significant change in the treatment of American Indians during the last half of the nineteenth century?

(A) The beginnings of negotiation with individual tribes
(B) The start of a removal policy
(C) The abandonment of the reservation system
(D) The admission of American Indians to United States citizenship
(E) The division of the tribal lands among individual members

(A) (B) (C) (D) (E)

27. The principal foreign policy issue confronting the Wilson administration between the outbreak of the First World War in 1914 and United States involvement in the conflict in 1917 was the

(A) future of United States overseas possessions
(B) territorial and political integrity of Poland
(C) freedom of the seas
(D) question of a Pan-American collective security organization
(E) issue of war debt repayment by the Allies

Ⓐ Ⓑ Ⓒ Ⓓ Ⓔ

28. "This, then, is held to be the duty of the man of wealth: to consider all surplus revenues which come to him simply as trust funds, which he is called upon to administer and strictly bound as a matter of duty to administer in the manner which, in his judgment, is best calculated to produce the most beneficial results for the community — the man of wealth thus becoming the mere agent and trustee for his poorer brethren."

The sentiments expressed above are most characteristic of

(A) transcendentalism
(B) pragmatism
(C) the Gospel of Wealth
(D) the Social Gospel
(E) Social Darwinism

Ⓐ Ⓑ Ⓒ Ⓓ Ⓔ

29. The Reconstruction Acts of 1867 provided for

(A) temporary Union military supervision of the former Confederacy
(B) federal monetary support of the resettlement of Black Americans in Africa
(C) denial of property-holding and voting rights to Black Americans
(D) implementation of anti-Black vagrancy laws in the South
(E) lenient readmission of the formerly Confederate states to the Union

Ⓐ Ⓑ Ⓒ Ⓓ Ⓔ

30. Which of the following is correct about the Washington Naval Conference of 1921-1922?

(A) It was convened to equalize naval strength among the five major powers.
(B) It imposed specific limitations on the number of battleships allowed to the signatory nations.
(C) It outlawed the use of submarines in warfare.
(D) It confirmed the isolationist nature of United States foreign policy during the 1920's.
(E) It underscored the Harding administration's indifference to Japanese expansion in the Far East.

Ⓐ Ⓑ Ⓒ Ⓓ Ⓔ

31. The so-called lost generation after the First World War was

(A) represented by Ernest Hemingway in the figures of Jake Barnes and Lady Brett Ashley
(B) depicted in Sylvia Plath's *The Bell Jar*
(C) glorified by T. S. Eliot in "The Love Song of J. Alfred Prufrock"
(D) portrayed as the principal subject of Sinclair Lewis' *Babbitt*
(E) portrayed as the principal subject of Theodore Dreiser's *An American Tragedy*

Ⓐ Ⓑ Ⓒ Ⓓ Ⓔ

32. "The reasons for the failures of the Chinese National Government appear in some detail in the attached record. They do not stem from any inadequacy of American aid. Our military observers on the spot have reported that Nationalist armies did not lose a single battle during the crucial year of 1948 through lack of arms or ammunition. The fact was that the decay which our observers had detected in Chungking early in the war had fatally sapped the powers of resistance of the Kuomintang."

The 1949 Department of State "White Paper," from which the excerpt above is taken, had which of the following effects?

(A) It led to a closer relationship between the United States and the Union of Soviet Socialist Republics.
(B) It led to friendly relations between the Union of Soviet Socialist Republics and the People's Republic of China.
(C) It convinced the "China Lobby" that the downfall of Nationalist China had been inevitable.
(D) It temporarily quieted the charges of Senator Joseph McCarthy that there were Communists in the Department of State.
(E) It heightened bitter domestic controversy about the Far Eastern policy of the United States.

Ⓐ Ⓑ Ⓒ Ⓓ Ⓔ

33. The Employment Act of 1946 did which of the following?

   (A) Guaranteed the right of collective bargaining for labor unions.
   (B) Provided for retraining of veterans of the armed forces.
   (C) Declared full employment to be an objective of the federal
       government.
   (D) Provided for large-scale public works to prevent a postwar
       depression.
   (E) Created goals for the hiring of women and minorities by the
       federal government.

   Ⓐ Ⓑ Ⓒ Ⓓ Ⓔ

34. The anticombination laws passed by numerous states in the late
    1880's were a response to which of the following organizational
    innovations?

   (A) The creation and growth of international cartels
   (B) The development of industry-wide trade associations
   (C) The joining of skilled and unskilled workers in industrial unions
   (D) The formation of agricultural marketing cooperatives
   (E) The use of stockholding trusts to create business oligopolies

   Ⓐ Ⓑ Ⓒ Ⓓ Ⓔ

35. Which of the following is correct about United States involvement in
    the Vietnam War?

   (A) It was justified by an appeal to the Open Door policy.
   (B) It was the exclusive responsibility of the Johnson and Nixon
       administrations.
   (C) It came about only after a formal declaration of war.
   (D) It was primarily anti-Soviet in purpose.
   (E) It grew out of policy assumptions and commitments dating from
       the end of the Second World War.

   Ⓐ Ⓑ Ⓒ Ⓓ Ⓔ

36. The main purpose of the Wagner Labor Relations Act of 1935 was to

   (A) end the sit-down strike in Flint, Michigan
   (B) settle the struggle between the AFL and the CIO
   (C) guarantee workers a minimum wage
   (D) ensure workers' right to organize and bargain collectively
   (E) exempt organized labor from the Sherman Antitrust Act

   Ⓐ Ⓑ Ⓒ Ⓓ Ⓔ

265

The Only Way We Can Save Her

Carey Orr. *The Tribune* (Chicago), 1939.

37. This cartoon from the 1930's suggests that the cartoonist

  (A) wished to see Europe destroyed
  (B) believed that Japan was a greater threat to the United States than Germany was
  (C) did not distinguish among the European belligerents in terms of war aims or forms of government
  (D) believed that the United States must enter the war to make the world safe for democracy
  (E) believed that Europe was doomed to communism

Ⓐ Ⓑ Ⓒ Ⓓ Ⓔ

38. Which of the following would have been most likely to vote for William Jennings Bryan in 1896 ?

    (A) A Kansas farmer
    (B) A Chicago industrial worker
    (C) A Philadelphia homemaker
    (D) A university professor of economics
    (E) A New York Republican party member

    Ⓐ Ⓑ Ⓒ Ⓓ Ⓔ

39. Franklin D. Roosevelt's farm policy was primarily designed to

    (A) reduce farm prices to make food cheaper for the consumer
    (B) increase production by opening new lands to farmers
    (C) reduce production in order to boost farm prices
    (D) use price and wage controls to stabilize farm prices
    (E) end federal controls over agriculture

    Ⓐ Ⓑ Ⓒ Ⓓ Ⓔ

40. The second Sioux War (1875-1876), in which Custer was defeated at the Battle of the Little Big Horn, was caused by all of the following EXCEPT

    (A) the extension of the route of the Northern Pacific Railroad
    (B) a concentrated effort on the part of the major Protestant
        denominations to convert the Sioux to Christianity
    (C) the gold rush in the Black Hills
    (D) corruption within the Department of the Interior
    (E) overland migration of settlers to the Pacific Northwest

    Ⓐ Ⓑ Ⓒ Ⓓ Ⓔ

Study Resources

The textbooks and reference books suggested for preparing for the American History I examination cover the full range of American history and can therefore be used in preparing for the American History II examination as well.

Human Growth and Development *(Infancy, Childhood, Adolescence)*

Description of the Examination

The Subject Examination in Human Growth and Development (Infancy, Childhood, Adolescence) covers material that is generally taught in a one-semester introductory course in child psychology, child development, or developmental psychology, with primary emphasis on infancy, early childhood, and middle childhood. An understanding of the major theories and research related to physical, cognitive, social, personality, and emotional development is required, as is the ability to apply this knowledge.

The exam is 90 minutes long and includes approximately 90 multiple-choice questions to be answered in two separately timed 45-minute sections.

Knowledge and Skills Required

Each question on the exam requires the student to demonstrate one or more of the following abilities.

- Knowledge of basic facts and terminology

- Understanding of generally accepted concepts and principles

- Understanding of theories and recurrent developmental issues

- Applications of knowledge to particular problems or situations

The examination questions are drawn from the 13 major categories listed below. For each category, several key words and phrases identify topics with which candidates should be familiar. The approximate percent of the examination devoted to each category is also shown below.

➤   *Approximate Percent of Examination*

10%   Theories of development
         Behavioral-learning
         Cognitive-developmental
         Psychoanalytic

Approximate Percent of Examination

5%   Research strategies and methodology
    Experimental
    Longitudinal
    Cross-sectional
    Correlational
    Case study

10%   Biological development
    Prenatal influences
    Perinatal influences
    Physical growth and maturation
    Development of nervous system
    Motor development
    Heredity, genetics, genetic counseling
    Nutritional influences
    Sexual maturation
    Influences of drugs

7%   Perceptual and sensorimotor development
    Vision
    Hearing
    Sensorimotor activities
    Critical periods
    Sensory deprivation

12%   Cognitive development
    Piaget
    Information-processing (e.g., attention, memory)
    Concept formation
    Cognitive styles and creativity
    Play
    Environmental influences on cognitive development

Approximate Percent of Examination

8%   Language development
      Vocalization and sounds
      Development of grammar
      Semantic development
      Language and thought
      Referential communication
      Environmental influences on language development

4%   Intelligence
      Concepts of intelligence
      Heredity and environment
      Developmental stability and change

10%   Social development
      Attachment
      Aggression
      Prosocial behavior
      Moral development
      Sex roles
      Peer relationships

8%   Family and society
      Parent-child relationships
      Cross-cultural and ethnic variations
      Social class influences
      Sibling and birth-order influences
      Influences of divorce, single-parent families
      Child abuse, parental neglect
      Mass media influences

8%   Personality and emotions
      Temperament
      Self-control
      Achievement strivings
      Locus of control
      Development of emotions

8%   Learning
   Habituation
   Classical conditioning
   Operant conditioning
   Observational learning and imitation
   Discrimination and generalization

5%   Schooling and intervention
   Applications of developmental principles within the school
   Preschool, day care
   Intervention programs and services
   Training in parenting skills

5%   Atypical development
   Giftedness
   Consequences of hereditary diseases
   Learning disabilities, handicapping conditions
   Retardation
   Hyperactivity
   Asocial behavior, fears, phobias, obsessions
   Antisocial behavior, delinquency
   Autism, childhood psychosis

Sample Questions

The 25 sample questions that follow are similar to questions on the Human Growth and Development examination, but they do not appear on the actual examination.

Before attempting to answer the sample questions, read all the information about the Human Growth and Development examination on the preceding pages. Additional suggestions for preparing for CLEP examinations are provided in chapter 4.

Try to answer correctly as many questions as possible. Then compare your answers with the correct answers, given in Appendix B.

Directions: Each of the questions or incomplete statements below is followed by five suggested answers or completions. Select the one that is best in each case.

1. The first negative emotion clearly exhibited during infancy is best described as

   (A) fear
   (B) anger
   (C) disgust
   (D) distress
   (E) jealousy

   Ⓐ Ⓑ Ⓒ Ⓓ Ⓔ

2. Which of the following variables is LEAST likely to be related to the quality of language displayed by a three-year-old child?

   (A) The child's sex
   (B) The child's environment
   (C) The child's general intelligence
   (D) The child's birth order
   (E) The child's body build

   Ⓐ Ⓑ Ⓒ Ⓓ Ⓔ

3. According to behavioral psychologists, which of the following treatments would be most likely to extinguish aggressive behavior in preschool children?

   (A) Threatening to isolate them immediately after such behavior
   (B) Ignoring them so that they do not receive the attention they are seeking
   (C) Severely scolding them
   (D) Discouraging them but not punishing them
   (E) Reasoning with them and explaining that their behavior is wrong

   Ⓐ Ⓑ Ⓒ Ⓓ Ⓔ

4. The length of time that it takes to toilet train a young child depends most on which of the following?

   (A) Presence or absence of older siblings
   (B) Severity of the training practices the parents use
   (C) Verbal ability of the parents
   (D) The child's feeding regimen in infancy
   (E) Age at which the parents begin to train the child

   Ⓐ Ⓑ Ⓒ Ⓓ Ⓔ

5. Which of the following conditions is most characteristic of autism?

   (A) An obsessive attachment to the mother
   (B) A lack of motor coordination
   (C) Unresponsiveness to others
   (D) Low intelligence
   (E) Physical deformity   Ⓐ Ⓑ Ⓒ Ⓓ Ⓔ

6. Anxiety over performance can positively motivate academic achievement in children as long as the degree of anxiety is

   (A) very high
   (B) high
   (C) moderate
   (D) low
   (E) very low   Ⓐ Ⓑ Ⓒ Ⓓ Ⓔ

7. According to Piaget, cognitive development begins with which of the following?

   (A) Preoperations
   (B) Concrete operations
   (C) Intuitive thought
   (D) Sensorimotor activities
   (E) Formal operations   Ⓐ Ⓑ Ⓒ Ⓓ Ⓔ

8. Social class differences in the amount of infant vocalization are primarily the result of social class differences in which of the following?

   (A) Maternal anxiety
   (B) Verbal stimulation
   (C) Paternal illness
   (D) Sibling rivalry
   (E) Marital discord   Ⓐ Ⓑ Ⓒ Ⓓ Ⓔ

9. Studies in which the same people are tested at different ages are called

   (A) longitudinal
   (B) cross-sectional
   (C) normative
   (D) naturalistic
   (E) experimental   Ⓐ Ⓑ Ⓒ Ⓓ Ⓔ

10. Which of the following is most central to the concept of "critical period"?

    (A) Growth spurts must occur at specific ages.
    (B) A certain chronological age must be reached before specific behaviors can occur.
    (C) A given function emerges automatically during a particular time period, regardless of learning experiences.
    (D) Particular experiences are crucial during a certain time period in development.
    (E) Children go through a negativistic stage as part of their cognitive development.

    Ⓐ Ⓑ Ⓒ Ⓓ Ⓔ

11. According to psychoanalytic theories of personality development, undue stress occurring at any given stage of development is most likely to lead to

    (A) dominance of the conflicts associated with that stage in later personality organization
    (B) an unstable personality unable to participate in normal social relations
    (C) Oedipal problems that may affect later relations with spouse or children
    (D) delinquent behavior during adolescence and excessively aggressive behavior later in life
    (E) atypical behavior with a high susceptibility to schizophrenia

    Ⓐ Ⓑ Ⓒ Ⓓ Ⓔ

12. If reinforcement is to be most effective in learning, it should be

    (A) provided as sparingly as possible
    (B) used on a regularly scheduled basis
    (C) used primarily with high achievers
    (D) delayed until the end of the learning period
    (E) provided soon after the desired behavior occurs

    Ⓐ Ⓑ Ⓒ Ⓓ Ⓔ

13. Studies of identical twins are particularly useful for

    (A) controlling observer bias
    (B) eliminating perceptual bias
    (C) controlling for parental bias
    (D) equating environmental factors
    (E) controlling hereditary factors

    Ⓐ Ⓑ Ⓒ Ⓓ Ⓔ

14. Which of the following statements regarding chronic malnutrition in pregnant women is true?

(A) It does not affect the birth weight of the infant but can impair central nervous system functioning.
(B) It is a minor problem because the unborn baby takes its needed nourishment before the mother's metabolic needs are met.
(C) It is associated with lower birth weight, as well as possible permanent damage to the central nervous system.
(D) The results of recent research have been inconclusive in showing that maternal malnutrition has any adverse effects on the fetus.
(E) It is of concern only in the overpopulated countries of the world.

(A) (B) (C) (D) (E)

15. In Harlow's experiments, infant monkeys raised with only wire or cloth "mothers" were LEAST fearful in strange situations in the presence of

(A) the "mother" who had provided food
(B) the "mother" who had provided contact comfort
(C) the "mother" who had provided primary drive reduction
(D) other young monkeys
(E) their natural mother

(A) (B) (C) (D) (E)

16. Which of the following characteristics of a stimulus pattern is LEAST likely to elicit attention or exploratory behavior in a child?

(A) Novelty
(B) Complexity
(C) Contrast
(D) Surprisingness
(E) Redundancy

(A) (B) (C) (D) (E)

17. Which of the following procedures would best predict what the intelligence test scores of a group of two-year-old children will be at age twenty-one?

(A) Using the children's scores on the Stanford-Binet Intelligence Scale
(B) Using the children's scores on a test of motor development
(C) Using the children's mothers' intelligence test scores
(D) Using the children's scores on a measure of temperament
(E) Predicting an adult IQ of 100 for every child

(A) (B) (C) (D) (E)

276

18. Sibling rivalry in a toddler is LEAST likely to be manifested in which of the following ways?

    (A) Whining or crying easily
    (B) Regressing to an earlier stage of development
    (C) Trying to get parental attention
    (D) Displaying hostility toward the new sibling
    (E) Acting with increased independence   Ⓐ Ⓑ Ⓒ Ⓓ Ⓔ

19. A sudden loud noise made in the vicinity of a newborn infant is likely to elicit the

    (A) Babinski reflex
    (B) Moro reflex
    (C) head-turning reflex
    (D) palmar grasp reflex
    (E) stepping reflex   Ⓐ Ⓑ Ⓒ Ⓓ Ⓔ

20. On which of the following types of problems would a four-year-old child and a seven-year-old child be expected to perform most similarly?

    (A) Conservation of number
    (B) Reversal shift
    (C) Transposition
    (D) Object constancy
    (E) Superordinate concepts   Ⓐ Ⓑ Ⓒ Ⓓ Ⓔ

21. Red-green color blindness is best described as

    (A) a sex-linked recessive trait
    (B) a sex-linked dominant trait
    (C) an autosomal recessive trait
    (D) an autosomal dominant trait
    (E) a trait resulting from chromosomal breakage   Ⓐ Ⓑ Ⓒ Ⓓ Ⓔ

22. The primary reason that the recall memory of an older child is generally better than that of a younger child is that the older child

    (A) has better perceptual abilities
    (B) can organize information better
    (C) engages in concrete thinking
    (D) does not have to categorize information
    (E) recognizes information more easily   Ⓐ Ⓑ Ⓒ Ⓓ Ⓔ

23. Which of the following theorists did NOT develop a "stage" theory?

    (A) Freud
    (B) Piaget
    (C) Skinner
    (D) Kohlberg
    (E) Erikson

    Ⓐ Ⓑ Ⓒ Ⓓ Ⓔ

24. Studies of maternal deprivation suggest that which of the following is most crucial for normal behavioral development during the first year of life?

    (A) Breast feeding
    (B) Social stimulation
    (C) Extensive discipline by the mother
    (D) Engaging the infant in vigorous motor activity
    (E) The infant's becoming attached to one and only one adult

    Ⓐ Ⓑ Ⓒ Ⓓ Ⓔ

25. According to psychoanalytic theory, which of the following mechanisms (and the attitude accompanying it) would be most important for working out a healthy solution of a little boy's Oedipus complex?

    (A) Identification with the father ("I am like Daddy.")
    (B) Object-choice of the father ("I love Daddy best.")
    (C) Identification with the mother ("I am like Mommy.")
    (D) Object-choice of the mother ("I love Mommy best.")
    (E) Projection onto the mother ("Mommy loves me best.")

    Ⓐ Ⓑ Ⓒ Ⓓ Ⓔ

Study Resources

The following list contains several textbooks that are typical of those used in child development and child psychology courses at the college level. To prepare for the Human Growth and Development examination, you should study the contents of at least one such textbook. Although most textbooks cover the topics listed in the test content outline, they may vary somewhat in content, approach, and emphasis. You are therefore advised to consult more than one textbook on the major topics. You may find it helpful to supplement your reading with books and articles listed in the bibliographies found in most developmental psychology textbooks.

Parents and others who work with children may have gained some preparation for this test through experience. However, knowledge of the basic facts, theories, and principles of child psychology and development is necessary to provide background for taking the test.

Additional suggestions for preparing for CLEP examinations are given in chapter 4.

Many libraries do not carry textbooks as a policy. If you can't find any of the following textbooks at the library, see whether the college bookstore has a used copy. If you can't locate the most recent edition, an edition that is one or two years older will suffice for most subject areas. As a final option, purchase a new copy of the suggested textbook as an investment in your education.

TEXTBOOKS

Bee, Helen, *The Developing Child*, 6th ed. New York: HarperCollins, 1992.

Clarke-Stewart, Alison and Joanne Koch, *Children: Development Through Adolescence.* New York: John Wiley & Sons, 1983.

Gardner, Howard, *Developmental Psychology: An Introduction*, 2nd ed. Boston: Little, Brown, 1982.

Hetherington, E. Mavis and Ross D. Parke, *Child Psychology: A Contemporary Viewpoint*, 3rd ed. New York: McGraw Hill, 1986.

Liebert, Robert M., Rita Wicks-Nelson, and Robert V. Kail, *Developmental Psychology*, 4th ed. Englewood Cliffs, NJ: Prentice-Hall, 1986.

Mussen, Paul H., John J. Conger, Jerome Kagan, and Aletha C. Huston, *Child Development and Personality*, 7th ed. New York: Harper & Row, 1990.

Papalia, Diane E. and Sally Wendkos Olds, *Human Development*, 5th ed. New York: McGraw-Hill, 1992.

Shaffer, David R., *Developmental Psychology: Childhood and Adolescence*, 3rd ed. Pacific Grove, CA: Brooks/Cole, 1992.

Introduction to Educational Psychology

Description of the Examination

The Subject Examination entitled Introduction to Educational Psychology covers the material that is usually taught in a one-semester undergraduate course in this subject. Emphasis is placed on principles of learning and cognition, teaching methods and classroom management, child growth and development, and evaluation and assessment of learning.

The examination contains approximately 100 multiple-choice questions to be answered in two separately timed 45-minute sections.

Knowledge and Skills Required

Questions on the exam require candidates to demonstrate one or more of the following abilities.

- Knowledge and comprehension of basic facts, concepts, and principles

- Association of ideas with given theoretical positions

- Awareness of important influences on learning and instruction

- Familiarity with research and statistical concepts and procedures

- Ability to apply various concepts and theories to particular teaching situations and problems

The subject matter of the Introduction to Educational Psychology examination is drawn from the following topics.

Approximate Percent of Examination

5%   Educational Aims or Philosophies

        Socialization

        Preparation for responsible citizenship

        Preparation for careers

        Lifelong learning

        Moral/character development

      →   *Approximate Percent of Examination*

15%   Cognitive Perspective
           Attention and perception
           Memory capacity
           Organization of long-term memory
           Chunking/encoding
           Mental imagery
           Metacognition
           Problem-solving
           Transfer

11%   Behavioristic Perspective
           Classical conditioning
           Law of Effect
           Operant conditioning
           Applications of behaviorism
           Behavioral modification programs
           Schedules of reinforcement
           Token economies
           Cognitive learning theory

15%   Development
           Cognitive
           Social
           Moral
           Language acquisition
           Gender identity/sex roles
           Adolescence
           Mental health
           School readiness

10%   Motivation
           Theories of motivation
           Achievement motivation
           Locus of control/attribution theory
           Learned helplessness
           Reinforcement contingencies
           Intrinsic motivation
           Anxiety/stress

➡ Approximate Percent of Examination

17%   Individual Differences

Nature vs. nurture

Intelligence

Aptitude/achievement

Reading ability

Exceptionalities in learning (e.g., giftedness, physical disabilities, and behavior disorders)

Creativity

Cultural influences

12%   Testing

Test construction (e.g., classroom tests)

Test validity

Test reliability

Norm- and criterion-referenced tests

Scaled scores/standard deviation

Bias in testing

Classroom assessment (e.g., grading procedures and formative evaluation)

Use and misuse of assessment techniques

Assessment of instructional objectives

Descriptive statistics

10%   Pedagogy

Psychology of content areas

Instructional design and technique

Classroom management

Advance organizers

Discovery and reception learning

Cooperative learning

Clarity/organization

Teacher expectations/Pygmalion effect/wait time

Bilingual/ESL instruction

5%   Research design and analysis

Experiments

Surveys

Longitudinal research

Qualitative research/case studies

Research analysis and statistics

Sample Questions

The 25 sample questions that follow are similar to questions on the Introduction to Educational Psychology examination, but they do not actually appear on the examination.

Before attempting to answer the sample questions, read all the information about the Introduction to Educational Psychology examination on the preceding pages. Additional suggestions for preparing for CLEP examinations are provided in chapter 4.

Try to answer correctly as many questions as possible. Then compare your answers with the correct answers, given in Appendix B.

Directions: Each of the questions or incomplete statements below is followed by five suggested answers or completions. Select the one that is best in each case.

1. Which of the following learning outcomes usually undergoes the largest loss within 24 hours of acquisition?

   (A) The learning of meaningful material
   (B) The learning of rote material
   (C) The formulation of concepts
   (D) The application of principles
   (E) The making of generalizations   Ⓐ Ⓑ Ⓒ Ⓓ Ⓔ

2. When Robert's classmates no longer showed approval of his clowning, his clowning behavior occurred less frequently. The concept best exemplified by Robert's change in behavior is

   (A) extinction   (B) discrimination
      (C) generalization   (D) transfer
         (E) learning set   Ⓐ Ⓑ Ⓒ Ⓓ Ⓔ

3. Which of the following procedures draws a subgroup from a larger population in such a way that each member of the defined population has an equal chance of being included?

   (A) Pattern similarity selection
   (B) Simple random sampling
   (C) Stratified sampling
   (D) Proportional selection
   (E) Quota sampling   Ⓐ Ⓑ Ⓒ Ⓓ Ⓔ

4. In a fifth-grade class that is working on a set of arithmetic problems, which of the following behaviors would be most characteristic of the pupil who is a divergent thinker?

   (A) Writing down the principle used to solve the problem as well as the solution itself
   (B) Making answers far more exact than is necessary
   (C) Working as fast as possible in order to be the first to finish the assignment
   (D) Finding a variety of ways to solve each problem
   (E) Providing the correct solution to the greatest number of problems

   Ⓐ Ⓑ Ⓒ Ⓓ Ⓔ

5. To measure students' understanding of a theorem in geometry, it is best for a teacher to have the students do which of the following?

   (A) Write out the theorem.
   (B) Recall the proof of the theorem.
   (C) Demonstrate that they have memorized the theorem.
   (D) Solve a problem that is given in the textbook.
   (E) Solve a related problem that is not in the textbook.

   Ⓐ Ⓑ Ⓒ Ⓓ Ⓔ

6. A child who is frightened by a dog and develops a fear of other dogs is exhibiting which of the following principles of learning?

   (A) Discrimination learning
   (B) Negative transfer
   (C) Behavior shaping
   (D) Stimulus generalization
   (E) Cognitive dissonance

   Ⓐ Ⓑ Ⓒ Ⓓ Ⓔ

7. In experimental studies of the motor development of identical twins, one twin is generally given practice at a particular skill at an earlier period of development and the other twin at a later period of development. The fact that it generally takes less practice for the later-trained twin to acquire the skill is evidence for the importance of

   (A) heredity   (B) maturation   (C) learning
     (D) individual differences   (E) early experience

   Ⓐ Ⓑ Ⓒ Ⓓ Ⓔ

8. In a fifth-grade class studying the ancient Inca culture, all of the following questions are likely to stimulate pupils to think creatively EXCEPT:

   (A) Why do you suppose the clothing of the Incas was so different from today's?
   (B) What weapons and tools did the Incas use for hunting?
   (C) What would be the reaction of an ancient Inca toward modern Peru?
   (D) If the Incas had defeated the Spanish, how might things be different in Peru today?
   (E) If you had lived in Peru during the time of the Incas, what are the things you would have liked and disliked?

   Ⓐ Ⓑ Ⓒ Ⓓ Ⓔ

9. The psychological frame of reference that deals extensively with the effects of unconscious motivation on behavior is

   (A) behaviorism (B) neobehaviorism (C) psychoanalysis
   (D) humanism (E) Gestalt psychology

   Ⓐ Ⓑ Ⓒ Ⓓ Ⓔ

10. Of the following, learning is best defined as

    (A) development that occurs without external stimulation
    (B) the process of overcoming obstacles during instinctual behavior
    (C) effort that is persistent, selective, and purposeful
    (D) the modification of behavior through experience
    (E) the gathering of data to test hypotheses

    Ⓐ Ⓑ Ⓒ Ⓓ Ⓔ

11. According to Kohlberg's theory of moral development, a teacher in the primary grades should expect that

    (A) children will learn and understand universal ethical principles
    (B) children will demonstrate ethical principles in their behavior, especially with their peers
    (C) children's moral development will proceed through a sequence of three broad levels
    (D) attempts to teach lessons on moral development will be useless
    (E) children will teach ethical principles to younger siblings

    Ⓐ Ⓑ Ⓒ Ⓓ Ⓔ

12. A preschool child sees a teacher roll a ball of clay into a sausage-like shape. The teacher asks, "Is the amount of clay the same as before?" The child insists that the sausage shape consists of more clay than the ball did. According to Piaget, this mistake by the child occurs principally because of which of the following?

    (A) A poorly stated question by the teacher
    (B) Erroneous earlier learning by the child
    (C) The greater attractiveness of the sausage shape
    (D) Functional retardation of the child
    (E) A lack of understanding of the conservation principle

    Ⓐ Ⓑ Ⓒ Ⓓ Ⓔ

13. A fourth-grade teacher wants her pupils to learn to recognize oak trees. Which of the following strategies would best lead to that goal?

    (A) Telling the pupils to visit the park after school and observe several oak trees
    (B) Showing the pupils sketches of oaks and other trees and pointing out the distinguishing characteristics of oaks
    (C) Giving each pupil one or two acorns to plant and presenting a lesson on how oak trees grow
    (D) Decorating the classroom bulletin boards with pictures of trees
    (E) Showing pupils a film of the major trees of North America and then giving the pupils a quiz on oak trees

    Ⓐ Ⓑ Ⓒ Ⓓ Ⓔ

14. Compared with traditional classroom teaching, a principal advantage of programmed instruction is that it

    (A) is easier to organize and make available to students
    (B) requires less concentration by the student
    (C) maintains student interest at a higher level
    (D) allows large-scale individualization of instruction
    (E) increases interaction between students and teachers

    Ⓐ Ⓑ Ⓒ Ⓓ Ⓔ

15. To say that a test is reliable is to say that the

    (A) results will be approximately the same if the test is given again under similar conditions
    (B) test measures what it was designed to measure
    (C) predictive validity of the test is high
    (D) objectives measured by the test are important
    (E) test scores can be interpreted objectively by anyone simply by using the test manual

    Ⓐ Ⓑ Ⓒ Ⓓ Ⓔ

16. The concept of developmental tasks refers to the

    (A) development of mental abilities, as distinguished from physical abilities
    (B) ability of the child to develop certain conceptual arrangements
    (C) behavior of the child that results from hereditary determinants
    (D) behaviors of the child that are expected at various ages
    (E) physiological development of the child

    Ⓐ Ⓑ Ⓒ Ⓓ Ⓔ

17. Which of the following correlation coefficients has the highest predictive value?

    (A) 0.80
    (B) 0.60
    (C) 0.00
    (D) −0.70
    (E) −0.90

    Ⓐ Ⓑ Ⓒ Ⓓ Ⓔ

18. Which of the following statistics is most affected by extreme scores?

    (A) Mean
    (B) Median
    (C) Mode
    (D) Rank correlation
    (E) Interquartile range

    Ⓐ Ⓑ Ⓒ Ⓓ Ⓔ

19. As compared with boys who have a low need to achieve, boys who have a high need to achieve are more likely to have parents who provide

    (A) social training and consistent approval independent of the child's level of performance
    (B) independence training and interest in the child's level of performance
    (C) high levels of aspiration and continual criticism independent of the child's level of performance
    (D) independence training and lack of interest in the child's level of performance
    (E) low levels of aspiration and infrequent criticism independent of the child's level of performance

    Ⓐ Ⓑ Ⓒ Ⓓ Ⓔ

20. Which of the following perspectives on teaching would most likely support the idea that instruction should emphasize a positive relationship between teachers and students?

    (A) Behavioral   (B) Humanistic   (C) Cognitive
    (D) Correlational   (E) Maturational

    Ⓐ Ⓑ Ⓒ Ⓓ Ⓔ

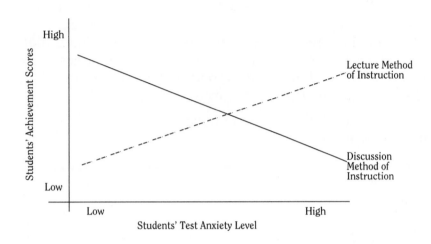

21. Which of the following statements best describes the relationships depicted in the graph above?

    (A) Differences among students in test anxiety result in different achievement levels depending on instructional method received.
    (B) Differences among students in test anxiety result in different achievement levels independent of instructional method received.
    (C) The effect of two different instructional methods on students' achievement is positively correlated with students' test anxiety levels.
    (D) The effect of two different instructional methods on students' achievement is negatively correlated with students' test anxiety levels.
    (E) Students' achievement levels are independent of their test anxiety levels.

    Ⓐ Ⓑ Ⓒ Ⓓ Ⓔ

22. Laura, a fifteen-year-old, is capable of reasoning abstractly without the use of real objects to assist her. According to Piaget, Laura is in which of the following cognitive development stages?

    (A) Concrete operations   (B) Tertiary circular reactions
    (C) Preoperations   (D) Formal operations   (E) Sensorimotor

    Ⓐ Ⓑ Ⓒ Ⓓ Ⓔ

23. Decisions about the values that are transmitted in schools are best related to the teacher's role as

    (A) instructional expert   (B) socialization agent
     (C) counselor   (D) motivator
       (E) classroom manager   Ⓐ Ⓑ Ⓒ Ⓓ Ⓔ

24. A teacher in a third-grade class presents each pupil with 20 small cardboard disks. Each pupil is asked to form separate small groups of disks, with a different number of disks in each group. Then the teacher asks that one disk be added to each group. When that is accomplished, pupils are to attempt to state a rule or generalization indicating what has happened to the number of disks in each group. This kind of learning is most accurately described as

    (A) rote   (B) directed   (C) discovery
     (D) deductive   (E) passive   Ⓐ Ⓑ Ⓒ Ⓓ Ⓔ

25. Using the principle of successive approximation involves which of the following?

    (A) Reinforcing responses that represent progress toward a desired response
    (B) Making a succession of trials designed to provide information about a problem
    (C) Acquiring a behavior change through imitation of models that demonstrate the behavior
    (D) Averaging repeated measures for adequate assessment of a variable
    (E) Testing possible solutions until success is obtained in problem solving

        Ⓐ Ⓑ Ⓒ Ⓓ Ⓔ

Study Resources

The following list contains several textbooks that are typical of those used in educational psychology courses at the college level. To prepare for the Introduction to Educational Psychology examination, you should study the contents of at least one such textbook. Although most texts cover the topics listed in the test content outline, they may vary somewhat in content, approach, and emphasis. You are therefore advised to consult more than one textbook on the major topics.

You will find it helpful to supplement your reading with books listed in the bibliographies that can be found in most educational psychology textbooks. The widely available periodical *Psychology Today* is a useful resource for newsworthy developments and general information about psychological research and its applications to education. The *Journal of Educational Psychology* provides recent research in topics that are important to the field.

Additional suggestions for preparing for CLEP examinations are provided in chapter 4.

Many libraries do not carry textbooks as a policy. If you can't find any of the following textbooks at the library, see whether the college bookstore has a used copy. If you can't locate the most recent edition, an edition that is one or two years older will suffice for most subject areas. As a final option, purchase a new copy of the suggested textbook as an investment in your education.

TEXTBOOKS

Biehler, Robert F. and Jack Snowman, *Psychology Applied to Teaching,* 6th ed. Boston: Houghton Mifflin, 1990.

Gage, N. L. and David C. Berliner, *Educational Psychology,* 5th ed. Boston: Houghton Mifflin, 1991.

Glover, John A. and Roger H. Bruning, *Educational Psychology, Principles and Applications,* 3rd ed. Glenview, IL: Scott, Foresman, 1990.

Mayer, Richard, *Educational Psychology: A Cognitive Approach.* Boston: Little, Brown, 1987.

Woolfolk, Anita, *Educational Psychology,* 4th ed. Englewood Cliffs, NJ: Prentice Hall, 1990.

Principles of Macroeconomics

Description of the Examination

The Subject Examination in Principles of Macroeconomics covers material that is usually taught in a one-semester undergraduate course in the principles of macroeconomics. This aspect of economics deals with principles of economics that apply to a total economic system, particularly the general levels of output and income and interrelations among sectors of the economy. The test places particular emphasis on the determinants of aggregate demand and on the monetary and fiscal policies that are appropriate to achieve particular policy objectives. Within this context, candidates are expected to understand concepts such as the multiplier, the accelerator, and balance-of-payments equilibrium; terms such as inflation, deflationary gap, and depreciation; and institutional arrangements such as open-market operations, deficit spending, and flexible exchange rates.

The examination consists of approximately 80 multiple-choice questions to be answered in two separately timed 45-minute sections.

Knowledge and Skills Required

Questions on the Principles of Macroeconomics examination require candidates to demonstrate one or more of the following abilities.

- Understanding of important economic terms and concepts

- Interpretation and manipulation of economic graphs

- Interpretation and evaluation of economic data

- Application of simple economic models

The outline below indicates the material covered by the examination and the approximate percentage of questions in each category.

Approximate Percent of Examination

8-12%   Basic economic concepts
      Scarcity: the nature of the economic system
      Opportunity costs and production possibilities curves
      Demand, supply, and price determination

10-18%   Measurement of economic performance
      Gross domestic and national products and national
        income concepts
      Inflation and price indices
      Unemployment

60-70%   National income and price determination
      Aggregate supply and demand: Keynesian and classical
        analysis (25-30%)
      Circular flow
      Components of aggregate supply and demand
      Multiplier
      Fiscal policy
      Long vs. short run

      Money and banking (15-20%)
      Definition of money and its creation
      Tools of central bank policy and monetary policy

      Fiscal and monetary policy combination (20-25%)
      Interaction of fiscal and monetary policy
      Debts and deficits
      Stabilization policies for aggregate demand and
        supply shocks
      Monetarist, supply-siders, and Keynesian
        controversies

10-15%   International economics and growth
      Comparative advantage, trade policy, international
        finance, and exchange rates
      Economic growth

Sample Questions

The 39 sample questions that follow are similar to questions on the Principles of Macroeconomics examination, but they do not appear on the actual examination.

Before attempting to answer the sample questions, read all the information about the Principles of Macroeconomics examination given above. Additional suggestions for preparing for CLEP examinations are provided in chapter 4.

Try to answer correctly as many questions as possible. Then compare your answers with the correct answers, given in Appendix B.

Directions: Each of the questions or incomplete statements below is followed by five suggested answers or completions. Select the one that is best in each case.

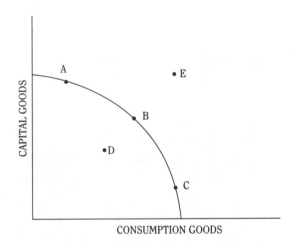

1. An economy that is fully employing all its productive resources but allocating less to investment than to consumption will be at which of the following positions on the production possibilities curve shown above?

   (A) A
   (B) B
   (C) C
   (D) D
   (E) E

   Ⓐ Ⓑ Ⓒ Ⓓ Ⓔ

2. Assume that land in an agricultural economy can be used either for producing grain or for grazing cattle to produce beef. The opportunity cost of converting an acre from cattle grazing to grain production is the

    (A) market value of the extra grain that is produced
    (B) total amount of beef produced
    (C) number of extra bushels of grain that are produced
    (D) amount by which beef production decreases
    (E) profits generated by the extra production of grain

    Ⓐ Ⓑ Ⓒ Ⓓ Ⓔ

3. Which of the following is a possible cause of stagflation (simultaneous high unemployment and high inflation)?

    (A) Increase in labor productivity
    (B) Increase in price for raw materials
    (C) The rapid growth and development of the computer industry
    (D) A decline in labor union membership
    (E) A low growth rate of the money supply

    Ⓐ Ⓑ Ⓒ Ⓓ Ⓔ

4. Which of the following will occur as a result of an improvement in technology?

    (A) The aggregate demand curve will shift to the right.
    (B) The aggregate demand curve will shift to the left.
    (C) The aggregate supply curve will shift to the right.
    (D) The aggregate supply curve will shift to the left.
    (E) The production possibilities curve will shift inward.

    Ⓐ Ⓑ Ⓒ Ⓓ Ⓔ

5. Increases in real income per capita are made possible by

    (A) improved productivity
    (B) a high labor/capital ratio
    (C) large trade surpluses
    (D) stable interest rates
    (E) high protective tariffs

    Ⓐ Ⓑ Ⓒ Ⓓ Ⓔ

6. Which of the following is an example of "investment" as the term is used by economists?

   (A) A schoolteacher purchases 10,000 shares of stock in an automobile company.
   (B) Newlyweds purchase a previously owned home.
   (C) One large automobile firm purchases another large automobile firm.
   (D) A farmer purchases $10,000 worth of government securities.
   (E) An apparel company purchases 15 new sewing machines.

   Ⓐ Ⓑ Ⓒ Ⓓ Ⓔ

7. The United States government defines an individual as unemployed if the person

   (A) does not hold a paying job
   (B) has been recently fired
   (C) works part-time but needs full-time work
   (D) is without a job but is looking for work
   (E) wants a job but is not searching because he or she thinks none is available

   Ⓐ Ⓑ Ⓒ Ⓓ Ⓔ

8. If businesses are experiencing an unplanned increase in inventories, which of the following is most likely to be true?

   (A) Aggregate demand is greater than output, and the level of spending will increase.
   (B) Aggregate demand is less than output, and the level of spending will decrease.
   (C) The economy is growing and will continue to grow until a new equilibrium level of spending is reached.
   (D) Planned investment is greater than planned saving, and the level of spending will decrease.
   (E) Planned investment is less than planned saving, and the level of spending will increase.

   Ⓐ Ⓑ Ⓒ Ⓓ Ⓔ

9. Which of the following workers is most likely to be classified as structurally unemployed?

   (A) A high school teacher who is unemployed during the summer months
   (B) A recent college graduate who is looking for her first job
   (C) A teenager who is seeking part-time employment at a fast-food restaurant
   (D) A worker who is unemployed because his skills are obsolete
   (E) A woman who reenters the job market after her child begins elementary school

   Ⓐ Ⓑ Ⓒ Ⓓ Ⓔ

10. According to the classical model, an increase in the money supply causes an increase in which of the following?

    I. The price level
    II. Nominal gross domestic product
    III. Nominal wages

    (A) I only
    (B) II only
    (C) III only
    (D) II and III only
    (E) I, II, and III

    Ⓐ Ⓑ Ⓒ Ⓓ Ⓔ

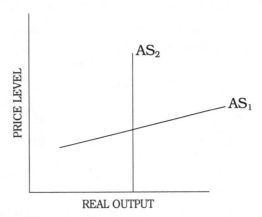

REAL OUTPUT

11. The diagram above shows two aggregate supply curves, AS$_1$ and AS$_2$. Which of the following statements most accurately characterizes the AS$_1$ curve relative to the AS$_2$ curve?

(A) AS$_1$ is Keynesian because it reflects greater wage and price flexibility.
(B) AS$_1$ is classical because it reflects greater wage and price flexibility.
(C) AS$_1$ is Keynesian because it reflects less wage and price flexibility.
(D) AS$_1$ is classical because it reflects less wage and price flexibility.
(E) AS$_1$ could be either classical or Keynesian because it reflects greater wage flexibility but less price flexibility.

Ⓐ Ⓑ Ⓒ Ⓓ Ⓔ

12. An increase in which of the following would cause the long-run aggregate supply curve to shift to the right?

(A) Corporate income tax rates
(B) Aggregate demand
(C) Potential output
(D) The average wage rate
(E) The price level

Ⓐ Ⓑ Ⓒ Ⓓ Ⓔ

13. According to the classical economists, which of the following is most sensitive to interest rates?

(A) Consumption
(B) Investment
(C) Government spending
(D) Transfer payments
(E) Intermediate goods

Ⓐ Ⓑ Ⓒ Ⓓ Ⓔ

14. In the circular flow diagram, which of the following is true?

    (A) Businesses pay wages, rent, interest, and profits to households in return for use of factors of production.
    (B) Businesses purchase goods and services from households in return for money payments.
    (C) Households pay wages, rent, interest, and profits to businesses in return for use of factors of production.
    (D) The relationship between households and businesses exists only in a traditional society.
    (E) The relationship between households and businesses exists only in a command economy.

    Ⓐ Ⓑ Ⓒ Ⓓ Ⓔ

15. Which of the following would most likely lead to a decrease in aggregate demand, that is, shift the aggregate demand curve leftward?

    (A) A decrease in taxes
    (B) A decrease in interest rates
    (C) An increase in household savings
    (D) An increase in household consumption
    (E) An increase in business firms' purchases of capital equipment from retained earnings

    Ⓐ Ⓑ Ⓒ Ⓓ Ⓔ

16. According to the Keynesian model, equilibrium output of an economy may be less than the full-employment level of output because at full employment

    (A) sufficient income may not be generated to keep workers above the subsistence level
    (B) there might not be enough demand by firms and consumers to buy that output
    (C) workers may not be willing to work the hours necessary to produce the output
    (D) interest rates might not be high enough to provide the incentive to finance the production
    (E) banks may not be willing to lend enough money to support the output

    Ⓐ Ⓑ Ⓒ Ⓓ Ⓔ

17. If the Federal Reserve lowers the reserve requirement, which of the following is most likely to happen to interest rates and gross domestic product?

	Interest Rates	Gross Domestic Product
(A)	Increase	Decrease
(B)	Increase	Increase
(C)	Decrease	Decrease
(D)	Decrease	Increase
(E)	No change	No change

Ⓐ Ⓑ Ⓒ Ⓓ Ⓔ

18. If the marginal propensity to consume is 0.9, what is the maximum amount that the equilibrium gross domestic product could change if government expenditures increase by $1 billion?

(A) It could decrease by up to $9 billion.
(B) It could increase by up to $0.9 billion.
(C) It could increase by up to $1 billion.
(D) It could increase by up to $9 billion.
(E) It could increase by up to $10 billion.

Ⓐ Ⓑ Ⓒ Ⓓ Ⓔ

19. Expansionary fiscal policy will be most effective when

(A) the aggregate supply curve is horizontal
(B) the economy is at or above full-employment output
(C) transfer payments are decreased, while taxes remain unchanged
(D) wages and prices are very flexible
(E) the Federal Reserve simultaneously increases the reserve requirement

Ⓐ Ⓑ Ⓒ Ⓓ Ⓔ

20. Which of the following would increase the value of the multiplier?

(A) An increase in government expenditure
(B) An increase in exports
(C) A decrease in government unemployment benefits
(D) A decrease in the marginal propensity to consume
(E) A decrease in the marginal propensity to save

Ⓐ Ⓑ Ⓒ Ⓓ Ⓔ

21. Assume that the reserve requirement is 25 percent. If banks have excess reserves of $10,000, which of the following is the maximum amount of additional money that can be created by the banking system through the lending process?

    (A) $2,500
    (B) $10,000
    (C) $40,000
    (D) $50,000
    (E) $250,000

    Ⓐ Ⓑ Ⓒ Ⓓ Ⓔ

22. The principal reason for requiring commercial banks to maintain reserve balances with the Federal Reserve is that these balances

    (A) provide the maximum amount of reserves a bank would ever need
    (B) give the Federal Reserve more control over the money-creating operations of banks
    (C) ensure that banks do not make excessive profits
    (D) assist the Treasury in refinancing government debt
    (E) enable the government to borrow cheaply from the Federal Reserve's discount window

    Ⓐ Ⓑ Ⓒ Ⓓ Ⓔ

23. The purchase of securities on the open market by the Federal Reserve will

    (A) increase the supply of money
    (B) increase the interest rate
    (C) increase the discount rate
    (D) decrease the number of Federal Reserve notes in circulation
    (E) decrease the reserve requirement

    Ⓐ Ⓑ Ⓒ Ⓓ Ⓔ

24. To counteract a recession, the Federal Reserve should

    (A) buy securities on the open market and raise the reserve requirement
    (B) buy securities on the open market and lower the reserve requirement
    (C) buy securities on the open market and raise the discount rate
    (D) sell securities on the open market and raise the discount rate
    (E) raise the reserve requirement and lower the discount rate

    Ⓐ Ⓑ Ⓒ Ⓓ Ⓔ

25. Total spending in the economy is most likely to increase by the largest amount if which of the following occur to government spending and taxes?

	Government Spending	Taxes
(A)	Decrease	Increase
(B)	Decrease	No change
(C)	Increase	Increase
(D)	Increase	Decrease
(E)	No change	Increase

26. According to the Keynesian model, an increase in the money supply affects output more if

(A) investment is sensitive to interest rates
(B) money demand is sensitive to interest rates
(C) the unemployment rate is low
(D) consumption is sensitive to the Phillips curve
(E) government spending is sensitive to public opinion

27. Supply-side economists argue that

(A) a cut in high tax rates results in an increased deficit and thus increases aggregate supply
(B) lower tax rates provide positive work incentives and thus shift the aggregate supply curve to the right
(C) the aggregate supply of goods can only be increased if the price level falls
(D) increased government spending should be used to stimulate the economy
(E) the government should regulate the supply of imports

Ⓐ Ⓑ Ⓒ Ⓓ Ⓔ

28. Which of the following policies would most likely be recommended in an economy with an annual inflation rate of 3 percent and an unemployment rate of 11 percent?

(A) An increase in transfer payments and an increase in the reserve requirement
(B) An increase in defense spending and an increase in the discount rate
(C) An increase in income tax rates and a decrease in the reserve requirement
(D) A decrease in government spending and the open-market sale of government securities
(E) A decrease in the tax rate on corporate profits and a decrease in the discount rate

Ⓐ Ⓑ Ⓒ Ⓓ Ⓔ

29. According to the monetarists, inflation is most often the result of

(A) high federal tax rates
(B) increased production of capital goods
(C) decreased production of capital goods
(D) an excessive growth of the money supply
(E) upward shifts in the consumption function

Ⓐ Ⓑ Ⓒ Ⓓ Ⓔ

30. According to the Keynesian model, an expansionary fiscal policy would tend to cause which of the following changes in output and interest rates?

	Output	Interest Rates
(A)	Increase	Increase
(B)	Increase	Decrease
(C)	Decrease	Increase
(D)	Decrease	Decrease
(E)	No change	Decrease

Ⓐ Ⓑ Ⓒ Ⓓ Ⓔ

31. Which of the following would result in the largest increase in aggregate demand?

    (A) A $30 billion increase in military expenditure and a $30 billion open-market purchase of government securities
    (B) A $30 billion increase in military expenditure and a $30 billion open-market sale of government securities
    (C) A $30 billion tax cut and a $30 billion open-market sale of government securities
    (D) A $30 billion tax increase and a $30 billion open-market purchase of government securities
    (E) A $30 billion increase in social security payments and a $30 billion open-market sale of government securities

    Ⓐ Ⓑ Ⓒ Ⓓ Ⓔ

32. Which of the following measures might be used to reduce a federal budget deficit?

    I. Raising taxes
    II. Reducing federal spending
    III. Lowering interest rates

    (A) I only
    (B) II only
    (C) III only
    (D) I and III only
    (E) I, II, and III

    Ⓐ Ⓑ Ⓒ Ⓓ Ⓔ

33. Which of the following would most likely be the immediate result if the United States increased tariffs on most foreign goods?

    (A) The United States standard of living would be higher.
    (B) More foreign goods would be purchased by Americans.
    (C) Prices of domestic goods would increase.
    (D) Large numbers of United States workers would be laid off.
    (E) The value of the United States dollar would decrease against foreign currencies.

    Ⓐ Ⓑ Ⓒ Ⓓ Ⓔ

34. Which of the following policies is most likely to encourage long-run economic growth in a country?

    (A) An embargo on high-technology imports
    (B) A decline in the number of immigrants to the country
    (C) An increase in government transfer payments
    (D) An increase in the per capita savings rate
    (E) An increase in defense spending

    Ⓐ Ⓑ Ⓒ Ⓓ Ⓔ

35. Which of the following would occur if the international value of the United States dollar decreased?

    (A) United States exports would rise.
    (B) More gold would flow into the United States.
    (C) United States demand for foreign currencies would increase.
    (D) The United States trade deficit would increase.
    (E) Americans would pay less for foreign goods.

    Ⓐ Ⓑ Ⓒ Ⓓ Ⓔ

36. If exchange rates are allowed to fluctuate freely and the United States demand for German marks increases, which of the following will most likely occur?

    (A) Americans will have to pay more for goods made in Germany.
    (B) Germans will find that American goods are getting more expensive.
    (C) The United States balance-of-payments deficit will increase.
    (D) The dollar price of marks will fall.
    (E) The dollar price of German goods will fall.

    Ⓐ Ⓑ Ⓒ Ⓓ Ⓔ

37. The replacement of some portion of the federal personal income tax with a general sales tax would most likely result in

    (A) greater overall progressivity in the tax structure
    (B) lesser overall progressivity in the tax structure
    (C) stronger automatic stabilization through the business cycle
    (D) increased consumption of liquor, cigarettes, and gasoline
    (E) a smaller federal budget deficit

    Ⓐ Ⓑ Ⓒ Ⓓ Ⓔ

38. A deficit in the United States trade balance can be described as

    (A) an excess of the value of commodity imports over the value of commodity exports
    (B) an excess of the value of commodity exports over the value of commodity imports
    (C) an excess of payments to foreigners over receipts from foreigners
    (D) an almost complete depletion of the gold stock
    (E) the consequence of an undervalued dollar

    Ⓐ Ⓑ Ⓒ Ⓓ Ⓔ

39. Problems faced by all economic systems include which of the following?

   I. How to allocate scarce resources among unlimited wants
  II. How to decentralize markets
 III. How to decide what to produce, how to produce, and for whom to produce
  IV. How to set government production quotas

(A) I only
(B) I and III only
(C) II and III only
(D) I, II, and III only
(E) I, II, III, and IV

Study Resources

There are many introductory economics textbooks that vary greatly in difficulty. The following books are among the more widely used for introductory courses in the principles of economics. All the books are published in one-volume editions, which cover both microeconomics and macroeconomics; most are also published in two-volume editions, with one volume covering macroeconomics and the other microeconomics. All the references cover the topics in the content outlines of the Principles of Macroeconomics and Principles of Microeconomics examinations, but their approaches and emphases differ. A companion study guide/workbook is available for all the textbooks. The study guides typically include brief reviews, definitions of key concepts, problem sets, and multiple-choice test questions with answers. Many publishers also make available computer-assisted learning packages.

To broaden your knowledge of economic issues, you may read relevant articles published in the economics periodicals that are available in most college libraries — for example, *The Economist, The Margin,* and *The American Economic Review. The Wall Street Journal* and the *New York Times,* along with local papers may also enhance your understanding of economic issues.

Additional suggestions for preparing for CLEP examinations are provided in chapter 4.

Many libraries do not carry textbooks as a policy. If you can't find any of the following textbooks at the library, see whether the college bookstore has a used copy. If you can't locate the most recent edition, an edition that is one or two years older will suffice for most subject areas. As a final option, purchase a new copy of the suggested textbook as an investment in your education.

TEXTBOOKS

Baumol, William J. and Alan S. Blinder, *Economics, Principles and Policy*, 5th ed. New York: Harcourt Brace Jovanovich, 1991.

Case, Karl E. and Ray C. Fair, *Principles of Economics*, 2nd ed. Englewood Cliffs, NY: Prentice Hall, 1991.

Hess, Peter N. and Clark G. Ross, *Principles of Economics*. St. Paul, MN: West Publishing, 1993.

Lipsey, Richard C., Peter O. Steiner and Douglas D. Purvis, *Economics*, 9th ed. New York: Harper and Row, 1990.

Mansfield, Edwin, *Economics: Principles, Problems, Decisions*, 7th ed. New York: W. W. Norton, 1992.

McConnell, Campbell R., *Economics: Principles, Problems and Policies*, 11th ed. New York: McGraw-Hill, 1990.

Miller, Roger LeRoy, *Economics Today*, 7th ed. New York: Harper and Row, 1991.

Ragan, James F. and Lloyd B. Thomas, *Principles of Economics*, 2nd ed. Fort Worth: Harcourt Brace Jovanovich, 1993.

Samuelson, Paul A. and William D. Nordhaus, *Economics*, 14th ed. New York: McGraw-Hill, 1992.

Principles of Microeconomics

Description of the Examination

The Subject Examination in Principles of Microeconomics covers material that is usually taught in a one-semester undergraduate course in the principles of microeconomics. This aspect of economics deals with the principles of economics that apply to the behavior of groups, organizations, and individuals within the larger economic system. Questions on the exam require candidates to apply analytic techniques to hypothetical situations and to analyze and evaluate government policies on the basis of simple theoretical models. The exam emphasizes analytical capabilities rather than a factual understanding of United States institutions and policies.

The examination consists of approximately 80 multiple-choice questions to be answered in two separately timed 45-minute sections.

Knowledge and Skills Required

Questions on the Principles of Microeconomics examination require candidates to demonstrate one or more of the following abilities.

- Understanding of important economic terms and concepts

- Interpretation and manipulation of economic graphs

- Interpretation and evaluation of economic data

- Application of simple economic models

The outline below indicates the material covered by the examination and the approximate percent of questions in each category.

➡ *Approximate Percent of Examination*

8-12%   Basic economic concepts
      Scarcity: nature of economic systems
      Opportunity costs and production possibilities
      Comparative advantage

60-70%   The nature and function of the product market
    Supply and demand (15-20%)
     Price and quantity demanded
     Basic implementation of policy
    Consumer demand (10-15%)
     Consumer choice: utility and demand theory
     Elasticity
    Firm's production, costs, and revenue (10-15%)
     Marginal product and diminishing returns
     Total, average, and marginal costs and revenue
     Long-run costs and economies of scale
    Profit maximization: pricing, revenue, and output both in the long run and the short run and in the firm and the market (25-30%)
     Perfect competition
     Imperfect competition
      Monopoly
      Oligopoly and monopolistic competition
    Efficiency and antitrust (4-6%)

10-15%   Factor Market
    Derived demand
    Determination of wages and other factor prices
    Distribution of income

4-6%   Market failures and the role of government
    Externalities
    Public goods

Sample Questions

The 39 sample questions that follow are similar to questions on the Principles of Microeconomics examination, but they do not appear on the actual examination.

Before attempting to answer the sample questions, read all the information about the Principles of Microeconomics examination given above. Additional suggestions for preparing for CLEP examinations are provided in chapter 4.

Try to answer correctly as many questions as possible. Then compare your answers with the correct answers, given in Appendix B.

Directions: Each of the questions or incomplete statements below is followed by five suggested answers or completions. Select the one that is best in each case.

Questions 1-2 are based on the following table.

PRODUCTION FUNCTION

(Figures in body of table represent amounts of output.)

Units of Labor	Units of Capital					
	1	2	3	4	5	6
1	141	200	245	282	316	346
2	200	282	346	400	448	490
3	245	346	423	490	548	600
4	282	400	490	564	632	692
5	316	448	548	632	705	775
6	346	490	—	692	775	846

1. Information given in the table can be used to illustrate the law of

   (A) diminishing returns
   (B) diminishing demand
   (C) diminishing utility
   (D) supply and demand
   (E) comparative advantage   Ⓐ Ⓑ Ⓒ Ⓓ Ⓔ

2. If there are constant returns to scale throughout the production process, the amount of output that can be produced with 3 units of capital and 6 units of labor must be

   (A) 490
   (B) 548
   (C) 600
   (D) 608
   (E) 693   Ⓐ Ⓑ Ⓒ Ⓓ Ⓔ

3. Which of the following best states the thesis of the law of comparative advantage?

   (A) Differences in relative costs of production are the key to determining patterns of trade.
   (B) Differences in absolute costs of production determine which goods should be traded between nations.
   (C) Tariffs and quotas are beneficial in increasing international competitiveness.
   (D) Nations should not specialize in the production of goods and services.
   (E) Two nations will not trade if one is more efficient than the other in the production of all goods.

   Ⓐ Ⓑ Ⓒ Ⓓ Ⓔ

4. A retail firm planning to increase the price of a product it sells would hope that

   (A) the good is an inferior good
   (B) the price of complements would also go up
   (C) the price of substitutes would go down
   (D) demand for the product is perfectly elastic
   (E) demand for the product is inelastic

   Ⓐ Ⓑ Ⓒ Ⓓ Ⓔ

5. If it were possible to increase the output of military goods and simultaneously to increase the output of the private sector of an economy, which of the following statements about the economy and its current position relative to its production possibilities curve would be true?

   (A) The economy is inefficient and inside the curve.
   (B) The economy is inefficient and on the curve.
   (C) The economy is efficient and on the curve.
   (D) The economy is efficient and inside the curve.
   (E) The economy is efficient and outside the curve.

   Ⓐ Ⓑ Ⓒ Ⓓ Ⓔ

6. Which of the following would necessarily cause a fall in the price of a product?

   (A) An increase in population and a decrease in the price of an input
   (B) An increase in population and a decrease in the number of firms producing the product
   (C) An increase in average income and an improvement in production technology
   (D) A decrease in the price of a substitute product and an improvement in production technology
   (E) A decrease in the price of a substitute product and an increase in the price of an input

   Ⓐ Ⓑ Ⓒ Ⓓ Ⓔ

7. Agricultural price supports will most likely result in

   (A) shortages of products if the price supports are above the equilibrium price
   (B) shortages of products if the price supports are at equilibrium price
   (C) surpluses of products if the price supports are above the equilibrium price
   (D) surpluses of products if the price supports are below the equilibrium price
   (E) a balance between quantity demanded and quantity supplied if the price floor is above the equilibrium price

   Ⓐ Ⓑ Ⓒ Ⓓ Ⓔ

8. The market equilibrium price of home heating oil is $1.50 per gallon. If a price ceiling of $1.00 per gallon is imposed, which of the following will occur in the market for home heating oil?

   I. Quantity supplied will increase.
   II. Quantity demanded will increase.
   III. Quantity supplied will decrease.
   IV. Quantity demanded will decrease.

   (A) II only
   (B) I and II only
   (C) I and IV only
   (D) II and III only
   (E) III and IV only

   Ⓐ Ⓑ Ⓒ Ⓓ Ⓔ

9. Assume a consumer finds that her total expenditure on compact discs stays the same after the price of compact discs declines. Which of the following is true for this consumer over the price range?

   (A) Compact discs are inferior goods.
   (B) The consumer's demand for compact discs increased in response to the price change.
   (C) The consumer's demand for compact discs is perfectly price elastic.
   (D) The consumer's demand for compact discs is perfectly price inelastic.
   (E) The consumer's demand for compact discs is unit price elastic.

   Ⓐ Ⓑ Ⓒ Ⓓ Ⓔ

10. An improvement in production technology for a certain good leads to

    (A) an increase in demand for the good
    (B) an increase in the supply of the good
    (C) an increase in the price of the good
    (D) a shortage of the good
    (E) a surplus of the good

    Ⓐ Ⓑ Ⓒ Ⓓ Ⓔ

11. If the demand for a product is price elastic, which of the following is true?

    (A) An increase in product price will have no effect on the firm's total revenue.
    (B) An increase in product price will increase the firm's total revenue.
    (C) A reduction in product price will increase the firm's total revenue.
    (D) A reduction in product price will decrease the firm's rate of inventory turnover.
    (E) A reduction in product price will decrease the total cost of goods sold.

    Ⓐ Ⓑ Ⓒ Ⓓ Ⓔ

12. If an increase in the price of good X causes a drop in demand for good Y, good Y is

    (A) an inferior good
    (B) a luxury good
    (C) a necessary good
    (D) a substitute for good X
    (E) a complement to good X

    Ⓐ Ⓑ Ⓒ Ⓓ Ⓔ

13. The demand curve for cars is downward sloping because an increase in the price of cars leads to

    (A) the increased use of other modes of transportation
    (B) a fall in the expected future price of cars
    (C) a decrease in the number of cars available for purchase
    (D) a rise in the prices of gasoline and other oil-based products
    (E) a change in consumers' tastes in car

    Ⓐ Ⓑ Ⓒ Ⓓ Ⓔ

14. Suppose that an effective minimum wage is imposed in a certain labor market above the equilibrium wage. If labor supply in that market subsequently increases, which of the following will occur?

    (A) Unemployment in that market will increase.
    (B) Quantity of labor supplied will decrease.
    (C) Quantity of labor demanded will increase.
    (D) Market demand will increase.
    (E) The market wage will increase.

    Ⓐ Ⓑ Ⓒ Ⓓ Ⓔ

15. Suppose that a family buys all its clothing from a discount store and treats these items as inferior goods. Under such circumstances, this family's consumption of discount store clothing will necessarily

    (A) increase when a family member wins the state lottery
    (B) increase when a family member gets a raise in pay at work
    (C) remain unchanged when its income rises or falls due to events beyond the family's control
    (D) decrease when a family member becomes unemployed
    (E) decrease when a family member experiences an increase in income

    Ⓐ Ⓑ Ⓒ Ⓓ Ⓔ

16. The primary distinction between the short run and the long run is that in the short run

    (A) firms make profits, but in the long run no firm makes economic profits
    (B) profits are maximized, but in the long run all costs are maximized
    (C) some costs of production are fixed, but in the long run all costs are fixed
    (D) some costs of production are fixed, but in the long run all costs are variable
    (E) marginal costs are rising, but in the long run they are constant

    Ⓐ Ⓑ Ⓒ Ⓓ Ⓔ

Questions 17-19 are based on the table below, which shows a firm's total cost for different levels of output.

Output	Total Cost
0	$24
1	33
2	41
3	48
4	54
5	61
6	69

17. Which of the following is the firm's marginal cost of producing the fourth unit of output?

(A) $54.00
(B) $13.50
(C) $ 7.50
(D) $ 6.00
(E) $ 1.50

(A) (B) (C) (D) (E)

18. Which of the following is the firm's average total cost of producing 3 units of output?

(A) $48.00
(B) $16.00
(C) $14.00
(D) $13.50
(E) $ 7.00

(A) (B) (C) (D) (E)

19. Which of the following is the firm's average fixed cost of producing 2 units of output?

(A) $24.00
(B) $20.50
(C) $12.00
(D) $ 8.00
(E) $ 7.50

(A) (B) (C) (D) (E)

20. Marginal revenue is the change in revenue that results from a one-unit increase in the

    (A) variable input
    (B) variable input price
    (C) output level
    (D) output price
    (E) fixed cost

    Ⓐ Ⓑ Ⓒ Ⓓ Ⓔ

21. In the short run, if the product price of a perfectly competitive firm is less than the minimum average variable cost, the firm will

    (A) raise its price
    (B) increase its output
    (C) decrease its output slightly but increase its profit margin
    (D) lose more by continuing to produce than by shutting down
    (E) lose less by continuing to produce than by shutting down

    Ⓐ Ⓑ Ⓒ Ⓓ Ⓔ

22. Suppose that the license paid by each business to operate in a city increases from $400 per year to $500 per year. What effect will this increase have on a firm's short-run costs?

	Marginal Cost	Average Total Cost	Average Variable Cost
(A)	Increase	Increase	Increase
(B)	Increase	Increase	No effect
(C)	No effect	No effect	No effect
(D)	No effect	Increase	Increase
(E)	No effect	Increase	No effect

    Ⓐ Ⓑ Ⓒ Ⓓ Ⓔ

23. Which of the following statements is true of perfectly competitive firms in long-run equilibrium?

    (A) Firm revenues will decrease if production is increased.
    (B) Total firm revenues are at a maximum.
    (C) Average fixed cost equals marginal cost.
    (D) Average total cost is at a minimum.
    (E) Average variable cost is greater than marginal cost.

    Ⓐ Ⓑ Ⓒ Ⓓ Ⓔ

24. If the chemical industry in an area has been dumping its toxic waste free of charge into a river, government action to ensure a more efficient use of resources would have which of the following effects on the industry's output and product price?

	Output	Price
(A)	Decrease	Decrease
(B)	Decrease	Increase
(C)	Increase	Decrease
(D)	Increase	Increase
(E)	Increase	No change

Ⓐ Ⓑ Ⓒ Ⓓ Ⓔ

25. Assume a perfectly competitive industry is in long-run equilibrium. A permanent increase in demand will eventually result in

(A) a decrease in demand because the price will increase and people will buy less of the output
(B) a decrease in supply because the rate of output and the associated cost will both increase
(C) an increase in price but no increase in output
(D) an increase in output
(E) a permanent shortage since the quantity demanded is now greater than the quantity supplied

Ⓐ Ⓑ Ⓒ Ⓓ Ⓔ

26. Economists are critical of monopoly principally because

(A) monopolists gain too much political influence
(B) monopolists are able to avoid paying their fair share of taxes
(C) monopolists are unfair to poor people
(D) monopoly leads to an inefficient use of scarce productive resources
(E) monopolists cause international political tension by competing with one another overseas for supplies of raw materials

Ⓐ Ⓑ Ⓒ Ⓓ Ⓔ

27. Which of the following statements has to be true in a perfectly competitive market?

(A) A firm's marginal revenue equals price.
(B) A firm's average total cost is above price in the long run.
(C) A firm's average fixed cost rises in the short run.
(D) A firm's average variable cost is higher than price in the long run.
(E) Large firms have lower total costs than small firms.

Ⓐ Ⓑ Ⓒ Ⓓ Ⓔ

28. A perfectly competitive firm produces in an industry whose product sells at a market price of $100. At the firm's current rate of production, marginal cost is rising and equal to $110. To maximize its profits, the firm should change its output and price in which of the following ways?

	Output	Price
(A)	Decrease	Increase
(B)	Decrease	No change
(C)	No change	Increase
(D)	Increase	No change
(E)	Increase	Decrease

29. The typical firm in a monopolistically competitive industry earns zero profit in long-run equilibrium because

(A) advertising costs make monopolistic competition a high-cost market structure rather than a low-cost market structure

(B) the firms in the industry do not operate at the minimum point on their long-run average cost curves

(C) there are no significant restrictions on entering or exiting from the industry

(D) the firms in the industry are unable to engage in product differentiation

(E) there are close substitutes for each firm's product

Ⓐ Ⓑ Ⓒ Ⓓ Ⓔ

30. In the long run, compared with a perfectly competitive firm, a monopolistically competitive firm with the same costs will have

(A) a higher price and higher output

(B) a higher price and lower output

(C) a lower price and higher output

(D) a lower price and lower output

(E) the same price and lower output

Ⓐ Ⓑ Ⓒ Ⓓ Ⓔ

31. Which of the following describes what will happen to market price and quantity if firms in a perfectly competitive market form a cartel and act as a profit-maximizing monopoly?

	Price	Quantity
(A)	Decrease	Decrease
(B)	Decrease	Increase
(C)	Increase	Increase
(D)	Increase	Decrease
(E)	Increase	No change

Ⓐ Ⓑ Ⓒ Ⓓ Ⓔ

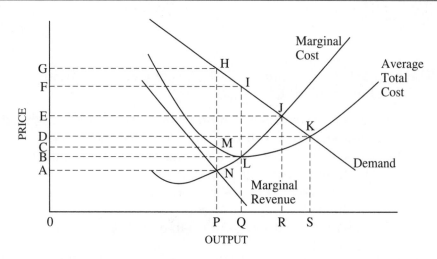

32. The diagram above depicts cost and revenue curves for a firm. What are the firm's profit-maximizing output and price?

	Output	Price
(A)	0S	0D
(B)	0R	0E
(C)	0Q	0F
(D)	0Q	0B
(E)	0P	0G

Ⓐ Ⓑ Ⓒ Ⓓ Ⓔ

33. Imperfectly competitive firms may be allocatively inefficient because they produce at a level of output such that

(A) average cost is at a minimum
(B) price equals marginal revenue
(C) marginal revenue is greater than marginal cost
(D) price equals marginal cost
(E) price is greater than marginal cost

Ⓐ Ⓑ Ⓒ Ⓓ Ⓔ

34. In a market economy, public goods such as community police protection are unlikely to be provided in sufficient quantity by the private sector because

    (A) private firms are less efficient at producing public goods than is the government
    (B) the use of public goods cannot be withheld from those who do not pay for them
    (C) consumers lack information about the benefits of public goods
    (D) consumers do not value public goods highly enough for firms to produce them profitably
    (E) public goods are inherently too important to be left to private firms to produce

    Ⓐ Ⓑ Ⓒ Ⓓ Ⓔ

35. Assume that both input and product markets are competitive. If the product price rises, in the short run firms will increase production by increasing

    (A) the stock of fixed capital until marginal revenue equals the product price
    (B) the stock of fixed capital until the average product of capital equals the price of capital
    (C) labor input until the marginal revenue product of labor equals the wage rate
    (D) labor input until the marginal product of labor equals the wage rate
    (E) labor input until the ratio of product price to the marginal product of labor equals the wage rate

    Ⓐ Ⓑ Ⓒ Ⓓ Ⓔ

36. In which of the following ways does the United States government currently intervene in the working of the market economy?

    I. It produces certain goods and services.
    II. It regulates the private sector in an effort to achieve a more efficient allocation of resources.
    III. It redistributes income through taxation and public expenditures.

    (A) I only
    (B) II only
    (C) III only
    (D) II and III only
    (E) I, II, and III

    Ⓐ Ⓑ Ⓒ Ⓓ Ⓔ

37. If hiring an additional worker would increase a firm's total cost by less than it would increase its total revenue, the firm should

    (A) not hire the worker
    (B) hire the worker
    (C) hire the worker only if another worker leaves or is fired
    (D) hire the worker only if the worker can raise the firm's productivity
    (E) reduce the number of workers employed by the firm

    Ⓐ Ⓑ Ⓒ Ⓓ Ⓔ

38. If a firm wants to produce a given amount of output at the lowest possible cost, it should use resources in such a manner that

    (A) it uses relatively more of the less expensive resource
    (B) it uses relatively more of the resource with the highest marginal product
    (C) each resource has just reached the point of diminishing marginal returns
    (D) the marginal products of each resource are equal
    (E) the marginal products per dollar spent on each resource are equal

    Ⓐ Ⓑ Ⓒ Ⓓ Ⓔ

39. If the firms in an industry pollute the environment and are not charged for the pollution, which of the following is true from the standpoint of the efficient use of resources?

    (A) Too much of the industry's product is produced, and the price of the product is too high.
    (B) Too much of the industry's product is produced, and the price of the product is too low.
    (C) Too little of the industry's product is produced, and the price of the product is too high.
    (D) Too little of the industry's product is produced, and the price of the product is too low.
    (E) The industry is a monopoly.

    Ⓐ Ⓑ Ⓒ Ⓓ Ⓔ

Study Resources

The study resources suggested for preparing for the Principles of Macroeconomics examination cover both microeconomics and macroeconomics and can be used in preparing for the Principles of Microeconomics examination.

Introductory Psychology

Description of the Examination

The Subject Examination in Introductory Psychology covers material that is usually taught in a one-semester undergraduate course in introductory psychology. It stresses basic facts, concepts, and generally accepted principles. Among the topics included on the exam are learning and cognition, behavior, personality, abnormal behavior, perception, motivation and emotion, and developmental and social psychology.

The exam is 90 minutes long and contains approximately 100 multiple-choice questions to be answered in two separately timed 45-minute sections.

Knowledge and Skills Required

Questions on the test require candidates to demonstrate one or more of the followng abilities.

- Knowledge of terminology, principles, and theory

- Comprehension, evaluation, and analysis of problem situations

- Application of knowledge to new situations

The Introductory Psychology examination requires knowledge of the following areas of psychology:

➡ Approximate Percent of Examination

8-9% History, approaches, methods
      History of psychology
      Approaches: biological, behavioral, cognitive, humanistic, psychodynamic
      Research methods: experimental, clinical, correlational
      Ethics in research

8-9% Biological bases of behavior
      Neuroanatomy
      Functional organization of the nervous system
      Endocrine system
      Physiological techniques
      Genetics

	Approximate Percent of Examination

7-8%   Sensation and perception
       Receptor processes: vision, audition
       Sensory mechanisms: thresholds, adaptation
       Other senses: kinesthetic, olfactory, gustatory
       Perceptual development
       Perceptual processes
       Attention

5-6%   States of consciousness
       Sleep and dreaming
       Hypnosis and meditation
       Psychoactive drug effects

10-11%   Learning
       Biological bases
       Classical conditioning
       Operant conditioning
       Cognitive processes in learning

8-9%   Cognition
       Cognitive development
       Memory
       Language
       Thinking and problem solving
       Intelligence and creativity

7-8%   Motivation and emotion
       Biological bases
       Theories of motivation
       Theories of emotion
       Hunger, thirst, sex, pain
       Social motivation

◆   *Approximate Percent of Examination*

8-9%   Developmental psychology

       Theories of development

       Dimensions of development: physical, cognitive, social, moral

       Research methods: longitudinal, cross-sectional

       Heredity-environment issues

       Gender identity and sex roles

7-8%   Personality

       Personality theories and approaches

       Assessment techniques

       Research methods: idiographic, nomothetic

       Self-concept, self-esteem

       Growth and adjustment

8-9%   Abnormal psychology

       Theories of psychopathology

       Anxiety disorders

       Affective disorders

       Dissociative disorders

       Somatoform disorders

       Personality disorders

       Psychoses

7-8%   Treatment of psychological disorders

       Insight therapies: psychodynamic/humanistic approaches

       Behavioral therapies

       Cognitive therapies

       Biological therapies

       Community and preventative approaches

◆   *Approximate Percent of Examination*

7-8%   Social psychology
      Group dynamics
      Attribution processes
      Interpersonal perception
      Conformity, compliance, obedience
      Attitudes and attitude change
      Aggression/Antisocial behavior

3-4%   Statistics, tests, and measurement
      Samples, populations, norms
      Reliability and validity
      Descriptive statistics
      Inferential statistics
      Types of tests
      Theories of intelligence
      Mental retardation

Sample Questions

The 35 questions that follow are similar to questions on the Introductory Psychology examination, but they do not appear on the actual examination.

Before attempting to answer the sample questions, read all the information about the Introductory Psychology examination given above. Additional suggestions for preparing for CLEP examinations are provided in chapter 4.

Try to answer correctly as many questions as possible. Then compare your answers with the correct answers, given in Appendix B.

Directions: Each of the questions or incomplete statements below is followed by five suggested answers or completions. Select the one that is best in each case.

1. A psychologist tests the hypothesis that students from small families are more competitive in their concern about grades than are students from large families. In this study, which of the following are the independent and the dependent variables, respectively?

    (A) Course grades . . competitiveness
    (B) Course grades . . family size
    (C) Competitiveness . . family size
    (D) Competitiveness . . course grades
    (E) Family size . . competitiveness

    Ⓐ Ⓑ Ⓒ Ⓓ Ⓔ

2. One theory of the effects of arousal holds that efficiency of behavior can be described as an inverted U-shaped function of increasing arousal. Which of the following accurately describes this relationship?

    (A) Greater arousal leads to better performance.
    (B) Greater arousal leads to poorer performance.
    (C) Low and high levels of arousal lead to poorest performance.
    (D) Overarousal leads to performance efficiency.
    (E) Underarousal leads to performance efficiency.

    Ⓐ Ⓑ Ⓒ Ⓓ Ⓔ

3. The total number of chromosomes found in a human cell is

    (A) 16
    (B) 20
    (C) 46
    (D) 86
    (E) 102

    Ⓐ Ⓑ Ⓒ Ⓓ Ⓔ

4. Shortly after learning to associate the word "dog" with certain four-legged furry animals, young children will frequently misidentify a cow or a horse as a dog. This phenomenon is best viewed as an example of

    (A) differentiation   (B) negative transfer
       (C) imprinting   (D) stimulus generalization
          (E) linear perspective

    Ⓐ Ⓑ Ⓒ Ⓓ Ⓔ

5. In adults, total sensory deprivation for long periods of time produces

(A) a feeling of well-being similar to that achieved through meditation
(B) no change in emotions or cognition, provided the subject was
    mentally stable before the deprivation
(C) increased efficiency in the senses of sight, hearing, and touch
(D) profound apathy and a subjective sensation of powerlessness
(E) hallucinations and impaired efficiency in all areas of intellectual
    functioning

Ⓐ Ⓑ Ⓒ Ⓓ Ⓔ

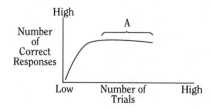

6. The portion of the performance curve above marked A represents

(A) extinction   (B) a plateau   (C) spontaneous recovery
   (D) a serial position effect   (E) response generalization

Ⓐ Ⓑ Ⓒ Ⓓ Ⓔ

7. In which of the following areas does psychological research show
most clearly that girls develop earlier than boys?

(A) Independence from parents
(B) Athletic competence
(C) Intellectual achievement
(D) Physical growth spurt
(E) Self-actualization

Ⓐ Ⓑ Ⓒ Ⓓ Ⓔ

8. Research on the effectiveness of psychotherapy has indicated that

(A) psychotherapists differ among themselves as to the most
    appropriate method of intervention
(B) nondirective techniques are generally superior to directive ones
(C) the effectiveness of a method depends on the length of time a
    therapist was trained in the method
(D) psychoanalysis is the most effective technique for eliminating
    behavior disorders
(E) psychoanalysis is the most effective technique for curing anxiety
    disorders

Ⓐ Ⓑ Ⓒ Ⓓ Ⓔ

9. If on the last day of a psychology class, a student is asked to remember what was done in class each day during the term, she will likely be able to remember best the activities of the first and last class meetings. This situation is an example of

    (A) retroactive inhibition   (B) positive transfer
    (C) the serial position effect   (D) interference
    (E) short-term memory

    Ⓐ Ⓑ Ⓒ Ⓓ Ⓔ

10. When insulted by a friend, Sally's first impulse was to strike him. Instead, she yelled loudly and kicked a door several times. This means of reducing aggressive impulses exemplifies which of the following?

    (A) Repression   (B) Abreaction   (C) Displacement
    (D) Cathexis   (E) Sublimation

    Ⓐ Ⓑ Ⓒ Ⓓ Ⓔ

11. Which of the following parts of the brain is primarily responsible for relaying incoming sensory information to the cerebral cortex?

    (A) Cerebellum   (B) Thalamus   (C) Medulla
    (D) Hypothalamus   (E) Reticular activating system

    Ⓐ Ⓑ Ⓒ Ⓓ Ⓔ

12. A school psychologist informs a ninth-grade teacher that Jimmy "identifies" with his twelfth-grade brother. What the psychologist means is that Jimmy tends to

    (A) feel inferior to his brother
    (B) envy and to be jealous of his brother
    (C) influence the way his brother views the world
    (D) recognize similarities between his brother and himself
    (E) accept his brother's values and to imitate his behavior

    Ⓐ Ⓑ Ⓒ Ⓓ Ⓔ

13. According to Freud, the superego is the portion of the psyche which is

    (A) socialized   (B) hedonistic   (C) narcissistic
    (D) reality-oriented   (E) pleasure-oriented

    Ⓐ Ⓑ Ⓒ Ⓓ Ⓔ

14. Brain waves during REM sleep generally appear as

    (A) alternating high- and low-amplitude waves
    (B) rapid low-amplitude waves
    (C) unevenly paced medium-amplitude waves
    (D) slow low-amplitude waves
    (E) slow high-amplitude waves   Ⓐ Ⓑ Ⓒ Ⓓ Ⓔ

15. Which of the following statements does NOT accurately describe the retina?

    (A) The rods are more dense in the fovea than in the periphery.
    (B) The blind spot is closer to the fovea than to the edge of the retina.
    (C) The image on the retina is upside down.
    (D) It is located at the back of the eye.
    (E) It contains two kinds of receptors: rods and cones.

    Ⓐ Ⓑ Ⓒ Ⓓ Ⓔ

16. Which of the following is a true statement about the relationship between test validity and test reliability?

    (A) A test can be reliable without being valid.
    (B) A test that has high content validity will have high reliability.
    (C) A test that has low content validity will have low reliability.
    (D) The higher the test's validity, the lower its reliability will be.
    (E) The validity of a test always exceeds its reliability.

    Ⓐ Ⓑ Ⓒ Ⓓ Ⓔ

17. Proactive inhibition describes a process by which

    (A) people remember digits better than words
    (B) people remember images better than words
    (C) people remember elements in pairs
    (D) prior learning interferes with subsequent learning
    (E) subsequent learning interferes with prior learning

    Ⓐ Ⓑ Ⓒ Ⓓ Ⓔ

18. Checking the coin return every time one passes a pay telephone or a vending machine is a type of behavior probably being maintained by which of the following schedules of reinforcement?

    (A) Fixed interval only
    (B) Fixed ratio only
    (C) Variable ratio only
    (D) Variable interval and fixed ratio
    (E) Fixed interval and variable ratio   Ⓐ Ⓑ Ⓒ Ⓓ Ⓔ

19. Which of the following is the most common form of psychological disorder?

    (A) Psychotic   (B) Somatoform   (C) Dissociative
       (D) Psychosexual   (E) Mood

    (A) (B) (C) (D) (E)

20. In an approach-avoidance conflict, as the person nears the goal, the levels of attraction and aversion change in which of the following ways?

    (A) Both increase.
    (B) Both decrease.
    (C) Attraction increases and aversion decreases.
    (D) Attraction decreases and aversion increases.
    (E) Both are extinguished.

    (A) (B) (C) (D) (E)

21. Which of the following kinds of therapy attempts to correct irrational beliefs that lead to psychological distress?

    (A) Behavioral   (B) Cognitive   (C) Existential
       (D) Gestalt   (E) Psychoanalytic

    (A) (B) (C) (D) (E)

22. "Give me a dozen healthy infants, well-formed, and my own specified world to bring them up in and I'll guarantee to take any one at random and train him to become any type of specialist I might select . . ."

    This statement was made by

    (A) James   (B) Thorndike   (C) Watson
       (D) Wertheimer   (E) Woodworth

    (A) (B) (C) (D) (E)

23. Similarity, proximity, and familiarity are important determinants of

    (A) observational learning
    (B) friendship formation
    (C) sexual orientation
    (D) aggression
    (E) imprinting

    (A) (B) (C) (D) (E)

24. A diagnosis of schizophrenia typically includes which of the following symptoms?

   (A) Delusions   (B) Panic attacks   (C) Hypochondriasis
      (D) Multiple personality   (E) Psychosexual dysfunction

   Ⓐ Ⓑ Ⓒ Ⓓ Ⓔ

25. A young child breaks her cookie into a number of pieces and asserts that "now there is more to eat." In Piaget's analysis, the child's behavior is evidence of

   (A) formal logical operations
   (B) concrete logical operations
   (C) conservation
   (D) preoperational thought
   (E) sensorimotor analysis

   Ⓐ Ⓑ Ⓒ Ⓓ Ⓔ

26. Carl G. Jung is associated with which of the following concepts?

   (A) Inferiority complex
   (B) Need for achievement
   (C) Collective unconscious
   (D) Self-esteem
   (E) Self-actualization

   Ⓐ Ⓑ Ⓒ Ⓓ Ⓔ

27. Which of the following types of research design is most appropriate for establishing a cause-and-effect relation between two variables?

   (A) Between subjects   (B) Within subjects   (C) Quantitative
      (D) Experimental   (E) Naturalistic

   Ⓐ Ⓑ Ⓒ Ⓓ Ⓔ

28. A neuron is said to be "polarized" when

   (A) it is in the refractory period
   (B) it is in a resting state
   (C) it responds to a strong stimulus
   (D) the synaptic terminals release chemicals into the synaptic gap
   (E) chemicals outside the cell body cross the cell membrane

   Ⓐ Ⓑ Ⓒ Ⓓ Ⓔ

29. Making the amount of time a child can spend playing video games contingent on the amount of time the child spends practicing the piano is an illustration of

    (A) Bentham's adaptive hedonism principle
    (B) Locke's law of association
    (C) aversive conditioning
    (D) classical conditioning
    (E) operant conditioning   Ⓐ Ⓑ Ⓒ Ⓓ Ⓔ

30. Which of the following has been identified as correlating most closely with heart disease?

    (A) Anxiety   (B) Physical overexertion   (C) Guilt
    (D) Muscle tension   (E) Hostility   Ⓐ Ⓑ Ⓒ Ⓓ Ⓔ

31. The term "etiology" refers to the study of which of the following aspects of an illness?

    (A) Origins and causes
    (B) Characteristic symptoms
    (C) Expected outcome following treatment
    (D) Frequency of occurrence
    (E) Level of contagiousness   Ⓐ Ⓑ Ⓒ Ⓓ Ⓔ

32. Erikson's and Freud's theories of personality development are most similar in that they both

    (A) emphasize the libido
    (B) focus on adult development
    (C) discount the importance of culture
    (D) are based on stages
    (E) view behavior as a continuum   Ⓐ Ⓑ Ⓒ Ⓓ Ⓔ

33. Higher-level cognitive processes, such as decision-making, and lower-level perceptual processes, such as color discrimination, respectively, involve primarily

    (A) features analysis and top-down processing
    (B) perceptual set and expectancy
    (C) bottom-up processing and expectancy
    (D) bottom-up processing and top-down processing
    (E) top-down processing and bottom-up processing

                                           Ⓐ Ⓑ Ⓒ Ⓓ Ⓔ

34. Developmental psychologists would most likely prefer longitudinal research designs to cross-sectional research designs because longitudinal designs

    (A) usually yield results much more quickly
    (B) offer the advantage of between-subjects comparisons
    (C) are much less likely to be influenced by cultural changes that occur over time
    (D) utilize the subjects as their own experimental controls
    (E) are more valid

    Ⓐ Ⓑ Ⓒ Ⓓ Ⓔ

35. An individual undergoing psychotherapy shows improvement due only to that person's belief in the therapy and not because of the therapy itself. This result illustrates a

    (A) transference effect
    (B) placebo effect
    (C) cathectic effect
    (D) primary gain
    (E) conditioned response

    Ⓐ Ⓑ Ⓒ Ⓓ Ⓔ

Study Resources

The following is a list of the textbooks most widely assigned in introductory psychology courses at CLEP-user institutions. To prepare for the Introductory Psychology examination, you should study the contents of at least one such textbook. Although most texts cover the topics listed in the test content outline, they may vary somewhat in content, approach, and emphasis. You are therefore advised to consult more than one textbook on the major topics.

You will find it helpful to supplement your reading with books listed in the bibliographies found in most psychology textbooks. Additional suggestions for preparing for CLEP examinations are given in chapter 4.

Many libraries do not carry textbooks as a policy. If you can't find any of the following textbooks at the library, see whether the college bookstore has a used copy. If you can't locate the most recent edition, an edition that is one or two years older will suffice for most subject areas. As a final option, purchase a new copy of the suggested textbook as an investment in your education.

TEXTBOOKS

Atkinson, Rita L., Richard C. Atkinson, Edwin E. Smith, and Darly J. Bem, *Introduction to Psychology,* 10th ed. San Diego: Harcourt Brace Jovanovich, 1990.

Coon, Dennis, *Introduction to Psychology: Exploration and Application,* 6th ed. St. Paul, MN: West, 1992.

Gerow, Joshua R., Thomas Brothen, and Jerry D. Newell, *Fundamentals of Psychology.* Glenview, IL: Scott, Foresman, 1989.

Gleitman, Henry, *Psychology,* 3rd ed. New York: W. W. Norton, 1991.

Myers, David G., *Psychology,* 3rd ed. New York: Worth, 1992.

Rathus, Spencer A., *Psychology,* 4th ed. New York: Holt, Rinehart & Winston, 1989.

Weiten, Wayne, *Psychology: Themes and Variations,* 2nd ed. Pacific Grove, CA: Brooks/Cole, 1992.

Wortman, Camille B., Elizabeth F. Loftus, and Mary E. Marshall, *Psychology,* 4th ed. New York: Alfred A. Knopf, 1992.

Zimbardo, Philip G., *Psychology and Life,* 13th ed. Glenview, IL: Scott, Foresman, 1992.

Introductory Sociology

Description of the Examination

The Subject Examination in Introductory Sociology covers material that is usually taught in a one-term introductory sociology course at most colleges and universities. Exam questions deal with social institutions; stratification; social patterns, processes, and changes; and the sociological perspective. The examination emphasizes basic facts and concepts as well as general theoretical approaches used by sociologists. Highly specialized knowledge of the subject and methodology of the discipline is not included.

The examination is composed of approximately 100 multiple-choice questions to be answered in two separately timed 45-minute sections.

Knowledge and Skills Required

Questions on the exam require candidates to demonstrate one or more of the following abilities.

- Identification of specific names, facts, and concepts from sociological literature

- Understanding of relationships between concepts, empirical generalizations, and theoretical propositions of sociology

- Understanding of the methods by which sociological relationships are established

- Application of concepts, propositions, and methods to hypothetical situations

- Interpretation of tables and charts

The subject matter of the Introductory Sociology examination is drawn from the following topics.

↞	*Approximate Percent of Examination*

20% Institutions
    Family
    Economic
    Political
    Educational
    Religious

30% Social stratification (process and structure)
    Social mobility
    Social class
    Power and social inequality
    Professions and occupations
    Race and ethnic relations
    Gender roles

15% Social patterns
    Community
    Demography
    Human ecology
    Rural-urban patterns

20% Social processes
    Roles
    Groups
    Aggregates
    Deviance and social control
    Social change
    Collective behavior
    Socialization
    Culture

15% The sociological perspective
    History of sociology
    Methods and measurement
    Sociological theory

Sample Questions

The 20 sample questions that follow are similar to questions on the Introductory Sociology examination, but they do not actually appear on the exam.

Before attempting to answer the sample questions, read all the information about the Introductory Sociology examination given above. Additional suggestions for preparing for CLEP examinations are provided in chapter 4.

Try to answer correctly as many questions as possible. Then compare your answers with the correct answers, given in Appendix B.

Directions: Each of the questions or incomplete statements below is followed by five suggested answers or completions. Select the one that is best in each case.

1. All of the following are examples of voluntary associations EXCEPT the

   (A) Republican party
   (B) League of Women Voters
   (C) Federal Bureau of Investigation
   (D) Veterans of Foreign Wars
   (E) Knights of Columbus

   Ⓐ Ⓑ Ⓒ Ⓓ Ⓔ

2. A sex ratio of 120 means that there are

   (A) 120 more males in a population than females
   (B) 120 more females in a population than males
   (C) 120 males for every 100 females in a population
   (D) 120 females for every 100 males in a population
   (E) 12% more men than women in a population

   Ⓐ Ⓑ Ⓒ Ⓓ Ⓔ

3. Industrialization is most likely to reduce the importance of which of the following functions of the family?

   (A) Economic production
   (B) Care of young children
   (C) Fulfillment of sexual needs
   (D) Socialization of the individual
   (E) Social control

   Ⓐ Ⓑ Ⓒ Ⓓ Ⓔ

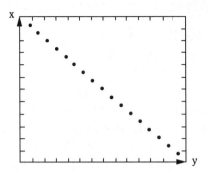

4. Which of the following best describes the relationship between x and y on the scattergram above?

(A) A perfect positive correlation
(B) A perfect negative correlation
(C) A perfect curvilinear correlation
(D) A low negative correlation
(E) A correlation of zero

Ⓐ Ⓑ Ⓒ Ⓓ Ⓔ

5. The process by which an individual learns how to live in his or her social surroundings is known as

(A) amalgamation   (B) association
   (C) collective behavior   (D) socialization
      (E) innovation

Ⓐ Ⓑ Ⓒ Ⓓ Ⓔ

6. Which of the following may properly be considered norms?

   I. Laws
  II. Folkways
 III. Mores

(A) I only   (B) III only   (C) I and II only
   (D) II and III only   (E) I, II, and III

Ⓐ Ⓑ Ⓒ Ⓓ Ⓔ

7. Which of the following theorists argued that class conflict was inevitable in a capitalistic society and would result in revolution?

(A) C. Wright Mills   (B) Karl Marx
   (C) Émile Durkheim   (D) Alva Myrdal
      (E) Karl Mannheim

Ⓐ Ⓑ Ⓒ Ⓓ Ⓔ

8. Which of the following relies most heavily on sampling methods?

    (A) Small group experiment
    (B) Case study
    (C) Participant observation
    (D) Survey
    (E) Laboratory experiment   Ⓐ Ⓑ Ⓒ Ⓓ Ⓔ

9. Humans can be found in many physical environments on the Earth's surface, and the basis for this adaptation is

    (A) instinct (B) heredity (C) culture
       (D) stratification (E) ethnocentrism   Ⓐ Ⓑ Ⓒ Ⓓ Ⓔ

10. According to Émile Durkheim, a society that lacks clear-cut norms to govern aspirations and moral conduct is characterized by

    (A) rationalism (B altruism (C) egoism
       (D) secularism (E) anomie   Ⓐ Ⓑ Ⓒ Ⓓ Ⓔ

11. The process by which an immigrant or an ethnic minority is absorbed socially into a receiving society is called

    (A) assimilation (B) accommodation
       (C) cooperation (D) interaction
          (E) equilibrium   Ⓐ Ⓑ Ⓒ Ⓓ Ⓔ

12. Which of the following characteristics is unique to human societies?

    (A) A normative order   (B) Territorial boundaries
       (C) Sustained interaction   (D) A division of labor
          (E) Group autonomy   Ⓐ Ⓑ Ⓒ Ⓓ Ⓔ

13. Demographic patterns have clearly demonstrated that more males than females are born in

    (A) technologically developing countries only
    (B) technologically developed countries only
    (C) virtually every known human society
    (D) highly urbanized developing countries only
    (E) countries with high nutritional standards only

                                     Ⓐ Ⓑ Ⓒ Ⓓ Ⓔ

14. Which of the following correctly lists Max Weber's three dimensions of social stratification?

    (A) Class, politics, education
    (B) Prestige, politics, occupation
    (C) Residence, occupation, religion
    (D) Status, class, party
    (E) Status, religion, prestige   Ⓐ Ⓑ Ⓒ Ⓓ Ⓔ

15. In order for an occupation to be considered a profession by a sociologist, it must be an occupation that

    (A) requires knowledge of a body of specialized information with a theoretical foundation
    (B) has high public visibility in the community
    (C) requires training from a specialized school rather than from a university
    (D) serves government and industry as well as individuals
    (E) is a full-time position paying a regular salary

       Ⓐ Ⓑ Ⓒ Ⓓ Ⓔ

16. In the study of social class, the sociologist would be LEAST likely to focus on problems of

    (A) power   (B) social mobility   (C) style of life
       (D) motivation   (E) occupational status

       Ⓐ Ⓑ Ⓒ Ⓓ Ⓔ

17. An example of a folkway in American society is

    (A) joining a religious cult
    (B) eating a sandwich for lunch
    (C) not paying income taxes on time
    (D) stopping for a red light
    (E) being fined for jaywalking   Ⓐ Ⓑ Ⓒ Ⓓ Ⓔ

18. Malthus' prediction that food production could not keep pace with the growth of population is based in part on which of the following propositions?

    (A) The law of large numbers
    (B) The law of diminishing returns
    (C) Economies of scale
    (D) The fallacy of composition
    (E) Constant costs   Ⓐ Ⓑ Ⓒ Ⓓ Ⓔ

19. Personality formation and the learning of social roles take place

    (A) only in childhood
    (B) mainly in adolescence
    (C) mainly in early adulthood
    (D) through the productive years only
    (E) throughout the life cycle   Ⓐ Ⓑ Ⓒ Ⓓ Ⓔ

20. According to the United States Bureau of the Census, the fastest
    growing household type in 1980 was the

    (A) traditional nuclear family   (B) extended family
       (C) single person   (D) couple without children
          (E) family with three or more children   Ⓐ Ⓑ Ⓒ Ⓓ Ⓔ

Study Resources

The following list provides the names of several sociology textbooks and
some supplementary readings. The textbooks will help you understand
the perspective and content of an introductory sociology course at the
college level. You should read two or three of these or similar books
because authors tend to emphasize different areas. The supplementary
reading list consists of books that provide in-depth discussions of
sociological topics for those desiring a better understanding of a
particular issue, theory, or concept.

As you read, take notes that address the following issues, which are
fundamental to most questions that appear on the test.

- What is society? What is culture? What is common to all societies, and
  what is characteristic of American society?

- What are other basic concepts in sociology that help to describe
  human nature, human interaction, and the collective behavior of
  groups, organizations, institutions, and societies?

- What methods do sociologists use to study, describe, analyze, and
  observe human behavior?

Additional suggestions for preparing for CLEP examinations are provided
in chapter 4.

Many libraries do not carry textbooks as a policy. If you can't find any
of the following textbooks at the library, see whether the college bookstore
has a used copy. If you can't locate the most recent edition, an edition
that is one or two years older will suffice for most subject areas. As a final
option, purchase a new copy of the suggested textbook as an investment
in your education.

TEXTBOOKS

Conklin, John E., *Sociology: An Introduction,* 2nd ed. New York:
   Macmillan, 1987.

Johnson, Allan G., *Human Arrangements: An Introduction to Sociology,*
   2nd ed. San Diego: Harcourt Brace Jovanovich, 1989.

Lenski, Gerhard E., Jean Lenski, and Patrick Nolan, *Human Societies: An
   Introduction to Macrosociology,* 6th ed. New York: McGraw-Hill, 1991.

Robertson, Ian, *Sociology,* 3rd ed. New York: Worth, 1987.

SUPPLEMENTARY READINGS

Cargan, Leonard and Jeanne Ballantine, *Sociological Footprints:
   Introductory Readings in Sociology,* 5th ed. Belmont, CA: Wadsworth,
   1991.

Henslin, James M., ed., *Down to Earth Sociology: Introductory Readings,*
   6th ed. New York: Free Press, 1991.

Both books are collections of previously published essays and articles
dealing with the major areas of sociological inquiry.

Western Civilization I: Ancient Near East to 1648

Description of the Examination

The Subject Examination in Western Civilization I: Ancient Near East to 1648 tests subject matter that is usually covered in the first semester of a two-semester course in Western Civilization. Questions deal with the civilizations of the Ancient Near East, Greece, and Rome; the Middle Ages; the Renaissance and Reformation; and early modern Europe. Candidates may be asked to choose the correct definition of a historical term, select the historical figure whose political viewpoint is described, identify the correct relationship between two historical factors, or detect the inaccurate pairing of an individual with a historical event. Groups of questions may require candidates to interpret, evaluate, or relate the contents of a passage, a map, a picture, or a cartoon to other information, or to analyze and utilize the data contained in a graph or table.

The examination is 90 minutes long and contains approximately 120 multiple-choice questions to be answered in two separately timed 45-minute sections.

Knowledge and Skills Required

Questions on the examination require candidates to demonstrate one or more of the following abilities.

- Understanding of important factual knowledge of developments in Western Civilization (about 25-35 percent of the examination)

- Ability to identify the causes and effects of major historical events (about 5-15 percent of the examination)

- Ability to analyze, interpret, and evaluate textual and graphic materials (about 20-30 percent of the examination)

- Ability to distinguish the relevant from the irrelevant (about 15-25 percent of the examination)

- Ability to reach conclusions on the basis of facts (about 10-20 percent of the examination)

The subject matter of the Western Civilization I examination is drawn from the following topics.

➤	*Approximate Percent of Examination*

8-11%   Ancient Near East

     Political evolution

     Religion, culture, and technical developments in Egypt, Mesopotamia, Palestine

15-17%   Ancient Greece and Hellenistic Civilization

     Political evolution to Periclean Athens

     Periclean Athens to Peloponnesian Wars

     Culture, religion, and thought of Ancient Greece

     The Hellenistic political structure

     The culture, religion, and thought of Hellenistic Greece

15-17%   Ancient Rome

     Political evolution of the Republic and of the Empire (economic and geographical context)

     Roman thought and culture

     Early Christianity

     The Germanic invasions

     The decline of Rome

23-27%   Medieval History

     Early medieval politics and culture through Charlemagne

     Feudal and manorial institutions

     The medieval Church

     Medieval thought and culture

     Rise of the towns and changing economic forms

     Feudal monarchies

     The decline of the Church

13-17%   Renaissance and Reformation

     The Renaissance in Italy

     The Renaissance outside Italy

     The New Monarchies

     Protestantism and Catholicism reformed and reorganized

◆ *Approximate Percent of Examination*

10-15%   Early Modern Europe, 1560-1648
        The opening of the Atlantic
        The Commercial Revolution
        Dynastic and religious conflicts
        Thought and culture

Sample Questions

The 25 sample questions that follow are similar to questions on the Western Civilization I examination, but they do not actually appear on the examination.

Before attempting to answer the sample questions, read all the information about the Western Civilization I examination on the preceding pages. Additional suggestions for preparing for CLEP examinations are provided in chapter 4.

Try to answer correctly as many questions as possible. Then compare your answers with the correct answers, given in Appendix B.

Directions: Each of the questions or incomplete statements below is followed by five suggested answers or completions. Select the one that is best in each case.

1. The earliest urban settlements arose in which of the following types of areas?

    (A) Coastal plains   (B) Inland deforested plains
      (C) Desert oases   (D) Fertile river valleys
        (E) Narrow valleys well protected by mountains

    Ⓐ Ⓑ Ⓒ Ⓓ Ⓔ

2. "The great wealth of the palaces and the widespread prosperity of the land were due to the profits of trade, protected or exploited by naval vessels equipped with rams. The palaces and towns were unfortified, and peaceful scenes predominated in the frescoes, which revealed a love of dancing, boxing, and a sport in which boys and girls somersaulted over the backs of charging bulls."

    The culture described above was that of the ancient

    (A) Minoans   (B) Hittites   (C) Macedonians
      (D) Assyrians   (E) Persians

    Ⓐ Ⓑ Ⓒ Ⓓ Ⓔ

3. "These people maintained their skill as seafarers, traders, and artists. They planted Carthage and other colonies in the western Mediterranean. They developed a new script in which a separate sign stood not for a syllable, but for a consonant or vowel sound."

The people described above were the

(A) Phoenicians
(B) Hittites
(C) Assyrians
(D) Mycenaeans
(E) Philistines

Ⓐ Ⓑ Ⓒ Ⓓ Ⓔ

4. Pharaoh Akhenaton of Egypt (c. 1375-1358 B.C.) is best known today for

(A) building the largest pyramid in the Valley of the Kings
(B) conquering large expanses of territory outside of the Nile Valley
(C) developing a monotheistic religion
(D) uniting upper and lower Egypt under a single administrative system
(E) writing down the first code of Egyptian law

Ⓐ Ⓑ Ⓒ Ⓓ Ⓔ

5. Among the ancient Hebrews, a prophet was

(A) a teacher who expounded the Scriptures
(B) a king with hereditary but limited powers
(C) a judge who administered traditional law
(D) a priest with exclusive rights to perform functions at the temple
(E) an individual who was inspired by God to speak to the people

Ⓐ Ⓑ Ⓒ Ⓓ Ⓔ

6. The outstanding achievement of King Hammurabi of Mesopotamia was that he

(A) issued a more comprehensive law code than had any known predecessor
(B) conquered and established dominion over all of Egypt
(C) built the hanging gardens of Babylon
(D) established the first democratic government
(E) successfully defended his kingdom against the Assyrians

Ⓐ Ⓑ Ⓒ Ⓓ Ⓔ

7. Of the following, which helps explain why the Roman Republic gave way to dictatorship during the first century B.C.?

    (A) The government that was suitable for a small city-state failed to meet the needs of an empire.
    (B) A strong leader was needed because the upper classes feared a rebellion on the part of the slave population.
    (C) Outside pressures on boundaries could not be resisted by republican armies.
    (D) Rome's period of expansion was over.
    (E) The Roman senatorial class was declining in number.

    Ⓐ Ⓑ Ⓒ Ⓓ Ⓔ

8. All of the following were emphasized by the early Christian church EXCEPT a

    (A) ritual fellowship meal in memory of Christ
    (B) toleration of other religious sects
    (C) belief in the value of the souls of women and slaves as well as those of free men
    (D) belief in life after death for all believers in Christ
    (E) belief in the value of martyrdom, defined as dying for the faith

    Ⓐ Ⓑ Ⓒ Ⓓ Ⓔ

9. All of the following invaded the Roman Empire EXCEPT the

    (A) Vikings
    (B) Ostrogoths
    (C) Visigoths
    (D) Vandals
    (E) Huns

    Ⓐ Ⓑ Ⓒ Ⓓ Ⓔ

10. The craft guilds of the Middle Ages had as their primary purpose the

    (A) promotion of trade and the protection of merchants
    (B) control of town government
    (C) regulation of production and quality
    (D) guardianship of the social and financial affairs of their members
    (E) accumulation of capital and the lending of money

    Ⓐ Ⓑ Ⓒ Ⓓ Ⓔ

11. The orders of Franciscan and Dominican friars founded in the thirteenth century differed from earlier monastic orders principally in that the friars

    (A) took vows of poverty, chastity, and obedience
    (B) broke away from the control of the pope
    (C) introduced the ideas of Plato and other early Greek philosophers into their teaching
    (D) devoted themselves mainly to copying ancient manuscripts
    (E) traveled among the people instead of living in monasteries

    Ⓐ Ⓑ Ⓒ Ⓓ Ⓔ

12. All of the following factors played a part in bringing about the Hundred Years' War EXCEPT:

    (A) The English king had lands in Gascony.
    (B) A French princess was the mother of an English king.
    (C) Flemish towns were dependent on England for raw wool.
    (D) The Holy Roman Emperor wanted to bring pressure on the Swiss cantons.
    (E) The Capetian dynasty had come to an end.

    Ⓐ Ⓑ Ⓒ Ⓓ Ⓔ

13. Civil peace and personal security were enjoyed to a greater degree in Norman England than in continental Europe principally because the Norman kings

    (A) maintained a large standing army
    (B) claimed the direct allegiance of the mass of the peasantry
    (C) avoided conflicts with the Church
    (D) kept their vassals occupied with continental conflicts
    (E) developed a centralized and efficient type of feudalism

    Ⓐ Ⓑ Ⓒ Ⓓ Ⓔ

14. Which of the following could have been made immediately available to the reading public in large quantities as soon as it was written?

    (A) *On Christian Liberty*, Martin Luther
    (B) *Travels*, Marco Polo
    (C) *The Divine Comedy*, Dante Alighieri
    (D) *Canterbury Tales*, Geoffrey Chaucer
    (E) English translation of the Bible, John Wycliffe

    Ⓐ Ⓑ Ⓒ Ⓓ Ⓔ

15. A central feature of the Catholic Reformation was the

   (A) Roman Catholic church's inability to correct abuses
   (B) establishment of new religious orders such as the Jesuits
   (C) transfer of authority from Rome to the bishoprics
   (D) rejection of Baroque art
   (E) toleration of Protestants in Roman Catholic countries

   Ⓐ Ⓑ Ⓒ Ⓓ Ⓔ

16. A sixteenth-century traveler would have been most likely to encounter the type of architecture shown above in which of the following European countries?

   (A) Spain
   (B) France
   (C) Germany
   (D) England
   (E) Sweden

   Ⓐ Ⓑ Ⓒ Ⓓ Ⓔ

17. The major and most immediate social consequence of the rise of towns in the eleventh and twelfth centuries was

   (A) a lessening of the distinction among social classes
   (B) the concept of the prosperous caring for the indigent
   (C) the decline of royal authority
   (D) a new social class enriched by manufacturing and trade
   (E) the decline in the social status of the lesser clergy

   Ⓐ Ⓑ Ⓒ Ⓓ Ⓔ

18. In *The Prince*, Machiavelli asserted that

    (A) historical examples are useless for understanding political behavior
    (B) the intelligent prince should keep his state neutral in the event of war
    (C) people are not trustworthy and cannot be relied on in time of need
    (D) the prince should be guided by the ethical principles of Christianity
    (E) luck is of no consequence in the success or failure of princes

    Ⓐ Ⓑ Ⓒ Ⓓ Ⓔ

19. On which of the following issues did Luther and Calvin DISAGREE?

    (A) Toleration for minority viewpoints
    (B) Relationship of the church to civil authority
    (C) The authority of the Scriptures
    (D) The existence of the Trinity
    (E) The retention of the sacrament of baptism

    Ⓐ Ⓑ Ⓒ Ⓓ Ⓔ

20. Between 1629 and 1639, Charles I of England tried to obtain revenues by all of the following means EXCEPT

    (A) the levying of ship money
    (B) income from crown lands
    (C) forced loans
    (D) the sale of monopolies
    (E) grants from Parliament

    Ⓐ Ⓑ Ⓒ Ⓓ Ⓔ

21. All of the following are associated with the commercial revolution in early modern Europe EXCEPT

    (A) an increase in the number of entrepreneurial capitalists
    (B) the appearance of state-run trading companies
    (C) a large influx of precious metals into Europe
    (D) an expansion of the guild system
    (E) a "golden age" for the Netherlands

    Ⓐ Ⓑ Ⓒ Ⓓ Ⓔ

22. Castiglione's *Book of the Courtier* (1528) was intended as

    (A) a collection of entertaining travel stories
    (B) a guide to the military affairs of the Italian peninsula
    (C) a collection of meditations and spiritual reflections
    (D) a guide to refined behavior and etiquette
    (E) an allegory of courtly love

    Ⓐ Ⓑ Ⓒ Ⓓ Ⓔ

23. Which of the following resulted from the defeat of the Spanish Armada in 1588?

    (A) Spanish domination of the Mediterranean was ended.
    (B) The invasion of England was prevented.
    (C) Dutch sympathies for the Spanish cause increased.
    (D) War broke out between England and France.
    (E) There was a series of uprisings in the Spanish colonies of Central and South America.

    Ⓐ Ⓑ Ⓒ Ⓓ Ⓔ

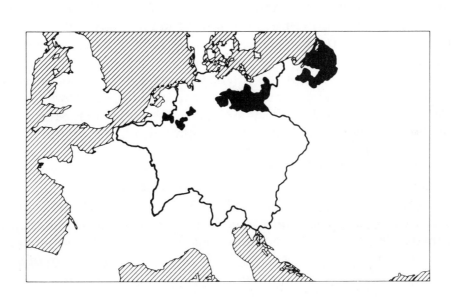

24. In the mid-seventeenth century, the area shaded black on the map above belonged to

    (A) Russia
    (B) Poland
    (C) Sweden
    (D) Austria
    (E) Brandenburg-Prussia

    Ⓐ Ⓑ Ⓒ Ⓓ Ⓔ

25. The theory concerning the solar system that was published by Copernicus in 1543 <u>denied</u> the popular belief that the

    (A) Earth revolves around the Sun
    (B) Earth revolves around the Moon
    (C) Earth is the center of the universe
    (D) Sun is the center of the universe
    (E) stars revolve around the Sun

    Ⓐ Ⓑ Ⓒ Ⓓ Ⓔ

Study Resources

To prepare for the Western Civilization I: Ancient Near East to 1648 and Western Civilization II: 1648 to the Present examinations, you should study the appropriate chapters in at least one college textbook in this subject. The books listed here cover the historical periods from the Ancient Near East to the Present and can, therefore, be used in preparing for either or both of the examinations. Most Western Civilization textbooks cover approximately the same chronological span, but the material they emphasize differs. The following are among the more widely used texts, though there are others that are equally good. Because texts are frequently revised, editions and publication dates are not given. It is recommended that you use the most recent edition of a text whenever possible.

You will find it helpful to supplement your reading with books listed in the bibliographies found in most history textbooks. In addition, contemporary novels and plays, as well as works by Homer, Shakespeare, and Dickens, provide rich sources of information. Classic works of nonfiction are equally valuable; for example, Machiavelli's *The Prince*, Mill's *On Liberty*, and Paine's *The Rights of Man*. Books of documents are an excellent source for sampling primary materials; *A Documentary History of Modern Europe*, edited by T. G. Barnes and G. D. Feldman (Little, Brown), is one such collection. Actual works of art in museums can bring to life not only the reproductions found in books but history itself, while films such as *A Man for All Seasons* and *The Return of Martin Guerre* and television series such as "Civilisation," "I, Claudius," "Elizabeth R," and the "Ascent of Man" provide enjoyable reinforcement to what is learned through reading.

Additional suggestions for preparing for CLEP examinations appear in chapter 4.

Many libraries do not carry textbooks as a policy. If you can't find any of the following textbooks at the library, see whether the college bookstore has a used copy or purchase a new copy as an investment in your education.

TEXTBOOKS

Chambers, Mortimer et al., *The Western Experience*, 3 vols. New York: McGraw-Hill. (This text is especially strong in its emphasis on social history. It includes maps, charts, recommended readings, illustrations, and art essays.)

Chodorow, Stanley et al., *The Mainstream of Civilization.* San Diego: Harcourt Brace Jovanovich. (A standard text that seeks to understand the basic characteristics of each civilization in history. It emphasizes a sense of each period through a study of the interrelations of politics, economics, art, and religion. Maps, illustrations, recommended readings, and excerpts from documents are included.)

Clough, Shepard B. et al., *European History in a World Perspective*, 3 vols. Lexington, MA: D. C. Heath. (A thorough history that looks at Western civilization and European history, in particular, from within and without. It contains maps, tables, illustrations, and suggested readings for both the beginning and the advanced student.)

Kagan, Donald et al., *The Western Heritage*, 2 vols. New York: Macmillan. (A standard text that presents an overview of Western civilization. It includes illustrations, maps, suggested readings, and excerpts from documents.)

Lerner, Robert E. et al., *Western Civilizations: Their History and Their Culture*, 2 vols. New York: W. W. Norton. (A comprehensive work, rich in detail, with many illustrations, maps, tables, and charts, and a well-rounded list of recommended readings.)

McKay, John P. et al., A *History of Western Society.* Boston: Houghton Mifflin. (A text that is particularly strong on social and cultural history and in relating historical episodes to what came before and what came after. The text reflects new areas of interest and discovery within the historical profession. Important questions are raised and answered in each chapter. Illustrations, recommended readings, maps, and quotations from primary sources are included.)

Palmer, Robert R. and Joel Colton, A *History of the Modern World, 2* vols. New York: McGraw-Hill. (A readable text that offers only summary information on Western civilization prior to the Middle Ages but is especially strong and thorough on periods after that. It includes maps, illustrations, picture essays, and a bibliography.)

Wallbank, T. Walter et al., *Civilization Past and Present,* 5 vols. New York: HarperCollins. (A text that emphasizes the interaction of world cultures. It has a global perspective and includes considerable material on non-Western peoples.)

Winks, Robin et al., *A History of Civilization,* 3 vols. Englewood Cliffs, NJ: Prentice Hall. (A standard text that has been revised over the years to incorporate recent historical approaches. It contains maps, illustrations, and lists of recommended readings, including historical fiction.)

Western Civilization II: 1648 to the Present

Description of the Examination

The Subject Examination in Western Civilization II: 1648 to the Present covers material that is usually taught in the second semester of a two-semester course in Western Civilization. Questions cover European history from the seventeenth century through the post-Second World War period including political, economic, and cultural developments such as Scientific Thought, the Enlightenment, the French and Industrial Revolutions, Nationalism, Imperialism, the Russian Revolution, and the First and Second World Wars. Candidates may be asked to choose the correct definition of a historical term, select the historical figure whose political viewpoint is described, identify the correct relationship between two historical factors, or detect the inaccurate pairing of an individual with a historical event. Groups of questions may require candidates to interpret, evaluate, or relate the contents of a passage, a map, a picture, or a cartoon to other information or to analyze and use the data contained in a graph or table.

The examination is 90 minutes long and includes approximately 120 questions to be answered in two separately timed 45-minute sections.

Knowledge and Skills Required

Questions on the examination require candidates to demonstrate one or more of the following abilities.

- Understanding of important factual knowledge of developments in Western Civilization (about 25-35 percent of the examination)

- Ability to identify the causes and effects of major historical events (about 5-15 percent of the examination)

- Ability to analyze, interpret, and evaluate textual and graphic materials (about 20-30 percent of the examination)

- Ability to distinguish the relevant from the irrelevant (about 15-25 percent of the examination)

- Ability to reach conclusions on the basis of facts (about 10-20 percent of the examination)

The subject matter of the Western Civilization II examination is drawn from the following topics.

➡ *Approximate Percent of Examination*

7-9%   Absolutism and Constitutionalism, 1648-1715
      The Dutch Republic
      The English Revolution
      The France of Louis XIV
      Formation of Austria and Prussia
      The "westernization" of Russia

4-6%   Competition for empire and economic expansion
      Global economy of the eighteenth century
      Western Europe after Utrecht 1713-1740
      Economic and demographic change in the eighteenth
        century

5-7%   The scientific view of the world
      Bacon, Descartes, and Newton
      New knowledge about the individual and society
      Political theory

7-9%   Enlightenment and enlightened despotism
      The Philosophes
      Enlightened despotism
      Partitions of Poland
      The British Reform Movement

10-12%   The French Revolution and Napoleonic Europe
      The Revolution of 1789
      The Revolution and Europe
      The Terror
      The Constitutional Republic
      The Consulate
      The French Empire
      The continental system
      The overthrow of Napoleon

Approximate Percent of Examination

7-9%   The Industrial Revolution
      Causes of the Industrial Revolution
      Impact of industrialization on the working and middle classes
      The advent of the "isms"

6-8%   Political developments, 1815-1848
      Conservative politics
      Liberalism
      Nationalism
      The Revolutions of 1830 and 1848

8-10% Politics and diplomacy in the Age of Nationalism, 1850-1914
      The Second French Empire, 1852-1870
      The unification of Italy
      The founding of the German Empire
      Austria-Hungary
      Russia
      The Third French Republic
      Socialism and labor unions
      Waning of classical liberalism
      European diplomacy, 1871-1900

7-9%   Economy, culture, and imperialism, 1850-1914
      Demography
      World economy of the nineteenth century
      Technological developments
      Science, philosophy, and the arts
      Imperialism in Africa and Asia
      The Russo-Japanese War
      The Balkan Wars

10-12%   The First World War, the Russian Revolution, and postwar
Europe, 1914-1924
    The causes of the First World War
    The economic and social impact of the war
    The Peace of Paris, 1919
    The Revolution of 1917
    The impact of the Russian Revolution on Europe

7-9%   Europe between the wars
    Stalin's five-year plans and purges
    International politics, 1919-1939
    The Great Depression
    Italy and Germany between the wars

8-10%   The Second World War and contemporary Europe
    The causes and course of the Second World War
    Postwar Europe
    Science, philosophy, the arts, and religion
    Contemporary social developments

Sample Questions

The 25 sample questions that follow are similar to questions on the
Western Civilization II examination, but they do not actually appear on
the examination.

Before attempting to answer the sample questions, read all the
information about the Western Civilization II examination on the
preceding pages. Additional suggestions for preparing for CLEP
examinations are provided in chapter 4.

Try to answer correctly as many questions as possible. Then compare
your answers with the correct answers, given in Appendix B.

Directions: Each of the questions or incomplete statements below is followed by five suggested answers or completions. Select the one that is best in each case.

1. Colbert's economic policies ran into difficulties chiefly because of the

   (A) relative poverty of France
   (B) loss of France's colonial empire
   (C) wars of Louis XIV
   (D) abandonment of the salt tax
   (E) reckless spending by the nobility

   Ⓐ Ⓑ Ⓒ Ⓓ Ⓔ

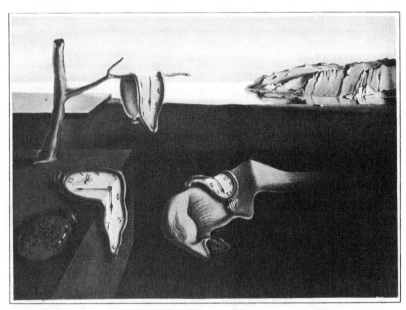

Collection, The Museum of Modern Art, New York.

2. Which of the following is a major theme depicted in the painting above?

   (A) A scientific view of the world
   (B) Enlightened rationalism
   (C) Romantic concern with nature
   (D) Realistic appraisal of industrial progress
   (E) The world of the unconscious mind

   Ⓐ Ⓑ Ⓒ Ⓓ Ⓔ

361

3. Which of the following occurred as a result of the War of the Austrian Succession (1740-1748) and the Seven Years' War (1756-1763)?

   (A) Prussia emerged as an important economic and military power.
   (B) Sweden ceased to be a great power.
   (C) Russia extended its territory to the shores of the Baltic Sea.
   (D) Hapsburg claims to Polish territory were dropped.
   (E) France acquired the provinces of Alsace and Lorraine.

   Ⓐ Ⓑ Ⓒ Ⓓ Ⓔ

4. Which of the following statements best describes Romanticism?

   (A) A belief that the rules of art are eternal and unchanging
   (B) Interest in expressing general and universal truths rather than particular and concrete ones
   (C) Emphasis on logical reasoning and exact factual knowledge
   (D) Emphasis on a high degree of emotional subjectivity
   (E) A value system that rejects idealism

   Ⓐ Ⓑ Ⓒ Ⓓ Ⓔ

5. All of the following were related to the Eastern Question EXCEPT

   (A) Pan-Slavism
   (B) the Congress of Berlin of 1878
   (C) the Crimean War
   (D) the Kruger Telegram
   (E) the Treaty of San Stefano

   Ⓐ Ⓑ Ⓒ Ⓓ Ⓔ

6. The cartoon above refers to the

   (A) Napoleonic Wars
   (B) Crimean War
   (C) Boer War
   (D) Russo-Japanese War
   (E) First World War

   Ⓐ Ⓑ Ⓒ Ⓓ Ⓔ

7. All of the following were instrumental in the emergence of Italy as a modern nation-state EXCEPT

(A) Mazzini
(B) Napoleon III
(C) Cavour
(D) Francis II
(E) Garibaldi

Ⓐ Ⓑ Ⓒ Ⓓ Ⓔ

8. "Men being by nature all free, equal, and independent, no one can be put out of this estate and subjected to the political power of another without his own consent, which is done by agreeing with other men, to join and unite into a community for their comfortable, safe, and peaceable living in a secure enjoyment of their properties."

The quotation above is from a work by

(A) John Locke
(B) Karl Marx
(C) Edmund Burke
(D) Voltaire
(E) Adam Smith

Ⓐ Ⓑ Ⓒ Ⓓ Ⓔ

9. Which of the following characterizes the size of the population of Europe during the eighteenth century?

(A) It increased rapidly.
(B) It stayed about the same.
(C) It declined.
(D) It dropped drastically in Western Europe, but rose in Eastern Europe.
(E) It dropped drastically in Eastern Europe, but rose in Western Europe.

Ⓐ Ⓑ Ⓒ Ⓓ Ⓔ

10. The term "collective security" would most likely be discussed in which of the following studies?

(A) A book on the twentieth-century welfare state
(B) A monograph on Soviet agricultural policy during the 1920's
(C) A book on Bismarckian imperialism
(D) A treatise on Social Darwinism
(E) A work on European diplomacy during the 1930's

Ⓐ Ⓑ Ⓒ Ⓓ Ⓔ

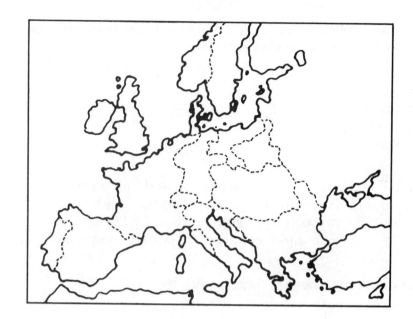

11. The map above shows national boundaries in which of the following years?

   (A) 1789
   (B) 1812
   (C) 1815
   (D) 1870
   (E) 1914   Ⓐ Ⓑ Ⓒ Ⓓ Ⓔ

12. The British economist John Maynard Keynes did which of the following?

   (A) He urged governments to increase mass purchasing power in
        times of deflation.
   (B) He defended the principles of the Versailles Treaty.
   (C) He helped to establish the British Labour party.
   (D) He prophesied the inevitable economic decline of capitalism.
   (E) He originated the concept of marginal utility to replace the labor
        theory of value.
                                                      Ⓐ Ⓑ Ⓒ Ⓓ Ⓔ

13. The vast increase in German military expenditures in the two decades
    preceding the First World War occurred primarily because Germany

   (A) had extended its imperialistic activities to the Far East
   (B) was planning to militarize the provinces of Alsace and Lorraine
   (C) was extending military aid to Russia
   (D) feared an attack from France
   (E) was rapidly expanding its navy   Ⓐ Ⓑ Ⓒ Ⓓ Ⓔ

14. In comparison to a preindustrial economy, the most distinctive feature of a modern economy is its

    (A) greater capacity to sustain growth over time
    (B) increased democratization of the workplace
    (C) lower wages for the literate middle class
    (D) lack of economic cycles
    (E) elimination of hunger and poverty   Ⓐ Ⓑ Ⓒ Ⓓ Ⓔ

15. The chief professed aim of Marxist socialists in the latter half of the nineteenth century was to

    (A) establish constitutional government
    (B) ensure equal rights for women
    (C) end government regulation of business
    (D) institute trial by jury in all criminal cases
    (E) abolish private ownership of the means of production

    Ⓐ Ⓑ Ⓒ Ⓓ Ⓔ

16. "Each individual, bestowing more time and attention upon the means of preserving and increasing his portion of wealth than is or can be bestowed by government, is likely to take a more effectual course than what, in this instance and on his behalf, would be taken by government."

    The quotation above best illustrates which of the following?

    (A) Fascism
    (B) Mercantilism
    (C) Syndicalism
    (D) Classical liberalism
    (E) Utopian socialism

    Ⓐ Ⓑ Ⓒ Ⓓ Ⓔ

17. The aim of the Soviet Union's First Five-Year Plan was to

    (A) acquire foreign capital
    (B) produce an abundance of consumer goods
    (C) encourage agricultural production by subsidizing the kulaks
    (D) build up heavy industry
    (E) put industrial policy in the hands of the proletariat

    Ⓐ Ⓑ Ⓒ Ⓓ Ⓔ

POPULATION DENSITY IN FRANCE PER SQUARE KILOMETER

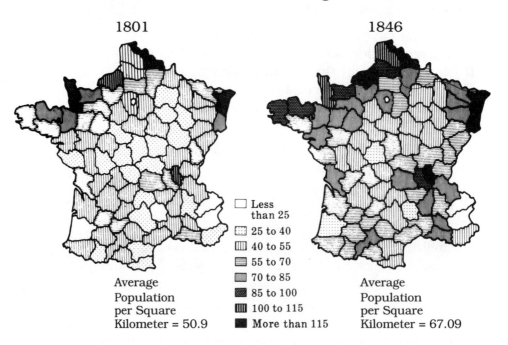

1801

1846

Average Population per Square Kilometer = 50.9

Legend:
- ☐ Less than 25
- 25 to 40
- 40 to 55
- 55 to 70
- 70 to 85
- 85 to 100
- 100 to 115
- ■ More than 115

Average Population per Square Kilometer = 67.09

18. The increase in population density between 1801 and 1846 shown above indicates that

(A) the growth of Paris absorbed any natural population increase

(B) there was a reversing trend in which industry moved to the center of France while agriculture moved to the north

(C) the population distribution in existence in 1801 was almost unchanged in 1846

(D) by 1846 southern France was declining in population

(E) by 1846 central France was declining in population

19. The National Assembly in France (1789-1791) did all of the following EXCEPT

    (A) issue assignats
    (B) ban strikes
    (C) pass the Civil Constitution of the Clergy
    (D) abolish guilds
    (E) abolish private property   Ⓐ Ⓑ Ⓒ Ⓓ Ⓔ

20. The cartoon above, published in 1955, suggested that

    (A) the Soviet Union intended to seize and control the bone of contention
    (B) France and Germany should cooperate with each other to meet the Soviet threat
    (C) France and Germany were industrially and economically weak
    (D) communism dominated Western Europe
    (E) France, Germany, and the communist nations should seek to form a tripartite pact in Europe

    Ⓐ Ⓑ Ⓒ Ⓓ Ⓔ

21. Historical explanations for nineteenth-century European imperialism include all of the following EXCEPT a

(A) need to discover new sources of raw materials
(B) need to find new markets for manufactured goods
(C) desire to establish world government
(D) need to invest excess financial resources
(E) desire to maintain the European balance of power

Ⓐ Ⓑ Ⓒ Ⓓ Ⓔ

22. All of the following factors contributed to the rise of the National Socialist German Workers' party (Nazis) EXCEPT

(A) the weakness of the Weimar Republic
(B) dissatisfaction with the Versailles Treaty
(C) the impact of the Great Depression
(D) the support of German conservatives
(E) the support of Socialist trade unions

Ⓐ Ⓑ Ⓒ Ⓓ Ⓔ

23. "He used extreme methods and mass repressions at a time when the Revolution was already victorious, when the Soviet state was strengthened, when the exploiting classes were already liquidated and Socialist relations were rooted solidly in all phases of the national economy, when our party was politically consolidated and had strengthened itself both numerically and ideologically."

In the quotation above, which of the following spoke and about whom?

(A) Khrushchev about Stalin
(B) Khrushchev about Trotsky
(C) Stalin about Trotsky
(D) Trotsky about Lenin
(E) Brezhnev about Lenin

Ⓐ Ⓑ Ⓒ Ⓓ Ⓔ

24. Albert Einstein's theory of relativity proposed

(A) a new structure for the atom
(B) a new conception of space and time
(C) the fundamental concepts for developing the computer
(D) the origin of the universe from the explosion of a single mass
(E) the particulate nature of light

Ⓐ Ⓑ Ⓒ Ⓓ Ⓔ

25. Which of the following is a central and essential component of the European welfare state?

    (A) Nationalization of all major sectors of the economy
    (B) Decentralization of the state
    (C) State responsibility for assuring access to medical care for all citizens
    (D) Elimination of large private fortunes through taxation
    (E) Elimination of independent trade unions

    (A) (B) (C) (D) (E)

Study Resources

The study resources for Western Civilization II: 1648 to the Present are the same as for Western Civilization I: Ancient Near East to 1648.

Calculus with Elementary Functions

Description of the Examination

The Subject Examination in Calculus with Elementary Functions covers skills and concepts that are usually taught in a one-year college course in calculus with elementary functions. Topics from both differential and integral calculus are included, as well as algebraic, trigonometric, exponential, and logarithmic functions. The examination is primarily concerned with an intuitive understanding of calculus and experience with its methods and applications. Knowledge of preparatory mathematics, including algebra, plane and solid geometry, trigonometry, and analytic geometry, is assumed.

A new edition of the Calculus with Elementary Functions examination that allows — but does not require — the use of a scientific, non-graphing calculator was introduced in the fall of 1994. The knowledge and skills required for the new edition are the same as those required for the former edition. The new edition, however, has no optional free-response section.

The examination includes approximately 45 multiple-choice questions to be answered in two separately timed 45-minute sections.

Knowledge and Skills Required

The following subject matter is included on the Calculus with Elementary Functions examination:

➡	*Approximate Percent of Examination*
20%	Elementary Functions (algebraic, trigonometric, exponential, and logarithmic)

Properties of functions

Definition, domain, range

Sum, product, quotient, composition

Absolute value, e.g., $|f(x)|$ and $f(|x|)$

Inverse

Odd and even

Periodicity

Graphs; symmetry and asymptotes

Zeros of a function

Properties of particular functions

Fundamental identities and addition formulas for trigonometric functions

Amplitude and periodicity of A sin (bx + c) and A cos (bx + c)

a^x(a > 0, a ≠ 1) and $\log_a$ x (a > 0, a ≠ 1, and x > 0) and their inverse relationship

Limits

Statement of properties, e.g., limit of a constant, sum, product, quotient

The number e such that $\lim_{n\to\infty}\left(1+\dfrac{1}{n}\right)^n = e$ and $\lim_{x\to 0}\dfrac{e^x-1}{x} = 1$

Limits that involve infinity, e.g., $\lim_{x\to 0}\dfrac{1}{x^2}$ is nonexistent and $\lim_{x\to\infty}\dfrac{\sin x}{x} = 0$

Continuity

40%   Differential Calculus

The derivative

Definitions of the derivative; e.g.,

$$f'(a) = \lim_{x\to a}\frac{f(x)-f(a)}{x-a} \text{ and}$$

$$f'(x) = \lim_{h\to 0}\frac{f(x+h)-f(x)}{h}$$

Derivatives of elementary functions

Derivatives of sum, product, quotient (including tan x and cot x)

Derivative of a composite function (chain rule); e.g., sin (ax + b), ae^{kx}, ln (kx)

Derivative of an implicitly defined function

Derivative of a rational power of a function

Derivative of the inverse of a function (including Arcsin x and Arctan x)

Logarithmic differentiation

Derivatives of higher order

Statement of Rolle's theorem without proof; mean value theorem; graphical illustration

Relation between differentiability and continuity

Applications of the derivative

Slope of a curve; tangent and normal lines to a curve

Curve sketching: increasing and decreasing functions; relative and absolute maximum and minimum points; concavity; points of inflection

Extreme value problems

Velocity and acceleration of a particle moving along a line

Average and instantaneous rates of change

Related rates of change

40% Integral Calculus

Antiderivatives

Applications of antiderivatives

Distance and velocity from acceleration with initial conditions

Solutions of $y' = ky$ and applications to growth and decay

Techniques of integration

Basic integration formulas

Integration by substitution (use of identities, change of variable)

Simple integration by parts, such as

$$\int xe^x \, dx \text{ and } \int \ln x \, dx$$

The definite integral

Concept of the definite integral as an area

Approximations to the definite integral using rectangles or trapezoids

Definition of the definite integral as the limit of a sum

Properties of the definite integral

The fundamental theorem —

$$\left(\frac{d}{dx}\int_a^x f(t)dt = f(x) \text{ and } \int_a^b f(x)dx = F(b) - F(a),\right.$$
$$\left.\text{where } F'(x) = f(x)\right)$$

Applications of the integral

Average (mean) value of a function on an interval

Area between curves

Volume of a solid of revolution

Interpretation of ln x as area under the graph of $y = x^{-1}$

Sample Questions

The 40 sample questions that follow are similar to questions on the Calculus with Elementary Functions examination, but they do not actually appear on the examination.

Before attempting to answer the sample questions, read all the information about the Calculus examination on the preceding pages. Additional suggestions for preparing for CLEP examinations are provided in chapter 4.

Try to answer correctly as many questions as possible. Then compare your answers with the correct answers, given in Appendix B.

Directions: Solve the following problems. Do not spend too much time on any one problem.

Notes: (1) In this examination, ln x denotes the natural logarithm of x (that is, logarithm to the base e). (2) Unless otherwise specified, the domain of a function f is assumed to be the set of all real numbers x for which f(x) is a real number.

1. If the graph of $y = 2^{-x} - 1$ is reflected in the x-axis, then an equation of the reflection is y =

   (A) $2^x - 1$
   (B) $1 - 2^x$
   (C) $1 - 2^{-x}$
   (D) $\log_2 (x + 1)$
   (E) $\log_2 (1 - x)$ Ⓐ Ⓑ Ⓒ Ⓓ Ⓔ

2. If $f(x) = (2x + 1)^4$, then the 4th derivative of $f(x)$ at $x = 0$ is

(A) 0
(B) 24
(C) 48
(D) 240
(E) 384

Ⓐ Ⓑ Ⓒ Ⓓ Ⓔ

3. What is $\lim\limits_{h \to 0} \dfrac{\cos\left(\frac{\pi}{2} + h\right) - \cos\frac{\pi}{2}}{h}$?

(A) $-\infty$
(B) -1
(C) 0
(D) 1
(E) $+\infty$

Ⓐ Ⓑ Ⓒ Ⓓ Ⓔ

4. Which of the following is equal to ln 4 ?

(A) $\ln 3 + \ln 1$

(B) $\dfrac{\ln 8}{\ln 2}$

(C) $\displaystyle\int_1^4 e^t \, dt$

(D) $\displaystyle\int_1^4 \ln x \, dx$

(E) $\displaystyle\int_1^4 \frac{1}{t} dt$

Ⓐ Ⓑ Ⓒ Ⓓ Ⓔ

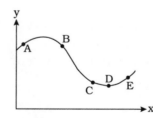

5. At which of the five points on the graph in the figure above are $\dfrac{dy}{dx}$ and $\dfrac{d^2y}{dx^2}$ both negative?

(A) A
(B) B
(C) C
(D) D
(E) E

Ⓐ Ⓑ Ⓒ Ⓓ Ⓔ

6. If $y = x + \sin(xy)$, then, where defined, $\dfrac{dy}{dx} =$

    (A) $1 + \cos(xy)$

    (B) $1 + y \cos(xy)$

    (C) $\dfrac{1}{1 - \cos(xy)}$

    (D) $\dfrac{1}{1 - x \; \cos(xy)}$

    (E) $\dfrac{1 + y \; \cos(xy)}{1 - x \; \cos(xy)}$
           Ⓐ Ⓑ Ⓒ Ⓓ Ⓔ

7. If $y = 10^{(x^2-1)}$, then $\dfrac{dy}{dx} =$

    (A) $(\ln 10) \; 10^{(x^2-1)}$

    (B) $(2x) \; 10^{(x^2-1)}$

    (C) $(x^2-1) \; 10^{(x^2-2)}$

    (D) $2x(\ln 10) \; 10^{(x^2-1)}$

    (E) $x^2(\ln 10) \; 10^{(x^2-1)}$
           Ⓐ Ⓑ Ⓒ Ⓓ Ⓔ

8. Which of the following statements about the curve $y = x^4 - 2x^3$ is true?

    (A) The curve has no relative extreme value.

    (B) The curve has one point of inflection and two relative extreme values.

    (C) The curve has two points of inflection and one relative extreme value.

    (D) The curve has two points of inflection and two relative extreme values.

    (E) The curve has two points of inflection and three relative extreme values.
           Ⓐ Ⓑ Ⓒ Ⓓ Ⓔ

9. If $y = \cos^2 x - \sin^2 x$, then $y' =$

    (A) -1

    (B) 0

    (C) $-2 \sin(2x)$

    (D) $-2(\cos x + \sin x)$

    (E) $2(\cos x - \sin x)$
           Ⓐ Ⓑ Ⓒ Ⓓ Ⓔ

10. The average value of $f(x) = x^2\sqrt{x^3+1}$ on the closed interval $[0,2]$ is

(A) $\dfrac{26}{9}$

(B) $\dfrac{13}{3}$

(C) $\dfrac{26}{3}$

(D) 13

(E) 26 ⒜ ⒝ ⒞ ⒟ ⒠

11. A smooth curve has the property that for all x the value of its slope at 2x is twice the value of its slope at x. The slope at 0 is

(A) not defined
(B) negative
(C) zero
(D) positive
(E) not determinable from the information given ⒜ ⒝ ⒞ ⒟ ⒠

12. If $f(x) = e^x$, which of the following is equal to $f'(e)$?

(A) $\displaystyle\lim_{h\to 0}\dfrac{e^{x+h}}{h}$

(B) $\displaystyle\lim_{h\to 0}\dfrac{e^{x+h}-e^e}{h}$

(C) $\displaystyle\lim_{h\to 0}\dfrac{e^{e+h}-e}{h}$

(D) $\displaystyle\lim_{h\to 0}\dfrac{e^{x+h}-1}{h}$

(E) $\displaystyle\lim_{h\to 0}\dfrac{e^{e+h}-e^e}{h}$ ⒜ ⒝ ⒞ ⒟ ⒠

13. Let $f(x) = \dfrac{1}{k}\cos(kx)$. For what value of k does f have period 3 ?

(A) $\dfrac{2}{3}$

(B) $\dfrac{2\pi}{3}$

(C) $\dfrac{3\pi}{2}$

(D) 6

(E) 6π ⒜ ⒝ ⒞ ⒟ ⒠

14. $\int_{1}^{2} x^{-3} \, dx =$

  (A) $-\dfrac{7}{8}$

  (B) $-\dfrac{3}{4}$

  (C) $\dfrac{15}{64}$

  (D) $\dfrac{3}{8}$

  (E) $\dfrac{15}{16}$ Ⓐ Ⓑ Ⓒ Ⓓ Ⓔ

15. $\int (x-1)\sqrt{x} \, dx =$

  (A) $\dfrac{3}{2}\sqrt{x} - \dfrac{1}{\sqrt{x}} + C$

  (B) $\dfrac{2}{3}x^{\frac{3}{2}} + \dfrac{1}{2}x^{\frac{1}{2}} + C$

  (C) $\dfrac{1}{2}x^2 - x + C$

  (D) $\dfrac{2}{5}x^{\frac{5}{2}} - \dfrac{2}{3}x^{\frac{3}{2}} + C$

  (E) $\dfrac{1}{2}x^2 + 2x^{\frac{3}{2}} - x + C$ Ⓐ Ⓑ Ⓒ Ⓓ Ⓔ

16. What is $\lim\limits_{x \to \infty} \dfrac{x^2 - 4}{2 + x - 4x^2}$?

  (A) -2

  (B) $-\dfrac{1}{4}$

  (C) $\dfrac{1}{2}$

  (D) 1

  (E) The limit does not exist.   Ⓐ Ⓑ Ⓒ Ⓓ Ⓔ

17. The area of the region in the first quadrant between the graph of $y = x\sqrt{4 - x^2}$ and the x-axis is

    (A) $\dfrac{2}{3}\sqrt{2}$

    (B) $\dfrac{8}{3}$

    (C) $2\sqrt{2}$

    (D) $2\sqrt{3}$

    (E) $\dfrac{16}{3}$ Ⓐ Ⓑ Ⓒ Ⓓ Ⓔ

18. For which of the following functions does the property $\dfrac{d^3y}{dx^3} = \dfrac{dy}{dx}$ hold?

    I. $y = e^x$
    II. $y = e^{-x}$
    III. $y = \sin x$

    (A) I only

    (B) II only

    (C) III only

    (D) I and II

    (E) II and III   Ⓐ Ⓑ Ⓒ Ⓓ Ⓔ

19. Let $a < c < b$ and let f be differentiable on [a, b]. Which of the following is NOT necessarily true?

    (A) $\displaystyle\int_a^b f(x)dx = \int_a^c f(x)dx + \int_c^b f(x)dx$

    (B) There exists d in [a, b] such that $f'(d) = \dfrac{f(b) - f(a)}{b - a}$.

    (C) $\displaystyle\int_a^b f(x)dx \geqq 0$

    (D) $\displaystyle\lim_{x \to c} f(x) = f(c)$

    (E) If k is a real number, then $\displaystyle\int_a^b kf(x)dx = k\int_a^b f(x)dx$.

    Ⓐ Ⓑ Ⓒ Ⓓ Ⓔ

20. The function $f(x) = \ln (\sin x)$ is defined for all x in which of the following intervals?

    (A) $0 < x < \pi$

    (B) $0 \leq x \leq \pi$

    (C) $\dfrac{3\pi}{2} < x < \dfrac{5\pi}{2}$

    (D) $\dfrac{3\pi}{2} \leq x \leq \dfrac{5\pi}{2}$

    (E) $\dfrac{3\pi}{2} < x < 2\pi$

    Ⓐ Ⓑ Ⓒ Ⓓ Ⓔ

21. $\lim\limits_{x \to 0} (x \csc x)$ is

    (A) $-\infty$
    (B) -1
    (C) 0
    (D) 1
    (E) ∞

    Ⓐ Ⓑ Ⓒ Ⓓ Ⓔ

22. $\int_{-3}^{3} |x + 2|\, dx =$

    (A) 0
    (B) 9
    (C) 12
    (D) 13
    (E) 14

    Ⓐ Ⓑ Ⓒ Ⓓ Ⓔ

23. The volume generated by revolving about the x-axis the region enclosed by the graphs of $y = 2x$ and $y = 2x^2$, for $0 \leq x \leq 1$, is

    (A) $\pi\int_0^1 (2x - 2x^2)^2\, dx$

    (B) $\pi\int_0^1 (4x^2 - 4x^4)\, dx$

    (C) $2\pi\int_0^1 x(2x - 2x^2)\, dx$

    (D) $\pi\int_0^2 \left(\sqrt{\dfrac{y}{2}} - \dfrac{y}{2}\right)^2 dy$

    (E) $\pi\int_0^2 \left(\dfrac{y}{2} - \dfrac{y^2}{2}\right) dy$

    Ⓐ Ⓑ Ⓒ Ⓓ Ⓔ

24. Let f be defined as follows, where a ≠ 0.

$$f(x) = \begin{cases} \dfrac{x^2 - a^2}{x - a}, & \text{for } x \neq a, \\ 0, & \text{for } x = a. \end{cases}$$

Which of the following are true about f ?

  I. $\lim\limits_{x \to a} f(x)$ exists.
 II. f(a) exists.
III. f(x) is continuous at x = a.

(A) None

(B) I only

(C) II only

(D) I and II only

(E) I, II, and III

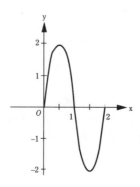

25. The figure above shows the graph of a sine function for one complete period. Which of the following is an equation for the graph?

(A) $y = 2 \sin\left(\dfrac{\pi}{2}x\right)$

(B) $y = \sin(\pi x)$

(C) $y = 2 \sin(2x)$

(D) $y = 2 \sin(\pi x)$

(E) $y = \sin(2x)$

26. Which of the following definite integrals is NOT equal to 0?

(A) $\displaystyle\int_{-\pi}^{\pi} \sin^3 x \, dx$

(B) $\displaystyle\int_{-\pi}^{\pi} x^2 \sin x \, dx$

(C) $\displaystyle\int_{0}^{\pi} \cos x \, dx$

(D) $\displaystyle\int_{-\pi}^{\pi} \cos^3 x \, dx$

(E) $\displaystyle\int_{-\pi}^{\pi} \cos^2 x \, dx$

Ⓐ Ⓑ Ⓒ Ⓓ Ⓔ

27. Let f be a continuous function on the closed interval [0,2].

If $2 \leq f(x) \leq 4$, then the greatest possible value of $\displaystyle\int_{0}^{2} f(x)dx$ is

(A) 0
(B) 2
(C) 4
(D) 8
(E) 16

Ⓐ Ⓑ Ⓒ Ⓓ Ⓔ

28. The acceleration at time t of a particle moving on the x-axis is $4\pi \cos t$. If the velocity is 0 at t = 0, what is the average velocity of the particle over the interval $0 \leq t \leq \pi$?

(A) 0

(B) $\dfrac{4}{\pi}$

(C) 4

(D) 8

(E) 8π

Ⓐ Ⓑ Ⓒ Ⓓ Ⓔ

29. $\displaystyle\int_{0}^{1} xe^{-x}dx =$

(A) $\dfrac{e-2}{e}$

(B) $\dfrac{2-e}{e}$

(C) $\dfrac{e+2}{e}$

(D) $\dfrac{e}{e-2}$

(E) $\dfrac{e}{2-e}$

Ⓐ Ⓑ Ⓒ Ⓓ Ⓔ

30. Let $f(x) = x^3 + x$. If h is the inverse function of f, then $h'(2) =$

(A) $\dfrac{1}{13}$

(B) $\dfrac{1}{4}$

(C) 1

(D) 4

(E) 13

Ⓐ Ⓑ Ⓒ Ⓓ Ⓔ

31. $\displaystyle\int \tan(2x)\, dx =$

(A) $-2 \ln|\cos(2x)| + C$

(B) $-\dfrac{1}{2} \ln|\cos(2x)| + C$

(C) $\dfrac{1}{2} \ln|\cos(2x)| + C$

(D) $2 \ln|\cos(2x)| + C$

(E) $\dfrac{1}{2} \sec(2x)\tan(2x) + C$

Ⓐ Ⓑ Ⓒ Ⓓ Ⓔ

32. $\displaystyle\int \cos^2 x \sin x\, dx =$

(A) $-\dfrac{\cos^3 x}{3} + C$

(B) $-\dfrac{\cos^3 x \sin^2 x}{6} + C$

(C) $\dfrac{\sin^2 x}{2} + C$

(D) $\dfrac{\cos^3 x}{3} + C$

(E) $\dfrac{\cos^3 x \sin^2 x}{6} + C$

Ⓐ Ⓑ Ⓒ Ⓓ Ⓔ

33. If $f(x) = \dfrac{\ln x}{x}$ for $x > 0$, which of the following is true?

(A) f is increasing for all x greater than 0.
(B) f is increasing for all x greater than 1.
(C) f is decreasing for all x between 0 and 1.
(D) f is decreasing for all x between 1 and e.
(E) f is decreasing for all x greater than e.

Ⓐ Ⓑ Ⓒ Ⓓ Ⓔ

383

34. If r is positive and increasing, for what value of r is the rate of increase of r³ twelve times that of r ?

(A) $\sqrt[3]{4}$
(B) 2
(C) $\sqrt[3]{12}$
(D) $2\sqrt{3}$
(E) 6

Ⓐ Ⓑ Ⓒ Ⓓ Ⓔ

35. An equation of the line tangent to $y = x^3 + 3x^2 + 2$ at its point of inflection is

(A) $y = -6x - 6$
(B) $y = -3x + 1$
(C) $y = 2x + 10$
(D) $y = 3x - 1$
(E) $y = 4x + 1$

Ⓐ Ⓑ Ⓒ Ⓓ Ⓔ

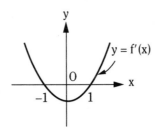

36. The graph of the derivative of f is shown in the figure above. Which of the following could be the graph of f ?

(A)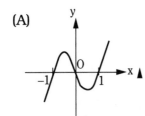
(B)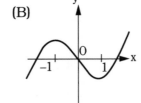
(C)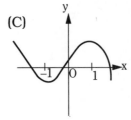

(D)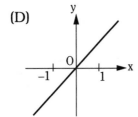
(E)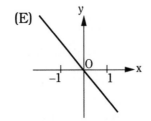

Ⓐ Ⓑ Ⓒ Ⓓ Ⓔ

37. If f is continuous for all x, which of the following integrals necessarily have the same value?

I. $\int_a^b f(x)dx$

II. $\int_0^{b-a} f(x+a)dx$

III. $\int_{a+c}^{b+c} f(x+c)dx$

(A) I and II only
(B) I and III only
(C) II and III only
(D) I, II, and III
(E) No two necessarily have the same value.

Ⓐ Ⓑ Ⓒ Ⓓ Ⓔ

38. The volume of a cone of radius r and height h is given by $V = \frac{1}{3}\pi r^2 h$. If the radius and the height both increase at a constant rate of $\frac{1}{2}$ centimeter per second, at what rate, in cubic centimeters per second, is the volume increasing when the height is 9 centimeters and the radius is 6 centimeters?

(A) $\frac{1}{2}\pi$
(B) 10π
(C) 24π
(D) 54π
(E) 108π

Ⓐ Ⓑ Ⓒ Ⓓ Ⓔ

39. If h is the inverse function of f and if $f(x) = \frac{1}{x}$, then h(x) =

(A) ln x
(B) $-\frac{1}{x^2}$
(C) $-\frac{1}{x}$
(D) x
(E) $\frac{1}{x}$

Ⓐ Ⓑ Ⓒ Ⓓ Ⓔ

40. The normal to the curve represented by the equation $y = x^2 + 6x + 4$ at the point $(-2, -4)$ also intersects the curve at $x =$

    (A) -6

    (B) $-\dfrac{9}{2}$

    (C) $-\dfrac{7}{2}$

    (D) -3

    (E) $-\dfrac{1}{2}$ Ⓐ Ⓑ Ⓒ Ⓓ Ⓔ

Study Resources

The following list contains a number of textbooks that are typical of those widely used in introductory calculus courses at the college level. All the books cover the topics in the outline given earlier, but their approach and emphasis may differ. To prepare for the Calculus examination, therefore, a candidate is advised to study one or more of these or other calculus textbooks. In addition, the Barron's book provides helpful test preparation suggestions, and the Schaum Outline provides a condensed version of the important topics usually covered in a college calculus course. Both of these books contain many sample problems; many of those in the Barron's book are taken from old forms of Advanced Placement and CLEP examinations.

   Many libraries do not carry textbooks as a policy. If you can't find any of the following textbooks at the library, see whether the college bookstore has a used copy. If you can't locate the most recent edition, an edition that is one or two years older will suffice for most subject areas. As a final option, purchase a new copy of the suggested textbook as an investment in your education.

TEXTBOOKS

Anton, Howard, *Calculus with Analytic Geometry,* 3rd ed. New York: John Wiley & Sons, 1988.

Edwards, C. H. and David E. Penney, *Calculus and Analytic Geometry,* 3rd ed. Englewood Cliffs, NJ: Prentice Hall, 1990.

Faires, Douglas and Barbara Faires, *Calculus and Analytic Geometry,* 2nd ed. New York: Random House, 1988.

Flanders, Harley, *Calculus.* New York: W. H. Freeman, 1985.

Grossman, Stanley, *Calculus, Part I: The Calculus of One Variable,* 2nd ed. Orlando, FL: Academic Press, 1986.

Larson, Roland E. and Robert P. Hostetler, *Calculus with Analytic Geometry,* 4th ed. Lexington, MA: D. C. Heath, 1990.

Leithold, Louis, *The Calculus with Analytical Geometry,* 6th ed. New York: Harper & Row, 1990.

Mizrahi, Abe and Michael Sullivan, *Calculus and Analytic Geometry,* 3rd ed. Belmont, CA: Wadsworth, 1986.

Silverman, Richard, *Calculus with Analytic Geometry.* Englewood Cliffs, NJ: Prentice Hall, 1985.

Simmons, G. F., *Calculus with Analytic Geometry.* New York: McGraw-Hill, 1985.

Swokowski, Earl W., *Calculus,* 5th ed. Boston: PWS-Kent, 1991.

Thomas, George B., Jr. and Ross L. Finney, *Calculus and Analytic Geometry,* 8th ed. Reading, MA: Addison-Wesley, 1992.

SUPPLEMENTARY REFERENCE MATERIALS

Hockett, Shirley, *Barron's How to Prepare for Advanced Placement Examinations, Mathematics,* 4th ed. New York: Barron's, 1992.

Ayres, Frank, Jr., and Elliot Mendelson, *Schaum's Outline of Theory and Problems of Differential and Integral Calculus,* 3rd ed. New York: McGraw-Hill, 1990.

SUPPLEMENTARY REFERENCE MATERIALS

Hockett, Shirley, *Barron's How to Prepare for Advanced Placement Examinations, Mathematics,* 4th ed. New York: Barron's, 1992.

Ayres, Frank, Jr., and Elliot Mendelson, *Schaum's Outline of Theory and Problems of Differential and Integral Calculus,* 3rd ed. New York: McGraw-Hill, 1990.

College Algebra

Description of the Examination

The Subject Examination in College Algebra covers the material that is usually taught in a one-semester college course in algebra. About half the exam is made up of routine problems requiring basic algebraic skills; the remainder involves solving nonroutine problems in which candidates must demonstrate their understanding of concepts. The examination includes questions on basic algebraic operations; linear and quadratic equations, inequalities, and graphs; algebraic, exponential, and logarithmic functions; and miscellaneous other topics. It is assumed that the candidate is familiar with currently taught algebraic vocabulary, symbols, and notation. The test places little emphasis on arithmetic calculations and it does not contain any questions that require the use of a calculator. However, the use of a scientific calculator (non-graphing, non-programmable) is permitted during the examination.

The examination consists of approximately 70 multiple-choice questions to be answered in two separately timed 45-minute sections.

Knowledge and Skills Required

The subject matter covered by the College Algebra examination is distributed approximately as follows:

⬤ Approximate Percent of Examination

25%   Algebraic operations
     Combining algebraic expressions
     Factoring
     Simplifying algebraic fractions
     Operating with powers and roots

20%   Equations, inequalities, and their graphs
     Linear equations and inequalities
     Quadratic equations and inequalities
     Systems of equations and inequalitie

Approximate Percent of Examination

25%   Algebraic, exponential, and logarithmic functions and their
          graphs
              Domain
              Range
              Composition
              Inverse of functions

30%   Miscellaneous topics
              Theory of equations
              Sets
              Real numbers
              Complex numbers
              Sequences and series

Within the subject matter described above, questions on the exam require candidates to demonstrate the abilities given below in the approximate proportions indicated.

- Solving routine, straightforward problems (about 50 percent of the examination)

- Solving nonroutine problems requiring an understanding of concepts and the application of skills and concepts (about 50 percent of the examination)

Sample Questions

The 28 questions that follow are similar to questions on the College Algebra examination, but they do not appear on the actual examination.

Before attempting to answer the sample questions, read all the information about the College Algebra examination on the preceding pages. Additional suggestions for preparing for CLEP examinations are provided in chapter 4.

Try to answer correctly as many questions as possible. Then compare your answers with the correct answers, given in Appendix B.

Directions: Solve the following problems. Do not spend too much time on any one problem.

Notes: (1) Unless otherwise specified, the domain of any function f is assumed to be the set of all real numbers x for which f(x) is a real number.

(2) i will be used to denote $\sqrt{-1}$.

(3) Figures that accompany the following problems are intended to provide information useful in solving the problems. They are drawn as accurately as possible EXCEPT when it is stated in a specific problem that its figure is not drawn to scale. All figures lie in a plane unless otherwise indicated.

1. If R = {1,2}, S = {2,3,4}, and T = {2,4}, then (R∪S)∩T is

   (A) {2}
   (B) {4}
   (C) {2,4}
   (D) {1,2,3,4}
   (E) The empty set

   Ⓐ Ⓑ Ⓒ Ⓓ Ⓔ

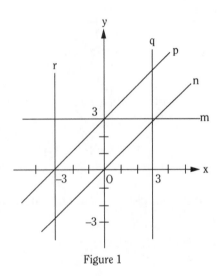

Figure 1

2. Which of the lines in Figure 1 is the graph of x = 3 ?

   (A) m
   (B) n
   (C) p
   (D) q
   (E) r

   Ⓐ Ⓑ Ⓒ Ⓓ Ⓔ

3. If f(x) = 2x – 1, then f(3x) =

    (A) 3x – 1
    (B) 6x – 1
    (C) 6x – 3
    (D) $6x^2 - 1$
    (E) $6x^2 - 3x$

Ⓐ Ⓑ Ⓒ Ⓓ Ⓔ

4. If x + 2 = y, what is the value of | x – y | + | y – x |?

    (A) – 4
    (B) 0
    (C) 2
    (D) 4
    (E) It cannot be determined from the information given.

Ⓐ Ⓑ Ⓒ Ⓓ Ⓔ

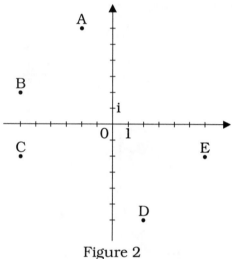

Figure 2

5. Which point in Figure 2 represents the complex number 6-2i ?

    (A) A   (B) B   (C) C   (D) D   (E) E

Ⓐ Ⓑ Ⓒ Ⓓ Ⓔ

6. Where defined, $(x^a)^a$ =

    (A) $x^{\frac{a}{2}}$
    (B) x^{a^2}
    (C) x^{a+2}
    (D) x^{2a}
    (E) $2x^a$

Ⓐ Ⓑ Ⓒ Ⓓ Ⓔ

7. Which of the shaded regions below represents the graph of
{(x,y) | x ≥ 2 and y ≤ 0} ?

(A)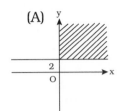

(B)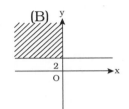

(C)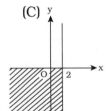

(D)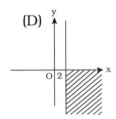

(E)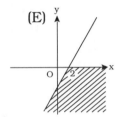

Ⓐ Ⓑ Ⓒ Ⓓ Ⓔ

8. Where defined, $\dfrac{x^3 - 1}{x - 1} =$
   (A) x + 1
   (B) $x^2 + 1$
   (C) $x^2 - x + 1$
   (D) $x^2 - x - 1$
   (E) $x^2 + x + 1$

Ⓐ Ⓑ Ⓒ Ⓓ Ⓔ

9. $\displaystyle\sum_{k=-1}^{3} k^2 =$

(A) 5   (B) 10   (C) 13   (D) 14   (E) 15

Ⓐ Ⓑ Ⓒ Ⓓ Ⓔ

10. Where defined, $\dfrac{x - \dfrac{4y^2}{9x}}{\dfrac{3x}{2} + y} =$

(A) $\dfrac{9x(3x - 2y)}{2y(3x + 2y)}$

(B) $\dfrac{2(3x + 2y)^2}{9(3x - 2y)}$

(C) $\dfrac{3x + 2y}{9}$

(D) $\dfrac{2(3x - 2y)}{9x}$

(E) $\dfrac{(3x - 2y)(3x + 2y)^2}{18x}$

Ⓐ Ⓑ Ⓒ Ⓓ Ⓔ

11. For what real numbers x is $y = 2^{-x}$ a negative number?

(A) All real x
(B) x > 0 only
(C) x ≥ 0 only
(D) x < 0 only
(E) No real x

Ⓐ Ⓑ Ⓒ Ⓓ Ⓔ

12. If $\log_x 16 = 8$, then x =

(A) $\dfrac{1}{2}$

(B) $\dfrac{1}{\sqrt{2}}$

(C) $\sqrt{2}$

(D) 2

(E) $2\sqrt{2}$

Ⓐ Ⓑ Ⓒ Ⓓ Ⓔ

13. The set of all real numbers that satisfy the inequality $|x - 2| \leq 5$ is

(A) {x: −5 ≤ x ≤ 5}
(B) {x: −3 ≤ x ≤ 7}
(C) {x: −7 ≤ x ≤ 3}
(D) {x: x < −5}
(E) {x: x < −7 or x > 3}

Ⓐ Ⓑ Ⓒ Ⓓ Ⓔ

14. If $f(x) = 2x + 1$ and $g(x) = 3x - 1$, then $f(g(x)) =$

    (A) $6x - 1$
    (B) $6x + 2$
    (C) $x - 2$
    (D) $5x$
    (E) $6x^2 + x - 1$

Ⓐ Ⓑ Ⓒ Ⓓ Ⓔ

15. If the remainder is 7 when $x^3 + kx^2 - 3x - 15$ is divided by $x - 2$, then $k =$

    (A) 5
    (B) 6
    (C) 7
    (D) 9
    (E) 11

Ⓐ Ⓑ Ⓒ Ⓓ Ⓔ

16. The set of all values of b for which the equation $4x^2 + bx + 1 = 0$ has one or two real roots is defined by

    (A) $b > 4$
    (B) $b < 4$
    (C) $b \geq 4$ or $b \leq -4$
    (D) $b > 4$ or $b < -4$
    (E) $b \geq 1$ or $b \leq -1$

Ⓐ Ⓑ Ⓒ Ⓓ Ⓔ

17. Given the two complex numbers $Z = p + qi$ and $\overline{Z} = p - qi$, where p and q are real numbers different from zero, which of the following statements involving Z and $\overline{Z}$ must be true?

    (A) $Z = -\overline{Z}$
    (B) $(\overline{Z})^2$ is a real number.
    (C) $Z \cdot \overline{Z}$ is a real number.
    (D) $(\overline{Z})^2 = Z^2$
    (E) $Z^2 = -(\overline{Z})^2$

Ⓐ Ⓑ Ⓒ Ⓓ Ⓔ

18. $\dfrac{(n+1)!}{n!} - n =$

    (A) 0
    (B) 1
    (C) n
    (D) $n + 1$
    (E) $n!$

Ⓐ Ⓑ Ⓒ Ⓓ Ⓔ

19. In how many points do the graphs of $x^2 + y^2 = 9$ and $x^2 = 8y$ intersect?

    (A) One
    (B) Two
    (C) Three
    (D) Four
    (E) More than four   Ⓐ Ⓑ Ⓒ Ⓓ Ⓔ

20. $\dfrac{1+2i}{1-2i} =$

    (A) $\dfrac{4-3i}{-3}$

    (B) $\dfrac{-3+4i}{5}$

    (C) 1

    (D) $\dfrac{3-4i}{5}$

    (E) $\dfrac{4-3i}{3}$ Ⓐ Ⓑ Ⓒ Ⓓ Ⓔ

21. A colony of bacteria starts with 2 bacteria at noon. If the number of bacteria triples every 40 minutes, how many bacteria will be present at 4:00 p.m. on the same day?

    (A) 486   (B) 729   (C) 1,458   (D) 46,656   (E) 118,098

                                          Ⓐ Ⓑ Ⓒ Ⓓ Ⓔ

$$\begin{cases} 2x + y - z = 3 \\ x + 3y - 2z = 7 \\ 3x - y + 4z = 11 \end{cases}$$

22. What is the value of z in the solution set of the system of equations above?

    (A) $-\dfrac{11}{3}$

    (B) $-\dfrac{3}{2}$

    (C) 1

    (D) 2

    (E) 3 Ⓐ Ⓑ Ⓒ Ⓓ Ⓔ

23. Which quadrants of the plane contain points of the graph of
2x – y > 4 ?

(A) First, second, and third only
(B) First, second, and fourth only
(C) First, third, and fourth only
(D) Second, third, and fourth only
(E) First, second, third, and fourth

Ⓐ Ⓑ Ⓒ Ⓓ Ⓔ

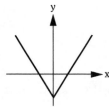

Figure 3

24. Figure 3 is the graph of y = f(x). Which of the following is the graph of
y = |f(x)| ?

(A)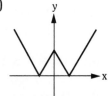

(B)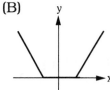

(C)

(D)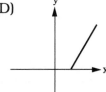

(E)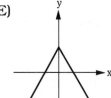

Ⓐ Ⓑ Ⓒ Ⓓ Ⓔ

25. If x, 3x + 2, and 8x + 3 are the first three terms of an arithmetic progression, then x =

(A) −1

(B) $-\dfrac{1}{5}$

(C) 0

(D) $\dfrac{1}{3}$

(E) 3

Ⓐ Ⓑ Ⓒ Ⓓ Ⓔ

26. What is the middle term in the expansion of $\left(x - \dfrac{1}{x}\right)^6$?

(A) $20x^3$

(B) $\dfrac{20}{x^3}$

(C) $-15x^2$

(D) -15

(E) -20

Ⓐ Ⓑ Ⓒ Ⓓ Ⓔ

27. A driver decides to stop her car by tapping the brake pedal once every 5 seconds. After each tap of the brake pedal her speed is 3/4 of what it was before the tap. If the initial speed of the car is 60 miles per hour (88 feet per second), how many feet will the car travel from the first tap of the brake until the car comes to a stop?

(A) 264   (B) 440   (C) 900   (D) 1,320   (E) 1,408

Ⓐ Ⓑ Ⓒ Ⓓ Ⓔ

28. The set of <u>real</u> solutions of $\dfrac{2}{3-x} = \dfrac{1}{3} - \dfrac{1}{x}$ is

(A) the empty set   (B) {3}   (C) {-3}

(D) {3, -3}   (E) {3i, -3i}

Ⓐ Ⓑ Ⓒ Ⓓ Ⓔ

Study Resources

The list below contains a number of textbooks that are typical of those widely used in algebra courses at the college level. All the textbooks cover the major topics in the outline given previously, but their approach and emphasis may differ. To prepare for the College Algebra examination, study one or more of these or similar textbooks.

Many libraries do not carry textbooks as a policy. If you can't find any of the following textbooks at the library, see whether the college bookstore has a used copy. If you can't locate the most recent edition, an edition that is one or two years older will suffice for most subject areas. As a final option, purchase a new copy of the suggested textbook as an investment in your education.

TEXTBOOKS

Barnett, Raymond A. and Michael R. Ziegler, *College Algebra*, 4th ed. New York: McGraw-Hill, 1989.

Beckenbach, Edwin et al., *Modern College Algebra and Trigonometry*, 5th ed. Belmont, CA: Wadsworth, 1986.

Keedy, M. L. and M. L. Bittinger, *College Algebra: A Functions Approach*, 4th ed. Reading, MA: Addison-Wesley, 1986.

Leithold, Louis, *College Algebra*, 2nd ed. New York: Macmillan, 1980.

Munem, Mustafa et al., *College Algebra*, 2nd ed. New York: Worth, 1979. [Study Guide included.]

Swokowski, Earl W., *Fundamentals of College Algebra*, 7th ed. Boston: PWS-Kent, 1989.

Trigonometry

Description of the Examination

The Subject Examination in Trigonometry covers material that is usually taught in a one-semester college course in trigonometry with primary emphasis on analytical trigonometry. More than half the exam is made up of routine problems requiring basic trigonometric skills; the remainder involves solving nonroutine problems in which candidates must demonstrate their understanding of concepts. The exam includes questions on trigonometric functions and their relationships, evaluation of trigonometric functions of positive and negative angles, trigonometric equations and inequalities, graphs of trigonometric functions, trigonometry of the triangle, and miscellaneous other topics. It is assumed that the candidate is familiar with currently taught trigonometric vocabulary and notation and with both radian and degree measure. The exam places little emphasis on arithmetic calculations, and the use of calculators and other computing devices is not permitted during the examination.

The examination consists of approximately 80 multiple-choice questions to be answered in two separately timed 45-minute sections.

Knowledge and Skills Required

The following subject matter is included on the Trigonometry examination.

    ➡   *Approximate Percent of Examination*

30%   Trigonometric functions and their relationships

        Cofunction relationships

        Reciprocal relationships

        Pythagorean relationships such as $\sin^2\theta + \cos^2\theta = 1$

        Functions of two angles such as $\sin(\alpha+\beta)$

        Functions of double angles such as $\cos 2\theta$

        Functions of half angles such as $\sin\dfrac{\theta}{2}$

        Identities

←	*Approximate Percent of Examination*

20%   Evaluation of trigonometric functions of angles with terminal sides in the various quadrants or on the axes, including positive and negative angles greater than 360° (or 2π radians)

10%   Trigonometric equations and inequalities

10%   Graphs of trigonometric functions

10%   Trigonometry of the triangle including the law of sines and the law of cosines

20%   Miscellaneous

Inverse functions (arc sin, arc cos, arc tan)

Trigonometric form (polar form) of complex numbers including DeMoivre's theorem

Within the subject matter described above, questions on the test require candidates to demonstrate the abilities given below in the approximate proportions indicated.

- Solving routine problems involving basic trigonometric skills (about 60 percent of the examination)

- Solving nonroutine problems requiring an understanding of concepts and the application of skills and concepts (about 40 percent of the examination)

Sample Questions

The 25 questions that follow are similar to questions on the Trigonometry examination, but they do not actually appear on the examination.

Before attempting to answer the sample questions, read all the information about the Trigonometry examination on the preceding pages. Additional suggestions for preparing for CLEP examinations are provided in chapter 4.

Try to answer correctly as many questions as possible. Then compare your answers with the correct answers, given in Appendix B.

Directions: Solve the following problems. Do not spend too much time on any one problem.

Note: On this test the inverse function of a trigonometric function f(x) may be expressed as either $f^{-1}(x)$ or arc f(x).

1. cos 60° sin 30° =

   (A) $\dfrac{1}{4}$ (B) $\dfrac{1}{2}$ (C) $\dfrac{3}{4}$ (D) 1   (E) 2

   Ⓐ Ⓑ Ⓒ Ⓓ Ⓔ

2. If $0 < x < \pi$ and tan x = 1, then x =

   (A) $\dfrac{\pi}{6}$ (B) $\dfrac{\pi}{4}$ (C) $\dfrac{\pi}{2}$ (D) $\dfrac{2\pi}{3}$ (E) $\dfrac{3\pi}{4}$

   Ⓐ Ⓑ Ⓒ Ⓓ Ⓔ

3. A circular gear turns 60 degrees per hour. Through how many radians does it turn in 12 hours?

   (A) $\dfrac{4}{\pi}$ (B) $\dfrac{36}{\pi}$ (C) 4π (D) 12π (E) 36π

   Ⓐ Ⓑ Ⓒ Ⓓ Ⓔ

4. If x is the measure of an acute angle such that $\tan x = \dfrac{k}{3}$, then sin x =

   (A) $\dfrac{k}{3+k}$ (B) $\dfrac{3}{\sqrt{9-k^2}}$ (C) $\dfrac{k}{\sqrt{9-k^2}}$

   (D) $\dfrac{3}{\sqrt{9+k^2}}$ (E) $\dfrac{k}{\sqrt{9+k^2}}$

   Ⓐ Ⓑ Ⓒ Ⓓ Ⓔ

5. cos 240° =
   (A) $-\sin 240°$
   (B) $-\cos 60°$
   (C) $\sin (-240°)$
   (D) $\sin 150°$
   (E) $\cos 60°$

   Ⓐ Ⓑ Ⓒ Ⓓ Ⓔ

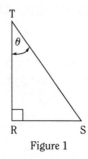

Figure 1

6. In right triangle RST in Figure 1, RS is 9 and $\tan \theta = \dfrac{3}{4}$.

What is the area of $\triangle$RST ?

(A) 18   (B) 27   (C) 36   (D) 54   (E) 108

Ⓐ Ⓑ Ⓒ Ⓓ Ⓔ

7. If θ is an angle in standard position such that the terminal ray of θ passes through the point (12, –5), then $\sin \theta =$

(A) $-\dfrac{12}{13}$ (B) $-\dfrac{5}{13}$ (C) $-\dfrac{5}{17}$ (D) $\dfrac{5}{17}$ (E) $\dfrac{12}{13}$

Ⓐ Ⓑ Ⓒ Ⓓ Ⓔ

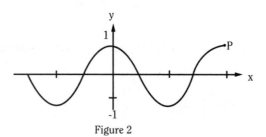

Figure 2

8. On the portion of the graph of $y = \cos \dfrac{2}{3} x$ in Figure 2, what is the x-coordinate of point P if the y-coordinate is 1 ?

(A) $\dfrac{2\pi}{3}$ (B) 2π (C) 3π (D) 4π (E) 6π

Ⓐ Ⓑ Ⓒ Ⓓ Ⓔ

9. If $\sin x = 2 \cos x$, what is $\tan x$?

(A) $\dfrac{1}{2}$ (B) $\dfrac{\sqrt{2}}{2}$ (C) $\sqrt{2}$ (D) 2

(E) It cannot be determined from the information given.

Ⓐ Ⓑ Ⓒ Ⓓ Ⓔ

10. If $\sin \theta = 0.8$, then $\cos 2\theta =$

(A) -0.36 (B) -0.28 (C) -0.20
(D) 0.20 (E) 0.36

Ⓐ Ⓑ Ⓒ Ⓓ Ⓔ

11. $\cos [\sin^{-1}(-\frac{1}{2})] =$

(A) $-\frac{\pi}{6}$ (B) $\frac{\pi}{3}$ (C) $\frac{1}{2}$ (D) $\frac{\sqrt{3}}{2}$ (E) $2\sqrt{3}$

Ⓐ Ⓑ Ⓒ Ⓓ Ⓔ

12. Wherever defined, $\dfrac{\csc x}{\sec x} =$

(A) $1 - \cos^2 x$ (B) $\cos x$ (C) $\cot x$
(D) $\sin x$ (E) $\tan x$

Ⓐ Ⓑ Ⓒ Ⓓ Ⓔ

13. For $0 \leq x \leq 2\pi$, $\sin x > \cos x$ if and only if

(A) $0 < x < \frac{\pi}{4}$ (B) $\frac{\pi}{6} < x < \frac{\pi}{2}$ (C) $0 < x \leq \frac{\pi}{2}$

(D) $\frac{\pi}{4} \leq x < \frac{\pi}{2}$ (E) $\frac{\pi}{4} < x < \frac{5\pi}{4}$

Ⓐ Ⓑ Ⓒ Ⓓ Ⓔ

14. $(\cos \theta \tan \theta)^2 =$

(A) 0 (B) 1 (C) $\cot^2 \theta$
(D) $\sin^2 \theta$ (E) $\cos^2 \theta \csc^2 \theta$

Ⓐ Ⓑ Ⓒ Ⓓ Ⓔ

15. How many values of t are there between 0° and 360°, inclusive, for which $\cos t = 0$?

(A) None   (B) One   (C) Two   (D) Three   (E) Four

Ⓐ Ⓑ Ⓒ Ⓓ Ⓔ

16. $\sin (\arctan 1) =$

(A) 0 (B) $\frac{1}{2}$ (C) $\frac{\sqrt{2}}{2}$ (D) $\frac{\sqrt{3}}{2}$ (E) 1

Ⓐ Ⓑ Ⓒ Ⓓ Ⓔ

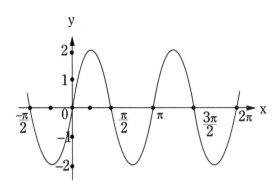

Figure 3

17. The graph shown in Figure 3 above is part of the graph of which of the following equations?

(A) $y = \sin \dfrac{x}{2} + 1$ (B) $y = \sin 2x$ (C) $y = 2 \sin \dfrac{x}{2}$

(D) $y = 2 \sin x$ (E) $y = 2 \sin 2x$

Ⓐ Ⓑ Ⓒ Ⓓ Ⓔ

18. If $0 < y < x < \dfrac{\pi}{2}$, which of the following are true?

 I. $\sin y < \sin x$
 II. $\cos y < \cos x$
 III. $\tan y < \tan x$

(A) None   (B) I and II only   (C) I and III only
(D) II and III only   (E) I, II, and III

Ⓐ Ⓑ Ⓒ Ⓓ Ⓔ

19. What is the solution set of $\cos^2 x + 2 \cos x = 0$, where

$-\dfrac{\pi}{2} \leq x \leq \dfrac{\pi}{2}$?

(A) $\left\{-\dfrac{\pi}{2}, \dfrac{\pi}{2}\right\}$ (B) $\left\{-\dfrac{\pi}{2}, \pi\right\}$ (C) $\{-\pi, \pi\}$

(D) $\{-\pi, 0, \pi\}$ (E) The empty set

Ⓐ Ⓑ Ⓒ Ⓓ Ⓔ

20. Where defined, $\dfrac{\sin x}{-1 + \sec x} + \dfrac{\sin x}{1 + \sec x} =$

(A) $-2 \cot x$ (B) $-2 \tan x$ (C) $2 \cot x$
(D) $2 \tan x$ (E) $\tan 2x$

Ⓐ Ⓑ Ⓒ Ⓓ Ⓔ

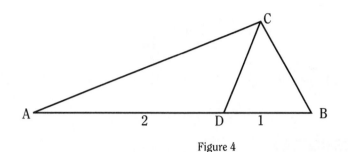

Figure 4

21. In Figure 4, if △BCD is equilateral, what is the length of side AC in △ABC ?

   (A) $\sqrt{5}$ (B) $\sqrt{7}$ (C) $2\sqrt{2}$ (D) 3
   (E) It cannot be determined from the information given.

   Ⓐ Ⓑ Ⓒ Ⓓ Ⓔ

22. What are all the real numbers x for which sin(–x) = sin x ?

   (A) No number
   (B) Zero
   (C) All integral multiples of π
   (D) All integral multiples of $\dfrac{\pi}{2}$
   (E) All numbers

   Ⓐ Ⓑ Ⓒ Ⓓ Ⓔ

23. Using DeMoivre's theorem, $[4 (\cos \dfrac{\pi}{3} + i \sin \dfrac{\pi}{3})]^3$ can be expressed as

   (A) – 64   (B) – 64i   (C) 12 + 12i
   (D) 12 – 12i   (E) –12 – 12i

   Ⓐ Ⓑ Ⓒ Ⓓ Ⓔ

24. Which of the following represents part of the graph of y = 3 sin 2x ?

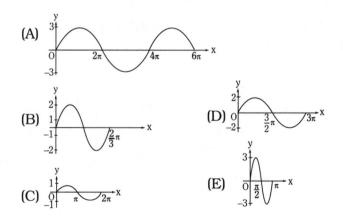

   Ⓐ Ⓑ Ⓒ Ⓓ Ⓔ

25. If $0 \leqq \theta \leqq \dfrac{\pi}{2}$ and, where defined, $\dfrac{2\tan\theta}{1 - \tan^2\theta} = \cot\theta$, then $\theta =$

(A) $\dfrac{\pi}{2}$ (B) $\dfrac{\pi}{3}$ (C) $\dfrac{\pi}{4}$ (D) $\dfrac{\pi}{6}$ (E) 0   Ⓐ Ⓑ Ⓒ Ⓓ Ⓔ

Study Resources

The list below contains textbooks that are typical of those widely used in trigonometry courses at the college level. All the textbooks cover the major topics in the outline given earlier, but the approaches to certain topics may differ. To prepare for the Trigonometry examination, therefore, a candidate is advised to study one or more of these or similar textbooks. The supplementary reference, by Farley et al., is a paperback designed for supplementary study.

Many libraries do not carry textbooks as a policy. If you can't find any of the following textbooks at the library, see whether the college bookstore has a used copy. If you can't locate the most recent edition, an edition that is one or two years older will suffice for most subject areas. As a final option, purchase a new copy of the suggested textbook as an investment in your education.

TEXTBOOKS

Barnett, Raymond A. and Michael R. Ziegler, *College Algebra with Trigonometry,* 4th ed. New York: McGraw-Hill, 1989.

Keedy, M. L. and M. L. Bittinger, *Trigonometry: Triangles and Functions,* 4th ed. Reading, MA: Addison-Wesley, 1986.

Swokowski, Earl W., *Fundamentals of Trigonometry,* 7th ed. Boston: PWS-Kent, 1989.

SUPPLEMENTARY REFERENCE MATERIAL

Farley, Reuben W. et al., *Trigonometry: A Unitized Approach.* Englewood Cliffs, NJ: Prentice Hall, 1975.

College Algebra — Trigonometry

Description of the Examination

The Subject Examination in College Algebra-Trigonometry covers material that is usually taught in a one-semester course that includes both algebra and trigonometry. Such a course is usually taken by students who have studied algebra and geometry in high school, but who need additional study of precalculus mathematics before enrolling in calculus and other advanced courses at the college level.

The College Algebra-Trigonometry examination requires all the knowledge and skills required by the examinations in College Algebra and in Trigonometry. The combined examination consists of two separately timed 45-minute sections, each containing approximately 40 multiple-choice questions. One section is devoted exclusively to College Algebra; the other to Trigonometry. The exam places little emphasis on arithmetic calculations, and the use of calculators is not permitted during the examination.

Separate scores are not reported for College Algebra and Trigonometry. Candidates wishing to earn credit for both of these courses by examination should take the separate examinations in these subjects.

Sample Questions

Sample questions for this examination can be found in the two preceding sections.

Study Resources

The textbooks and supplementary reference materials suggested for both the College Algebra and the Trigonometry examinations can also be used to prepare for the College Algebra-Trigonometry examination. However, the textbooks listed below are typical of those used in a one-semester course that covers both algebra and trigonometry. These books assume a basic knowledge of algebra and geometry and therefore provide less explanation of fundamental topics than do the textbooks suggested for the College Algebra and the Trigonometry examinations.

Many libraries do not carry textbooks as a policy. If you can't find any of the following textbooks at the library, see whether the college bookstore has a used copy. If you can't locate the most recent edition, an edition that is one or two years older will suffice for most subject areas. As a final option, purchase a new copy of the suggested textbook as an investment in your education.

TEXTBOOKS

Barnett, Raymond A. and Michael R. Ziegler, *College Algebra with Trigonometry*, 4th ed. New York: McGraw-Hill, 1989.

Beckenbach, Edwin F. et al., *Modern College Algebra and Trigonometry*, 5th ed. Belmont, CA: Wadsworth, 1986.

Christy, Dennis T., *Algebra and Trigonometry*, 4th ed. New York: Wm. C. Brown, 1989.

Goodman, A. W., *A Short Course in Algebra and Trigonometry* (illus.). New York: Ardsley House, 1985.

Keedy, Mervin L. and Marvin L. Bittinger, *Algebra and Trigonometry: A Functions Approach*, 5th ed. Reading, MA: Addison-Wesley, 1990.

Lial, Margaret L., Charles D. Miller, and David I. Schneider, *Algebra and Trigonometry*, 5th ed. Glenview, IL: Scott, Foresman, 1990.

Munem, M. A. and J. P. Yizze, *Precalculus: Functions and Graphs*, 5th ed. New York: Worth, 1990.

Swokowski, Earl W., *Precalculus: Functions and Graphs*, 5th ed. Boston: Prindle, Weber & Schmidt, 1987.

SUPPLEMENTARY REFERENCE MATERIAL

Larson, Loren C., *Algebra and Trigonometry Refresher for Calculus Students*. New York: W. H. Freeman, 1979.

General Biology

Description of the Examination

The Subject Examination in General Biology covers material that is usually taught in a one-year biology course at the college level. The subject matter tested covers the broad field of the biological sciences, organized into three major areas: molecular and cellular biology, organismal biology, and population biology. The examination gives approximately equal weight to these three areas, and the questions relating to them are interspersed randomly throughout the test.

The examination consists of approximately 120 multiple-choice questions to be answered in two separately timed 45-minute sections.

Knowledge and Skills Required

Questions on the examination require candidates to demonstrate one or more of the following abilities.

- Knowledge of facts, principles, and processes of biology

- Understanding of the means by which information is collected, and how it is interpreted.

- Understanding of how one hypothesizes from available information, and how one draws conclusions and makes further predictions

- Understanding that science is a human endeavor with social consequences

The subject matter of the General Biology examination is drawn from the following topics.

⬤   *Approximate Percent of Examination*

33%   Molecular and Cellular Biology

Chemical composition of organisms

Simple chemical reactions and bonds

Properties of water

Chemical structure of carbohydrates, lipids, proteins, organic acids, nucleic acids

Approximate Percent of Examination

Cells
> Structure and function of cell organelles
>
> Properties of cell membranes
>
> Comparison of prokaryotic and eukaryotic cells

Enzymes
> Enzyme-substrate complex
>
> Role of coenzymes
>
> Inorganic cofactors
>
> Prosthetic groups

Energy transformations
> Glycolysis, respiration, anaerobic pathways
>
> Photosynthesis

Cell division
> Structure of chromosomes
>
> Mitosis, meiosis, and cytokinesis in plants and animals

Chemical nature of the gene
> Watson-Crick model of nucleic acids
>
> DNA replication
>
> Mutations
>
> Control of protein synthesis: transcription, translation, post-transcriptional processing
>
> Structural and regulatory genes
>
> Transformation and transduction

The origin of life
> Modern theories
>
> Experimental evidence

34% Organismal Biology
> Structure and function in plants with emphasis on angiosperms
>> Root, stem, leaf, flower, seed, fruit
>>
>> Water and mineral absorption and transport
>>
>> Food translocation and storage

Plant reproduction and development

Alternation of generations in ferns, pines, and flowering plants

Gamete formation and fertilization

Growth and development: hormonal control

Tropism and photoperiodicity

Structure and function in animals with emphasis on vertebrates

Major systems

Homeostatic mechanisms

Hormonal control in homeostasis and reproduction

Animal reproduction and development

Gamete formation, fertilization

Cleavage, gastrulation, germ layer formation, differentiation of organ systems

Experimental analysis of vertebrate development

Extraembryonic membranes of vertebrates

Formation and function of the mammalian placenta

Blood circulation in the human embryo

Principles of heredity

History of early experiments in heredity

Mendelian inheritance (dominance, segregation, independent assortment)

Chromosomal basis of inheritance

Linkage

Sex-linked, sex-influenced, sex-limited inheritance

Polygenic inheritance (height, skin color)

Multiple alleles (human blood groups)

33%   Population Biology

Principles of ecology

Energy flow and productivity in ecosystems

Biogeochemical cycles

Population growth and regulation (natality, mortality, competition, migration, density)

Community structure, growth, regulation (major biomes, succession and climax communities)

Habitat (biotic and abiotic factors)

Concept of niche

Principles of evolution

History of evolutionary concepts, Lamarckian and Darwinian theories

Modern concepts of natural selection (differential reproduction, mutation, Hardy-Weinberg equilibrium, speciation)

Adaptive radiation

Major features of plant and animal evolution

Concepts of homology and analogy

Convergence, extinction, balanced polymorphism, genetic drift

Classification of living organisms

Evolutionary history of humans

Principles of behavior

Stereotyped, learned social behavior

Societies (ants, bees, birds, primates)

Social biology

Problem of human population growth (age composition, birth and fertility rates, theory of demographic transition)

Human intervention in the natural world (management of resources, environmental pollution)

Implications of biomedical progress (control of human reproduction, genetic engineering)

Sample Questions

The 25 sample questions that follow are similar to questions on the General Biology examination, but they do not actually appear on the examination.

Before attempting to answer the sample questions, read all the information about the General Biology examination given above. Additional suggestions for preparing for CLEP examinations are provided in chapter 4.

Try to answer correctly as many questions as possible. Then compare your answers with the correct answers, given in Appendix B.

Directions: Each of the questions or incomplete statements below is followed by five suggested answers or completions. Select the one that is best in each case.

1. In which of the following ways do social insects benefit most from having several types or castes within the species?

   (A) Each colony is able to include a large number of individuals.
   (B) The secretions or odors produced by the protective caste are an effective defense.
   (C) The division of the species into castes ensures the survival of the fittest.
   (D) Large numbers of the worker caste can migrate to start new colonies.
   (E) The specialized structure of each caste permits division of labor and greater efficiency.

   Ⓐ Ⓑ Ⓒ Ⓓ Ⓔ

2. The greatest diversity of structure and of methods of locomotion is exhibited in the individuals of

   (A) a class
   (B) a family
   (C) an order
   (D) a species
   (E) a phylum

   Ⓐ Ⓑ Ⓒ Ⓓ Ⓔ

3. Of the following, which is an example of a mutualistic relationship?

   (A) The protozoan *Trichonympha* digesting wood in the gut of termites
   (B) The sporozoan *Plasmodium* reproducing in human blood cells and liberating toxins into the human body
   (C) Two species of *Paramecium* deriving food from a common laboratory culture
   (D) Rabbits being eaten by foxes
   (E) Humans inadvertently providing food for cockroaches

   Ⓐ Ⓑ Ⓒ Ⓓ Ⓔ

4. Evidence that multicellular green plants may have evolved from green algae is supplied by the fact that in both

   (A) the gametophyte generation is dominant
   (B) the sporophyte generation is dominant
   (C) chlorophylls *a* and *b* are photosynthetic pigments
   (D) xylem vessels are pitted and spiraled
   (E) male gametes are nonflagellated

   Ⓐ Ⓑ Ⓒ Ⓓ Ⓔ

5. All of the following statements concerning the light-dependent phase of photosynthesis are true EXCEPT:

   (A) An initial event is the excitation of electrons from chlorophyll by light energy.
   (B) The excited electrons are raised to a higher energy level.
   (C) If not captured in the reaction, the excited electrons drop back to their initial energy levels.
   (D) If captured in the reaction, some of the energy of the excited electrons is used to split carbon dioxide to carbon and oxygen.
   (E) The reaction occurs in grana.

   Ⓐ Ⓑ Ⓒ Ⓓ Ⓔ

6. Which of the following statements best explains the hypothesis that the development of sexual reproduction has resulted in acceleration of the rate of evolution?

   (A) Mutations are more likely to occur in spermatogenesis and oogenesis than in mitotically dividing cells.
   (B) Sexual reproduction results in more offspring than does asexual reproduction.
   (C) Those members of a species that are best adapted to their environment are most likely to be successful in sexual reproduction.
   (D) Mutations usually do not occur in the production of spores or in cells dividing by fission.
   (E) Sexual reproduction is more likely to result in genetic recombination than is asexual reproduction.

   Ⓐ Ⓑ Ⓒ Ⓓ Ⓔ

A frog gastrocnemius muscle gives a smooth tetanic contraction at any rate of stimulation above 20 per second. At threshold stimulus intensity, a response of some specific strength will be obtained. Increase of the stimulus intensity by 50 percent will increase the strength of response nearly 50 percent. If the intensity is again increased 50 percent, the response will increase only about another 25 percent. Further increase in the stimulus intensity produces no further increase in response.

7. The observations above are best explained by which of the following?

   (A) A muscle functions with an all-or-none mechanism.
   (B) Muscle-fiber sarcolemma is electrically resistant.
   (C) The fibers of a muscle do not all contract at the same rate.
   (D) The fibers of a muscle fatigue at varying rates.
   (E) The fibers of a muscle have varying thresholds for response.

   Ⓐ Ⓑ Ⓒ Ⓓ Ⓔ

8. In an amphibian gastrula, transplantation experiments that involve the dorsal lip of the blastopore indicate that this tissue

    (A) is destined to be ectoderm
    (B) does not differ from other tissues of the blastula in any significant manner
    (C) will cause a concentration of yolk in adjacent cells
    (D) has the power to initiate differentiation of the embryonic neural tube
    (E) is so sensitive that it will develop into any embryonic structure depending on its surroundings

    Ⓐ Ⓑ Ⓒ Ⓓ Ⓔ

9. Deposits of coal in Greenland and the Antarctic indicate that

    (A) these regions once contained numerous mollusks that deposited carbohydrates in their shells
    (B) the Earth's crust in these regions contains vast amounts of limestone
    (C) these regions were once thickly vegetated
    (D) there is a rich store of dissolved carbon dioxide in the seas surrounding these regions
    (E) a geologic uplift of coral rock and ocean bed has recently occurred in these regions

    Ⓐ Ⓑ Ⓒ Ⓓ Ⓔ

10. Thirst, loss of weight, and sugar in the urine result from the undersecretion of a hormone by which of the following?

    (A) Thyroid
    (B) Parathyroids
    (C) Islets of Langerhans
    (D) Adrenals
    (E) Thymus

    Ⓐ Ⓑ Ⓒ Ⓓ Ⓔ

11. Considering the role of mitochondria in cells, one would expect to find mitochondria most abundant in which of the following?

    (A) Mature red blood cells
    (B) Callous cells of the skin
    (C) Cells of the heart muscle
    (D) Epithelial cells of the cheek lining
    (E) Fat cells

    Ⓐ Ⓑ Ⓒ Ⓓ Ⓔ

12. All of the following statements about enzymes are true EXCEPT:

    (A) A single enzyme molecule can be used over and over again.
    (B) Most enzymes are highly specific with regard to the reactions they catalyze.
    (C) Some enzymes contain an essential nonprotein component.
    (D) Enzymes can function only within living cells.
    (E) Enzymes are destroyed by high temperatures.

    Ⓐ Ⓑ Ⓒ Ⓓ Ⓔ

13. Which of the following factors figures most significantly in limiting the size to which an animal cell may grow?

    (A) The ratio of cell surface to cell volume
    (B) The abundance of mitochondria in the cytoplasm
    (C) The chemical composition of the cell membrane
    (D) The presence of an inelastic cell wall
    (E) The relative number of nucleoli

    Ⓐ Ⓑ Ⓒ Ⓓ Ⓔ

14. Which of the following best describes the effect on heart action of the stimulation of the parasympathetic nerve fibers of the vagus nerve?

    (A) There is a decrease in the volume of blood pumped and an increase in the heartbeat rate.
    (B) There is an increase in the volume of blood pumped without a decrease in the heartbeat rate.
    (C) There is a prolonged acceleration in the heartbeat rate.
    (D) There is a decrease in the heartbeat rate.
    (E) There is an initial increase in the heartbeat rate, followed by a decrease.

    Ⓐ Ⓑ Ⓒ Ⓓ Ⓔ

15. If poorly drained soils encourage the growth of bacteria that convert nitrate to nitrogen, the effect on higher plants will be to

    (A) increase lipid production
    (B) decrease protein production
    (C) increase carbohydrate production
    (D) produce unusually large fruits
    (E) stimulate chlorophyll production

    Ⓐ Ⓑ Ⓒ Ⓓ Ⓔ

16. A patient is placed on a restricted diet of water, pure cooked starch, olive oil, adequate minerals, and vitamins. If a urinalysis several weeks later reveals the presence of relatively normal amounts of urea, the urea probably came from the

    (A) food eaten during the restricted diet
    (B) withdrawal of reserve urea stored in the liver
    (C) chemical combination of water, carbon dioxide, and free nitrogen
    (D) deamination of cellular proteins
    (E) urea synthesized by kidney tubule cells

    Ⓐ Ⓑ Ⓒ Ⓓ Ⓔ

Directions: The following group of questions consists of five lettered headings followed by a list of numbered phrases. For each numbered phrase select the one heading that is most closely related to it. A heading may be used once, more than once, or not at all.

Questions 17-19

    (A) Fertilization
    (B) Meiosis
    (C) Mitosis
    (D) Pollination
    (E) Nondisjunction

17. The process by which a zygote is formed

    Ⓐ Ⓑ Ⓒ Ⓓ Ⓔ

18. The process by which somatic (body) cells divide

    Ⓐ Ⓑ Ⓒ Ⓓ Ⓔ

19. The process by which monoploid (haploid) cells are formed from diploid cells

    Ⓐ Ⓑ Ⓒ Ⓓ Ⓔ

Directions: Each group of questions below concerns an experimental situation. In each case, first study the description of the situation. Then choose the best answer to each question following it.

Questions 20-22

Expenditures of solar energy, calculated by C. Juday for Lake Mendota in southern Wisconsin, appear in the table below.

Reflected or otherwise lost 49.5%
Absorbed in evaporation of water 25.0%
Raising of temperatures in the lake 21.7%
Melting of ice in the spring 3.0%
Directly used by organisms 0.8%

The pyramid of biomass for this same lake is represented by the following diagram.

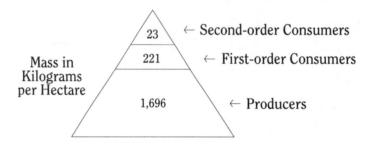

20. The most probable explanation for the relative masses of the first- and second-order consumers is that

   (A) each link in the food chain of an ecosystem has less available energy than the previous link has
   (B) only a small fraction of sunlight that reaches the Earth is transformed into chemical energy by photosynthesis
   (C) the total energy of the decomposers is greater than that of the rest of the organisms put together
   (D) seasonal fluctations in weather limit the number of consumers
   (E) second-order consumers require more total energy than first-order consumers do

   Ⓐ Ⓑ Ⓒ Ⓓ Ⓔ

21. The energy incorporated into this ecosystem is most dependent on the

   (A) photoperiod
   (B) total amount of photosynthesis
   (C) predator-prey relationships
   (D) length of the food chains
   (E) total amount of respiration

   Ⓐ Ⓑ Ⓒ Ⓓ Ⓔ

22. If the lake is assumed to be a typical ecosystem, the percent of radiant energy from the Sun that is trapped in photosynthesis is about

(A) 100%
(B)   10%
(C)   1%
(D) 0.1%
(E) 0.01%

Ⓐ Ⓑ Ⓒ Ⓓ Ⓔ

Questions 23-25

Inheritance of certain characteristics of the fruit fly, *Drosophila*, is as indicated by the table below.

Characteristic	Dominant	Recessive
Body color	Gray	Black
Eye color	Red	White

A female fruit fly had a gray body and white eyes. After being mated with a male fruit fly, she laid 112 eggs that developed into the following kinds of offspring.

Number	Body	Eyes
28	Gray	Red
29	Gray	White
28	Black	Red
27	Black	White

23. With respect to body color, the male parent of the 112 offspring was most probably

(A) homozygous gray
(B) heterozygous gray
(C) homozygous black
(D) heterozygous black
(E) of a genotype that cannot be determined from the data given

Ⓐ Ⓑ Ⓒ Ⓓ Ⓔ

24. Examination revealed that all of the 56 red-eyed offspring were females and all of the 56 white-eyed offspring were males. This observation indicates that

    (A) red and white eye colors segregate independently of sex
    (B) all of the red-eyed offspring inherited their eye color from their female parent
    (C) all of the red-eyed offspring were homozygous
    (D) the gene for eye color is linked to the gene for body color
    (E) the gene for red or for white eye color is carried on the X-chromosome

    Ⓐ Ⓑ Ⓒ Ⓓ Ⓔ

25. In this experiment, the number of offspring that exhibit both recessive characters is

    (A) 1
    (B) 27
    (C) 28
    (D) 55
    (E) 56

    Ⓐ Ⓑ Ⓒ Ⓓ Ⓔ

Study Resources

The following list contains textbooks that are typical of those widely used in college-level introductory biology courses. All the books cover the topics in the outline given earlier, but their approaches to certain topics and the emphases given to them may differ. To prepare for the General Biology examination, a candidate is advised to study one or more of these or other similar books. In addition, candidates would do well to consult pertinent articles from the monthly magazine *Scientific American*, available in most libraries.

Many libraries do not carry textbooks as a policy. If you can't find any of the following textbooks at the library, see whether the college bookstore has a used copy. If you can't locate the most recent edition, an edition that is one or two years older will suffice for most subject areas. As a final option, purchase a new copy of the suggested textbook as an investment in your education.

TEXTBOOKS

Arms, Karen and Pamela S. Camp, *Biology*, 3rd ed. New York: Saunders College Publications, 1987.

Campbell, Neil A., *Biology*, 2nd ed. Menlo Park, CA: Benjamin-Cummings, 1990.

Curtis, Helena and N. Sue Barnes, *Biology*, 5th ed. New York: Worth, 1989.

Johnson, Leland G., *Biology*, 2nd ed. Dubuque, IA: Wm. C. Brown, 1987.

Keeton, William T. and James L. Gould, *Biological Science*, 4th ed. New York: W. W. Norton, 1986.

Purves, William K., Gordon H. Orians, and H. Craig Heller, *Life, The Science of Biology*. Sunderland, MA: Sinauer Associates, 1992.

Raven, Peter H. and George B. Johnson, *Biology*, 3rd ed. St. Louis, MO: Mosby-Year Book, 1992.

Villee, Claude A., Eldra P. Solomon, and P. William Davis, *Biology*, 2nd ed. Philadelphia: Saunders College Publications, 1989.

Wallace, Robert A., Gerald P. Sanders, and Robert J. Ferl, *Biology, The Science of Life*, 3rd ed. New York: HarperCollins, 1991.

Wessells, Norman K. and Janet L. Hopson, *Biology*. New York: Random House, 1988.

General Chemistry

Description of the Examination

The Subject Examination in General Chemistry covers material usually taught in a one-year introductory course in general chemistry. Understanding of the structure and states of matter, reaction types, equations and stoichiometry, equilibrium, kinetics, thermodynamics, and descriptive and experimental chemistry is required, as is the ability to interpret and apply this material to new and unfamiliar problems.

Battery-operated hand-held calculators may be used during the examination; however, all calculator memories must be cleared of both programs and data and no peripheral devices such as magnetic cards or tapes are permitted. It may be helpful to use a calculator for some questions on the examination. A Periodic Chart of the elements is included in the examination booklet.

The exam contains approximately 80 multiple-choice questions to be answered within two separately timed 45-minute periods.

Knowledge and Skills Required

Questions on the examination require candidates to demonstrate one or more of the following abilities.

- Recall: remember specific facts; demonstrate straightforward knowledge of information and familiarity with terminology

- Application: understand concepts and reformulate information into other equivalent terms; apply knowledge to unfamiliar and/or practical situations; solve mathematical problems

- Interpretation: infer and deduce from data available and integrate information to form conclusions; recognize unstated assumptions

The subject matter of the General Chemistry examination is drawn from the following topics.

Approximate Percent of Examination

20%   Structure of Matter

   Atomic theory and atomic structure

   Evidence for the atomic theory

   Atomic masses; determination by chemical and physical means

   Atomic number and mass number; isotopes and mass spectroscopy

   Electron energy levels: atomic spectra, quantum numbers, atomic orbitals

   Periodic relationships including, for example, atomic radii, ionization energies, electron affinities, oxidation states

   Chemical bonding

   Binding forces

   Types: covalent, ionic, metallic, macromolecular (or network), van der Waals, hydrogen bonding

   Relationships to structure and to properties

   Polarity of bonds, electronegativities

   Geometry of molecules, ions, and coordination complexes; structural isomerism; dipole moments of molecules; relation of properties to structure

   Molecular models

   Valence bond theory; hybridization of orbitals, resonance, sigma and pi bonds

   Other models; for example, molecular orbital

   Nuclear chemistry: nuclear equations, half-lives, and radioactivity; chemical applications

19%   States of Matter

   Gases

   Laws of ideal gases; equations of state for an ideal gas

   Kinetic-molecular theory

   Interpretation of ideal gas laws on the basis of this theory

   Dependence of kinetic energy of molecules on temperature: Boltzmann distribution

   Deviations from ideal gas laws

Liquids and solids

Liquids and solids from the kinetic-molecular viewpoint

Phase diagrams of one-component systems

Changes of state, critical phenomena

Crystal structure

Solutions

Types of solutions and factors affecting solubility

Methods of expressing concentration

Colligative properties; for example, Raoult's law

Effect of interionic attraction on colligative properties and solubility

12%   Reaction Types

Formation and cleavage of covalent bonds

Acid-base reactions; concepts of Arrhenius, Brönsted-Lowry, and Lewis; amphoterism

Reactions involving coordination complexes

Precipitation reactions

Oxidation-reduction reactions

Oxidation number

The role of the electron in oxidation-reduction

Electrochemistry; electrolytic cells, standard half-cell potentials, prediction of the direction of redox reactions, effect of concentration changes

10%   Equations and Stoichiometry

The mole concept; Avogadro's number

Ionic and molecular species present in chemical systems; net ionic equations

Stoichiometry: mass and volume relations with emphasis on the mole concept

Balancing of equations including those for redox reactions

Approximate Percent of Examination

7%   Equilibrium

Concept of dynamic equilibrium, physical and chemical; Le Chatelier's principle; equilibrium constants

Quantitative treatment

Equilibrium constants for gaseous reactions in terms of both molar concentrations and partial pressure (K_c, K_p)

Equilibrium constants for reactions in solutions

Constants for acids and bases; pK; pH

Solubility product constants and their application to precipitation and the dissolution of slightly soluble compounds

Constants for complex ions

Common ion effect; buffers

4%   Kinetics

Concept of rate of reaction

Order of reaction and rate constant: their determination from experimental data

Effect of temperature change on rates

Energy of activation; the role of catalysts

The relationship between the rate-determining step and a mechanism

5%   Thermodynamics

State functions

First law: heat of formation; heat of reaction; change in enthalpy; Hess's law; heat capacity; heats of vaporization and fusion

Second law: free energy of formation; free energy of reaction; dependence of change in free energy on enthalpy and entropy changes

Relationship of change in free energy to equilibrium constants and electrode potentials

---

14%   Descriptive Chemistry

The accumulation of certain specific facts of chemistry is essential to enable students to comprehend the development of principles and concepts, to demonstrate applications of principle, to relate fact to theory and properties to structure, and to develop an understanding of systematic nomenclature, which facilitates communication. The following areas are normally included on the examination:

Chemical reactivity and products of chemical reactions

Chemistry of the main groups and transition elements, including typical examples of each

Organic chemistry, including such topics as functional groups and isomerism (may be treated as a separate unit or as exemplary material in other areas, such as bonding)

9%   Experimental Chemistry

Some questions are based on laboratory experiments widely performed in general chemistry and ask about the equipment used, observations made, calculations performed, and interpretation of the results. The questions are designed to provide a measure of students' understanding of the basic tools of chemistry and their applications to simple chemical systems.

Sample Questions

The 28 sample questions that follow are similar to questions on the General Chemistry examination, but they do not appear on the actual examination. Because a Periodic Chart is provided with the actual examination, you should refer to a Periodic Chart as needed when working through the sample questions.

Before attempting to answer the sample questions, read all the information about the General Chemistry examination on the preceding pages. Additional suggestions for preparing for CLEP examinations are provided in chapter 4.

Try to answer correctly as many questions as possible. Then compare your answers with the correct answers, given in Appendix B.

Directions: The group of questions below consists of five lettered headings followed by a list of numbered phrases. For each numbered phrase, select the one heading that is most closely related to it. Each heading may be used once, more than once, or not at all.

Questions 1-3

    (A) Trigonal pyramidal
    (B) Tetrahedral
    (C) Trigonal bipyramidal
    (D) Square pyramidal
    (E) Square planar

1. The shape of the PCl_5 molecule in the vapor state   Ⓐ Ⓑ Ⓒ Ⓓ Ⓔ

2. The shape of NH_4^+ Ⓐ Ⓑ Ⓒ Ⓓ Ⓔ

3. The shape of XeF_4 Ⓐ Ⓑ Ⓒ Ⓓ Ⓔ

Directions: Each of the questions or incomplete statements below is followed by five suggested answers or completions. Select the one that is best in each case.

$$1s^2\ 2s^2 2p^6\ 3s^2 3p^3$$

4. An atom of phosphorus has the electronic configuration indicated above. In the ground state, the number of orbitals occupied by at least one electron is

    (A) 3
    (B) 5
    (C) 9
    (D) 11
    (E) 15   Ⓐ Ⓑ Ⓒ Ⓓ Ⓔ

5. For which of the following pairs of species is the difference in radius the greatest?

    (A) Y^{3+} and La^{3+}
    (B) Fe^{2+} and Co^{2+}
    (C) S^{2-} and Cl^-
    (D) Na^+ and Mg^{2+}
    (E) F^- and Cl^- Ⓐ Ⓑ Ⓒ Ⓓ Ⓔ

6. The half-life of ^{55}Cr is 1.8 hours. The delivery of a sample of this isotope from the reactor to your laboratory requires about 10.8 hours. What is the minimum amount of such material that should be shipped so that you receive 1.0 milligram of ^{55}Cr ?

(A) 128 mg
(B) 64 mg
(C) 32 mg
(D) 11 mg
(E) 1.0 mg

Ⓐ Ⓑ Ⓒ Ⓓ Ⓔ

7. As the volume of a sample of a real gas is increased at constant temperature, the behavior of the gas more closely approximates that of an ideal gas because the

(A) collisions with the walls of the container become less frequent
(B) average molecular speed decreases
(C) molecules have expanded
(D) average distance between molecules becomes greater
(E) average molecular kinetic energy decreases

Ⓐ Ⓑ Ⓒ Ⓓ Ⓔ

8. A sealed vessel contains 0.200 mole of oxygen gas, 0.100 mole of nitrogen gas, and 0.200 mole of argon gas. The total pressure of the gas mixture is 5.00 atmospheres. The partial pressure of the argon is

(A) 0.200 atmosphere
(B) 0.500 atmosphere
(C) 1.00 atmosphere
(D) 2.00 atmospheres
(E) 5.00 atmospheres

Ⓐ Ⓑ Ⓒ Ⓓ Ⓔ

9. The critical temperature of a substance gives information about all of the following EXCEPT the

(A) slope of the solid-liquid line on a phase diagram
(B) relative attractive forces among the molecules
(C) highest boiling point the liquid can exhibit
(D) ease of liquefying a gas by pressure
(E) lowest temperature above which only one phase can exist

Ⓐ Ⓑ Ⓒ Ⓓ Ⓔ

10. For a solid solute that has an endothermic heat of solution when dissolved in water, which of the following is true?

(A) Its lattice energy is less than its energy of hydration.
(B) Its solubility will increase with an increase in temperature.
(C) Its solubility increases significantly with an increase in pressure.
(D) The value of ΔG for the solution process is positive.
(E) The entropy of the system decreases as the solute is dissolved.

Ⓐ Ⓑ Ⓒ Ⓓ Ⓔ

11. A 2.6-gram sample of a nonvolatile solute (molar mass 52 grams) is dissolved in 50. grams of a solvent (molar mass 100. grams) that has a vapor pressure of 33 millimeters of mercury at 20°C. Assuming the solution to be ideal, the vapor pressure of the solution at 20°C is

(A) 3.0 mm Hg   (B) 20. mm Hg   (C) 23 mm Hg
   (D) 27 mm Hg   (E) 30. mm Hg

Ⓐ Ⓑ Ⓒ Ⓓ Ⓔ

12. A solution prepared by mixing 10 milliliters of 1-molar HCl and 10 milliliters of 2-molar NaOH has a pH of

(A) 0.0   (B) 0.3   (C) 7.0   (D) 13.7   (E) 14.0

Ⓐ Ⓑ Ⓒ Ⓓ Ⓔ

13. All of the following reactions can be defined as Lewis acid-base reactions EXCEPT

(A) $Al(OH)_3 + OH^- \rightarrow Al(OH)_4^-$
(B) $Cl_2 + H_2O \rightarrow HOCl + H^+ + Cl^-$
(C) $SnCl_4 + 2\ Cl^- \rightarrow SnCl_6^{2-}$
(D) $NH_4^+ + NH_2^- \rightarrow 2\ NH_3$
(E) $H^+ + NH_3 \rightarrow NH_4^+$

Ⓐ Ⓑ Ⓒ Ⓓ Ⓔ

14. Which of the species below contains a group V element in an oxidation state different from that of the others?

(A) NO_3^- (B) $POCl_3$ (C) $H_2PO_4^-$
   (D) $KAsF_4$ (E) Sb_4O_{10}

Ⓐ Ⓑ Ⓒ Ⓓ Ⓔ

$$Cd^{2+} + 2e^- \rightleftharpoons Cd \qquad E^0 = -0.40\ volt$$
$$Cu^+ + e^- \rightleftharpoons Cu \qquad E^0 = +0.52\ volt$$
$$Ag^+ + e^- \rightleftharpoons Ag \qquad E^0 = +0.80\ volt$$

15. Based on the standard electrode potentials given above, which of the following is the strongest reducing agent?

(A) Cd   (B) Cd^{2+} (C) Cu   (D) Ag   (E) Ag^+

Ⓐ Ⓑ Ⓒ Ⓓ Ⓔ

16. A sample of $CaCO_3$ (molar mass 100. grams) was reported as being 28.0 percent Ca. If no calcium was present in any impurities, the percent of $CaCO_3$ in the sample is

(A) 28.0%   (B) 42.0%   (C) 56.0%
   (D) 70.0%   (E) 100.0%

Ⓐ Ⓑ Ⓒ Ⓓ Ⓔ

$$2 \text{ Al(s)} + 6 \text{ HCl(aq)} \rightarrow 2 \text{ AlCl}_3\text{(aq)} + 3 \text{ H}_2\text{(g)}$$

17. According to the reaction above at 25°C and 1.00 atmosphere, about how many grams of aluminum (atomic mass 27) are necessary to produce 0.60 mole of hydrogen gas?

    (A) 1.2 grams
    (B) 11 grams
    (C) 16 grams
    (D) 24 grams
    (E) 32 grams Ⓐ Ⓑ Ⓒ Ⓓ Ⓔ

$$...\text{IO}_3^- + ...\text{S}_2\text{O}_3^{2-} + ...\text{H}^+ \rightarrow ...\text{I}^- + ...\text{S}_4\text{O}_6^{2-} + ...\text{H}_2\text{O}$$

18. When the equation above is balanced and all coefficients are reduced to lowest whole number terms, the coefficient for the reducing agent is

    (A) 1
    (B) 3
    (C) 4
    (D) 6
    (E) 8 Ⓐ Ⓑ Ⓒ Ⓓ Ⓔ

19. The ionization constant for acetic acid is 1.8×10^{-5}; that for hydrocyanic acid is 4×10^{-10}. In 0.1-molar solutions of sodium acetate and sodium cyanide, it is true that

    (A) [H⁺] equals [OH⁻] in each solution
    (B) [H⁺] exceeds [OH⁻] in each solution
    (C) [H⁺] of the sodium acetate solution is less than that of the sodium cyanide solution
    (D) [OH⁻] of the sodium acetate solution is less than that of the sodium cyanide solution
    (E) [OH⁻] of the two solutions is the same Ⓐ Ⓑ Ⓒ Ⓓ Ⓔ

$$\text{HCl} > \text{HC}_2\text{H}_3\text{O}_2 > \text{HCN} > \text{H}_2\text{O} > \text{NH}_3$$

20. Five acids are listed above in order of decreasing acid strength. Which of the following reactions must have an equilibrium constant with a value less than 1?

    (A) $\text{HCl} + \text{CN}^- \rightleftharpoons \text{HCN} + \text{Cl}^-$
    (B) $\text{HCl} + \text{H}_2\text{O} \rightleftharpoons \text{H}_3\text{O}^+ + \text{Cl}^-$
    (C) $\text{HC}_2\text{H}_3\text{O}_2 + \text{OH}^- \rightleftharpoons \text{C}_2\text{H}_3\text{O}_2^- + \text{H}_2\text{O}$
    (D) $\text{H}_2\text{O} + \text{NH}_2^- \rightleftharpoons \text{NH}_3 + \text{OH}^-$
    (E) $\text{HCN} + \text{C}_2\text{H}_3\text{O}_2^- \rightleftharpoons \text{HC}_2\text{H}_3\text{O}_2 + \text{CN}^-$ Ⓐ Ⓑ Ⓒ Ⓓ Ⓔ

$$2\ NO + Cl_2 \rightarrow 2\ NOCl$$

21. Doubling the concentration of both reactants in the reaction above increases the rate by a factor of 8. Doubling the chlorine concentration alone doubles the rate. What is the overall order of the reaction?

(A) 0   (B) 1   (C) 2   (D) 3   (E) 4

Ⓐ Ⓑ Ⓒ Ⓓ Ⓔ

22. All of the following statements about the nitrogen family of elements are true EXCEPT:

(A) It contains both metals and nonmetals.
(B) The electronic configuration of the valence shell of the atom is ns^2np^3.
(C) The only oxidation states exhibited by members of this family are $-3, 0, +3, +5$.
(D) The atomic radii increase with increasing atomic number.
(E) The boiling points increase with increasing atomic number.

Ⓐ Ⓑ Ⓒ Ⓓ Ⓔ

$$A \rightarrow X$$

23. The enthalpy change for the reaction above is ΔH_T. This reaction can be broken down into a series of steps as shown in the diagram below.

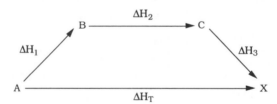

A relationship that must exist among the various enthalpy changes is

(A) $\Delta H_T - \Delta H_1 - \Delta H_2 - \Delta H_3 = 0$
(B) $\Delta H_T + \Delta H_1 + \Delta H_2 + \Delta H_3 = 0$
(C) $\Delta H_3 - (\Delta H_1 + \Delta H_2) = \Delta H_T$
(D) $\Delta H_2 - (\Delta H_3 + \Delta H_1) = \Delta H_T$
(E) $\Delta H_T + \Delta H_2 = \Delta H_1 + \Delta H_3$

Ⓐ Ⓑ Ⓒ Ⓓ Ⓔ

24. Which of the following formulas would be expected for a binary compound of barium and nitrogen?

(A) Ba_3N_2 (B) Ba_2N_3 (C) Ba_2N
(D) BaN_2 (E) BaN

Ⓐ Ⓑ Ⓒ Ⓓ Ⓔ

25. Which of the following salts when dissolved in water forms a basic solution?

(A) NaCl   (B) $(NH_4)_2SO_4$ (C) $CuSO_4$
(D) K_2CO_3 (E) NH_4NO_3

Ⓐ Ⓑ Ⓒ Ⓓ Ⓔ

26. Of the following organic compounds, which is LEAST soluble in water?

(A) CH_3OH
(B) $CH_3CH_2CH_2OH$
(C) $CH_3CH_2CH_2OCH_2CH_2CH_3$

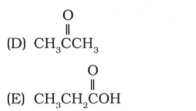

(D) $CH_3\overset{\displaystyle O}{\overset{\|}{C}}CH_3$

(E) $CH_3CH_2\overset{\displaystyle O}{\overset{\|}{C}}OH$

Ⓐ Ⓑ Ⓒ Ⓓ Ⓔ

27. Of the laboratory equipment listed below, which has the greatest relative uncertainty in a measurement?

(A) 50-ml burette when used to measure 25 ml
(B) 25-ml pipette when used to measure 25 ml
(C) 50-ml graduated cylinder when used to measure 25 ml
(D) Analytical balance when used to weigh 25 grams
(E) Centigram balance when used to weigh 25 grams

Ⓐ Ⓑ Ⓒ Ⓓ Ⓔ

		RESULTS	
SAMPLE	REAGENT USED	LIMITED AMOUNT OF REAGENT	EXCESS REAGENT
I	NaOH	White precipitate	Precipitate dissolves
II	NH_3(aq)	White precipitate	White precipitate

28. The table above summarizes the reactions of two samples of a certain unknown solution when treated with bases.

Which of the following metallic ions could be present in the unknown solution?

(A) Ca^{2+} (B) Zn^{2+} (C) Ni^{2+} (D) Al^{3+} (E) Ag^+

Ⓐ Ⓑ Ⓒ Ⓓ Ⓔ

Study Resources

Following is a list of textbooks that are frequently used in first-year chemistry courses that you can use to prepare for the General Chemistry examination. Most cover the topics in the test outline given earlier, but their approaches to and their emphases on certain topics may differ, so you may want to study more than one textbook.

Additional suggestions for preparing for CLEP examinations appear in chapter 4.

Many libraries do not carry textbooks as a policy. If you can't find any of the following textbooks at the library, see whether the college bookstore has a used copy. If you can't locate the most recent edition, an edition that is one or two years older will suffice for most subject areas. As a final option, purchase a new copy of the suggested textbook as an investment in your education.

TEXTBOOKS

Brady, James E., *General Chemistry: Principles and Structure*, 5th ed. New York: John Wiley & Sons, 1990.

Brown, Theodore L., H. Eugene LeMay, Jr., and Bruce Edward Bursten, *Chemistry: The Central Science*, 5th ed. Englewood Cliffs, NJ: Prentice Hall, 1991.

Dickerson, R. E. et al., *Chemical Principles*, 4th ed. Menlo Park, CA: Benjamin Cummings, 1984.

Holtzclaw, Henry F., Jr. and William R. Robinson, *College Chemistry: With Qualitative Analysis*, 8th ed. Lexington, MA: D. C. Heath, 1988.

Masterton, William L. et al., *Chemical Principles, with Qualitative Analysis*, 6th ed. Philadelphia: Saunders College Publications, 1986.

Petrucci, Ralph H., *General Chemistry: Principles and Modern Applications*, 5th ed. New York: Macmillan, 1989.

Zumdahl, S. S., *Chemistry*, 2nd ed. Lexington, MA: D. C. Heath, 1989.

Information Systems and Computer Applications

Description of the Examination

The Subject Examination in Information Systems and Computer Applications covers material that is usually taught in an introductory college-level business course. Questions on the examination are about equally divided between those testing knowledge of terminology and basic concepts and those asking students to apply that knowledge. Although the examination assumes a general familiarity with information systems and computer applications, it does not emphasize the details of hardware design, language-specific programming techniques, or specific application packages. There are occasional references to applications such as word processing, spreadsheets, and data management, but questions that involve these applications do not draw heavily on one's knowledge of a specific product. Rather, the focus is on concepts and techniques applicable to a variety of products and environments.

The examination contains approximately 100 multiple-choice questions to be answered in two separately timed 45-minute sections.

Knowledge and Skills Required

Questions on the examination require candidates to demonstrate the following abilities in the approximate proportions indicated. A single question may require both abilities.

- Knowledge of terminology and basic concepts (about 50 percent of the examination)

- Application of knowledge (about 50 percent of the examination)

The subject matter of the Information Systems and Computer Applications examination is drawn from the following topics.

Approximate Percent of Examination

15%   Computer Hardware and Its Functions

Processing, storage, and I/O devices

Data concepts and representation

⬤	*Approximate Percent of Examination*

10% Computer Software
- Systems software
- Programming languages
- Standards

15% System Development Life Cycle
- System development life cycle methodologies
- Analysis/design tools and techniques

5% Computer Programming
- Program life cycle (analysis, design, coding, testing)
- Program design tools
- Programming logic (sequence, selection, repetition, case)

10% Data Management
- File organization (direct, sequential, indexed)
- Database concepts and models (hierarchical, network, relational)

10% Telecommunications
- Equipment and its functions
- Networks

20% Organizational and User Support Systems: Concepts and Applications
- Design support systems
- Artificial intelligence and expert systems
- Office systems (conferencing, voice mail, fax, electronic mail)
- End-user applications (word processing, spreadsheet, data management, graphics)

10%   Information Processing Management

　　　Types of information processing (batch, real-time, transaction)

　　　Controls in information processing (I/O, security, backup, recovery)

　　　Information processing careers

5%   Social and Ethical Issues (economic, privacy, security, legal)

Sample Questions

The 25 sample questions given here are similar to questions on the Information Systems and Computer Applications examination, but they do not appear on the actual examination.

Before attempting to answer the sample questions, read all the information about the Information Systems and Computer Applications examination on the preceding pages. Additional suggestions for preparing for CLEP examinations are provided in chapter 4.

Try to answer correctly as many questions as possible. Then compare your answers with the correct answers, given in Appendix B.

Directions: Each of the questions or incomplete statements below is followed by five suggested answers or completions. Select the one that is best in each case.

1. A spreadsheet can be described as

   (A) a type of expert system
   (B) an integrated applications package
   (C) a symbolic string-manipulation processor
   (D) a word processor for numeric information
   (E) an applications package for performing "what-if" analysis

   Ⓐ Ⓑ Ⓒ Ⓓ Ⓔ

2. In most computer languages, the absence of parentheses implies that the order of mathematical operation from highest to lowest precedence is

  (A) exponentiation, addition and subtraction, multiplication and division
  (B) addition and subtraction, multiplication and division, exponentiation
  (C) multiplication and division, exponentiation, addition and subtraction
  (D) exponentiation, multiplication and division, addition and subtraction
  (E) exponentiation, multiplication, division, addition and subtraction

  Ⓐ Ⓑ Ⓒ Ⓓ Ⓔ

3. The ability of computerized systems to store and exchange information represents a potential threat to our right of

  (A) free speech   (B) assembly   (C) equal access to information
    (D) privacy   (E) consumer protection

  Ⓐ Ⓑ Ⓒ Ⓓ Ⓔ

4. Should there be a power failure, the contents of RAM will be

  (A) automatically printed out
  (B) automatically saved on disk
  (C) displayed on the screen
  (D) lost
  (E) refreshed

  Ⓐ Ⓑ Ⓒ Ⓓ Ⓔ

5. Which of the following levels of computer programming language is closest to machine language?

  (A) Symbolic
  (B) Problem oriented
  (C) Procedural
  (D) Virtual
  (E) Declarative

  Ⓐ Ⓑ Ⓒ Ⓓ Ⓔ

6. In a spreadsheet formula, what type of cell address is fixed and does not change when the formula is copied?

  (A) Relative address   (B) Absolute address
    (C) Fixed address   (D) Static address
      (E) Constant address

  Ⓐ Ⓑ Ⓒ Ⓓ Ⓔ

7. Which of the following specifies running two or more programs concurrently on the same computer and sharing the computer's resources?

   (A) Booting   (B) Paging   (C) Multiprogramming
      (D) Multiprocessing   (E) Thrashing

   Ⓐ Ⓑ Ⓒ Ⓓ Ⓔ

8. Which DBMS data model uses 2-dimensional tables to describe data structures?

   (A) Relational   (B) Hierarchical
      (C) Network   (D) Navigational
         (E) CODASYL

   Ⓐ Ⓑ Ⓒ Ⓓ Ⓔ

9. Data values A and B are stored in memory locations X and Y, respectively. Which of the following is true after execution of an instruction that moves A to Y?

   (A) B is erased.
   (B) Y contains A, and X contains B.
   (C) A is eliminated from location X.
   (D) The sum A + B is stored at location Y.
   (E) Y contains A + B, and X contains B.

   Ⓐ Ⓑ Ⓒ Ⓓ Ⓔ

10. The following pseudocode depicts the logic in a section of a computer program.

    ```
    SET A TO 1
    SET B TO 3
    SET A TO A + B
    WHILE A < 20
         SET A TO (A*A)/2
    END WHILE
    ```

    The value of variable A following execution of the program segment is

    (A) 16   (B) 20   (C) 21   (D) 32   (E) 64

    Ⓐ Ⓑ Ⓒ Ⓓ Ⓔ

11. The time taken to locate and read or write data on a disk is known as

    (A) access motion time
    (B) rotational delay time
    (C) head movement time
    (D) disk access time
    (E) fetch time

    Ⓐ Ⓑ Ⓒ Ⓓ Ⓔ

12. Over which type of transmission line do data travel in both directions simultaneously?

(A) Simplex   (B) Half-duplex   (C) Full-duplex
(D) Double-duplex   (E) Parallel-duplex

Ⓐ Ⓑ Ⓒ Ⓓ Ⓔ

13. Which of the following would NOT be used as an input device for a computer system?

(A) Optical scanner   (B) Tape drive   (C) Hard disk
(D) Floppy disk   (E) Microfilm reader

Ⓐ Ⓑ Ⓒ Ⓓ Ⓔ

14. In many computers, input/output (I/O) devices are connected to primary storage by devices that enable I/O operations to overlap with CPU operations. These devices are called

(A) buffers   (B) channels   (C) selectors
(D) cables   (E) busses

Ⓐ Ⓑ Ⓒ Ⓓ Ⓔ

15. In parallel transmission, the bits representing a byte are sent out

(A) over separate lines
(B) over the same line
(C) with start and stop bits
(D) asynchronously
(E) synchronously

Ⓐ Ⓑ Ⓒ Ⓓ Ⓔ

16. If A = 4, B = 2, C = 6, and D = 2, then the execution of the statement

$X = A*B + C/D$

would set X to

(A) 7   (B) 8   (C) 11   (D) 16   (E) 10

Ⓐ Ⓑ Ⓒ Ⓓ Ⓔ

17. Which of the statements concerning real-time processing is generally FALSE?

(A) A real-time system requires online processing methods.
(B) A real-time system requires sequential file access.
(C) A real-time system requires online files.
(D) A real-time processing operation is one in which all transactions are processed soon after they occur.
(E) Real-time processing requires direct access storage.

Ⓐ Ⓑ Ⓒ Ⓓ Ⓔ

442

18. One responsibility that is NOT traditionally given to a beginning programmer is

    (A) coding   (B) debugging   (C) program testing
    (D) documentation   (E) systems design

    Ⓐ Ⓑ Ⓒ Ⓓ Ⓔ

19. The person responsible for establishing a data dictionary that standardizes data item definitions is usually the

    (A) systems analyst
    (B) applications programmer
    (C) data definition analyst
    (D) database administrator
    (E) librarian

    Ⓐ Ⓑ Ⓒ Ⓓ Ⓔ

20. In a large organization, which of the following applications is (are) usually considered appropriate for end-user development?

    I. Writing a program that creates reports to be used by a single department for a short period of time
    II. Developing an inquiry system that uses records downloaded from the corporate database
    III. Developing a system to process sales transactions for uploading to the corporate database

    (A) I only
    (B) II only
    (C) III only
    (D) I and II only
    (E) I, II, and III

    Ⓐ Ⓑ Ⓒ Ⓓ Ⓔ

21. Pseudocode is frequently a useful aid in all of the following activities EXCEPT

    (A) writing the program
    (B) running the program
    (C) debugging the program
    (D) explaining the program to others who are not programmers
    (E) making changes in the program after it is completed and checked out

    Ⓐ Ⓑ Ⓒ Ⓓ Ⓔ

22. In which phase of the system development life cycle is the user LEAST involved?

    (A) Analysis   (B) Design   (C) Development
    (D) Implementation   (E) Maintenance

    Ⓐ Ⓑ Ⓒ Ⓓ Ⓔ

23. The use of a computer with a modem in the office allows for data communications to take place in which of the following forms?

    I. Electronic mail
    II. Computer conferencing
    III. Voice mail

    (A) I only   (B) II only   (C) III only
      (D) I and II only   (E) I, II, and III

    Ⓐ Ⓑ Ⓒ Ⓓ Ⓔ

24. The major difference between direct access storage devices and magnetic tape is that records on direct access devices

    (A) are recorded serially
    (B) can be of fixed or variable length
    (C) can be blocked or unblocked
    (D) can be accessed directly or sequentially
    (E) are more easily verified

    Ⓐ Ⓑ Ⓒ Ⓓ Ⓔ

25. When applied to the development of computer systems, the term "ergonomics" means

    (A) designing computer systems to maximize the cost-benefit ratio
    (B) applying human factors principles to maximize the efficiency of the human-machine interface
    (C) following the systems development life cycle
    (D) fostering development team interaction through the use of computer-aided software engineering tools
    (E) optimizing the throughput rate by adjusting the operating system interrupts

    Ⓐ Ⓑ Ⓒ Ⓓ Ⓔ

Study Resources

The references given below have been updated from a list of textbooks used in introductory college courses in information systems and computer applications in 1989. The original list was obtained through a survey of approximately 400 faculty who were teaching such courses. The references are divided into two categories:

- textbooks that deal with general computer concepts and applications software.

- textbooks that focus on information processing.

If you plan to obtain credit at a particular institution, check the textbooks that are currently being used in the relevant course; the examination is likely to be reasonably consistent with introductory information processing textbooks at most institutions. If you plan to prepare for the examination and have no specific institution in mind, select a textbook from each of the two categories listed below. As you prepare for the examination, keep in mind the test description given earlier as well as the topic outline.

Many libraries do not carry textbooks as a policy. If you can't find any of the following textbooks at the library, see whether the college bookstore has a used copy. If you can't locate the most recent edition, an edition that is one or two years older will suffice for most subject areas. As a final option, purchase a new copy of the suggested textbook as an investment in your education.

GENERAL REFERENCES

Davis, William S., *Computing Fundamentals: Concepts,* 3rd ed. Reading, MA: Addison-Wesley, 1991.

Ingalsbe, Lon, *Business Applications Software for IBM and Compatible Microcomputers,* 3rd ed. Columbus, OH: Merrill, 1990.

Sanders, Donald H., *Computers Today, with BASIC,* 3rd ed. New York: McGraw-Hill, 1988.

Shelly, Gary B., Thomas J. Cashman, and Gloria A. Waggoner, *Computer Concepts with Microcomputer Applications: WordPerfect 5.0/5.1, Lotus 1-2-3, dBase III Plus.* Boston: Boyd & Fraser, 1990.

Trainor, Timothy N. and Diane Krasnecvich, *Computers!* Santa Cruz, CA: Mitchell, 1989.

INFORMATION PROCESSING TEXTBOOKS

Athey, Thomas H. and Robert W. Zmud, *Introduction to Computers and Information Systems with BASIC*, 2nd ed. Glenview, IL: Scott, Foresman/Little, Brown College Division, 1988.

Kroenke, David and Kathleen A. Dolan, *Business Computer Systems: An Introduction*, 4th ed. New York: Mitchell, McGraw-Hill, 1990.

Laudon, Kenneth C. and Jane Price Laudon, *Management Information Systems: A Contemporary Perspective*, 2nd ed. New York: MacMillan, 1991.

Long, Larry E., *Introduction to Computers and Information Processing*, 3rd ed. Englewood Cliffs, NJ: Prentice Hall, 1991.

Parker, Charles S., *Understanding Computers and Information Processing: Today and Tomorrow*, 4th ed. Chicago: Dryden Press, 1992.

Principles of Management

Description of the Examination

The Subject Examination in Principles of Management covers the material that is usually taught in an introductory course in the essentials of management and organization. The fact that such courses are offered by different types of institutions and in a number of fields other than business has been taken into account in the preparation of this examination. The exam requires a knowledge of human resources and operational and functional aspects of management, but primary emphasis is placed on functional aspects of management.

The examination is 90 minutes long and includes approximately 100 multiple-choice questions to be answered in two separately timed 45-minute sections.

Knowledge and Skills Required

Questions on the test require candidates to demonstrate one or more of the following abilities.

- Specific factual knowledge, recall, and general understanding of purposes, functions, and techniques of management (about 10 percent of the examination)

- Understanding of and ability to associate the meaning of specific terminology with important management ideas, processes, techniques, concepts, and elements (about 40 percent of the examination)

- Understanding of theory and significant underlying assumptions, concepts, and limitations of management data, including a comprehension of the rationale of procedures, methods, and analyses (about 40 percent of the examination)

- Application of knowledge, general concepts, and principles to specific problems (about 10 percent of the examination)

The subject matter of the Principles of Management examination is drawn from the following topics.

⬤ Approximate Percent of Examination

20%   Organization and Human Resources
      Personnel administration
      Collective bargaining
      Human relations and motivation
      Training and development
      Performance appraisal
      Organizational development
      Effective communication
      Legal concerns
      Work force diversity

15%   Operational Aspects of Management
      Operations planning and control
      Work scheduling
      Quality management (TQM, e.g.)
      Information processing and management
      Strategic planning and analysis
      Productivity

50%   Functional Aspects of Management
         Planning
         Organizing
         Directing
         Controlling
         Authority
         Decision making
         Organization charts
         Leadership
         Organizational structure
         Budgeting
         Communication
         Problem solving
         Group dynamics
         Conflict resolution
         Effective communication
         Change
         Organizational theory

15%   Miscellaneous Aspects of Management
         Historical aspects
         Social responsibilities of business
         Systems
         International management and competition
         Environment
         Ethics
         Government regulation
         Management theory and theorists

Sample Questions

The 24 sample questions that follow are similar to questions on the Principles of Management examination, but they do not appear on the actual examination.

Before attempting to answer the sample questions, read all the information about the Principles of Management examination on the preceding pages. Additional suggestions for preparing for CLEP examinations are provided in chapter 4.

Try to answer correctly as many questions as possible. Then compare your answers with the correct answers, given in Appendix B.

Directions: Each of the questions or incomplete statements below is followed by five suggested answers or completions. Select the one that is best in each case.

1. Which of the following words is NOT logically related to the others?

    (A) Planning   (B) Directing   (C) Producing
       (D) Controlling   (E) Organizing

   Ⓐ Ⓑ Ⓒ Ⓓ Ⓔ

2. Program Evaluation and Review Technique (PERT) is a system for

    (A) developing the organization chart for a company
    (B) scheduling and finding the critical path for production
    (C) evaluating the performance of workers
    (D) reviewing the overall financial condition of the company
    (E) programming a computer

   Ⓐ Ⓑ Ⓒ Ⓓ Ⓔ

3. Which of the following is a correct statement about controlling as a management function?

    (A) It can be performed independently of planning.
    (B) It is performed only by the controller of an organization.
    (C) It is more prevalent in business than in government.
    (D) It assumes a certain approach to motivating employees.
    (E) To work effectively, it must be closely related to planning.

   Ⓐ Ⓑ Ⓒ Ⓓ Ⓔ

4. Decentralization tends to be encouraged by which of the following business trends?

   I. Product diversification
  II. Use of electronic computers
 III. Geographical expansion of operations

(A) I only   (B) II only   (C) III only
  (D) I and III only   (E) II and III only

Ⓐ Ⓑ Ⓒ Ⓓ Ⓔ

5. Which of the following can be best determined by consulting an organization chart?

(A) The size of the company
(B) The relationships of people
(C) The nature of work performed
(D) The relationship of positions
(E) The quality of management of the firm

Ⓐ Ⓑ Ⓒ Ⓓ Ⓔ

6. Which of the following best illustrates informal organization?

(A) Line authority, such as that of the field marshal and battalion commander in the military
(B) Staff authority, such as that of personnel or cost control in manufacturing
(C) Functional authority, such as corporate supervision of the legal aspect of pension plans in branch plants
(D) The acceptance of authority by subordinates
(E) Groupings based on such things as technical ability, seniority, and personal influence

Ⓐ Ⓑ Ⓒ Ⓓ Ⓔ

7. The number of subordinates who directly report to a superior refers to the manager's

(A) span of control   (B) organizational role
  (C) organizational structure   (D) chain of command
   (E) general staff

Ⓐ Ⓑ Ⓒ Ⓓ Ⓔ

8. The choice of organizational structure to be used in a business should be

    (A) made by mutual agreement among all the people affected
    (B) based on consideration of the type of organizational structures used by competitors
    (C) subject to definite and fixed rules
    (D) based on the objectives of each individual business
    (E) made by organization specialists rather than managers

    Ⓐ Ⓑ Ⓒ Ⓓ Ⓔ

9. The concept of hierarchy of needs attempts to explain which of the following?

    (A) Functional supervision   (B) Unity of command
      (C) Line-staff conflict   (D) Heuristic programming
        (E) Personal motivation

    Ⓐ Ⓑ Ⓒ Ⓓ Ⓔ

10. Frederick Taylor is considered a pioneer in the school of management referred to as the

    (A) management-process school
    (B) empirical school
    (C) scientific-management school
    (D) behaviorist school
    (E) social-system school

    Ⓐ Ⓑ Ⓒ Ⓓ Ⓔ

11. Preparation of which of the following is the most logical first step in developing an annual operating plan?

    (A) A sales forecast by product
    (B) A production schedule by product
    (C) A flow-of-funds statement by product
    (D) A plant and equipment requirement forecast
    (E) A pro forma income statement and balance sheet

    Ⓐ Ⓑ Ⓒ Ⓓ Ⓔ

12. A large span of control throughout an organization invariably results in

    (A) low morale
    (B) high morale
    (C) an excess work load for each manager
    (D) a flat (horizontal) organizational structure
    (E) a tall (vertical) organizational structure

    Ⓐ Ⓑ Ⓒ Ⓓ Ⓔ

13. Which of the following is an example of a line position in a manufacturing organization?

  (A) The sales manager concerned with selling a product in a given territory
  (B) The head of research and development concerned with new products
  (C) The controller concerned with establishing budgets
  (D) The personnel manager concerned with employing workers
  (E) The quality control manager concerned with maintaining quality standards in a production plant

  Ⓐ Ⓑ Ⓒ Ⓓ Ⓔ

14. Which of the following is a conflict-resolution practice that seeks to satisfy both parties to a conflict?

  (A) Avoidance
  (B) Stipulation
  (C) Competition
  (D) Collaboration
  (E) Appeal to authority

  Ⓐ Ⓑ Ⓒ Ⓓ Ⓔ

15. Which of the following goals is most likely to produce the desired results?

  (A) "Do your best."
  (B) "Outproduce your competitor by 5%."
  (C) "Introduce new products to the market at an unprecedented rate."
  (D) "Increase sales volume by 10% while maintaining current rate of expenditures."
  (E) "Reduce defects due to poor work habits."

  Ⓐ Ⓑ Ⓒ Ⓓ Ⓔ

16. The practice in large companies of establishing autonomous divisions whose heads are entirely responsible for what happens is referred to as

  (A) management by exception
  (B) decentralization of authority
  (C) delegation of authority
  (D) integration
  (E) informal organization

  Ⓐ Ⓑ Ⓒ Ⓓ Ⓔ

17. Which of the following control techniques is most likely to emphasize the importance of time?

    (A) Break-even charts
    (B) Physical standards
    (C) Quality circles
    (D) Variable budgeting
    (E) PERT (program evaluation and review technique)

    Ⓐ Ⓑ Ⓒ Ⓓ Ⓔ

18. In profit-decentralized companies, which of the following responsibilities of division managers should be subject to the LEAST restriction by top managers?

    (A) approval of advertising and product promotion programs
    (B) approval of the selection of key division executives
    (C) approval of major capital expenditures
    (D) establishment of procedures in functional areas
    (E) setting of long-range objectives and annual goals

    Ⓐ Ⓑ Ⓒ Ⓓ Ⓔ

19. Isabel Myers, Katherine Briggs, and Carl Jung have developed different models to help individuals understand

    (A) different approaches to decision making
    (B) personal aptitude for international careers
    (C) the relevance of cultural background
    (D) the stages of human relationships
    (E) the limitations of measures of the intelligence quotient

    Ⓐ Ⓑ Ⓒ Ⓓ Ⓔ

20. In a labor negotiation, if a third party has the power to determine a solution to a labor dispute between two parties, the negotiation is known as

    (A) a grievance
    (B) an arbitration
    (C) a conciliation
    (D) a mediation
    (E) a concession

    Ⓐ Ⓑ Ⓒ Ⓓ Ⓔ

21. A type of control device for assessing the progress of planned activities and the expenditure of resources allocated to their accomplishments is referred to as

    (A) a strategic plan
    (B) an organizational chart
    (C) a tactical plan
    (D) a budget
    (E) a proposal

    Ⓐ Ⓑ Ⓒ Ⓓ Ⓔ

22. Which of the following do managerial/leadership grids, team-building, and sensitivity training have in common?

    (A) They are crucial to operations management.
    (B) They are tools for organizational development.
    (C) They were developed by Peter Drucker.
    (D) They are necessary to the budgeting process.
    (E) They are the key elements of positive-reinforcement programs

    Ⓐ Ⓑ Ⓒ Ⓓ Ⓔ

23. According to Maslow, the need to feel genuinely respected by peers, both in and out of the work environment, is included in which of the following need classifications?

    (A) Physiological
    (B) Safety
    (C) Stability
    (D) Esteem
    (E) Self-actualization

    Ⓐ Ⓑ Ⓒ Ⓓ Ⓔ

24. Which of the following management activities is most typically described as a controlling function?

    (A) Goal setting
    (B) Purchasing
    (C) Coordinating
    (D) Budgeting
    (E) Recruiting

    Ⓐ Ⓑ Ⓒ Ⓓ Ⓔ

Study Resources

The following list contains several textbooks that are typical of those used in introductory management courses at the college level. To prepare for the Principles of Management examination, you should study the contents of at least one such textbook. Although most textbooks cover the topics listed in the test content outline, they may vary somewhat in content, approach, and emphasis. You may therefore wish to consult more than one textbook on the major topics.

Many libraries do not carry textbooks as a policy. If you can't find any of the following textbooks at the library, see whether the college bookstore has a used copy. If you can't locate the most recent edition, an edition that is one or two years older will suffice for most subject areas. As a final option, purchase a new copy of the suggested textbook as an investment in your education.

TEXTBOOKS

Bartol, Kathryn M. and David C. Martin, *Management*. New York: McGraw-Hill, 1991.

Daft, Richard L., *Management*, 2nd ed. Chicago: The Dryden Press, 1991.

Donnelly, James H., Jr. et al., *Fundamentals of Management*, 8th ed. Homewood, IL: Irwin, 1992.

Hellreigel, Don and John W. Slocum, Jr., *Management*, 6th ed. Reading, MA: Addison-Wesley, 1992.

Mondy, R. Wayne, Arthur Sharplin, and Shane R. Primeaux, *Management Concepts, Practices and Skills*, 5th ed. Needham Heights, MA: Allyn and Bacon, Inc., 1991.

Robbins, Stephen P., *Management*, 3rd ed. Englewood Cliffs, NJ: Prentice-Hall, 1991.

Introductory Accounting

Description of the Examination

The Subject Examination in Introductory Accounting covers the information and skills taught in two semesters (or the equivalent) of college-level accounting. The emphasis of the exam is on financial and managerial accounting. Colleges may award credit for a one- or two-semester course in financial accounting including some managerial accounting topics, or for one semester of financial accounting and one semester of managerial accounting.

Battery-operated, hand-held calculators may be used during the examination, but all calculator memories must be cleared of both programs and data and no peripheral devices such as magnetic cards or tapes are permitted. Although the examination was designed to be taken without a calculator, candidates may find one helpful for some of the questions.

The test is 90 minutes long and includes approximately 80 multiple-choice questions to be answered in two separately timed 45-minute sections.

Knowledge and Skills Required

Questions on the examination require candidates to demonstrate one or more of the following abilities.

- Familiarity with accounting concepts and terminology
- Preparation and use of financial reports issued for both internal and external purposes
- Application of accounting techniques to simple problem situations involving computations
- Understanding of the rationale for generally accepted accounting principles and procedures

The subject matter of the Introductory Accounting examination is drawn from the following topics.

Approximate Percent of Examination

60-70% Financial accounting (concerned with providing financial statements, reports, etc., of interest to company managers as well as bankers, investors, and other outsiders who must make a financial assessment of a company)

>Generally accepted accounting principles
>
>Rules of double-entry accounting
>
>The accounting cycle
>
>Presentation of and relationships between general-purpose financial statements
>
>Valuation of accounts and notes receivable
>
>Valuation of inventories
>
>Initial costs of plant assets
>
>Depreciation
>
>Long-term debt
>
>Capital
>
>Cash and stock dividends
>
>Treasury stock
>
>Purchase and sale of merchandise
>
>Revenue and cost apportionments
>
>Cash control
>
>Division of profits and losses in partnership accounting

30-40% Managerial accounting (concerned with the use of accounting data for internal purposes to help management in planning and controlling functions of the company)

>Analysis of departmental operations
>
>Process and job-order cost systems
>
>Standard costs and variances
>
>Direct costing and absorption costing
>
>Cost-volume profit (break-even) analysis
>
>Funds flow analysis
>
>Use of differential (relevant) cost
>
>Budgeting
>
>Performance evaluation
>
>Financial statement analysis

Sample Questions

The 25 sample questions that follow are similar to questions on the Introductory Accounting examination, but they do not actually appear on the examination.

Before attempting to answer the sample questions, read all the information about the Introductory Accounting examination given on the preceding pages. Additional suggestions for preparing for CLEP examinations are provided in chapter 4.

Try to answer correctly as many questions as possible. Then compare your answers with the correct answers, given in Appendix B.

Directions: Each of the questions or incomplete statements below is followed by five suggested answers or completions. Select the one that is best in each case.

1. The owner's equity in a business may derive from which of the following sources?

    I. Excess of revenue over expenses
    II. Investment by the owner
    III. Accounts payable

    (A) I only
    (B) II only
    (C) III only
    (D) I and II only
    (E) I, II, and III   Ⓐ Ⓑ Ⓒ Ⓓ Ⓔ

2. Entries made on the books at the end of a period to take care of changes occurring in accounts are called

    (A) fiscal entries
    (B) closing entries
    (C) reversing entries
    (D) correcting entries
    (E) adjusting entries   Ⓐ Ⓑ Ⓒ Ⓓ Ⓔ

3. In accounting, net income should be defined as an increase in

    (A) assets
    (B) cash
    (C) merchandise
    (D) sales
    (E) capital   Ⓐ Ⓑ Ⓒ Ⓓ Ⓔ

4. Treasury stock is correctly defined as

   (A) a corporation's own stock that has been issued and then
        reacquired
   (B) new issues of a corporation's stock before they are sold on the
        open market
   (C) stock issued by the United States Office of the Treasury
   (D) any stock that a corporation acquires and holds for more than 90
        days
   (E) any stock held by a corporation that receives dividends in excess
        of 5 percent of initial cost of the stock

   Ⓐ Ⓑ Ⓒ Ⓓ Ⓔ

5. The Accumulated Depreciation account should be shown in the
   financial statements as

   (A) an operating expense
   (B) an extraordinary loss
   (C) a liability
   (D) stockholders' equity
   (E) a contra (deduction) to an asset account

   Ⓐ Ⓑ Ⓒ Ⓓ Ⓔ

6. If fixed expenses are $26,000 and variable expenses are 75 percent of
   sales, the net income that would result from $500,000 in sales is

   (A) $75,000
   (B) $99,000
   (C) $200,000
   (D) $375,000
   (E) $401,000

   Ⓐ Ⓑ Ⓒ Ⓓ Ⓔ

7. Cost of goods sold is determined by which of the following?

   (A) Beginning inventory plus net purchases minus ending inventory
   (B) Beginning inventory plus purchases plus purchase returns minus
        ending inventory
   (C) Beginning inventory minus net purchases plus ending inventory
   (D) Purchases minus transportation-in plus beginning inventory
        minus ending inventory
   (E) Net sales minus ending inventory

   Ⓐ Ⓑ Ⓒ Ⓓ Ⓔ

8. Company X produces chairs of a single type, has a plant capacity of 50,000 chairs per year, and has total fixed expenses of $100,000 per year. Variable costs per chair are $2 and the current selling price is $5 per chair. At the beginning of a given year, the company purchases a specialized machine that costs $10,000, lasts one year, and reduces variable costs to $1.50 per chair. If the company produces and sells at 90 percent of capacity, what is the net income for that year?

(A) $8,750
(B) $23,000
(C) $47,500
(D) $50,000
(E) $83,000

        Ⓐ Ⓑ Ⓒ Ⓓ Ⓔ

9. All the following T-accounts contain the correct sides that would be used for increasing and decreasing an account EXCEPT

(A)
Revenue	
Decrease	Increase

(B)
Assets	
Increase	Decrease

(C)
Expenses	
Increase	Decrease

(D)
Owner's Equity	
Increase	Decrease

(E)
Liabilities	
Decrease	Increase

        Ⓐ Ⓑ Ⓒ Ⓓ Ⓔ

10. The Green Corporation, with assets of $5,000,000 and liabilities of $2,000,000, has 6,000 shares of capital stock outstanding (par value $300). What is the book value per share?

(A) $200
(B) $300
(C) $500
(D) $833
(E) $1,800

        Ⓐ Ⓑ Ⓒ Ⓓ Ⓔ

11. Of the following, the best description of a controlling account is that it is a

(A) schedule of accounts payable
(B) purchase form that itemizes merchandise bought
(C) ledger that contains a single type of account
(D) statement that lists the individual account balances in the creditors' ledger
(E) general ledger account that summarizes the balance in the accounts of a subsidiary ledger

        Ⓐ Ⓑ Ⓒ Ⓓ Ⓔ

12. At the end of the fiscal year, a company estimates that $4,300 of Accounts Receivable will be uncollectible. If, prior to adjustment, the company's Allowance for Bad Debts account has a credit balance of $1,600, what is the appropriate adjusting entry?

DEBIT	CREDIT	AMOUNT
(A) Allowance for Bad Debts	Bad Debts Expense	$4,300
(B) Allowance for Bad Debts	Accounts Receivable	$4,300
(C) Accounts Receivable	Allowance for Bad Debts	$1,600
(D) Bad Debts Expense	Allowance for Bad Debts	$2,700
(E) Bad Debts Expense	Accounts Receivable	$2,700

Ⓐ Ⓑ Ⓒ Ⓓ Ⓔ

13. A fast-moving widget stamping machine was purchased for cash. The list price was $4,000 with an applicable trade discount of 20 percent and a cash discount allowable of 2/10, n/30. Payment was made within the discount period. Freight costs of $100, F.O.B. origin, were paid. To install the machine properly, a platform was built and wiring installed for a total cost of $200. The trial run costs were $300 for labor and $50 for materials. The cost of the machine would be recorded as

(A) $3,626
(B) $3,628
(C) $3,786
(D) $3,828
(E) $4,178

Ⓐ Ⓑ Ⓒ Ⓓ Ⓔ

14. All of the following expenditures should be charged to an asset account rather than to an expense account of the current period EXCEPT the cost of

(A) overhauling a delivery truck, which extends its useful life by two years
(B) purchasing a new component for a machine. which serves to increase the machine's productive capacity
(C) constructing a parking lot for a leased building
(D) installing a new piece of equipment
(E) replacing worn-out tires on a delivery truck

Ⓐ Ⓑ Ⓒ Ⓓ Ⓔ

15. In a period of rising prices, which of the following inventory methods results in the highest cost of goods sold?

    (A) FIFO
    (B) LIFO
    (C) Average cost
    (D) Periodic inventory
    (E) Perpetual inventory   Ⓐ Ⓑ Ⓒ Ⓓ Ⓔ

16. A company forecasts that during the next year it will be able to sell 80,000 units of its special product at a competitive selling price of $10 per unit. The company has the capacity to produce 120,000 units per year. Its total fixed costs are $528,000. Its variable costs are estimated at $3 per unit. The company has the opportunity to sell 10,000 additional units during the same year at a special contract price of $50,000. This special contract will not affect the regular sales volume or price. Acceptance of the contract will cause the year's net income to

    (A) increase by $20,000
    (B) increase by $26,000
    (C) increase by $50,000
    (D) decrease by $50,000
    (E) decrease by $24,000   Ⓐ Ⓑ Ⓒ Ⓓ Ⓔ

17. Which of the following standard cost variances provides information about the extent to which the manufacturing plant of a company was used at normal capacity?

    (A) Materials quantity (usage) variance
    (B) Labor efficiency (time) variance
    (C) Labor rate variance
    (D) Overhead spending (controllable) variance
    (E) Overhead volume variance   Ⓐ Ⓑ Ⓒ Ⓓ Ⓔ

18. The following information refers to the purchase of merchandise by L Company. List price of merchandise, $1,050; trade discount 20 percent, 2/10, n/30; F.O.B. shipping point; freight cost prepaid by seller and added to the invoice, $100.

    What is the net amount to be paid to the vendor, within the discount period, for the merchandise?

    (A) $819.00
    (B) $901.60
    (C) $919.00
    (D) $921.20
    (E) $923.20   Ⓐ Ⓑ Ⓒ Ⓓ Ⓔ

19. X Corporation declares and issues a 5 percent stock dividend on common stock, payable in common stock, shortly after the close of the year. All of the following statements about the nature and effect of the dividend are true EXCEPT:

    (A) The total stockholders' equity in the corporation is not changed.
    (B) The dividend does not constitute income to the stockholders.
    (C) The book value per share of common stock is not changed.
    (D) The amount of retained earnings is reduced.
    (E) The amount of total assets is not changed.

    Ⓐ Ⓑ Ⓒ Ⓓ Ⓔ

20. The financial statement prepared to report the financing and investing activities of a business entity for a period of time is called the

    (A) Income Statement
    (B) Statement of Retained Earnings
    (C) Balance Sheet
    (D) Statement of Changes in Owners' Equity
    (E) Statement of Changes in Financial Position

    Ⓐ Ⓑ Ⓒ Ⓓ Ⓔ

21. A feature of the process cost system that is NOT a feature of the job order cost system is

    (A) computation of the equivalent units of production
    (B) compilation of the costs of each batch or job produced
    (C) use of the Raw Materials Inventory account
    (D) preparation of a Cost of Goods Manufactured Statement for each accounting period
    (E) application of manufacturing overhead on a predetermined basis

    Ⓐ Ⓑ Ⓒ Ⓓ Ⓔ

22. Net purchases for the year amounted to $80,000. The merchandise inventory at the beginning of the year was $19,000. On sales of $120,000, thirty percent of the selling price was gross profit. The inventory at the end of the year was

    (A) $13,000
    (B) $15,000
    (C) $17,000
    (D) $25,000
    (E) $63,000

    Ⓐ Ⓑ Ⓒ Ⓓ Ⓔ

23. The balance sheet of Harold Company shows current assets of $200,000 and current liabilities of $100,000. The company uses cash to acquire merchandise inventory. As a result of this transaction, which of the following is true of working capital and the current ratio?

    (A) Both are unchanged.
    (B) Working capital is unchanged; the current ratio increases.
    (C) Both decrease.
    (D) Working capital decreases; the current ratio increases.
    (E) Working capital decreases; the current ratio is unchanged.

    Ⓐ Ⓑ Ⓒ Ⓓ Ⓔ

In determining net income from business operations, the costs involved in generating revenue should be charged against that revenue.

24. The statement above best describes which of the following?

    (A) The cost principle
    (B) The going-concern principle
    (C) The profit principle
    (D) The matching principle
    (E) The business entity principle

    Ⓐ Ⓑ Ⓒ Ⓓ Ⓔ

25. Which of the following is the best explanation of the amount reported on the balance sheet as accumulated depreciation?

    (A) Self-insurance fund to protect against losses of the related assets from fire or other casualty
    (B) Decrease in market value of the related assets
    (C) Cash accumulated to purchase replacements as the related assets wear out
    (D) Cost of the related assets that has been allocated to operations
    (E) Estimated amount needed to replace the related assets as they wear out

    Ⓐ Ⓑ Ⓒ Ⓓ Ⓔ

Study Resources

To prepare for the Introductory Accounting examination you should study the contents of at least one textbook designed for a full-year undergraduate course in introductory accounting. A few of the more commonly used textbooks are listed here. While all of them cover both financial and managerial accounting topics, their approach and emphasis varies. You may therefore wish to consult more than one textbook on the more important topics.

Additional suggestions for preparing for CLEP examinations are given in chapter 4.

Many libraries do not carry textbooks as a policy. If you can't find any of the following textbooks at the library, see whether the college bookstore has a used copy. If you can't locate the most recent edition, an edition that is one or two years older will suffice for most subject areas. As a final option, purchase a new copy of the suggested textbook as an investment in your education.

FINANCIAL/MANAGERIAL REFERENCES

Horngren, Charles T. and Walter T. Harrison, Jr., *Accounting*, 2nd ed. Englewood Cliffs, NJ: Prentice Hall, 1992.

Meigs, Robert F. and Walter B. Meigs, *Accounting: The Basis for Business Decisions*, 8th ed. New York: McGraw-Hill, 1990.

Needles, Belverd E., Jr., et al., *Financial and Managerial Accounting*, 2nd ed. Boston: Houghton Mifflin, 1991.

Walgenbach, Paul H. et al., *Principles of Accounting*, 5th ed. San Diego: Harcourt Brace Jovanovich, 1990.

Warren, Carl S. and Philip E. Fess, *Principles of Financial and Managerial Accounting*, 3rd ed. Cincinnati: South-Western, 1992.

FINANCIAL

Hermanson, Roger H. and James Don Edwards, *Financial Accounting*, 5th ed. Homewood, IL: Irwin, 1992.

Meigs, Robert F. and Walter B. Meigs, *Financial Accounting*, 7th ed. New York: McGraw-Hill, 1992.

Nikolai, Loren A. and John Bazley, *Financial Accounting*, 3rd ed. Boston: PWS-Kent, 1990.

Skousen, K. Fred et al., *Financial Accounting*, 4th ed. Cincinnati: South-Western, 1991.

Solomon, Lanny M. et al., *Financial Accounting*, 3rd ed. St. Paul: West, 1992.

Walgenbach, Paul H. and Ernest I. Hanson, *Financial Accounting: An Introduction*, 6th ed. San Diego: Harcourt Brace Jovanovich, 1990.

MANAGERIAL

Engler, C. *Managerial Accounting*, 2nd ed. Homewood, IL: Irwin, 1990.

Garrison, Ray H., *Managerial Accounting: Concepts for Planning, Control, Decision Making*, 6th ed. Homewood, IL: Irwin, 1991.

Horngren, Charles T. and Gary L. Sundem, *Introduction to Management Accounting*, 8th ed. Englewood Cliffs, NJ: Prentice Hall, 1990.

Introductory Business Law

Description of the Examination

The Subject Examination in Introductory Business Law covers subject matter usually taught in an introductory one-semester college course in this subject. The examination places major emphasis on understanding the functions of contracts in American business law, but also includes questions on the history and sources of American law, legal systems and procedures, agency and employment, sales, and other topics.

The examination is 90 minutes long and includes approximately 100 multiple-choice questions to be answered in two separately timed 45-minute sections.

Knowledge and Skills Required

Questions on the test require candidates to demonstrate one or more of the following abilities.

- Knowledge of basic facts and terms (about 30-35 percent of the examination)

- Understanding of concepts and principles (about 30-35 percent of the examination)

- Ability to apply knowledge to specific case problems (about 30-35 percent of the examination)

The subject matter of the Introductory Business Law examination is drawn from the following topics.

➡	*Approximate Percent of Examination*
11%	History and sources of American law
12%	American legal systems and procedures

▶ *Approximate Percent of Examination*

60%   Contracts
      Meaning of terms
      Formation of contracts
      Consideration
      Joint obligations
      Contracts for the benefit of third parties
      Assignment/Delegation
      Statute of frauds
      Scope and meaning of contracts
      Breach of contract
      Bar to remedies for breach of contract
      Discharge of contracts
      Illegal contracts

3%   Agency and employment

4%   Sales

10%   Miscellaneous
      Torts
      Property
      Product liability
      Commercial paper
      Consumer protection

Sample Questions

The 24 sample questions that follow are similar to questions on the Introductory Business Law examination, but they do not appear on the actual examination.

Before attempting to answer the sample questions, read all the information about the Introductory Business Law examination on the preceding pages. Additional suggestions for preparing for CLEP examinations are provided in chapter 4.

Try to answer correctly as many questions as possible. Then compare your answers with the correct answers, given in Appendix B.

470

Directions: Each of the questions or incomplete statements below is followed by five suggested answers or completions. Select the one that is best in each case.

1. The authority of a court to hear and decide cases is known as

   (A) jurisdiction (B) habeas corpus
   (C) demurrer (D) quo warranto
   (E) stare decisis

   Ⓐ Ⓑ Ⓒ Ⓓ Ⓔ

2. Law that is formed by a group of individuals, acting as representatives for other individuals, is best termed

   (A) criminal law (B) civil law
   (C) legislative law (D) adjective law
   (E) tort law

   Ⓐ Ⓑ Ⓒ Ⓓ Ⓔ

3. A contract will be unenforceable if

   (A) one party to the contract feels he or she has been taken
       advantage of
   (B) a statute declares such a contract illegal
   (C) performance becomes difficult
   (D) public authorities voice disapproval of the contract
   (E) the parties involved believe the contract to be illegal

   Ⓐ Ⓑ Ⓒ Ⓓ Ⓔ

4. Angela promises to work for Barbara during the month of July, and Barbara promises to pay Angela $600 for her services. In this situation, what kind of contract has been made?

   (A) Unilateral (B) Executed (C) Quasi
   (D) Bilateral (E) Bilingual

   Ⓐ Ⓑ Ⓒ Ⓓ Ⓔ

5. Which of the following is an essential element of fraud?

   (A) Injury to a business interest
   (B) Misrepresentation of a material fact
   (C) Destruction of property
   (D) Knowledge of the consequences
   (E) Mistake about the identity of the subject matter

   Ⓐ Ⓑ Ⓒ Ⓓ Ⓔ

6. Clyde received the following letter from Joe: "I will sell you the books you examined yesterday for $10 each or $100 for the entire set." Clyde, not sure he would get much use from the books, told his brother, Michael, about the offer. Michael tendered Joe $100 for the books, but Joe refused to sell the books to Michael.

If Michael sued Joe, the court would probably hold that Michael

(A) can accept the offer because he is Clyde's brother
(B) can accept the offer if he will do so within a reasonable period of time
(C) cannot accept the offer until Clyde's rejection is communicated to Joe
(D) cannot accept the offer because it was not made to him
(E) cannot accept the offer unless he does so in writing

Ⓐ Ⓑ Ⓒ Ⓓ Ⓔ

7. All of the following have the right to enforce a contract EXCEPT

(A) a third-party creditor beneficiary
(B) an assignee
(C) a third-party donee beneficiary
(D) a transferee
(E) a third-party incidental beneficiary

Ⓐ Ⓑ Ⓒ Ⓓ Ⓔ

8. A method of discharging a contract that returns each party to his or her original position is

(A) an assignment
(B) an accord
(C) a revocation
(D) a rescission
(E) a novation

Ⓐ Ⓑ Ⓒ Ⓓ Ⓔ

9. A contract clause that requires both parties to act simultaneously is called a

(A) condition subsequent
(B) condition concurrent
(C) condition precedent
(D) negative condition
(E) restrictive condition

Ⓐ Ⓑ Ⓒ Ⓓ Ⓔ

10. Benson, a seventeen-year-old college freshman, was adequately supplied with clothes by his father. Smith, a clothing merchant, learned that Benson was spending money freely and solicited clothing orders from him. Benson bought $750 worth of ready-made clothing from Smith on credit. Benson failed to pay Smith.

    If Smith sued Benson, the court would probably hold that

    (A) Benson is liable for the $750 because by accepting and wearing the clothes he ratified the contract
    (B) Benson is not liable for the reasonable value of the clothing because Smith solicited the sales
    (C) Benson can disaffirm the contract, return the clothing, and escape liability
    (D) Benson is liable for the $750 because under these circumstances the clothing was a necessity
    (E) Benson's father is liable to Smith for the $750

    Ⓐ Ⓑ Ⓒ Ⓓ Ⓔ

11. The enforcement of a contract may be barred, according to operation of law, by

    (A) a merger
    (B) a consolidation
    (C) a material breach
    (D) the statute of limitations
    (E) a novation

    Ⓐ Ⓑ Ⓒ Ⓓ Ⓔ

12. A purchase from each of the following would be considered a purchase in the ordinary course of trade or business EXCEPT a purchase from a

    (A) pawnshop
    (B) department store
    (C) supermarket
    (D) discount department store
    (E) used car lot

    Ⓐ Ⓑ Ⓒ Ⓓ Ⓔ

13. Which of the following promises would be enforceable by the majority of courts?

(A) Avery finds Bond's dog and returns it to Bond. Later Bond promises to pay Avery a reward.

(B) Husband, in consideration of the love and affection given him by Wife, promises to pay her $1,000.

(C) Avery is extremely ill and placed in a hospital. Avery's neighbor, Bond, mows Avery's yard while Avery is recuperating. Later Avery promises to pay Bond the reasonable value of his services.

(D) Avery owes Bond $100, which debt is discharged in bankruptcy. Later Avery writes Bond a letter promising to pay Bond the $100.

(E) Daughter mows the family yard. In absence of an express agreement, Daughter can claim an implied promise on Father's part to pay for her services.

Ⓐ Ⓑ Ⓒ Ⓓ Ⓔ

14. Base Electric Company has entered an agreement to buy its actual requirements of brass wiring for six months from the Valdez Metal Wire Company, and Valdez Metal Wire Company has agreed to sell all the brass wiring Base Electric Company will require for six months. The agreement between the two companies is

(A) valid and enforceable
(B) unenforceable because of lack of consideration
(C) unenforceable because it is too indefinite
(D) lacking in mutuality of obligations
(E) illusory

Ⓐ Ⓑ Ⓒ Ⓓ Ⓔ

15. Ordinarily an employer is liable for which of the following acts committed by an employee for the benefit of the employer and in the scope of the employment?

 I. Torts
 II. Contracts
III. Misrepresentations

(A) I only
(B) II only
(C) III only
(D) II and III only
(E) I, II, and III

Ⓐ Ⓑ Ⓒ Ⓓ Ⓔ

16. Abbott was orphaned at the age of five. For the next fifteen years his material needs were met by his uncle, Barton. On his thirtieth birthday, Abbott wrote Barton and promised to pay him $100 per month as long as Barton lived. Abbott never made any payments. Barton died ten months later.

If Barton's estate sued Abbott for the amount of the promised payments, the court would probably hold that Barton's estate is

(A) not entitled to recover because past consideration will not support Abbott's promise
(B) not entitled to recover because of the statute of limitations
(C) not entitled to recover unless it can be shown that Barton's relatives were in desperate need
(D) entitled to recover on the promise
(E) entitled to recover because of Barton's previous aid to Abbott

Ⓐ Ⓑ Ⓒ Ⓓ Ⓔ

17. An agreement among creditors that each will accept a certain percentage of his or her claim as full satisfaction is called

(A) accord and satisfaction (B) creditor agreement
(C) composition of creditors (D) liquidation
(E) bankruptcy

Ⓐ Ⓑ Ⓒ Ⓓ Ⓔ

18. Which of the following decisions could NOT be made by an appellate court?

(A) Ordering a case to be tried in the appellate court
(B) Affirming a decision of a lower court
(C) Instructing a lower court to enter a judgment in accordance with the appellate court's opinion
(D) Remanding a case for a new trial
(E) Reversing the decision of a lower court

Ⓐ Ⓑ Ⓒ Ⓓ Ⓔ

19. Upon delivery of nonconforming goods, a buyer may do which of the following?

I. Reject all the goods.
II. Accept all the goods.
III. Accept those units which conform and reject the rest.

(A) I only (B) III only (C) I and II only
(D) II and III only (E) I, II, and III

Ⓐ Ⓑ Ⓒ Ⓓ Ⓔ

20. All of the following are usual functions performed by judges of trial courts having general jurisdiction EXCEPT

(A) issuing writs of habeas corpus
(B) conducting pretrial conferences in civil cases
(C) determining questions of fact in equity cases
(D) guiding the jury on questions of law in criminal and civil cases
(E) imposing pretrial settlements on parties who cannot agree

Ⓐ Ⓑ Ⓒ Ⓓ Ⓔ

21. Which of the following will apply if the parties to a contract knew or should have known that a word has a customary usage in their particular trade or community?

(A) No contract will result if the parties cannot voluntarily agree on the definition of the word.
(B) Parol evidence may not be used to define the meaning of the word.
(C) Parol evidence may be used to define the meaning of the word.
(D) Courts will not impose a definition that is contrary to the meaning supported by one party.
(E) A mistaken assumption regarding the definition by one of the parties will result in a voidable contract.

Ⓐ Ⓑ Ⓒ Ⓓ Ⓔ

22. Webster insured her residence with Old Home Insurance Company. Assuming that the policy contained no provision with respect to assignment, which of the following statements is correct?

(A) Webster may assign the policy to any person having capacity to contract.
(B) If Webster suffers an insured loss, she may assign the amount due under the policy to anyone.
(C) If Webster sells her residence, she must assign the policy to the purchaser.
(D) If Webster suffers an insured loss, she may assign the amount due under the policy only to a party furnishing material or labor for repair of the residence.
(E) Webster may assign the policy to any person having capacity to contract who agrees to pay the premium.

Ⓐ Ⓑ Ⓒ Ⓓ Ⓔ

23. Recovery in quasi contract is based on a judgment that determines the presence of

    (A) unjust enrichment
    (B) an express contract
    (C) an implied in fact contract
    (D) a violation of the statute of frauds
    (E) mutual mistake $\quad$ Ⓐ Ⓑ Ⓒ Ⓓ Ⓔ

24. A modern-day body of law that can be traced to the early law merchant is

    (A) the administrative system
    (B) the Uniform Commercial Code
    (C) constitutional law
    (D) civil law
    (E) the court of equity $\quad$ Ⓐ Ⓑ Ⓒ Ⓓ Ⓔ

Study Resources

The following list contains several textbooks that are typical of those used in business law courses at the college level. To prepare for the Introductory Business Law examination, you should study the contents of at least one such textbook, focusing on the topics listed in the test outline and omitting topics that are not included in the outline. Most textbooks contain many cases and case problems in addition to text material on theory and principles. Most also contain the complete text of the Uniform Commercial Code and a glossary of law terms. Although most textbooks cover the topics listed in the test content outline, they may vary somewhat in content, approach, and emphasis. You may therefore wish to consult more than one textbook on the major topics.

Additional suggestions for preparing for CLEP examinations are given in chapter 4.

Many libraries do not carry textbooks as a policy. If you can't find any of the following textbooks at the library, see whether the college bookstore has a used copy. If you can't locate the most recent edition, an edition that is one or two years older will suffice for most subject areas. As a final option, purchase a new copy of the suggested textbook as an investment in your education.

TEXTBOOKS

Anderson, Ronald A. et al., *Business Law,* rev. ed., UCC Standard Volume. Cincinnati: South-Western, 1988. (Designed for a one-semester course, condensed from *Business Law,* UCC Comprehensive Volume, which is designed for a two-semester course.)

Anderson, Ronald A. et al., *Business Law: Principles, Cases, Legal Environment,* 11th ed. Cincinnati: South-Western, 1992. (Note: A study guide by Anderson is available for both of his books.)

Corley, Robert N. and Peter J. Shedd, *Principles of Business Law,* 14th ed. Englewood Cliffs, NJ: Prentice-Hall, 1989.

Frascona, Joseph et al., *Principles of Business Law and the Legal Environment.* Rockleigh, NJ: Allyn & Bacon, 1988.

Mann, Richard A. and Barry S. Roberts, *Smith and Roberson's Business Law,* 8th ed. St. Paul: West, 1991.

Scaletta, Phillip and George D. Cameron, *Foundations of Business Law,* 2nd ed. Homewood, IL: BPI/Irwin, 1990.

Principles of Marketing

Description of the Examination

The Principles of Marketing examination covers the material that is commonly taught in a one-semester introductory course in marketing. Such a course is usually known as Basic Marketing, Introduction to Marketing, Fundamentals of Marketing, Marketing, or Marketing Principles. The examination covers the role of marketing in society and within a firm, understanding consumer and organizational markets, marketing strategy planning, the marketing mix, marketing institutions, and other selected topics such as international marketing, ethics, marketing research, services, and not-for-profit marketing. The candidate is also expected to have a basic knowledge of the economic/demographic, social/cultural, political/legal, and technological trends that are important to marketing.

The test is 90 minutes long and includes approximately 100 multiple-choice questions to be answered in two separately timed 45-minute sections.

Knowledge and Skills Required

Questions on the test require candidates to demonstrate one or more of the following abilities.

- Knowledge of basic terms used in marketing today

- Understanding, analysis, interpretation, and application of concepts and principles

- Ability to apply knowledge, concepts, and principles to specific situations or problems

- Ability to demonstrate basic computational skills as they relate to marketing

The subject matter of the Principles of Marketing examination is drawn from the following topics.

	Approximate Percent of Examination
5 - 8%	The role of marketing in society, including the historical development of marketing in the United States, marketing in different economic systems, and basic marketing functions
7 - 11%	The role of marketing within a firm, the marketing concept, planning and organization, and the marketing environment, e.g., the political/legal, social/cultural, economic/demographic, and technological environments
15 - 20%	Consumer and industrial markets, including their demographic and behavioral dimensions, measuring and forecasting demand, and marketing segmentation, targeting, and positioning
40 - 50%	The marketing mix, including product planning and management, pricing policies and methods, channels of distribution, advertising and sales promotion, and sales management
8 - 10%	Marketing institutions, including aspects of the structure of wholesale and retail markets and the role of intermediaries
11 - 14%	Other topics such as international marketing, marketing of services, marketing information and research, ethics, and not-for-profit marketing

Sample Test Questions

The 32 sample questions that follow are similar to questions on the Principles of Marketing examination, but they do not actually appear on the examination.

Before attempting to answer the sample questions, read all the information about the Principles of Marketing examination on the preceding pages. Additional suggestions for preparing for CLEP examinations are provided in chapter 4.

Try to answer correctly as many questions as possible. Then compare your answers with the correct answers, given in Appendix B.

Directions: Each of the questions or incomplete statements below is followed by five suggested answers or completions. Select the one that is best in each case.

1. Which of the following has the greatest influence on the amount of aggregate marketing demand?

   (A) Product supply
   (B) Current level of taxes
   (C) Purchasing power
   (D) Availability of raw materials
   (E) Production cost

   Ⓐ Ⓑ Ⓒ Ⓓ Ⓔ

2. A manufacturer of car batteries, who has been selling through an automotive parts wholesaler to garages and service stations, decides to sell directly to retailers. Which of the following will necessarily occur?

   (A) Elimination of the wholesaler's profit will result in a lower price to the ultimate consumer.
   (B) Elimination of the wholesaler's marketing functions will increase efficiency.
   (C) The total cost of distribution will be reduced because of the elimination of the wholesaler.
   (D) The marketing functions performed by the wholesaler will be eliminated.
   (E) The wholesaler's marketing functions will be shifted to or shared by the manufacturer and the retailer.

   Ⓐ Ⓑ Ⓒ Ⓓ Ⓔ

3. Which of the following strategies for entering the international market would involve the highest risk?

   (A) Joint ventures   (B) Exporting
      (C) Licensing   (D) Direct investment
         (E) Franchising

   Ⓐ Ⓑ Ⓒ Ⓓ Ⓔ

4. For a United States manufacturer of major consumer appliances, the most important leading indicator for forecasting sales is

   (A) automobile sales
   (B) furniture sales
   (C) educational level of consumers
   (D) housing starts
   (E) number of business failures

   Ⓐ Ⓑ Ⓒ Ⓓ Ⓔ

5. Which of the following is an example of a societal marketing approach?

   (A) Revamping the sales force training program
   (B) Making constant product improvements
   (C) Recalling voluntarily a product that is rumored to be defective
   (D) Implementing a marketing information system
   (E) Increasing efficiency by improving production facilities

   Ⓐ Ⓑ Ⓒ Ⓓ Ⓔ

6. In contrast to a selling orientation, a marketing orientation to business management seeks to

   (A) increase market share by emphasizing promotion
   (B) increase sales volume by lowering price
   (C) lower the cost of distribution by direct marketing
   (D) satisfy the needs of targeted consumers at a profit
   (E) market products that make efficient use of the firm's resources

   Ⓐ Ⓑ Ⓒ Ⓓ Ⓔ

7. All of the following are characteristics of services EXCEPT

   (A) intangibility   (B) inconsistency   (C) inseparability
     (D) perishability   (E) inflexibility

   Ⓐ Ⓑ Ⓒ Ⓓ Ⓔ

8. A fertilizer manufacturer who traditionally markets to farmers through farm supply dealers and cooperatives decides to sell current products to home gardeners through lawn and garden shops. This decision is an example of

   (A) market penetration   (B) market development
     (C) product development   (D) diversification
       (E) vertical integration

   Ⓐ Ⓑ Ⓒ Ⓓ Ⓔ

9. A manufacturer who refuses to sell to dealers its popular line of office copiers unless the dealers also agree to stock the manufacturer's line of paper products would most likely be in violation of which of the following?

   (A) Robinson–Patman Act
   (B) Clayton Act
   (C) Magnusson–Moss Act
   (D) Miller–Tydings Act
   (E) Interstate Commerce Act

   Ⓐ Ⓑ Ⓒ Ⓓ Ⓔ

10. Prior to ultimate consumption, the last member in an indirect distribution channel is the

(A) retailer   (B) wholesaler   (C) manufacturer
   (D) factor   (E) freight forwarder

Ⓐ Ⓑ Ⓒ Ⓓ Ⓔ

11. In which of the following situations is the number of buying influences most likely to be greatest?

(A) A university buys large quantities of paper for computer printers on a regular basis.
(B) A computer manufacturer is building a new headquarters and is trying to choose a line of office furniture.
(C) A consumer decides to buy a different brand of potato chips because they are on sale.
(D) A retail chain is searching for a vendor of lower-priced cleaning supplies.
(E) A purchasing manager has been asked to locate a second source of supply for corrugated shipping cartons.

Ⓐ Ⓑ Ⓒ Ⓓ Ⓔ

12. If a small firm with many competitors is able to segment the market successfully and develop a unique marketing mix for each target market, the firm will most likely face which of the following kinds of competition?

(A) Static oligopoly   (B) Oligopoly   (C) Monopoly
   (D) Monopolistic competition   (E) Pure competition

Ⓐ Ⓑ Ⓒ Ⓓ Ⓔ

13. What price should a retailer charge for an item that costs the retailer $12 if the retailer wants a 25 percent markup on the selling price?

(A) $ 9
(B) $15
(C) $16
(D) $22
(E) It cannot be determined without knowledge of the retailer's fixed costs.

Ⓐ Ⓑ Ⓒ Ⓓ Ⓔ

14. Because of demographic shifts in the United States over the last twenty years, marketing strategy planners must take into account the

    (A) increase in the number of farm families
    (B) increased number of working women
    (C) increasing population growth in the "snow belt" states
    (D) decline in the number of consumers who are over age 55
    (E) decreasing total population

    (A) (B) (C) (D) (E)

15. Roy Smith sells sets of encyclopedias door-to-door to families in low-income neighborhoods. Although the encyclopedias are priced above $300, they can be purchased for weekly installments of only $3. Roy's favorite sales pitch is "Would you deny your child a chance to become President of the United States someday just to save $3 per week?" Roy's selling approach appears to be an example of

    (A) deceptive advertising
    (B) questionable ethics
    (C) trade promotion
    (D) bait-and-switch pricing
    (E) customer-oriented selling

    (A) (B) (C) (D) (E)

16. Cooperative advertising is usually undertaken by manufacturers in order to

    (A) secure the help of the retailer in promoting a given product
    (B) divide responsibilities between the retailers and wholesalers within a channel of distribution
    (C) satisfy legal requirements
    (D) create a favorable image of a particular industry in the minds of consumers
    (E) provide a subsidy for smaller retailers that enables them to match the prices set by chain stores

    (A) (B) (C) (D) (E)

17. Which of the following is usually the major disadvantage of keeping the level of a retail store's inventory low?

    (A) Inventory turnover will be slow.
    (B) Insurance costs per item will multiply dramatically.
    (C) Buyer resistance will increase.
    (D) Markups will be low.
    (E) Items customers want may frequently be out of stock.

    (A) (B) (C) (D) (E)

18. A marketer usually offers a noncumulative quantity discount in order to

    (A) reward customers for repeat purchases
    (B) reduce advertising expenses
    (C) encourage users to purchase in large quantities
    (D) encourage buyers to submit payment promptly
    (E) ensure the prompt movement of goods through the channel of distribution

    Ⓐ Ⓑ Ⓒ Ⓓ Ⓔ

19. A toy manufacturing firm sold its product through a toy wholesaler, who in turn sold to appropriate retailers. The manufacturer's price is $20 to the wholesaler, whose markup is usually 20 percent on the selling price to the retailer. If the retailer's markup on the selling price to the customer is 50 percent, what is the price to the customer?

    (A) $24.00
    (B) $30.00
    (C) $36.00
    (D) $37.50
    (E) $50.00

    Ⓐ Ⓑ Ⓒ Ⓓ Ⓔ

20. Missionary salespersons are most likely to do which of the following?

    (A) Sell cosmetics directly to consumers in their own homes
    (B) Explain how air conditioners can be used in cold climates
    (C) Describe drugs and other medical supplies to physicians
    (D) Secure government approval to sell heavy machinery to a foreign government
    (E) Take orders for custom-tailored garments or other specially produced items

    Ⓐ Ⓑ Ⓒ Ⓓ Ⓔ

21. The demand for industrial goods is sometimes called "derived" because it depends on

    (A) economic conditions
    (B) demand for consumer goods
    (C) governmental activity
    (D) availability of labor and materials
    (E) the desire to make a profit

    Ⓐ Ⓑ Ⓒ Ⓓ Ⓔ

22. Behavioral research generally indicates that consumers' attitudes

    (A) do not usually change very easily or quickly
    (B) are usually very easy to change through promotion
    (C) cannot ever be changed
    (D) can only be developed through actual experience with products
    (E) are very accurate predictors of actual purchasing behavior

    Ⓐ Ⓑ Ⓒ Ⓓ Ⓔ

23. A channel of distribution refers to the

    (A) routing of goods through distribution centers
    (B) sequence of marketing intermediaries from producer to consumer
    (C) methods of transporting goods from producer to consumer
    (D) marketing intermediaries who perform a variety of functions
    (E) traditional handlers of a product line

    Ⓐ Ⓑ Ⓒ Ⓓ Ⓔ

24. A major advantage of distributing products by truck is

    (A) speed relative to rail or air
    (B) low probability of loss or damage to cargo
    (C) accessibility to pick-up and delivery locations
    (D) low cost relative to rail or water
    (E) ability to handle a wider variety of products than other means

    Ⓐ Ⓑ Ⓒ Ⓓ Ⓔ

25. If a firm is using penetration pricing for its new product, the firm is most likely trying to achieve which of the following pricing objectives?

    (A) Product quality leadership
    (B) Market-share maximization
    (C) High gross margin
    (D) Status quo
    (E) Geographic flexibility

    Ⓐ Ⓑ Ⓒ Ⓓ Ⓔ

26. The basic marketing functions include all of the following EXCEPT

    (A) transporting and storing
    (B) producing and consuming
    (C) buying and selling
    (D) standardization and grading
    (E) financing and risk-taking

    Ⓐ Ⓑ Ⓒ Ⓓ Ⓔ

27. The marketer of which of the following products would be most likely to use a promotional mix with a heavy emphasis on personal selling?

    (A) Life insurance   (B) Pencils   (C) Transistor radios
        (D) Bread   (E) Crackers

    Ⓐ Ⓑ Ⓒ Ⓓ Ⓔ

28. When manufacturers attempt to determine differences among buyers that may affect marketing to those buyers, the manufacturers are practicing a policy of

    (A) product diversification
    (B) product differentiation
    (C) product–line maximization
    (D) market segmentation
    (E) market expansion   Ⓐ Ⓑ Ⓒ Ⓓ Ⓔ

29. Marketing strategy planning consists of

    (A) supervising the activities of the firm's sales force
    (B) determining the most efficient way to manufacture products
    (C) selecting a target market and developing the marketing mix
    (D) redefining the firm's mission and setting its goals
    (E) monitoring how customers are responding to the firm's
        marketing mix   Ⓐ Ⓑ Ⓒ Ⓓ Ⓔ

30. During the early 1990's, in which of the following countries did exports account for the lowest percentage of the country's gross national product?

    (A) The United States
    (B) The United Kingdom
    (C) Saudi Arabia
    (D) Japan
    (E) The Netherlands   Ⓐ Ⓑ Ⓒ Ⓓ Ⓔ

31. A brand that has achieved brand insistence and is considered a specialty good by the target market suggests which of the following distribution objectives?

    (A) Widespread distribution near probable points of use
    (B) Limited or exclusive distribution
    (C) Intensive distribution
    (D) Enough exposure to facilitate price comparison
    (E) Widespread distribution at low cost   Ⓐ Ⓑ Ⓒ Ⓓ Ⓔ

32. Market segmentation that is concerned with people over 65 years of age is called

    (A) geographic   (B) socioeconomic   (C) demographic
       (D) psychographic   (E) behavioral   Ⓐ Ⓑ Ⓒ Ⓓ Ⓔ

Study Resources

The following list contains textbooks that are often used in marketing courses at the college level. To prepare for the Principles of Marketing examination, you should study the contents of at least one textbook that covers the basic principles of marketing. Although such textbooks cover the topics listed in the test content outline, they do vary in content, approach, and emphasis. You are therefore advised to consult more than one textbook on the major topics. Please note that textbooks are updated frequently; it is important to use the latest editions of the textbooks you choose. Most textbooks now have study guides, computer applications, and case studies to accompany them, and these learning aids could prove useful in the understanding and application of marketing concepts and principles.

You can broaden your understanding of marketing principles and their applications by keeping abreast of current developments in the field from articles in newspapers and news magazines as well as in business publications such as *The Wall Street Journal, Business Week, Harvard Business Review, Fortune, Ad Week*, and *Advertising Age*. Journals found in most college libraries that will help you expand your knowledge of marketing principles are, among others, *Journal of Marketing, Marketing Today, Journal of the Academy of Marketing Sciences, American Demographics*, and *Marketing Week*. Books of readings, such as *Annual Editions – Marketing*, also are sources of current thinking.

Additional suggestions for preparing for CLEP examinations are given in chapter 4.

Many libraries do not carry textbooks as a policy. If you can't find any of the following textbooks at the library, see whether the college bookstore has a used copy, or purchase a new copy of the suggested textbook as an investment in your education.

TEXTBOOKS

(Because these textbooks are updated frequently, editions and dates of publication have not been listed here.)

Berkowitz, Eric N., Roger A. Kerin, and William Rudelius, *Marketing.* Homewood IL: Irwin.

Boone, Louis E. and David L. Kurtz, *Contemporary Marketing.* Fort Worth: Dryden Press.

Evans, Joel R. and Barry Berman, *Marketing.* New York: Macmillan.

Kotler, Philip and Gary Armstrong, *Principles of Marketing.* Englewood Cliffs, NJ: Prentice Hall.

McCarthy, E. Jerome and William D. Perreault, Jr., *Basic Marketing: A Managerial Approach.* Homewood, IL: Irwin.

Pride, William M. and O.C. Ferrell, *Marketing: Concepts and Strategies.* Boston: Houghton Mifflin.

Schoell, William F. and Joseph P. Guiltinan, *Marketing: Contemporary Concepts and Practices.* Boston: Allyn & Bacon.

Appendixes

Appendix A
Sample Answer Sheet

COLLEGE-LEVEL EXAMINATION PROGRAM®
The College Board

ANSWER SHEET FOR NATIONAL ADMINISTRATIONS

| PAGE 1 |

DO NOT WRITE ON THIS PAGE.
DO NOT OPEN YOUR TEST BOOK UNTIL YOU ARE TOLD TO DO SO.
DO NOT, AT ANY TIME, PUT YOUR ANSWER SHEET INSIDE YOUR TEST BOOK.

Refer to the instructions below as you complete your answer sheet. Since the information you supply on the answer sheet will be used to report your scores, accuracy is essential.

If you will be using more than one answer sheet because you are taking more than one test, be sure your identifying information is entered in exactly the same way on each answer sheet.

Use only a No. 2 (HB or soft-lead) pencil to complete your answer sheet. Do NOT use a pen or other marker.

Make sure you fill in the corresponding circle below each letter and digit you enter in the boxes at the top of the columns. Each mark should be dark and completely fill the circle. If you make any changes, erase the unwanted marks carefully and completely.

Further explanations of selected items on the answer sheet follow.

Item 1: Your Name — Omit any spaces, hyphens, apostrophes, and "Jr." or "III" that normally appear in your name.

Item 3: Date of Birth — Any single digit must be preceded by a zero. For example, if your birthday is March 8, you should enter 03 for Month and 08 for Day. Be sure you enter the last two digits of your year of birth, not the current year.

Item 5: Your Mailing Address — If your street address is too long to fit in the spaces provided, refer to the abbreviations listed on page 4 and use whichever ones are appropriate. Indicate a space in your address by leaving a blank box and filling in the empty circle immediately below it. Indicate your state with the abbreviation listed on page 4.

Item 7: Foreign Country Codes — Codes for other countries can be found in the *CLEP Test Center Handbook.*

Item 8: Current Educational Level — Fill in the circle next to the level you have reached. For example, if you have finished your freshman year in college, fill in the circle for College Sophomore.

Item 9: Ethnic Group — Providing this information is optional. It is requested to help ensure that CLEP tests are fair and useful to all students.

Item 12: Test Center — Ask the test administrator for this code number or refer to *CLEP Colleges.*

Item 13: Score Report Recipient — The code number you enter here identifies the institution to which you want a copy of your scores sent.

If you want scores reported to the college at which you are being tested, ask the test administrator for the code number.

If your scores are to be reported to another institution and you do not know the code number, ask the test administrator for a copy of *CLEP Colleges* and look up the number. Enter the code number on your answer sheet, fill in the corresponding circle below each box, and then print the name and address of your score recipient on the lines provided.

If your score recipient is not listed in *CLEP Colleges,* enter "9999" in the boxes. Don't forget to fill in the corresponding circles and to print the recipient's name and address on the lines provided.

Do not put your own name and address in the space. If you want to be the only recipient of your scores, leave item 13 blank.

Item 18: Test Code — To insure accurate processing of your answer sheet and timely reporting of your scores, it is essential that you indicate the proper *test code number* on your answer sheet. The test code number is printed on the front cover of your test book.

Item 19: Test Book — Fill in the test book serial number, which can be found on the upper right-hand side of the front cover of your test book.

Item 20: Signature and Date — Be sure to sign and date the answer sheet in this box.

ANSWER SHEET FOR NATIONAL ADMINISTRATIONS

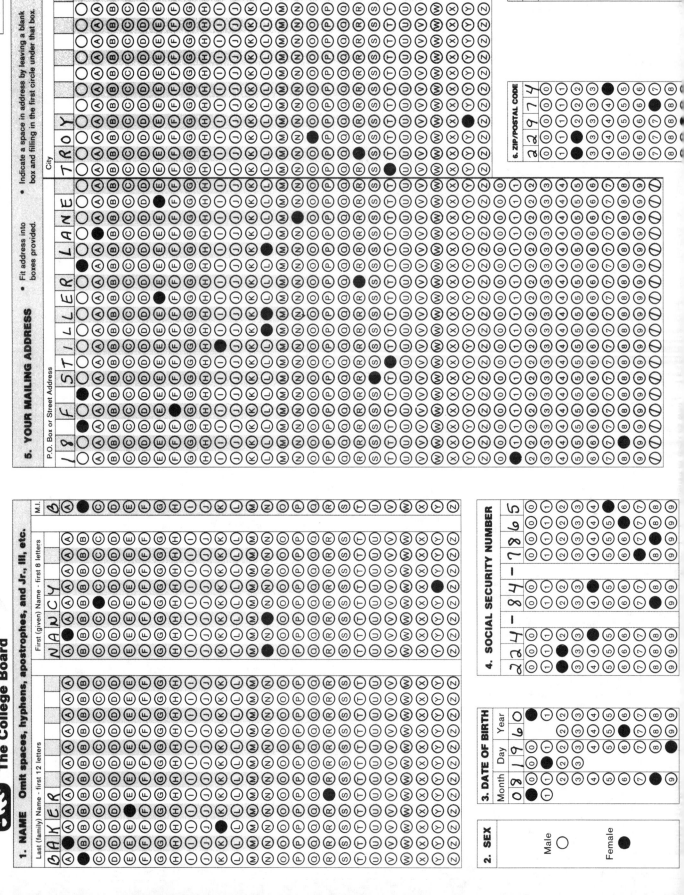

COLLEGE-LEVEL EXAMINATION PROGRAM
The College Board

Be sure each mark is dark and completely fills the intended circle. If you erase, do so completely. Mark your answers to both Section 1 and Section 2 on this page. If there are more circles than test questions, leave the extra circles blank.

EDUCATIONAL LEVEL

① Native American/American Indian
② Black or African American
③ Mexican American or Chicano
④ Asian, Asian American, or Pacific Islander
⑤ Puerto Rican
⑥ Latin American, South American, Central American, or other Hispanic
⑦ White
⑧ Other

① High School
② High School Graduate
③ College Freshman
④ College Sophomore
⑤ College Junior
⑥ College Senior
⑦ College Graduate

English at least as well as any other language?
● Yes ○ No

11. Mark here if you have a disability or physical impairment. ○

12. TEST CENTER
Enter the code number in these boxes. `1 2 3 4`

18. TEST CODE
`9 9 4 0`

13. SCORE REPORT RECIPIENT
If you do not have the code number, write 9999 in the boxes, fill in the appropriate circles, and print the institution's name and address.

CODE `0 1 9 4`

Institution
NAME CENTRAL UNIVERSITY
STREET
CITY CENTRAL CITY
STATE MISSOURI
ZIP CODE

19. TEST BOOK
SERIAL NUMBER `0 0 0 9 9 9`

14. FEES PAID
Examination Fee. . . . . ●
Special Administration Fee . ○ (If Any)
Total Paid . . $ `40`

17. TEST DATE
MONTH DAY YEAR
`0 7` `0 7` `9 2`

15. Are you taking the optional essay portion of this examination?
○ Yes ● No

16. Examination Name (Print)
AMERICAN HISTORY I: EARLY COLONIZATION TO 1877
Form Designation (Print)
2 ABC3

20. SIGNATURE AND DATE
I accept the conditions set forth with the CLEP registration information concerning the administration of the tests and reporting of scores.

Nancy Baber   7/7/93
Today's Date:

DO NOT WRITE ON THIS PAGE.

ABBREVIATIONS AND CODES FOR ITEM 5 OF THIS ANSWER SHEET

Abbreviations for use in street address

Avenue	**AVE**	Heights	**HTS**	Route	**RTE**
Boulevard	**BLVD**	Highway	**HWY**	Second	**2ND**
Circle	**CIR**	Mount	**MT**	South	**S**
Court	**CT**	North	**N**	Southeast	**S E**
Drive	**DR**	Northeast	**N E**	Southwest	**S W**
East	**E**	Northwest	**N W**	Square	**SQ**
Expressway	**EXPWY**	Parkway	**PKY**	Street	**ST**
First	**1ST**	Place	**PL**	Terrace	**TER**
Fort	**FT**	Post Office	**P O**	Third	**3RD**
Fourth	**4TH**	Road	**RD**	West	**W**

State Codes

AL	Alabama	**HI**	Hawaii	**MI**	Michigan	**NC**	North Carolina	**UT**	Utah
AK	Alaska	**ID**	Idaho	**MN**	Minnesota	**ND**	North Dakota	**VT**	Vermont
AZ	Arizona	**IL**	Illinois	**MS**	Mississippi	**OH**	Ohio	**VA**	Virginia
AR	Arkansas	**IN**	Indiana	**MO**	Missouri	**OK**	Oklahoma	**WA**	Washington
CA	California	**IA**	Iowa	**MT**	Montana	**OR**	Oregon	**WV**	West Virginia
CO	Colorado	**KS**	Kansas	**NE**	Nebraska	**PA**	Pennsylvania	**WI**	Wisconsin
CT	Connecticut	**KY**	Kentucky	**NV**	Nevada	**RI**	Rhode Island	**WY**	Wyoming
DE	Delaware	**LA**	Louisiana	**NH**	New Hampshire	**SC**	South Carolina	**PR**	Puerto Rico
DC	Dist. of Col.	**ME**	Maine	**NJ**	New Jersey	**SD**	South Dakota		
FL	Florida	**MD**	Maryland	**NM**	New Mexico	**TN**	Tennessee		
GA	Georgia	**MA**	Massachusetts	**NY**	New York	**TX**	Texas		

Appendix B
Answers to Sample Questions

English Composition

1. D		26. E	
2. D		27. A	
3. A		28. B	
4. E		29. D	
5. D		30. A	
6. C		31. B	
7. B		32. D	
8. A		33. C	
9. E		34. B	
10. C		35. E	
11. C		36. D	
12. B		37. C	
13. B		38. B	
14. A		39. E	
15. C		40. D	
16. D		41. A	
17. E		42. C	
18. A		43. D	
19. B		44. A	
20. D		45. C	
21. B		46. B	
22. C		47. E	
23. B		48. A	
24. D		49. E	
25. C		50. C	

Humanities

1. D
2. E
3. C
4. E
5. A
6. A
7. C
8. E
9. A
10. E
11. D
12. B
13. A
14. D
15. B
16. A
17. E
18. E
19. A
20. D
21. C
22. D
23. B
24. B
25. A

Mathematics

1. B
2. C
3. A
4. A
5. B
6. A
7. C
8. D
9. D
10. D
11. A
12. B
13. D
14. B
15. C
16. C
17. A
18. C
19. C
20. A
21. D
22. B
23. B
24. B
25. C

Natural Sciences

1. D
2. E
3. E
4. B
5. D
6. C
7. A
8. D
9. C
10. C
11. D
12. E
13. D
14. E
15. E
16. B
17. C
18. B
19. C
20. A
21. A
22. D
23. A
24. A
25. B

Social Sciences and History

1. E		26. C	
2. E		27. A	
3. A		28. D	
4. B		29. B	
5. D		30. D	
6. C		31. B	
7. A		32. A	
8. E		33. D	
9. A		34. A	
10. B		35. B	
11. C		36. B	
12. D		37. D	
13. D		38. C	
14. D		39. E	
15. C		40. C	
16. D			
17. B			
18. C			
19. C			
20. D			
21. A			
22. C			
23. E			
24. C			
25. E			

American Literature

1. B
2. A
3. B
4. D
5. A
6. D
7. E
8. B
9. B
10. E
11. D
12. C
13. C
14. A
15. C
16. E
17. E
18. B
19. D
20. C
21. D
22. A
23. B
24. A
25. B

Analysis and Interpretation of Literature

1. E
2. A
3. C
4. D
5. A
6. B
7. D
8. B
9. C
10. B
11. E
12. E
13. A
14. A
15. C
16. B
17. E
18. B
19. D
20. A
21. A
22. A
23. C
24. E
25. D

English Literature

1. C
2. C
3. D
4. D
5. A
6. B
7. A
8. E
9. A
10. C
11. A
12. D
13. B
14. E
15. E
16. A
17. C
18. C
19. C
20. B
21. D
22. B
23. E
24. D
25. B

Freshman College Composition

1. D	26. B
2. D	27. D
3. C	28. A
4. E	29. A
5. D	30. B
6. C	31. E
7. B	32. E
8. B	33. C
9. A	34. D
10. D	35. A
11. B	36. B
12. B	37. B
13. A	38. E
14. C	39. A
15. D	40. E
16. D	41. C
17. C	42. A
18. B	43. C
19. B	44. C
20. C	45. A
21. B	46. D
22. D	47. A
23. C	48. E
24. E	49. B
25. A	50. E

College French — Levels 1 and 2

1. C	
2. C	
3. A	
4. D	
5. A	
6. D	
7. D	
8. C	
9. A	
10. C	
11. A	
12. D	
13. B	
14. D	
15. B	
16. A	
17. B	
18. C	
19. C	
20. B	
21. A	
22. C	
23. B	
24. D	
25. D	

College German — Levels 1 and 2

1. D	
2. C	
3. B	
4. B	
5. C	
6. C	
7. A	
8. B	
9. B	
10. D	
11. D	
12. B	
13. C	
14. A	
15. C	
16. A	
17. D	
18. C	
19. B	
20. A	
21. B	
22. B	
23. A	
24. D	
25. C	
26. C	

College Spanish — Levels 1 and 2

1. D	
2. D	
3. B	
4. D	
5. B	
6. A	
7. D	
8. B	
9. C	
10. D	
11. C	
12. B	
13. C	
14. D	
15. D	
16. C	
17. A	
18. C	
19. B	
20. C	
21. B	
22. A	
23. C	
24. C	
25. D	

American Government

1. C	26. C
2. B	27. E
3. B	28. C
4. D	29. C
5. B	30. D
6. B	31. A
7. A	32. B
8. C	33. B
9. C	34. A
10. C	35. A
11. B	36. D
12. E	37. E
13. D	38. C
14. C	39. A
15. C	40. D
16. E	
17. E	
18. A	
19. A	
20. C	
21. A	
22. C	
23. D	
24. A	
25. B	

American History I: Early Colonizations to 1877

1. B	26. D
2. B	27. D
3. A	28. D
4. E	29. D
5. B	30. E
6. B	31. E
7. A	32. C
8. E	33. E
9. D	34. A
10. D	35. C
11. B	36. D
12. E	37. B
13. E	38. B
14. D	39. B
15. B	40. C
16. C	
17. C	
18. C	
19. C	
20. E	
21. A	
22. D	
23. C	
24. B	
25. A	

American History II: 1865 to the Present

1. C	26. E
2. E	27. C
3. B	28. C
4. E	29. A
5. A	30. B
6. A	31. A
7. B	32. E
8. C	33. C
9. A	34. E
10. C	35. E
11. D	36. D
12. E	37. C
13. C	38. A
14. D	39. C
15. B	40. B
16. D	
17. E	
18. A	
19. B	
20. C	
21. B	
22. A	
23. D	
24. A	
25. D	

Human Growth and Development

1. D	
2. E	
3. B	
4. E	
5. C	
6. C	
7. D	
8. B	
9. A	
10. D	
11. A	
12. E	
13. E	
14. C	
15. B	
16. E	
17. C	
18. E	
19. B	
20. D	
21. A	
22. B	
23. C	
24. B	
25. A	

Introduction to Educational Psychology		Principles of Macroeconomics			Principles of Microeconomics			Introductory Psychology	
1. B		1. C	26. A		1. A	26. D		1. E	26. C
2. A		2. D	27. B		2. C	27. A		2. C	27. D
3. B		3. B	28. E		3. A	28. B		3. C	28. B
4. D		4. C	29. D		4. E	29. C		4. D	29. E
5. E		5. A	30. A		5. A	30. B		5. E	30. E
6. D		6. E	31. A		6. D	31. D		6. B	31. A
7. B		7. D	32. E		7. C	32. E		7. D	32. D
8. B		8. B	33. C		8. D	33. E		8. A	33. E
9. C		9. D	34. D		9. E	34. B		9. C	34. D
10. D		10. E	35. A		10. B	35. C		10. C	35. B
11. C		11. C	36. A		11. C	36. E		11. B	
12. E		12. C	37. B		12. E	37. B		12. E	
13. B		13. B	38. A		13. A	38. E		13. A	
14. D		14. A	39. B		14. A	39. B		14. B	
15. A		15. C			15. E			15. A	
16. D		16. B			16. D			16. A	
17. E		17. D			17. D			17. D	
18. A		18. E			18. B			18. C	
19. B		19. A			19. C			19. E	
20. B		20. E			20. C			20. A	
21. A		21. C			21. D			21. B	
22. D		22. B			22. E			22. C	
23. B		23. A			23. D			23. B	
24. C		24. B			24. B			24. A	
25. A		25. D			25. D			25. D	

Introductory Sociology	Western Civilization I: Ancient Near East to 1648	Western Civilization II: 1648 to the Present	Calculus with Elementary Functions	
1. C	1. D	1. C	1. C	26. E
2. C	2. A	2. E	2. E	27. D
3. A	3. A	3. A	3. B	28. D
4. B	4. C	4. D	4. E	29. A
5. D	5. E	5. D	5. B	30. B
6. E	6. A	6. E	6. E	31. B
7. B	7. A	7. D	7. D	32. A
8. D	8. B	8. A	8. C	33. E
9. C	9. A	9. A	9. C	34. B
10. E	10. C	10. E	10. A	35. B
11. A	11. E	11. B	11. C	36. B
12. A	12. D	12. A	12. E	37. A
13. C	13. E	13. E	13. B	38. C
14. D	14. A	14. A	14. D	39. E
15. A	15. B	15. E	15. D	40. B
16. D	16. A	16. D	16. B	
17. B	17. D	17. D	17. B	
18. B	18. C	18. C	18. D	
19. E	19. B	19. E	19. C	
20. C	20. E	20. B	20. A	
	21. D	21. C	21. D	
	22. D	22. E	22. D	
	23. B	23. A	23. B	
	24. E	24. B	24. D	
	25. C	25. C	25. D	

College Algebra		Trigonometry	General Biology	General Chemistry		Information Systems and Computer Applications
1. C	26. E	1. A	1. E	1. C	26. C	1. E
2. D	27. D	2. B	2. E	2. B	27. C	2. D
3. B	28. A	3. C	3. A	3. E	28. D	3. D
4. D		4. E	4. C	4. C		4. D
5. E		5. B	5. D	5. E		5. A
6. B		6. D	6. E	6. B		6. B
7. D		7. B	7. E	7. D		7. C
8. E		8. C	8. D	8. D		8. A
9. E		9. D	9. C	9. A		9. A
10. D		10. B	10. C	10. B		10. D
11. E		11. D	11. C	11. E		11. D
12. C		12. C	12. D	12. D		12. C
13. B		13. E	13. A	13. B		13. E
14. A		14. D	14. D	14. D		14. B
15. A		15. C	15. B	15. A		15. A
16. C		16. C	16. D	16. D		16. C
17. C		17. E	17. A	17. B		17. B
18. B		18. C	18. C	18. D		18. E
19. B		19. A	19. B	19. D		19. D
20. B		20. C	20. A	20. E		20. D
21. C		21. B	21. B	21. D		21. B
22. E		22. C	22. C	22. C		22. C
23. C		23. A	23. C	23. A		23. D
24. A		24. E	24. E	24. A		24. D
25. D		25. D	25. B	25. D		25. B

Principles of Management	Introductory Accounting	Introductory Business Law	Principles of Marketing	
1. C	1. D	1. A	1. C	26. B
2. B	2. E	2. C	2. E	27. A
3. E	3. E	3. B	3. D	28. D
4. D	4. A	4. D	4. D	29. C
5. D	5. E	5. B	5. C	30. A
6. E	6. B	6. D	6. D	31. B
7. A	7. A	7. E	7. E	32. C
8. D	8. C	8. D	8. B	
9. E	9. D	9. B	9. B	
10. C	10. C	10. C	10. A	
11. A	11. E	11. D	11. B	
12. D	12. D	12. A	12. D	
13. A	13. C	13. D	13. C	
14. D	14. E	14. A	14. B	
15. D	15. B	15. E	15. B	
16. B	16. A	16. A	16. A	
17. E	17. E	17. C	17. E	
18. D	18. E	18. A	18. C	
19. A	19. C	19. E	19. E	
20. B	20. E	20. E	20. C	
21. D	21. A	21. C	21. B	
22. B	22. B	22. B	22. A	
23. D	23. A	23. A	23. B	
24. C	24. D	24. B	24. C	
	25. D		25. B	

Appendix C
List of Participating Colleges and Universities

Following is a list by city and state of institutions that grant credit for satisfactory scores on one or more CLEP examinations. Each college is assigned a four-digit code number by CLEP, which appears to the left of the college's name. Use this number when you are designating a college to receive your test scores to speed the process.

Some of these institutions administer CLEP examinations only to their own students, others administer the exams to anyone who properly registers to take them. For a free copy of *CLEP Colleges*, which contains a list of test centers and their address, write to or call: CLEP, P.O. Box 6601, Princeton, NJ 08541-6601; (609) 771-7865.

ALABAMA

Alexander City
1037 Alexander City State Junior College

Andalusia
1429 Lurleen B. Wallace State Junior College

Anniston
3334 Harry M. Ayers State Technical College

Athens
1024 Athens State College

Auburn
1005 Auburn University

Bay Minette
1939 James H. Faulkner State Community College

Bessemer
3231 Bessemer State Technical College

Birmingham
1064 Birmingham – Southern College
1352 Jefferson State Community College
1933 Lawson State Community College
1468 Miles College
1302 Samford University
1723 Southeastern Bible College
1856 University of Alabama in Birmingham

Boaz
1721 Snead State Community College

Brewton
1355 Jefferson Davis State Junior College

Decatur
1356 John C. Calhoun State Community College

Dothan
1824 Troy State University – Dothan
1264 Wallace Community College

Enterprise
1213 Enterprise State Junior College

Fayette
1038 Brewer State Junior College

Florence
1735 University of North Alabama

Gadsden
1262 Gadsden State Junior College

Hanceville
8685 Wallace State Community College

Huntsville
1586 Oakwood College
1854 University of Alabama in Huntsville

Jacksonville
1736 Jacksonville State University

Jasper
1943 Rocky Mountain College of Art & Design
7965 Walker College

Livingston
1737 Livingston University

Marion
1349 Judson College
1447 Marion Military Institute

Mobile
1517 S. D. Bishop State Junior College
1733 Spring Hill College
1515 University of Mobile
1880 University of South Alabama

Monroeville
1644 Patrick Henry State Junior College

Montevallo
1004 University of Montevallo

Montgomery
1006 Alabama State University
1036 Auburn University at Montgomery
1034 Faulkner University of Alabama – Christian
1303 Huntingdon College
1798 Troy State University in Montgomery

Muscle Shoals
7650 Shoals Community College

Normal
1003 Alabama A&M University

Opp
3333 Douglas MacArthur State Technical College

Phil Campbell
1577 Northwest Alabama Community College

Phoenix City
7189 Chattahoochee Valley Community College
7849 Troy State University

Rainsville
1576 Northeast Alabama State Junior College

Selma
1989 Concordia College
1792 Selma University
3146 Wallace State Community College

Talladega
1800 Talladega College

Troy
1738 Troy State University

Tuscaloosa
3338 Shelton State Community College – Junior Division
3330 Shelton State Community College of Technology
1739 Stillman College
1830 University of Alabama

Tuskegee
1813 Tuskegee University

Wadley
1728 Southern Union State Junior College

ALASKA

Anchorage
4201 Alaska Pacific University
4896 University of Alaska – Anchorage
7866 Wayland Baptist University

Barrow
0469 Arctic Sivunmun Ilisagvik College

Bethel
4370 University of Alaska – Fairbanks, Kuskokwim

Dillingham
7949 University of Alaska – Bristol Bay Campus

Fairbanks
4866 University of Alaska – Fairbanks

Juneau
4897 University of Alaska – Juneau, Southeast

Ketchikan
4379 University of Alaska – Southeast Ketchikan

Kodiak
4372 University of Alaska – Kodiak College

Kotzebue
7656 University of Alaska – Fairbanks, Chukchi

Nome
4545 University of Alaska – Fairbanks, Northwest

Palmer
4509 University of Alaska – Anchorage, Matanuska

Sitka
4742 Sheldon Jackson College
4754 University of Alaska – Southeast Sitka

Soldotna
4373 University of Alaska – Kenai Peninsula

Unalaska
7884 Unalaska Rural Educational Center

Valdez
4636 Prince William Sound Community College

ARIZONA

Coolidge
4122 Central Arizona College

Douglas
4097 Cochise College

Flagstaff
4006 Northern Arizona University

Glendale
4003 American Graduate School of International Management
4338 Glendale Community College

Holbrook
9251 Northland Pioneer College

Kingman
4495 Mohave County Community College

Mesa
4513 Mesa Community College

Phoenix
4223 Arizona College of the Bible
4518 Gateway Community College
4331 Grand Canyon University
4594 Ottawa University – Arizona
4606 Phoenix College
0997 Rio Salado Community College
4734 South Mountain Community College
4736 Southwestern College
4911 University of Phoenix
1316 Western International University

Prescott
4631 Prescott Center for Alternate Education
4996 Yavapai College

Scottsdale
4755 Scottsdale Community College

Tempe
4007 Arizona State University

Thatcher
4297 Eastern Arizona College

Tsaile
4550 Navajo Community College

Tucson
4623 Pima Community College
4622 Pima Community College – Downtown
7807 Southwestern University
4832 University of Arizona
4913 University of Phoenix – Tucson

Yuma
4013 Arizona Western College

ARKANSAS

Arkadelphia
6272 Henderson State University
6549 Ouachita Baptist University

Batesville
6009 Arkansas College

Beebe
6026 Arkansas State University – Beebe

Bentonville
7686 Northwest Arkansas Community College

Blytheville
6447 Mississippi County Community College

Camden
6704 Southern Arkansas University Tech.

Clarksville
6111 University of the Ozarks

College City
6658 Southern Baptist College

Conway
6273 Hendrix College
6012 University of Central Arkansas

El Dorado
6697 Southern Arkansas Community College

Fayetteville
6866 University of Arkansas – Fayetteville

Forrest City
6207 East Arkansas Community College

Fort Smith
6033 Arkansas Christian College
6220 Westark Community College

Harrison
6517 North Arkansas Community College

Helena
6583 Phillips County Community College

Hot Springs
6243 Garland County Community College

Little Rock
6753 Arkansas Baptist College
6578 Philander Smith College
6368 University of Arkansas – Little Rock

Magnolia
6661 Southern Arkansas University

Mena
7746 Rich Mountain Community College

Monticello
6007 University of Arkansas – Monticello

North Little Rock
6649 Shorter College

Paragould
6131 Crowley's Ridge College

Pine Bluff
6004 University of Arkansas – Pine Bluff

Russellville
6010 Arkansas Technical University

Searcy
6267 Harding University

Siloam Springs
6321 John Brown University

State University
6011 Arkansas State University

CALIFORNIA

Alameda
4118 College of Alameda

Angwin
4600 Pacific Union College

Aptos
4084 Cabrillo College

Arcata
4345 Humboldt State University

Atherton
4483 Menlo College

Azusa
4596 Azusa Pacific University

Bakersfield
4015 Bakersfield College
4110 California State University – Bakersfield

Barstow
4020 Barstow Community College
4138 Chapman College – Res. Education Center

Belmont
4063 College of Notre Dame – California

Berkeley
4008 Armstrong University

4724 Dominican School of Philosophy/ Theology
4833 University of California – Berkeley
7921 Vista College

Blythe
4603 Palo Verde College

Burbank
4955 Woodbury University

Calexico
4743 San Diego State University

Camarillo
4673 St. John's Seminary/College

Carson
4098 California State University – Dominguez Hills

Chico
4048 California State University – Chico

Chula Vista
4726 Southwestern College

Claremont
4054 Claremont McKenna College
4341 Harvey Mudd College
4619 Pitzer College
4607 Pomona College
4693 Scripps College

Coalinga
4056 West Hills Community College

Columbia
4108 Columbia College

Compton
4095 Claretian Junior Seminary
4078 Compton Community College

Costa Mesa
4584 Orange Coast College
4701 Southern California College

Culver City
4964 West Los Angeles College

Cupertino
4057 Cogswell Polytechnical College
4286 De Anza College

Cypress
4104 Cypress College

Davis
4834 University of California – Davis

El Cajon
4150 Christian Heritage College
4252 Cuyamaca College
4334 Grossmont College

El Camino
4302 El Camino College

Encino
4873 San Fernando College of Law

Eureka
4100 College of the Redwoods

Fountain Valley
7198 Coastline Community College
4822 University of Phoenix – Southern California Division
4703 William Howard Taft University

Fremont
4579 Ohlone College

Fresno
4123 California Christian College
4312 California State University – Fresno

4311 Fresno City College
4616 Fresno Pacific College
4748 San Joaquin College of Law
4970 West Coast Bible College

Fullerton
4589 California State University – Fullerton
4314 Fullerton College
4614 Pacific Christian College
4392 Southern California College of Optometry
7969 Western State University

Gilroy
4678 Gavilan College

Glendale
4327 Glendale Community College
7409 Glendale University College of Law

Glendora
4051 Citrus College

Hayward
4011 California State University – Hayward
4725 Chabot College

Huntington Beach
4339 Golden West College

Imperial
4358 Imperial Valley College

Inglewood
4558 National University – Inglewood
7962 University of West Los Angeles School of Law

Irvine
4069 Christ College – Irvine
4773 Irvine Valley College
7638 National University
4859 University of California – Irvine
7970 Western State University

La Mesa
4254 Coleman College

La Mirada
4017 Biola University

La Verne
4381 University of La Verne
7897 University of La Verne – Vandenberg

Lancaster
4005 Antelope Valley College
4143 Chapman College – Res. Educational Center

Lawndale
7848 University of Phoenix – South Bay

Loma Linda
4062 Loma Linda University

Long Beach
4389 California State University – Long Beach
4388 Long Beach City College
4626 Pacific Coast University School of Law

Los Altos Hills
4315 Foothill College

Los Angeles
4399 California State University – Los Angeles
7165 Committee of Bar Examiners of California
4457 Fashion Institute of Technology
4391 Los Angeles City College

4409 Los Angeles Southwest College
4403 Loyola/Marymount University
4493 Mount St. Mary's College – Chalon
4581 Occidental College
4394 Otis School of Art & Design
4880 University of California – Honors Office
4837 University of California – Los Angeles
4876 University of Judaism
7957 University of West Los Angeles
4966 West Coast University – Main Campus
4997 Yeshiva University – Los Angeles

Malibu
4630 Pepperdine University
4326 Pepperdine University – Los Angeles

Marina Del Rey
4210 Antioch University of Los Angeles

Marysville
4994 Yuba College

Merced
4500 Merced College

Mission Viejo
4747 Saddleback College

Modesto
4721 Fresno Pacific College – Extension Division
4486 Modesto Junior College

Monterey
4507 Monterey Institute of International Studies
4490 Monterey Peninsula College

Monterey Park
4296 East Los Angeles College

Moorpark
4512 Moorpark College

Moraga
4675 Saint Mary's College of California

Mountain View
7706 Peninsula University College of Law
4677 Saint Joseph's College

Napa
4530 Napa Valley College

Newhall
4411 The Masters College

Northridge
4548 Edison Technical College
4707 California State University – Northridge

Norwalk
4083 Cerritos College

Novato
4361 Marin Community College – Indian Valley Campus

Oakland
4031 California College Arts & Crafts
4059 Holy Names College
4376 Kaiser Foundation School
4406 Laney College
4502 Merritt College
4485 Mills College
4620 Patten College
4750 Samuel Merritt College of Nursing

Oceanside
4582 Mira Costa College

Orange
4139 Chapman College
4047 Chapman University

Orinda
4365 John F. Kennedy University

Oroville
4226 Butte College

Oxnard
4591 Oxnard College
4812 University of LaVerne – Ventura

Palm Desert
4085 College of the Desert

Pasadena
4010 Ambassador College
4009 Art Center College of Design
4034 California Institute of Technology
4612 Pacific Oaks College
4604 Pasadena City College

Pittsburg
4396 Los Medanos College

Pleasant Hill
4295 Diablo Valley College

Pomona
4082 California State Polytechnic University – Pomona

Porterville
4608 Porterville College

Quincy
4318 Feather River College

Ranch Cucamonga
4046 Chaffey Community College

Ranch Palos Verdes
4515 Marymount College

Redding
4698 Simpson College

Redlands
4368 Johnston Center University – Redlands
4848 University of Redlands – Whitehead

Redwood City
4109 Canada College

Reedley
4655 Kings River Community College

Ridgecrest
4027 Cerro Coso Community College

Riverside
4094 California Baptist College
4380 La Sierra University
4658 Riverside Community College
4839 University of California – Riverside

Rohnert Park
4723 Sonoma State University

Rosemead
4279 Don Bosco Technical Institute

Sacramento
4004 American River College
4208 American River College – PL
4671 California State University – Sacramento
4121 Cosumnes River College
4320 Golden Gate University
4556 National University
4670 Sacramento City College
7653 University of Phoenix – Sacramento

Salinas
4340 Hartnell College

San Bernardino
4099 California State – San Bernardino
4679 San Bernardino Valley College

San Bruno
4746 Skyline College

San Diego
4557 National University
4605 Point Loma Nazarene College
4681 San Diego City College
4669 San Diego Evening College
4735 San Diego Mesa College
4728 San Diego Miramar College
4682 San Diego State University
7874 The Union Institute
7876 University of Phoenix – San Diego
4849 University of San Diego
4039 U.S. International University – San Diego
7971 Western State University

San Fernando
4404 Los Angeles Mission College

San Francisco
7090 American College of Nursing
4032 California College of Podiatric Medicine
4052 City College of San Francisco
4329 Golden Gate University
4555 New College of California
4036 San Francisco Art Institute
4765 San Francisco College of Mortuary Science
4744 San Francisco Conservatory of Music
4684 San Francisco State University
4840 University of California San Francisco Medical Center
7986 University of Phoenix – Online
4850 University of San Francisco

San Jacinto
4501 Mount San Jacinto College

San Jose
4273 Evergreen Valley College
4386 Lincoln University – The Law School
4686 Regis University
4756 San Jose Bible College
4687 San Jose State University
4914 University of Phoenix – San Jose

San Luis Obispo
4038 California Polytechnic State University
4101 Cuesta Community College

San Marcos
4602 Palomar College

San Mateo
4070 College of San Mateo

San Pablo
4943 Contra Costa College

San Rafael
4284 Dominican College of San Rafael

San Ramon
4917 University of Phoenix – San Ramon

Santa Ana
4689 Rancho Santiago College

Santa Barbara
7586 Antioch University – Santa Barbara
4228 Brooks Institute of Photography

4835 University of California – Santa Barbara
4950 Westmont College

Santa Clara
7587 Mission College of California
4851 Santa Clara University

Santa Cruz
4021 Bethany Bible College
4860 University of California – Santa Cruz

Santa Maria
4002 Allan Hancock College

Santa Monica
4691 Santa Monica College

Santa Paula
4828 Thomas Aquinas College

Santa Rosa
4275 Empire College
4692 Santa Rosa Junior College

Saratoga
4958 West Valley College

South Lake Tahoe
4420 Lake Tahoe Community College

Stanford
4704 Stanford University

Stockton
4346 Humphrey's College
4706 San Joaquin Delta College
4065 University of the Pacific

Suisun City
4930 Solano Community College

Sunnyvale
4561 Palmer College of Chiropractic – West

Susanville
4383 Lassen College

Taft
4820 Taft College

Talmadge
4282 Dharma Realm Buddhist University

Thousand Oaks
4088 California Lutheran University

Turlock
4713 California State University – Stanislas

Valencia
4049 California Institute of the Arts
4117 College of the Canyons

Vallejo
4035 California Maritime Academy

Van Nuys
4401 Los Angeles Valley College
7881 University of Phoenix – Van Nuys
4978 Westminster University

Ventura
4931 Ventura College
7983 Ventura College of Law

Victorville
4932 Victor Valley College

Visalia
4071 College of the Sequoias

Vista
7641 National University – Vista

Walnut
4494 Mount San Antonio College

Weed
4087 College of the Siskiyous

Whittier
4663 Rio Hondo College
4952 Whittier College

Wilmington
4395 Los Angeles Harbor College

Woodland Hills
4398 Los Angeles Pierce College

Yucaipa
4126 Crafton Hills College

CANADA

Lennoxville
0962 Champlain Regional College – Lennoxville

North York
0894 York University

Oshawa
7550 Kingsway College

COLORADO

Alamosa
4001 Adams State College

Aspen
4102 Colorado Mountain College – Aspen

Aurora
4132 Columbia College – Colorado
4918 University of Phoenix – Colorado Division

Boulder
3342 Naropa Institute
4841 University of Colorado – Boulder

Breckenridge
4124 Colorado Mountain College

Carbondale
4107 Colorado Mountain College

Colorado Springs
4072 Colorado College
4133 Colorado Technical College
4291 Pikes Peak Community College
4666 Regis College – Colorado Springs
4874 University of Colorado – Colorado Springs
4830 U.S. Air Force Academy

Craig
7218 Colorado Northwestern Community College

Denver
4137 Community College of Denver
4505 Metropolitan State College
4656 Regis University
4711 Saint Thomas Seminary College
4875 University of Colorado – Denver
4877 University of Colorado – Health Science
4842 University of Denver

Durango
4310 Fort Lewis College

Eagle
7137 Colorado Mountain College – Eagle Center

Fort Collins
4075 Colorado State University

Fort Morgan
4516 Morgan Community College

Glenwood Springs
4120 Colorado Mountain College – Glenwood Center
4112 Colorado Mountain College – Glenwood Springs

Golden
4073 Colorado School of Mines

Grand Junction
7114 Colorado Christian University

Greeley
4204 Aims Community College
4074 University of Northern Colorado

Grand Junction
4484 Mesa State College

Gunnison
4946 Western State College

La Junta
4588 Otero Junior College

Lakewood
7132 Colorado Christian College
4659 Colorado Christian University
4130 Red Rocks Community College

Lamar
4382 Lamar Community College

Leadville
4113 Colorado Mountain College – East

Littleton
4014 Arapahoe Community College

Pueblo
9059 Pueblo Business College
4634 Pueblo Community College
4611 University of Southern Colorado

Rangely
4665 Colorado Northwestern Community College

Rifle
7145 Colorado Mountain College – Rifle

Steamboat Springs
4140 Colorado Mountain College – Alpine
4995 U.S. International University – Alpine

Sterling
4537 Northeastern Junior College

Trinidad
4821 Trinidad State Junior College

Vail
7140 Colorado Mountain College – Vail

Westminster
4119 Front Range Community College

CONNECTICUT

Bloomfield
3758 Saint Thomas Seminary

Bridgeport
3446 Housatonic Community-Technical College
3789 St. Vincent College of Nursing
3914 University of Bridgeport

Cromwell
3439 Holy Apostles College

Danbury
3350 Western Connecticut State University

Danielson
3716 Quinebaug Valley Community-Technical College

Enfield
3656 Asnuntuck Community-Technical College

Fairfield
3093 Bridgeport Engineering Institute
3390 Fairfield University
3780 Sacred Heart University

Farmington
3897 Tunxis Community-Technical College
3931 University of Connecticut

Groton
7944 University of New Haven

Hamden
3699 Paier College of Art
3712 Quinnipiac College

Hartford
3421 Capitol Community Technical College
3431 Hartford College for Women
3539 Morse School of Business
3899 Trinity College

Manchester
3544 Manchester Community-Technical College

Middletown
3551 Middlesex Community-Technical College
3959 Wesleyan University
3556 Wilcox College of Nursing

New Britain
3898 Central Connecticut State University

New Haven
3001 Albertus Magnus College
3792 Gateway Community-Technical College
7595 New Hampshire College
3662 Southern Connecticut State University

New London
3284 Connecticut College
3528 Mitchell College
5807 U.S. Coast Guard Academy

Newington
3292 Charter Oak State College

North Haven
3425 Gateway Community-Technical College

Norwalk
3470 Katherine Gibbs School
3677 Norwalk Community-Technical College

Norwich
3558 Three Rivers Community-Technical College

Southington
3121 Briarwood College

Stamford
3750 Saint Basil's College

Storrs
3915 University of Connecticut

Suffield
3784 Saint Alphonsus College

West Hartford
3299 University of Hartford – Basic Study

Waterbury
3550 Naugatuck Valley Community-Technical College
3698 Teikyo-Post University
3978 Waterbury State Technical College

West Hartford
3754 Saint Joseph College
3436 University of Hartford

West Haven
3663 University of New Haven

Willimantic
3966 Eastern Connecticut State University

Winsted
3652 Northwestern Connecticut Community-Technical College

DELAWARE

Dover
5153 Delaware State College
5201 Delaware Technical Community College – Terry Campus
5326 Kent Christian College
5894 Wesley College

Georgetown
5169 Delaware Technical Community College – Southern

New Castle
5925 Wilmington College

Newark
5204 Delaware Technical Community College – Stanton

Wilmington
5154 Delaware Technical Community College – Wilmington
5255 Goldey-Beacon College
5081 Widener University – University College of Delaware

DISTRICT OF COLUMBIA

Washington, D.C.
5050 AMCAS – American Medical College Applied Services
5007 American University
5749 Beacon College
5104 Catholic University of America
5705 Corcoran School of Art
5246 George Washington University
5244 Georgetown University
5297 Howard University – College of Liberal Arts
5422 Mount Vernon College
5524 Oblate College
5622 Southeastern University
5632 Strayer College
7836 Strayer College – Takoma Park
5796 Trinity College
5929 University of District of Columbia

FLORIDA

Avon Park
5666 South Florida Community College

Babson Park
5893 Webber College

Boca Raton
5229 Florida Atlantic University
5437 Lynn University

Bradenton
5427 Manatee Community College

Brooksville
5578 Pasco-Hernando Community
       College North

Clearwater
5142 Clearwater Christian College
5658 St. Petersburg Junior College –
       Clearwater

Cocoa
5073 Brevard Community College

Coral Gables
5815 University of Miami

Dade City
5562 Pasco-Hernando Community
       College East

Daytona Beach
5061 Bethune-Cookman College
5159 Daytona Beach Community College
4305 Embry-Riddle Aeronautical
       University – Arizona
5190 Embry-Riddle Aeronautical
       University – Florida

Deland
5630 Stetson University

Fort Lauderdale
5040 Art Institute of Fort Lauderdale
5074 Broward Community College
5171 Fort Lauderdale College
5712 National Education Center
5514 Nova University

Fort Myers
5191 Edison Community College

Fort Pierce
5322 Indian River Community College

Fort Walton Beach
5791 Troy State University – Florida

Gainesville
5653 Santa Fe Community College
5812 University of Florida

Graceville
5386 Baptist Bible Institute

Haines City
5388 Landmark Baptist College

Hobe Sound
5306 Hobe Sound Bible College

Hollywood
5741 Broward Community College –
       Hollywood
5969 Prospect Hall College

Jacksonville
5182 Edward Waters College
5232 Florida Community College – Kent
5331 Jacksonville University
5343 Jones College – Main Campus
5490 University of North Florida

Key West
5236 Florida Keys Community College

Kissimmee
5202 Florida Bible College

Lake City
5377 Lake City Community College

Lake Wales
5883 Warner Southern College

Lake Worth
5531 Palm Beach Community College

Lakeland
5218 Florida Southern College
5621 Southeastern College

Leesburg
5376 Lake Sumter Community College

Madison
5503 North Florida Junior College

Marianna
5106 Chipola Junior College

Melbourne
5080 Florida Institute of Technology

Miami
5206 Florida International University
5217 Florida Memorial College
5327 International Fine Arts College
5465 Miami Dade Community College –
       Medical Center
5160 Miami Dade Community College
       North
5458 Miami Dade Community College
       South
5457 Miami-Dade Community College –
       Wolfson Campus
5650 St. John Vianney College Seminary
5076 St. Thomas University
5463 Trinity College at Miami

Miami Shores
5053 Barry University

New Port Richey
5559 Pasco-Hernado Community College
       West

Niceville
5526 Okaloosa-Walton Community
       College

Ocala
5127 Central Florida Community College

Orlando
5345 Orlando College
5679 Southern College
5233 University of Central Florida
5869 Valencia Community College –
       West Campus

Palatka
5641 St. John's River Community
       College

Panama City
5271 Gulf Coast Community College

Pensacola
5970 Pensacola Christian College
5535 Pensacola Junior College
5833 University of West Florida

Pinellas Park
5606 St. Petersburg Junior College – St.
       Petersburg

Pompano Beach
5735 Broward Community College –
       North

Saint Augustine
5235 Flagler College

Saint Leo
5638 Saint Leo College

Saint Petersburg
5223 Eckerd College
7460 International Credentialing
       Association

Sanford
5662 Seminole Community College

Sarasota
5506 New College of University of South
       Florida
5573 Ringling School of Art & Design

Tallahassee
5215 Florida Agricultural & Mechanical
       University
5219 Florida State University
5794 Tallahassee Community College

Tampa
5304 Hillsborough Community College –
       Mabry
5311 Hillsborough Community College –
       Ybor
7669 National-Louis University
9907 Tampa College
5828 University of South Florida
5819 University of Tampa

Tarpon
5611 St. Petersburg Junior College

Temple Terrace
5216 Florida College

Titusville
5046 Brevard Community College

West Palm Beach
5553 Palm Beach Atlantic College
7730 Palm Beach County Schools

Winter Haven
5548 Polk Community College

Winter Park
5572 Rollins College

GEORGIA

Albany
5004 Albany State College
5026 Darton College

Americus
5250 Georgia Southwestern College

Athens
5813 University of Georgia

Atlanta
5429 Art Institute of Atlanta
5030 Atlanta Area Technical School
5014 Atlanta College of Art
5725 Atlanta Metropolitan College
5015 Atlanta University
5070 Bauder Fashion College – Atlanta
5110 Clark College
5187 Emory University
5196 Emory University Medical Center –
       Allied Health
5248 Georgia Institute of Technology
5251 Georgia State University
5344 John Marshall University of Law
5025 Mercer University in Atlanta
5623 Mercer University Southern School
       of Pharmacy
5415 Morehouse College
5417 Morris Brown College
7676 National-Louis University
7736 Office of Bar Admissions
5521 Oglethorpe University
5628 Spelman College

Augusta
5336 Augusta College
5406 Medical College of Georgia
5530 Paine College

Bainbridge
5062 Bainbridge College

Barnesville
5256 Gordon College

Brunswick
5078 Brunswick College

Carrollton
5900 West Georgia College

Clarkston
5165 DeKalb College Central
5694 DeKalb College North

Cleveland
5798 Truett McConnell College

Cochran
5411 Middle Georgia College

Columbus
5123 Columbus College

Cuthbert
5009 Andrew College

Dahlonega
5497 North Georgia College

Dalton
5167 Dalton College

Decatur
5711 DeKalb College South

Demorest
5537 Piedmont College

Douglas
5619 South Georgia College

East Point
5029 Atlanta Christian College

Fort Benning
5797 Troy State University – Fort
       Benning

Fort Valley
5220 Fort Valley State College

Franklin Springs
5184 Emmanuel College

Gainesville
5066 Brenau College
5273 Gainesville College

LaGrange
5362 LaGrange College

Lookout Mountain
6124 Covenant College

Macon
5439 Macon College
5409 Mercer University
5895 Wesleyan College

Marietta
5441 Chattahoochee Technical Institute
5359 Kennesaw State College
5614 Shorter College
5626 Southern College of Technology

Milledgeville
5252 Georgia College
5249 Georgia Military College

Morrow
5145 Clayton State College

Mount Berry
5059 Berry College

Mt. Vernon
5068 Brewton-Parker College

Oxford
5186 Emory University – Oxford College

Rome
5237 Floyd College
5616 Shorter College

Savannah
5012 Armstrong State College
5631 Savannah College of Art & Design
5609 Savannah State College
5157 South College

Statesboro
5253 Georgia Southern University

Swainsboro
5671 Swainsboro Technical Institute

Thomasville
5072 Thomas College

Tifton
5001 Abraham Baldwin Agricultural College

Toccoa Falls
5799 Toccoa Falls College

Valdosta
5855 Valdosta State University

Waleska
5568 Reinhardt College

Waycross
5889 Waycross College

Young Harris
5990 Young Harris College

GUAM

Magilao
0959 University of Guam

HAWAII

Hilo
4869 University of Hawaii – Hilo

Honolulu
4324 Cannons Business College
4105 Chaminade University – Honolulu
4352 Hawaii Pacific University
4350 Honolulu Community College
4362 International College
4377 Kapiolani Community College
4867 University of Hawaii – Manoa

Kaneohe
4976 Windward Community College

Laie Oahu
4106 Brigham Young University

Lihue Kauai
4378 Kauai Community College

Pearl City
4410 Leeward Community College
4959 West Oahu College – UH

IDAHO

Boise
4018 Boise State University

Caldwell
4060 Albertson College of Idaho

Coeur d'Alene
4539 North Idaho College

Lewiston
4385 Lewis-Clark State College

Moscow
4843 University of Idaho

Nampa
4544 Northwest Nazarene College

Pocatello
4355 Idaho State University

Rexburg
4657 Ricks College

Twin Falls
4114 College of Southern Idaho

ILLINOIS

Aurora
1027 Aurora University

Belleville
1057 Belleville Area College

Bloomington
1320 Illinois Wesleyan University

Cahokia
1621 Parks College of St. Louis University

Canton
1154 Spoon River College

Carbondale
1726 Southern Illinois University – Carbondale

Carlinville
1065 Blackburn College

Carterville
1357 John A. Logan College

Centralia
1108 Kaskaskia College

Champaign
1619 Parkland College

Charleston
1199 Eastern Illinois University

Chicago
1041 Aero Space Institute
1013 American Academy of Art
1014 American Conservatory of Music
1150 Chicago City-Wide College
7153 Chicago National College of Naprapathy
1118 Chicago State University
7146 City Colleges of Chicago
1135 Columbia College
1165 De Paul University
1089 Harold Washington College
0940 Harrington Institute
1317 Illinois College of Optometry
1318 Illinois Institute of Technology
1910 Kennedy King College
1412 Loyola University of Chicago
1520 MacCormac Junior College
1144 Malcolm X College

1220 Montay College
1486 Moody Bible Institute
1556 North Park College
1090 Northeastern Illinois University
1604 Northwestern University Medical Center – Nursing School
1578 Northwestern University of Continued Education
1584 Olive-Harvey College
2908 Ray College of Design
1093 Richard J. Daley College
1670 Robert Morris College
1666 Roosevelt University
3262 Rush University
1713 School of the Art Institute of Chicago
1716 Sherwood Conservatory of Music
1128 Spertus College of Judaica
0697 St. Augustine College
1708 St. Xavier University
1111 Truman College
1832 University of Chicago
1851 University of Illinois – Chicago
1872 Vandercook College Music
1925 Wilbur Wright College

Chicago Heights
1077 Prairie State College

Cicero
1489 Morton College

Crystal Lake
1525 McHenry County College

Danville
1160 Danville Area Community College

De Kalb
1559 Northern Illinois University

Decatur
1470 Millikin University
1976 Richland Community College

Deerfield
1810 Trinity College

Des Plaines
1573 Oakton Community College

Dixon
1780 Sauk Valley Community College

East Peoria
1312 Illinois Central College

East St. Louis
1749 State Community College

Edwardsville
1759 Southern Illinois University – Edwardsville

Elgin
1203 Elgin Community College
1351 Judson College

Elmhurst
1204 Elmhurst College

Elsah
1630 Principia College

Eureka
1206 Eureka College

Evanston
1366 Kendall College
1551 National-Louis University
1565 Northwestern University – Arts/Science
1546 Northwestern University of Kellogg – South Carolina
1747 Saint Francis Hospital – School of Nursing

Fairfield
7318 Frontier Community College

Freeport
1233 Highland Community College – Illinois

Galesburg
1982 Carl Sandburg College
1372 Knox College

Glen Ellyn
1083 College of DuPage

Godfrey
1430 Lewis & Clark Community College

Grayslake
1983 College of Lake County

Greenville
1256 Greenville College

Harrisburg
1777 Southeastern Illinois College

Ina
1673 Rend Lake College

Jacksonville
1315 Illinois College
1435 MacMurray College

Joliet
1130 College of St. Francis
1346 Joliet Junior College
7823 St. Joseph's College of Nursing

Kankakee
1380 Kankakee Community College
1596 Olivet Nazarene University

Kewanee
1537 Black Hawk College

Lake Forest
1052 Barat College
1392 Lake Forest College
7592 Lake Forest Graduate School of Management

Lebanon
1456 McKendree College

Lincoln
1405 Lincoln Christian College/Seminary
1406 Lincoln College

Lisle
1707 Illinois Benedictine College

Lombard
1567 National College Chiropractic

Macomb
1900 Western Illinois University

Malta
1385 Kishwaukee College

Mattoon
1424 Lake Land College

Moline
1483 Black Hawk College
4426 Moline Public Hospital – Nursing

Monmouth
1484 Monmouth College

Morrison
1269 Morrison Institute of Technology

Mount Carmel
1936 Wabash Valley College

Naperville
1555　North Central College

Niles
1755　Niles College/Loyola University

Normal
1319　Illinois State University

Oak Lawn
1210　Evangelical School of Nursing

Oak Park
1927　West Suburban College of Nursing

Oglesby
1397　Illinois Valley Community College

Olney
1305　Illinois Eastern Community College
1613　Olney Central College

Palatine
1932　William Rainey Harper College

Palos Heights
1820　Trinity Christian College

Palos Hills
1524　Moraine Valley Community College

Peoria
1070　Bradley University
1503　Methodist Medical Center – Illinois
3329　Midstate College

Quincy
1374　John Wood Community College
1645　Quincy University

River Forest
1140　Concordia University
1667　Rosary College

River Grove
1821　Triton College

Robinson
1242　Lincoln Trail College – IECC

Rock Island
1025　Augustana College

Rockford
1674　Rock Valley College
1665　Rockford College

Romeoville
1404　Lewis University

Skokie
1288　Hebrew Theological College

South Holland
1806　South Suburban College

Springfield
1428　Lincoln Land Community College
1787　Sangamon State University
1734　Springfield College in Illinois

Sugar Grove
1938　Waubonsee Community College

Ullin
1683　Shawnee Community College

University Park
1263　Governors State University

Urbana
1836　University of Illinois – Urbana/
　　　Champaign

Waukegan
1717　Shimer College

Westchester
7639　MIMA – The Management
　　　Association

Wheaton
3259　Illinois Institute of Technology
7672　National-Louis University
1905　Wheaton College

Wilmette
1438　Mallinckrodt College

Winnetka
7455　Health Professional International

INDIANA

Anderson
1016　Anderson University

Angola
1811　Tri-State University

Bloomington
1324　Indiana University – Bloomington
7483　Ivy Technical College/Bloomington

Columbus
1286　Indiana Vocational-Technical
　　　College – Columbus

Crawfordsville
1895　Wabash College

Donaldson
1015　Ancilla College

Evansville
1277　Indiana Vocational-Technical
　　　College – Evansville
3218　Lockyear College
1208　University of Evansville
1335　University of Southern Indiana

Fort Harrison
7937　Vincennes University Extension

Fort Wayne
1323　Indiana Institute of Technology
1336　Indiana University/Purdue
　　　University – Fort Wayne
1278　Indiana Vocational Technical
　　　College
1330　International Business College
1533　Interstate Technical Institute
1416　Lutheran College – Health
　　　Professionals
1637　Purdue University – Fort Wayne
　　　Campus
1693　Saint Francis College
1760　St. Joseph's Hospital School of
　　　Nursing
1227　Taylor University – Fort Wayne

Franklin
1228　Franklin College of Indiana

Gary
1338　Indiana University – Northwest
1281　Indiana Vocational-Technical
　　　College – Gary

Goshen
1251　Goshen College

Greencastle
1166　DePauw University

Hammond
1638　Purdue University – Calumet
　　　Campus

Hanover
1290　Hanover College

Huntington
1304　Huntington College

Indianapolis
1073　Butler University
1272　George Rogers Clark College
1343　Herron School of Art
1325　Indiana University – Purdue
　　　University at Indianapolis
1311　Indiana Vocational-Technical
　　　College – Indianapolis
1442　Marian College
1321　University of Indianapolis

Kokomo
1337　Indiana University at Kokomo
1329　Indiana Vocational-Technical
　　　College – Kokomo

Lafayette
1282　Indiana Vocational-Technical
　　　College – Lafayette

Madison
1334　Indiana Vocational-Technical
　　　College

Marion
1446　Indiana Wesleyan University

Mishawaka
1079　Bethel College

Muncie
1051　Ball State University
1279　Indiana Vocational-Technical
　　　College – Muncie

New Albany
7408　Graceland University
1314　Indiana University Southeast

North Manchester
1440　Manchester College

Notre Dame
1309　Holy Cross College
1702　St. Mary's College
1841　University of Notre Dame

Oakland City
1585　Oakland City College

Rensselaer
1697　Saint Joseph's College

Richmond
1195　Earlham College
1194　Indiana University East
1283　Indiana Vocational-Technical
　　　College – Richmond

Saint Mary of the Woods
1704　Saint Mary of the Woods College

Saint Meinrad
1705　St. Meinrad College

Sellersburg
1273　Indiana Vocational-Technical
　　　College

South Bend
1339　Indiana University – South Bend
1280　Indiana Vocational-Technical
　　　College – South
3140　Michiana College of Commerce

Terre Haute
1322　Indiana State University
1284　Indiana Vocational-Technical
　　　College – Terre Haute
1668　Rose-Hulman Institute of
　　　Technology

Upland
1802　Taylor University

Valparaiso
1873　Valparaiso Technical Institute
1874　Valparaiso University

Vincennes
1877　Vincennes University

West Lafayette
1631　Purdue University – West Lafayette

Westville
1640　Purdue University – North Central
　　　Westville

Whiting
1776　Calumet College of St. Joseph

Winona Lake
1252　Grace College – Indiana

IOWA

Ames
6306　Iowa State University

Ankeny
6177　Des Moines Area Community
　　　College – Ankeny
6214　Faith Baptist Bible College

Bettendorf
6712　Scott Community College – Eastern
　　　Iowa

Boone
6044　Des Moines Area Community
　　　College – Boone

Calmar
6751　Northeast Iowa Technical Institute
　　　– North

Cedar Falls
6307　University of Northern Iowa

Cedar Rapids
6101　Coe College
6027　Kirkwood Community College
6417　Mount Mercy College

Clarinda
6098　Iowa Western Community College
　　　– Clarinda

Clinton
6100　Clinton Community College –
　　　Eastern Iowa
6418　Mount St. Clare College

Council Bluffs
6302　Iowa Western Community College

Creston
6122　Southwestern Community College

Davenport
6585　Scott Community College – Palmer
6617　St. Ambrose University
6397　Teikyo Marycrest University

Decorah
6375　Luther College

Des Moines
6168　Drake University
6251　Grand View College

Dubuque
6099　Clarke College
1215　Emmaus Bible College
6370　Loras College
6869　University of Dubuque

Eagle Grove
6185 Iowa Central Community College – Eagle Grove

Epworth
6174 Divine Word College

Estherville
6196 Iowa Lakes Community College

Fairfield
4497 Maharishi International University

Fayette
6885 Upper Iowa University

Forest City
6925 Waldorf College

Fort Dodge
6217 Iowa Central Community College – Fort Dodge

Grinnell
6252 Grinnell College

Indianola
6650 Simpson College

Iowa City
6681 University of Iowa

Iowa Falls
6193 Ellsworth Community College – Iowa Valley

Keokuk
6340 Southeastern Community College – South

Lamoni
6249 Graceland College

Le Mars
6936 Teikyo-Westmar University

Marshalltown
6394 Marshalltown Community College – Iowa Valley

Mason City
6400 North Iowa Area Community College

Mount Pleasant
6308 Iowa Wesleyan College

Mount Vernon
6119 Cornell College

Muscatine
6422 Muscatine Community College – Eastern Iowa

Orange City
6490 Northwestern College

Oskaloosa
6943 William Penn College

Ottumwa
6299 Indian Hills Community College

Pella
6087 Central College

Peosta
6754 Northeast Iowa Technical Institute – South

Sheldon
6504 Northwest Iowa Technical College

Sioux Center
6171 Dordt College

Sioux City
6046 Briar Cliff College
6415 Morningside College
6950 Western Iowa Technical Community College

Storm Lake
6047 Buena Vista College

Waterloo
6288 Hawkeye Community College

Waverly
6926 Wartburg College

Webster City
6932 Iowa Central Community College – Webster City

West Burlington
6048 Southeastern Community College – North

West Des Moines
3219 National Institute of Technology

KANSAS

Arkansas City
6008 Cowley Community College

Atchison
6056 Benedictine College – South

Chanute
6093 Neosho County Community College

Coffeyville
6102 Coffeyville Community College

Colby
6129 Colby Community College

Concordia
6137 Cloud County Community College

Dodge City
6166 Dodge City Community College

El Dorado
6191 Butler County Community College

Emporia
6335 Emporia Kansas State College
6103 Way College of Emporia

Fort Scott
6219 Fort Scott Community College

Garden City
6246 Garden City Community College

Great Bend
6060 Barton County Community College

Haviland
6228 Barclay College

Hays
6218 Fort Hays State University

Hesston
6274 Hesston College

Highland
6276 Highland Community College

Hillsboro
6815 Tabor College

Hutchinson
6281 Hutchinson Community College

Independence
6304 Independence Community College

Iola
6305 Allen County Community College

Kansas City
6167 Donnelly College
6333 Kansas City Kansas Community College

Lawrence
6871 University of Kansas

Leavenworth
6630 Saint Mary College

Liberal
6714 Seward County Community Junior College

Lindsborg
6034 Bethany College

Manhattan
6334 Kansas State University
6392 Manhattan Christian College

McPherson
6088 Central College
6404 McPherson College

North Newton
6037 Bethel College

Olathe
6437 Mid-America Nazarene College

Ottawa
6547 Ottawa University – Kansas

Overland Park
6031 Baker University – Springs
6325 Johnson County Community College
6548 Ottawa University – Kansas City

Parsons
6576 Labette Community College

Pittsburg
6336 Pittsburg State University

Pratt
6581 Pratt Community College

Salina
6345 Kansas College of Technology
6337 Kansas Wesleyan

Sterling
6684 Sterling College

Topeka
6928 Washburn University

Wichita
6224 Friends University
6615 Kansas Newman College
6884 Wichita State University

Winfield
6670 Southwestern College

KENTUCKY

Ashland
1023 Ashland Community College

Barbourville
1825 Union College

Berea
1060 Berea College

Bowling Green
1901 Western Kentucky University

Campbellsville
1097 Campbellsville College

Columbia
1409 Lindsey Wilson College

Crestview Hills
1876 Thomas More College

Cumberland
1770 Southeast Community College

Danville
1109 Centre College

Elizabethtown
1211 Elizabethtown Community College

Fort Knox
1234 University of Kentucky – Fort Knox

Frankfort
1368 Kentucky State University

Georgetown
1249 Georgetown College

Grayson
1377 Kentucky Christian College

Hazard
1275 Hazard Community College

Henderson
1307 Henderson Community College

Highland Heights
1574 Northern Kentucky University

Hopkinsville
1274 Hopkinsville Community College

Jackson
1402 Lees College

Lexington
1474 Lexington Technical Institute
1808 Transylvania University
1837 University of Kentucky

London
1741 Sue Bennett College

Louisville
1056 Bellarmine College
1328 Jefferson Community College
4170 Kentucky College of Technology
1411 Louisville Presbyterian Theological Seminary
1552 Spalding University
3250 Sullivan Junior College of Business
1838 University of Louisville
1929 Watterson College

Madisonville
1544 Madisonville Community College

Maysville
1545 Maysville Community College

Midway
1467 Midway College

Morehead
1487 Morehead State University

Murray
1494 Murray State University

Owensboro
1071 Brescia College
1369 Kentucky Wesleyan College

Paducah
1620 Paducah Community College

Pikeville
1625 Pikeville College

Pippa Passes
1098 Alice Lloyd College

Prestonburg
1650 Prestonsburg Community College

Richmond
1200 Eastern Kentucky University

Saint Catharine
1690 St. Catharine College

Somerset
1779 Somerset Community College

Williamsburg
1145 Cumberland College

Wilmore
1019 Asbury College

Wilmore
1020 Asbury Theological Seminary

LOUISIANA

Alexandria
1632 Louisiana State University – Alexandria

Baton Rouge
6373 Louisiana State University – Baton Rouge
6663 Southern University A&M College

Bossier City
6073 Bossier Parish Community College

Chalmette
6715 Saint Bernard Parish Community College

Eunice
6386 Louisiana State University – Eunice

Grambling
6250 Grambling State University

Hammond
6656 Southeastern Louisiana University

Lafayette
6672 University of Southwestern Louisiana

Lake Charles
6403 McNeese State University

Monroe
6482 Northeast Louisiana University

Natchitoches
6492 Northwestern State University of Louisiana

New Orleans
6176 Delgado Community College
6164 Dillard University
6353 Louisiana State University – Nursing
6374 Loyola University – New Orleans
6472 New Orleans Baptist Theological Seminary
6471 Newcombe College
6002 Our Lady of Holy Cross College
9415 Phillips College
6711 Southern University – New Orleans
6841 Tulane University – University College
6379 University of New Orleans
6518 University Without Walls – New Orleans

6975 Xavier University of Louisiana

Pineville
6371 Louisiana College

Ruston
6372 Louisiana Technical University

Saint Benedict
6689 St. Joseph's Seminary

Shreveport
6082 Centenary College of Louisiana
6355 Louisiana State University – Shreveport
6719 Southern University – Bossier

Thibodaux
6221 Nicholls State University

MAINE

Auburn
3309 Central Maine Vocational
3014 Mid-State College

Augusta
3929 University of Maine – Augusta

Bangor
3074 Bangor Theological Seminary
3114 Beal College
3440 Husson College
3373 Husson College/EMMC Nursing
9732 Samaritan Hospital – School of Nursing

Bar Harbor
3305 College of the Atlantic

Biddeford
3751 University of New England

Brunswick
3089 Bowdoin College

Castine
3505 Maine Maritime Academy

Fairfield
3475 Kennebec Valley Technical College

Farmington
3506 University of Maine – Farmington

Fort Kent
3393 University of Maine at Fort Kent

Lewiston
3076 Bates College

Machias
3956 University of Maine – Machias

Orono
3916 University of Maine at Orono

Portland
3700 Casco Bay College
3441 Husson College South
3701 Maine College of Art
3691 University of Southern Maine
3960 Westbrook College

Presque Isle
3631 Northern Maine Vocational-Technical Institute
3008 University of Maine – Presque Isle

South Portland
3535 Southern Maine Vocational-Technical Institute

Unity
3925 Unity College

Waterville
3280 Colby College
3903 Thomas College

Windham
3755 Saint Joseph's College
3764 St. Joseph's College – Distance Education Program

MARYLAND

Annapolis
5598 Saint John's College – Main Campus
5809 U.S. Naval Academy

Arnold
5019 Anne Arundel Community College

Baltimore
5696 Arlington Bible College
5051 Baltimore City Community College
5114 College of Notre Dame of Maryland
5122 Coppin State College
5176 Dundalk Community College
5192 Essex Community College
5332 Johns Hopkins University
5370 Loyola College
5399 Maryland Institute College of Art
5416 Morgan State University
5131 New Community College – Baltimore Harbor
5657 Sojourner-Douglass College
5602 Saint Mary's Seminary and University
5810 University of Baltimore
5761 University of Maryland – Baltimore City
5835 University of Maryland – Baltimore County
7915 University of Maryland – School of Nursing

Bel Air
5303 Harford Community College
5746 Eastern Christian College

Bowie
5401 Bowie State University

Catonsville
5137 Catonsville Community College

Chestertown
5888 Washington College

College Park
5814 University of Maryland
5804 University of Maryland University College

Columbia
5308 Howard Community College

Cumberland
5028 Allegany Community College

Emmitsburg
5421 Mount Saint Mary's College

Frederick
5230 Frederick Community College
5296 Hood College

Frostburg
5402 Frostburg State University

Germantown
5414 Montgomery College – Takoma Park
5393 Montgomery Community College

Hagerstown
5738 Antietam Bible College
5290 Hagerstown Junior College

La Plata
5144 Charles County Community College

Lanham
5884 Washington Bible College

Largo
5545 Prince Georges Community College

Laurel
5101 Capitol College

McHenry
5279 Garrett Community College

North East
5091 Cecil Community College

Rockville
5440 Montgomery College – Rockville
7661 Potomoc College

Saint Mary's City
5601 Saint Mary's College of Maryland

Salisbury
5403 Salisbury State College
5400 University of Maryland – Eastern Shore

Silver Springs
5466 Maryland College of Art & Design

Stevenson
5856 Villa Julie College

Takoma Park
5890 Columbia Union College

Towson
5257 Goucher College
5404 Towson State University

Westminster
5898 Western Maryland College

Wye Mills
5143 Chesapeake College

MASSACHUSETTS

Amherst
3003 Amherst College
3447 Hampshire College
3769 Stockbridge School of Agriculture
3917 University of Massachusetts – Amherst
3945 University of Massachusetts – Continuing Education

Bedford
3554 Middlesex Community College

Beverly
3369 Endicott College

Boston
3120 Bay State Junior College
3107 Berklee College of Music
1168 Boston Architectural Center
3084 Boston Conservatory of Music
3087 Boston University
3123 Bunker Hill Community College
3099 Burdett School
3367 Emerson College
3368 Emmanuel College
3391 Fisher College – Boston
3392 Forsyth School of Dental Hygienists
3394 Franklin Institute of Boston
3473 Katharine Gibbs School
3287 Laboure College
3516 Massachusetts College of Art
3512 Massachusetts College of Pharmacy/Allied Health

3513 Massachusetts General Hospital – Institute of Health
3659 New England Conservancy of Music
3645 New England School of Art and Design
3641 Northeast Institute of Industrial Technology
3667 Northeastern University
3638 Northeastern University – Physician Assistants
3740 Roxbury Community College
3794 School Museum of Fine Arts
3761 Simmons College
3771 Suffolk University
3924 University of Massachusetts – Harbor Campus
3958 Wentworth Institute of Technology
3964 Wheelock College

Bradford
3091 Bradford College

Bridgewater
3517 Bridgewater State College

Brighton
3295 Saint John's Seminary College

Brockton
3549 Massasoit Community College

Brookline
3435 Hebrew College
3449 Holy Cross School of Theology
3639 Newbury College – Brookline

Buzzards Bay
3515 Massachusetts College of Art

Cambridge
7177 Cambridge College
7435 Harvard University – Extension School
3483 Lesley College
7581 Lesley College – Outreach
7577 Lesley College – School of Management

Chestnut Hill
3083 Boston College
3689 Pine Manor College

Chicopee
3283 Elms College

Danvers
3651 North Shore Community College

Dudley
3666 Nichols College

Fall River
3110 Bristol Community College

Fitchburg
3518 Fitchburg State College

Framingham
3519 Framingham State College
3397 Framingham Union State College of Nursing

Franklin
3352 Dean Junior College

Gardner
3545 Mount Wachusett Community College

Great Barrington
3795 Simons Rock of Bard College

Greenfield
3420 Greenfield Community College

Hanscom Air Force Base
3974 Western New England College

Haverhill
3674 Northern Essex Community College

Holyoke
3437 Holyoke Community College

Leicester
3482 Becker Junior College – Leicester

Lenox
3105 Berkshire Christian College

Longmeadow
3078 Bay Path College

Lowell
3911 University of Lowell

Medford
3901 Tufts University

Milton
3011 Aquinas Junior College – Milton
3285 Curry College

Newton
3013 Aquinas College Newton
3481 Lasell Junior College
3530 Mount Ida College

Newton Center
3277 Chamberlayne Junior College
3650 Northeast Institute of Art & Science – Mount Ida

North Adams
3521 North Adams State College

North Andover
3525 Merrimack College

North Dartmouth
3786 University of Massachusetts at Dartmouth

North Easton
3770 Stonehill College

Northampton
3762 Smith College

Norton
3963 Wheaton College

Paxton
3005 Anna Maria College for Men/ Women

Pittsfield
3102 Berkshire Community College

Quincy
3365 Eastern Nazarene College
3713 Quincy Junior College

Reading
7044 Austin Preparatory School

Salem
3522 Salem State College

South Hadley
3529 Mount Holyoke College

South Lancaster
3010 Atlantic Union College

Springfield
3002 American International College
3787 Baystate Medical Center – Nursing
3763 Springfield College
3791 Springfield Technical Community College
3962 Western New England College

Swampscott
9100 Marian Court Junior College

Waltham
3096 Bentley College
3092 Brandeis University

Wellesley
3075 Babson College
3957 Wellesley College

Wellesley Hills
3294 Massachusetts Bay Community College

Wenham
3417 United College Gordon Barrington

West Barnstable
3289 Cape Cod Community College

Westboro
3387 Fisher College – Westboro

Westfield
3523 Westfield State College

Weston
3723 Regis College

Williamstown
3965 Williams College

Worcester
3009 Assumption College
3079 Becker Junior College – Worcester
3308 Central New England Colleges
3279 Clark University
3282 College of the Holy Cross
3714 Quinsigamond Community College
3969 Worcester Polytechnic Institute
3524 Worcester State College

MEXICO

Monterrey
0843 Institute Tecn. de Monterrey

Puebla
0938 University de Las Americas

MICHIGAN

Adrian
1001 Adrian College
1719 Siena Heights College

Albion
1007 Albion College

Allendale
1258 Grand Valley State College

Alma
1010 Alma College

Alpena
1011 Alpena Community College

Ann Arbor
1094 Concordia College
1839 University of Michigan – Ann Arbor
1935 Washtenaw Community College

Auburn Heights
1606 Oakland Community College – Auburn Hills

Battle Creek
1375 Kellogg Community College

Benton Harbor
1137 Lake Michigan College

Berrien Springs
1030 Andrews University

Big Rapids
1222 Ferris State University

Bloomfield Hills
1607 Oakland Community College – Bloomfield Hills

Cedar Springs
1952 Jordan College

Centreville
1261 Glen Oaks Community College

Dearborn
1181 Detroit College of Business
1293 Henry Ford Community College

Detroit
1035 Center for Creative Studies
1425 Lewis Business College
1452 Marygrove College
1460 Mercy College of Detroit
1686 Sacred Heart Seminary
1835 University of Detroit
1964 University of Detroit – Evening College of Business
1894 Walsh College of Accounting & Business
1937 Wayne County Community College – Downtown
1898 Wayne State University

Dowagiac
1783 Southwestern Michigan College

East Lansing
1465 Michigan State University

Escanaba
1049 Bay de Noc Community College

Farmington Hills
1609 Oakland Community College – Orchard
1167 William Tyndale College

Flint
1225 Charles Stewart Mott College
1246 GMI Engineering/Management Institute
1853 University of Michigan – Flint

Grand Rapids
1018 Aquinas College
1095 Calvin College
1183 Davenport College of Business
1265 Grace Bible College
1253 Grand Rapids Baptist College & Seminary
1254 Grand Rapids Junior College
1376 Kendall College of Design
1672 Reformed Bible College

Hancock
1743 Suomi College

Harrison
1523 Mid Michigan Community College

Highland Park
1294 Highland Park Community College

Hillsdale
1295 Hillsdale College

Holland
1301 Hope College

Houghton
1464 Michigan Technical University

Howell
1209 Cleary College – Livingston

Ironwood
1250 Gogebic Community College

Jackson
1340 Jackson Community College

Kalamazoo
3254 Bronson Hospital – School of Nursing
1365 Kalamazoo College
1378 Kalamazoo Valley Community College
1902 Western Michigan University

Lansing
3127 Lansing Business Institute
1414 Lansing Community College

Livonia
1437 Madonna University
1764 Schoolcraft College

Marquette
1560 Northern Michigan University

Midland
1568 Northwood Institute

Monroe
1514 Monroe County Community College

Mount Pleasant
1106 Central Michigan University

Muskegon
1527 Baker College
1495 Muskegon Community College

Olivet
1595 Olivet College

Orchard Lake
1753 Saint Mary's College

Petoskey
1569 North Central Michigan College

Port Huron
1628 St. Clair County Community College

Rochester
1516 Michigan Christian College
1497 Oakland University

Roscommon
1382 Kirtland Community College

Sault Ste. Marie
1421 Lake Superior State University

Scottville
1941 West Shore Community College

Sidney
1522 Montcalm Community College

Southfield
1399 Lawrence Technical University
7267 Oakland Community College – Southeast

Spring Arbor
1732 Spring Arbor College

Union Lake
1612 Oakland Community College – Highland Lakes

University Center
1816 Delta College
1766 Saginaw Valley State College

Warren
1722 Macomb County Community College – South

Ypsilanti
1123 Cleary College – Washtenaw
1201 Eastern Michigan University

MINNESOTA

Alexandria
7062 Alexandria Technical College

Austin
6017 Austin Community College

Bemidji
6676 Bemidji State University

Bloomington
6501 Normandale Community College

Brainerd
6045 Brainerd Community College

Brooklyn Park
6498 North Hennepin Community College

Collegeville
6624 Saint John's University

Coon Rapids
6024 Anoka-Ramsey Community College

Crookston
6893 University of Minnesota – Crookston

Duluth
6107 College of St. Scholastica
6873 University of Minnesota – Duluth

Ely
6194 Vermilion Community College

Fergus Falls
6227 Fergus Falls Community College

Grand Rapids
6309 Itasca Community College

Hibbing
6275 Hibbing Community College

International Falls
6613 Rainy River Community College

Inver Grove Heights
6314 Inver Hills Community College

Mankato
6035 Bethany Lutheran College
6677 Mankato State University

Marshall
6703 Southwest State University

Minneapolis
6014 Augsburg College
6701 College of St. Catherine/St. Mary's
9116 Minneapolis Adult Vocational-Technical Institute
6411 Minneapolis College of Art and Design
6434 Minneapolis Community College
6505 North Central Bible College
7828 St. Mary's College Graduate Center
6874 University of Minnesota

Moorhead
6113 Concordia College
6678 Moorhead State University

Morris
6890 University of Minnesota – Morris

New Ulm
6435 Dr. Martin Luther College

Northfield
6081 Carleton College
6638 Saint Olaf College

Rochester
6412 Minnesota Bible College
6610 Rochester Community College

Roseville
6489 Northwestern College

Saint Bonifacius
6639 Saint Paul Bible College

Saint Cloud
6679 Saint Cloud State University
7824 Saint Cloud Technical College

Saint Paul
6038 Bethel College
6105 College of St. Catherine
6110 College of St. Thomas
6114 Concordia College – St. Paul
6265 Hamline University
6377 Luther Northwestern Seminarians
6390 MacAlester College
6445 Metropolitan State University
6687 School of the Associated Arts
7680 University of St. Thomas

Saint Peter
6253 Gustavus Adolphus College

Thief River Falls
6500 Northland Community College

Virginia
6432 Mesabi Community College

White Bear Lake
6388 Lakewood Community College

Willmar
6949 Willmar Community College

Winona
6632 Saint Mary's College
6680 Winona State University

Worthington
6945 Worthington Community College

MISSISSIPPI

Blue Mountain
1066 Blue Mountain College

Booneville
1557 Northeast Mississippi Community College

Clarksdale
1126 Coahoma Community College

Cleveland
1163 Delta State University

Clinton
1477 Mississippi College

Columbus
1481 Mississippi University for Women

Decatur
1196 East Central Junior College

Ellisville
1347 Jones County Junior College

Florence
1923 Wesley College

Fulton
1326 Itawamba Community College

Gautier
1354 Mississippi Gulf Coast Community College – JAC

Goodman
1299 Holmes Community College

Gulfport
1353 Mississippi Gulf Coast Community College – Jeff Davis Campus

Hattiesburg
1479 University of Southern Mississippi
1907 William Carey College

Holly Springs
1669 Rust College

Itta Bena
1482 Mississippi Valley State University

Jackson
1055 Belhaven College
1341 Jackson State University
1471 Millsaps College
1879 University of Mississippi – Jackson
1884 University of Mississippi Medical Center

Laurel
1781 Southeastern Baptist College

Lorman
1008 Alcorn State University

Mathiston
1924 Wood Junior College

Mayhew
7254 East Mississippi Community College – Gold Triangle Campus

Meridian
1461 Meridian Community College
3336 Mississippi State University – Meridian

Mississippi State
1480 Mississippi State University

Moorhead
1742 Mississippi Delta Community College

Natchez
1572 Natchez Junior College

Perkinston
1623 Mississippi Gulf Coast Community College – Perkinston

Poplarville
1622 Pearl River Junior College

Prentiss
1629 Prentiss Normal Industrial Institute

Raymond
1296 Hinds Community College

Scooba
1197 East Mississippi Community College

Senatobia
1562 Northwest Mississippi Community College

Summit
1729 Southwest Mississippi Community College

Tougaloo
1807 Tougaloo College

University
1840 University of Mississippi

Utica
1858 Hinds Community College – Utica

Wesson
1142 Copiah-Lincoln Community College

West Point
1450 Mary Holmes College

MISSOURI

Bolivar
6664 Southwest Baptist University

Boonville
6338 Kemper Military Junior College

Canton
6123 Culver-Stockton College

Cape Girardeau
6655 Southeast Missouri State University

Chillicothe
6858 University of Missouri Extension

Columbia
6095 Columbia College
6683 Stephen's College
6875 University of Missouri – Columbia

Conception
6112 Conception Seminary College

Fayette
6089 Central Methodist College

Flat River
6323 Mineral Area College

Florissant
6728 St. Louis Christian College
6225 St. Louis Community College at Florissant Valley

Forest Park
6226 St. Louis Community College – Forest Park

Fort Leonard Wood
7247 Drury College

Fulton
6937 Westminster College
6944 William Woods University

Hannibal
6266 Hannibal-LaGrange College

Hillsboro
6320 Jefferson College

Jefferson City
6366 Lincoln University

Joplin
6322 Missouri Southern State College
6542 Ozark Christian College

Kansas City
6109 Avila College
6331 Calvary Bible College
6330 Kansas City Art Institute
6436 Maple Woods Community College
6324 Penn Valley Community College
6612 Research College of Nursing
6611 Rockhurst College
6872 University of Missouri – Kansas City

Kirksville
6483 Northeast Missouri State University

Kirkwood
6430 St. Louis Community College at Meramec

Lees Summit
6359 Longview Community College

Lexington
6934 Wentworth Military Academy

Liberty
6941 William Jewell College

Marshall
6413 Missouri Valley College

Maryville
6488 Northwest Missouri State University

Moberly
6414 Moberly Area Community College

Neosho
6138 Crowder College

Nevada
6120 Cottey College

Parkville
6574 Park College

Point Lookout
6713 The School of the Ozarks

Poplar Bluff
6836 Three Rivers Community College

Portageville
7890 University of Missouri – Delta Center

Rolla
6876 University of Missouri – Rolla

Saint Charles
6367 Lindenwood College

Saint Joseph
6625 Missouri Western State College
6854 University of Missouri Extension Center

Saint Louis
0793 Barnes College
6216 Fontbonne College
7309 Fontbonne College Options
6269 Harris Stowe State College
6329 Jewish Hospital College
6399 Maryville College
6461 National-Louis University
6439 Missouri Baptist College – St. Louis
6626 St. Louis College of Pharmacy
6629 St. Louis University
6889 University of Missouri – St. Louis
6929 Washington University
6933 Webster University

Sedalia
6709 State Fair Community College

Springfield
7038 Assemblies of God Theological Seminary
6085 Central Bible College
6169 Drury College
6198 Evangel College
6665 Southwest Missouri State University

Tarkio
6816 Tarkio College

Trenton
6830 North Central Missouri College

Union
6200 East Central College

Warrensburg
6090 Central Missouri State University

MONTANA

Billings
4298 Eastern Montana College
4660 Rocky Mountain College

Bozeman
4488 Montana State University

Browning
4443 Blackfeet Community College

Butte
4487 Montana College of Mineral Science and Technology

Dillon
4945 Western Montana College

Glendive
4280 Dawson Community College

Great Falls
4058 College of Great Falls
7691 Northern Montana College

Havre
4538 Northern Montana College

Helena
4041 Carroll College

Lame Deer
4442 Dull Knife Memorial College

Miles City
4081 Miles Community College

Missoula
4489 University of Montana

NEBRASKA

Beatrice
6795 Southeast Community College

Bellevue
6053 Bellevue College

Blair
6157 Dana College

Chadron
6466 Chadron State College

Columbus
6584 Central Community College – Platte

Crete
6165 Doane College

Fremont
6406 Midland Lutheran College

Hastings
6136 Central Community College
6270 Hastings College

Kearny
6467 University of Nebraska at Kearny

Lincoln
7748 Doane College – Lincoln
6470 Nebraska Wesleyan University
6865 Union College
6877 University of Nebraska – Lincoln

McCook
6401 McCook Community College

Milford
6502 Southeast Community College – Milford Campus

Norfolk
6473 Northeast Community College

North Platte
6433 Mid-Plains Community College

Omaha
6049 Bishop Clarkson College
6106 College of St. Mary
6121 Creighton University
6248 Grace College of the Bible
6538 Metropolitan Technical Community College
6496 Nebraska College of Business
9366 Omaha College of Health Careers
6420 University of Nebraska at Omaha
6896 University of Nebraska Medical Center

Peru
6468 Peru State College

Scottsbluff
6648 Western Nebraska Community College

Seward
6116 Concordia College

Wayne
6469 Wayne State College

York
6984 York College

NEVADA

Carson City
4972 Western Nevada Community College – South

Elko
4293 Northern Nevada Community College

Incline Village
4757 Sierra Nevada College

Las Vegas
4861 University of Nevada – Las Vegas

North Las Vegas
4136 Community College of Southern Nevada

Reno
4960 Truckee Meadows Community College
4844 University of Nevada

Via Dyer
4281 Deep Springs College

NEW HAMPSHIRE

Bedford
3562 Magdalen College

Berlin
7899 College of Lifelong Learning
3646 New Hampshire Vocational-Technical College – Berlin

Chester
3977 White Pines College

Claremont
3684 New Hampshire Vocational-Technical College – Claremont

Concord
3389 Franklin Pierce College
3647 New Hampshire Technical Institute – Concord

Dover
3553 Mcintosh College

Durham
3814 College of Lifelong Learning
3918 University of New Hampshire

Hanover
3351 Dartmouth College

Henniker
3657 New England College

Keene
3694 Antioch University – New England
3472 Keene State College

Lebanon
7741 College of Lifelong Learning

Manchester
3452 Hesser College
3649 New Hampshire College
3660 New Hampshire Vocational-Technical College – Manchester
3670 Notre Dame College
3748 St. Anselm College

Nashua
3648 Daniel Webster College
3388 Franklin Pierce College
3643 New Hampshire Vocational-Technical College – Nashua
3728 Rivier College

New London
3281 Colby-Sawyer College

Plymouth
3690 Plymouth State College

Rindge
3395 Franklin Pierce College

Stratham
3661 New Hampshire Vocational-Technical College – Stratham

Windham
3310 Castle Junior College

NEW JERSEY

Blackwood
2121 Camden County College

Bloomfield
2044 Bloomfield College

Bridgewater
2862 Somerset County Technical Institute

Caldwell
2072 Caldwell College

Camden
2742 Rutgers State University College – Camden

Cape May
2813 Shelton College

Carney's Point
2868 Salem Community College

Clark
4173 Lyons Institute

Cranford
2921 Union County College

East Orange
2930 Upsala College

Edison
2441 Middlesex County College

Elizabeth
3150 Union College – Elizabeth Campus

Essex Falls
2566 Northeastern Bible College

Glassboro
2515 Rowan College of New Jersey

Hackensack
2232 Edward Williams College of Fairleigh Dickinson University

Hackettstown
2080 Centenary College

Hoboken
2819 Stevens Institute of Technology

Jersey City
2291 Hudson County Community College
2516 Jersey City State College
2806 St. Peter's College

Lakewood
2274 Georgian Court College

Lawrenceville
2758 Rider University

Lincroft
2181 Brookdale Community College

Little Falls
2061 Berkeley School – Little Falls

Lodi
2321 Felician College

Madison
2193 Drew University
2262 Fairleigh Dickinson University – Madison

Mahwah
2884 Ramapo College of New Jersey

Mays Landing
2024 Atlantic Community College

Mendham
2009 Assumption College for Sisters

Montclair
2348 Katherine Gibbs School
2427 Mountainside Hospital School of Nursing

Morristown
2090 College of St. Elizabeth

New Brunswick
2170 Cook College
2384 Livingston College
2192 Rutgers-Douglass College
2765 Rutgers State University – Rutgers College
2736 Rutgers University School of Arts
2777 Rutgers University – University College

Newark
2237 Essex County College
2513 New Jersey Institute of Technology
2789 Rutgers University – College of Nursing
2512 Rutgers University – College of Arts/Science

Newton
2191 Don Bosco College
2711 Sussex County Community College

Paramus
2032 Bergen Community College

Paterson
2694 Passaic County Community College

Pemberton
2180 Burlington County College

Perth Amboy
2686 Raritan Bay Medical Center – Nursing

Piscataway
2838 Rutgers University College of Engineering
2839 Rutgers University College of Pharmacy

Pomona
2889 Stockton State College

Princeton
2974 Westminster Choir College

Randolph
2124 County College of Morris

Rutherford
2255 Fairleigh Dickinson University

Sea Girt
2590 New Jersey Military Academy

Sewell
2281 Gloucester County College

Somerville
2867 Raritan Valley Community College

South Orange
2322 Immaculate Conception Seminary
2811 Seton Hall University

Sussex
2958 Upsala College – Wirths Campus

Teaneck
2263 Fairleigh Dickinson University – Teaneck

Toms River
2630 Ocean County College

Trenton
2444 Mercer County Community College
2442 Mercer Medical Center – Nursing
2748 Thomas A. Edison College
2519 Trenton State College

Union
2517 Kean College of New Jersey

Upper Montclair
2520 Montclair State College

Vineland
2118 Cumberland County College

Washington
2722 Warren County Community College

Wayne
2518 William Paterson College

West Long Branch
2416 Monmouth College

NEW MEXICO

Alamogordo
4012 New Mexico State University

Albuquerque
4220 Albuquerque Technical Vocational Institute
4845 University of New Mexico
4924 University of Phoenix – New Mexico Regional

Carlsbad
4547 New Mexico State University – Carlsbad

Clovis
4921 Clovis Community College
4290 Eastern New Mexico University

El Rito
4560 Northern New Mexico Community College

Farmington
4732 San Juan College

Gallup
4895 University of New Mexico – Gallup

Grants
4552 New Mexico State University – Grants

Hobbs
4116 College of the Southwest
4553 New Mexico Junior College

Las Cruces
4531 New Mexico State University

Las Vegas
4532 New Mexico Highlands University

Los Alamos
4809 University of New Mexico – Los Alamos

Los Lunas
4810 University of New Mexico – Valencia

Portales
4299 Eastern New Mexico University – Portales

Roswell
4662 Eastern New Mexico University – Roswell
4534 New Mexico Military Institute

Santa Fe
4676 College of Santa Fe
4737 St. Johns College – Santa Fe
4816 Santa Fe Community College

Silver City
4535 Western New Mexico University

Socorro
4533 New Mexico Institute of Mine/Technology

NEW YORK

Albany
2018 Albany Business College
2013 Albany College of Pharmacy
2015 Albany Medical Center – School of Nursing
2091 College of Saint Rose
2434 Maria College
7703 New York State Department of Education – Professional Licensing
7737 New York State Department of Education – Teacher Certification
2899 Regents College
2771 Russell Sage College – Evening

2343 Russell Sage Junior College of Albany
2532 State University of New York Center – Albany

Alfred
2005 Alfred University
2522 State University of New York College of Technology – Alfred

Amherst
2762 Daemen College

Annandale on Hudson
2037 Bard College

Auburn
2010 Cayuga County Community College

Aurora
2971 Wells College

Batavia
2272 Genesee Community College

Binghamton
2048 Broome Community College
2535 State University of New York – Binghamton

Brentwood
2604 C.W. Post – Long Island University – Suffolk
2849 Suffolk County Community College – West

Briarcliff Manor
2352 King's College

Brockport
2537 State University of New York College – Brockport

Bronx
2051 City University of New York – Bronx Community College
2303 City University of New York – Eugenio de Hostos Community College
2312 City University of New York – Herbert H. Lehman Community College
2088 College of Mount Saint Vincent
2259 Fordham University
2395 Manhattan College
2463 Monroe Business Institute
2536 State University of New York - Maritime College

Bronxville
2096 Concordia College
2810 Sarah Lawrence College

Brooklyn
2046 City University of New York – Brooklyn College
2358 City University of New York – Kingsboro Community College
2460 City University of New York – Medgar Evers College
2369 Long Island University – Brooklyn Center
2550 New York City Technical College – Brooklyn
2669 Pratt Institute
2668 Polytechnic University
2796 Saint Francis College
2802 Saint Joseph's College
2068 Schwartz College of Pharmacy
2534 State University of New York Health Sciences Center – Brooklyn

Brookville
2070 C.W. Post – Long Island University

Buffalo
2058 Bryant Stratton Business Institute
2073 Canisius College
2197 D'Youville College
2213 Erie Community College City Campus
2422 Medaille College
2533 State University of New York College – Buffalo
2892 State University of New York Health Science Center – Buffalo
2925 State University of New York University Center – Buffalo
2856 Trocaire College
2962 Villa Maria College – Buffalo

Canadaigua
2134 Finger Lakes Community College

Canton
2805 Saint Lawrence University
2523 State University of New York College of Technology – Canton

Cazenovia
2078 Cazenovia College

Clinton
2286 Hamilton College

Cobleskill
2524 State University of New York College of Agricultural Technology

Corning
2106 Corning Community College

Cortland
2538 State University of New York College – Cortland

Delhi
2525 State University of New York College of Technology – Delhi

Dobbs Ferry
2409 Mercy College

Douglaston
2075 Cathedral College Immaculate Conception

Dryden
2904 Tompkins Cortland Community College

Elmira
2226 Elmira College

Farmingdale
2695 Polytechnic University
2526 State University of New York College of Technology – Farmingdale

Flushing
2750 City University of New York – Queens College
2001 College of Aeronautics

Fredonia
2539 State University of New York College at Fredonia

Garden City
2003 Adelphi University
2563 Nassau Community College

Geneseo
2540 State University of New York College at Geneseo

Geneva
2294 Hobart College
2978 William Smith College

Glen Cove
2970 Webb Institute of Naval Architects

Glen Head
2169 New York Chiropractic College

Glens Falls
2017 Adirondack Community College

Hamburg
2334 Hilbert College

Hamilton
2086 Colgate University

Hempstead
2295 Hofstra University

Herkimer
2316 Herkimer County Community College

Houghton
2299 Houghton College

Hudson
2138 Columbia-Greene Community College

Hyde Park
3301 Culinary Institute of America

Ithaca
2098 Cornell University
2105 Cornell University College Engineering
2325 Ithaca College
2528 State University of New York College of Agriculture Life Science

Jamaica
2799 Saint John's University
2992 York College – City University of New York

Jamestown
2254 Fulton-Montgomery Community College
2346 Jamestown Business College
2335 Jamestown Community College

Jordanville
2298 Holy Trinity Orthodox Seminary

Keuka Park
2350 Keuka College

Kings Point
2923 United States Merchant Marine Academy

Loch Sheldrake
2855 Sullivan County Community College

Long Island City
2246 City University of New York – Fiorello H. LaGuardia Community College

Loudonville
2814 Siena College

Melville
4169 Katherine Gibbs School – Huntington

Middletown
7683 New School of Social Research
2625 Orange County Community College

Morrisville
2527 State University of New York – Morrisville

New Paltz
2541 State University of New York College – New Paltz

New Rochelle
2089 College of New Rochelle
2324 Iona College

New York
7047 A. Phillip Randolph Campus
2603 American Academy of Dramatic Arts
0967 Bar-Ilan University – Israel
2038 Barnard College
2034 Bernard Baruch College – City University of New York
2901 Boricua College
2063 Boro of Manhattan Community College – City University of New York
2428 City College School of Nursing – City University of New York
2147 City University of New York
2083 City College New York – City University of New York
7188 City University of New York BA/BS Program
2950 City University of New York – University Application Processing Center
2112 College of Insurance
2095 Columbia University
2116 Columbia University – Columbia College
2111 Columbia University School of Engineering
2905 Columbia University Teachers College
2097 Cooper Union
7724 Edna M. Clark School of Nursing
2257 Fashion Institute of Technology
2482 Germain School of Photography
2302 Helene Fuld School of Nursing
2301 Hunter College
2326 Institute of International Education
2339 Jewish Theological Seminary of America
2340 Juilliard School, The
2355 Katharine Gibbs School
2380 Lab Institute of Merchandising
2115 John Jay College of Criminal Justice – City University of New York
2396 Manhattan School of Music
2398 Mannes College of Music
2405 Marymount Manhattan College
2521 New School for Social Research
2963 New York City Technical College VHR
2562 New York University
2595 New York University – Gallatin Division
2555 New York University College of Business & Administration
2557 New York University School of Continuing Education
2635 Pace University – New York Campus
2638 Parsons School of Design
2751 Queensborough Community College – City University of New York
2776 Rabbinical Seminary of America
2835 School of Visual Arts
2897 State University of New York College of Optometry
2755 Technical Career Institute
2913 Tobe Coburn School of Fashion
2902 Touro College
3258 Wood School
2990 Yeshiva University

Newburgh
2423 Mount Saint Mary's College

Niagara University
2558 Niagara University

Nyack
2560 Nyack College
7660 Nyack College Adult Program

Oakdale Long Island
2011 Dowling College

Ogdensburg
2436 Mater Dei College
2965 Wadhams Hall Seminary-College

Old Westbury
2209 Empire State College – Long Island
     State University of New York
2561 New York Institute of Technology –
     Main
2866 State University of New York
     College – Old Westbury

Olean
2329 Jamestown Community College –
     Cattaraugus

Oneonta
2288 Hartwick College
2542 State University of New York
     College – Oneonta

Orangeburg
2190 Dominican College of Blauvelt

Orchard Park
2211 Erie Community College South
     Campus

Oswego
2543 State University of New York
     College – Oswego

Patchogue
2841 Saint Joseph's College – Patchogue

Paul Smiths
2640 Paul Smiths College

Plattsburgh
2135 Clinton Community College
2544 State University of New York
     College – Plattsburgh

Pleasantville
2685 Pace University – Pleasantville-
     Briarcliff

Potsdam
2084 Clarkson University
2545 State University of New York
     College – Potsdam

Poughkeepsie
2198 Dutchess Community College
2400 Marist College
2956 Vassar College

Purchase
2397 Manhattanville College
2878 State University of New York
     College – Purchase

Riverhead
2846 Suffolk County Community College
     – East

Rochester
2224 Eastman School of Music –
     Rochester
2733 Empire State College
2429 Monroe Community College
2511 Nazareth College of Rochester
2759 Roberts Wesleyan College
2770 Rochester Business Institute
2760 Rochester Institute of Technology

2798 Saint John Fisher College
2928 University of Rochester

Rockville Centre
2415 Molloy College

Rome
2508 The New School of Social Research

Sanborn
2568 Niagara County Community College

Saranac Lake
2571 North Country Community College

Saratoga Springs
2214 Empire State College – State
     University of New York
2815 Skidmore College

Schenectady
2879 Schenectady County Community
     College
2920 Union College

Seaford
3142 Five Towns College

Selden
2827 Suffolk County Community College
     – Selden

Southampton
2248 Friends World Program at Long
     Island University
2853 Southampton College of Long
     Island University

Sparkill
2807 Saint Thomas Aquinas College

Saint Bonaventure
2793 Saint Bonaventure University

Staten Island
2778 College of Staten Island
2845 Saint John's University – Staten
     Island
2966 Wagner College

Stone Ridge
2938 Ulster County Community College

Stony Brook
2548 State University of New York –
     Stony Brook

Suffern
2767 Rockland Community College

Syracuse
7201 Columbia College – Hancock Field
2366 Lemoyne College
2627 Onondaga Community College
2823 Syracuse University
2840 Syracuse University – Project
     Advance
2530 State University of New York
     College of Envirnomental
     Science & Forestry
2547 State University of New York Health
     Science – Syracuse

Tarrytown
2406 Marymount College

Troy
2300 Hudson Valley Community College
2757 Rensselaer Polytechnic Institute
2764 Russell Sage College – Main
     Campus

Utica
2414 Mohawk Valley Community College
7690 New School of Social Research
2847 Saint Elizabeth Hospital School of
     Nursing

2896 State University of New York
     College of Technology – Utica/
     Rome
2932 Utica College of Syracuse
     University

Valhalla
2972 Westchester Community College

Watertown
2345 Jefferson Community College

West Point
2924 United States Military Academy

White Plains
2064 Berkeley School – White Plains
2276 Pace University

Williamsville
2228 Erie Community College – North

Yonkers
2894 Cochran School of Nursing
2231 Elizabeth Seton College

NORTH CAROLINA

Ahoskie
5564 Roanoke-Chowan Technical College

Albemarle
5644 Stanly Community College

Ansonville
5020 Anson Community College

Asheboro
5585 Randolph Technical College

Asheville
5033 Asheville-Buncombe Technical
     Community College
5077 Blantons Junior College
5708 Cecils College
5013 University of North Carolina –
     Asheville

Banner Elk
5364 Lees-McRae College

Belmont
5055 Belmont Abbey College

Boiling Springs
5242 Gardner-Webb University

Boone
5010 Appalachian State University

Brevard
5067 Brevard College

Buies Creek
5100 Campbell University

Chapel Hill
5816 University of North Carolina –
     Chapel Hill

Charlotte
5102 Central Piedmont Community
     College
5231 East Coast Bible College
5333 Johnson C. Smith University
5361 King's College
5560 Queens College
5105 University of North Carolina –
     Charlotte

Clinton
5661 Sampson Community College

Clyde
5289 Haywood Community College

Concord
5136 Louise Harkey School of Nursing
5052 Barber-Scotia College

Cullowhee
5897 Western Carolina University

Dallas
5262 Gaston College

Davidson
5150 Davidson College

Dobson
5656 Surry Community College

Dublin
5044 Bladen Community College

Durham
5172 Durham Technical Community
     College
5495 North Carolina Central University

Elizabeth City
5597 Roanoke Bible College
5133 College of the Albemarle
5629 Elizabeth City State University

Elon College
5183 Elon College

Fayetteville
5212 Fayetteville State University
5208 Fayetteville Technical Community
     College
5391 Manna Christian College
5426 Methodist College

Flat Rock
5043 Blue Ridge Community College

Fort Bragg
7219 Campbell University – Fort Bragg

Goldsboro
5923 William Carter College
5926 Wayne Community College

Graham
5790 Technical College of Alamance

Grantsboro
5529 Pamlico Community College

Greensboro
5058 Bennett College
5260 Greensboro College
5261 Guilford College
5003 North Carolina A&T State
     University
5330 Rutledge College – Greensboro
5913 University of North Carolina –
     Greensboro

Greenville
5180 East Carolina University
5556 Pitt Community College

Hamlet
5588 Richmond Community College

Henderson
5876 Vance-Granville Community
     College

Hickory
5365 Lenoir Rhyne College
5098 Catawba Valley Community College

High Point
7029 Brookstone College Business
5293 High Point College
5348 John Wesley College – High Point

Jacksonville
5134 Carolina Coastal Community College

Jamestown
5275 Guilford Technical Community College

Kenansville
5350 James Sprunt College

Kinston
5378 Lenoir Comm College

Laurinburg
5214 Saint Andrews Presbyterian College

Lenoir
5146 Caldwell Community College & Technical Institute

Lexington
5170 Davidson County Community College

Louisburg
5369 Louisburg College

Lumberton
5594 Robeson Community College

Marion
5454 McDowell Technical Community College

Mars Hill
5395 Mars Hill College

Misenheimer
5536 Pfeiffer College

Montreat
5423 Montreat-Anderson College

Morehead City
5092 Carteret Community College

Morganton
5922 Western Piedmont Community College

Mount Olive
5435 Mount Olive College

Murfreesboro
5107 Chowan College

Murphy
5785 Tri-County Technical College

New Bern
5148 Craven Community College

Pembroke
5534 Pembroke State University

Pinehurst
5649 Sandhills Community College

Raleigh
5410 Meredith College
5496 North Carolina State University
5533 Peace College
5596 Saint Augustine's College
5600 Saint Mary's College
5612 Shaw University
5928 Wake Technical Community College

Rocky Mount
5491 Nash Technical College
5501 North Carolina Wesleyan College

Roxboro
5518 Piedmont Community College

Salisbury
5103 Catawba College

5367 Livingstone College
5589 Rowan-Cabarrus Community College

Sanford
5147 Central Carolina Community College

Shelby
5088 Cleveland Community College

Smithfield
5351 Johnston Community College

Spindale
5319 Isothermal Community College

Spruce Pine
5459 Mayland Community College

Statesville
5412 Mitchell Community College

Swannanoa
5886 Warren Wilson College

Sylva
5667 Southwestern Community College

Tarboro
5199 Edgecombe Community College

Washington
5086 Beaufort County Community College

Wentworth
5582 Rockingham Community College

Whiteville
5651 Southeastern Community College

Wilkesboro
5921 Wilkes Community College

Williamston
5445 Martin Community College

Wilmington
5094 Cape Fear Technical Institute
5907 University of North Carolina – Wilmington

Wilson
5016 Barton College
5930 Wilson County Technical College

Wingate
5908 Wingate College

Winston-Salem
5084 Bowman Gray School of Medicine
5512 North Carolina State College of the Arts
5555 Piedmont Bible College
5943 Rutledge College
5607 Salem College
5885 Wake Forest University
5909 Winston-Salem State University

NORTH DAKOTA

Bismarck
6041 Bismarck State Community College
6428 University of Mary

Devils Lake
6163 University of North Dakota – Lake Region

Dickinson
6477 Dickinson State University

Ellendale
0356 Trinity Bible College

Fargo
6474 North Dakota State University

Grand Forks
6878 University of North Dakota

Jamestown
6318 Jamestown College

Mayville
6478 Mayville State University

Minot
6479 Minot State University
9929 Trinity Medical Center School of Nursing

Valley City
6480 Valley City State University

Wahpeton
6476 North Dakota State College of Science

Williston
6905 University of North Dakota – Williston

OHIO

Ada
1591 Ohio Northern University

Akron
1829 University of Akron

Alliance
1492 Mount Union College

Archbold
1235 Northwest Technical College

Ashland
1021 Ashland University

Athens
1593 Ohio University

Berea
1050 Baldwin-Wallace College

Bluffton
1067 Bluffton College

Bowling Green
1069 Bowling Green University

Burton
1387 Kent State University – Geauga Campus

Canton
1439 Malone College
1688 Stark Technical College
1926 Walsh University

Cedarville
1151 Cedarville College

Celina
1947 Wright State University – Western Ohio

Chillicothe
1582 Ohio University – Chillicothe

Cincinnati
1002 Art Academy of Cincinnati
1091 Cincinnati Bible College/Seminary
1984 Cincinnati Technical College
1129 College of Mount Saint Joseph
1794 Southern Ohio College – Cincinnati
7850 Temple Baptist College
1966 Union for Experiment Colleges
1833 University of Cincinnati
1965 Xavier University

Circleville
1088 Circleville Bible College

Cleveland
1105 Case Western Reserve University
1152 Cleveland Institute of Art
1124 Cleveland Institute of Music
1221 Cleveland State University
1159 Cuyahoga Community College – Metro
1178 Dyke College
3264 Frances P. Bolton Nursing
1342 John Carroll University
1566 Notre Dame College
1589 Ohio College of Podiatric Medicine

Columbus
1048 Bliss College
1099 Capital University
1085 Columbus College of Art & Design
1148 Columbus State Community College
1229 Franklin University
1131 Ohio Dominican College
1592 The Ohio State University
1348 The Pontifical College Josephinum

Dayton
1827 Air Force Institute of Technology
1528 Miami-Jacobs Junior College Business
1720 Sinclair Community College
1834 University of Dayton
1179 Wright State University

Defiance
1162 The Defiance College

Delaware
1594 Ohio Wesleyan University

Elyria
1417 Lorain County Community College

Fairfield
3576 Southern Ohio College – Fairfield

Findlay
1223 University of Findlay

Gambier
1370 Kenyon College

Granville
1164 Denison University

Hamilton
1526 Miami University – Hamilton

Hillsboro
1752 Southern State Community College

Hiram
1297 Hiram College

Huron
1045 Bowling Green State University – Firelands

Kent
1367 Kent State University – Main Campus

Lancaster
1610 Ohio University – Lancaster

Mansfield
7693 North Central Technical College

Marietta
1444 Marietta College
7963 Washington State Community College

Mentor
1422 Lakeland Community College

Middletown
1509 Miami University – Middletown Branch

Mount Vernon
1531 Mount Vernon Nazarene College

Nelsonville
1822 Hocking Technical College

New Concord
1496 Muskingum College

Oberlin
1587 Oberlin College

Orrville
1892 Wayne General & Technical College

Oxford
1463 Miami University

Painesville
1391 Lake Erie College

Parma Heights
1985 Cuyahoga Community College – Western

Pepper Pike
1848 Ursuline College

Piqua
1191 Edison State Community College

Portsmouth
1790 Shawnee State University

Rio Grande
1663 Rio Grande College & Community College

Salem
7529 Kent State University – Salem Regional Campus

Springfield
1127 Clark State Community College
1922 Wittenberg University

Saint Clairsville
1072 Belmont Technical College
1617 Ohio University – Belmont County Branch

Saint Martin
1143 Chatfield College

Steubenville
1133 Franciscan University – Steubenville
1333 Jefferson Technical College

Sylvania
1427 Lourdes College

Tiffin
1292 Heidelberg College
1817 Tiffin University

Toledo
1175 Davis College
1643 Michael J. Owens Technical College
3241 Saint Vincent Medical Center – Nursing
1845 The University of Toledo

Urbana
1847 Urbana University

Warrensville
1978 Cuyahoga Community College – Eastern

Westerville
1597 Otterbein College

Wickliffe
1660 Rabbinical College – Telshe

Wilberforce
1107 Central State University
1906 Wilberforce University

Wilmington
1909 Wilmington College

Wooster
1134 College of Wooster

Yellow Springs
1017 Antioch College – Ohio
1652 Antioch University Sct Adult Learning

Youngstown
1975 Youngstown State University

Zanesville
1535 Muskingum Area Technical College
1647 Ohio University of Zanesville

OKLAHOMA

Ada
6186 East Central University

Altus
6020 Western Oklahoma State College

Alva
6493 Northwestern Oklahoma State University

Bartlesville
6135 Bartlesville Wesleyan College

Bethany
6036 Southern Nazarene University
6555 Southwestern College – Christian

Chickasha
6544 University of Science & Arts of Oklahoma

Claremore
6545 Rogers State College

Durant
6657 Southeastern Oklahoma State University

Edmond
6091 University of Central Oklahoma

El Reno
6192 Redlands Community College

Enid
6579 Phillips University

Goodwell
6571 Panhandle State University

Langston
6361 Langston University

Lawton
6080 Cameron University

Miami
6484 Northeastern Oklahoma A&M College

Midwest City
6559 Rose State College

Muskogee
6030 Bacone College

Norman
6879 University of Oklahoma

Oklahoma City
6257 Mid-America Bible College
6086 Oklahoma Christian College
6640 Oklahoma City Community College
6543 Oklahoma City University
6556 Oklahoma State University Technical Institute
6902 University of Oklahoma – Health Science

Poteau
6586 Carl Albert Junior College

Sayre
6646 Southwesten Oklahoma State University – Sayre

Seminole
6717 Seminole Junior College

Shawnee
6541 Oklahoma Baptist University
6621 Saint Gregory's College

Stillwater
6546 Oklahoma State University

Stilwell
6211 Flaming Rainbow University

Tahlequah
6485 Northeastern State University – Tahlequah

Tishomingo
6421 Murray State College

Tonkawa
6486 Northern Oklahoma College

Tulsa
6552 Oral Roberts University
6839 Tulsa Junior College
6883 The University of Tulsa
7989 University Center at Tulsa

Warner
6117 Connors State College

Weatherford
6673 Southwestern Oklahoma State University

Wilburton
6189 Eastern Oklahoma State College

OREGON

Albany
4413 Linn-Benton Community College

Ashland
4702 Southern Oregon State College

Astoria
4089 Clatsop Community College

Coos Bay
4729 Southwestern Oregon Community College

Corvallis
4586 Oregon State University

Eugene
4407 Lane Community College
4543 Northwest Christian College
4846 University of Oregon

Forest Grove
4601 Pacific University

Grants Pass
4653 Rogue Community College

Gresham
4508 Mount Hood Community College

Klamath Falls
4587 Oregon Institute of Technology

La Grande
4300 Eastern Oregon State College

Marylhurst
4480 Marylhurst College

McMinnville
4387 Linfield College

Monmouth
4585 Western Oregon State College

Newberg
4325 George Fox College

Ontario
4825 Treasure Valley Community College

Oregon City
4111 Clackamas Community College

Pendleton
4025 Blue Mountain Community College

Portland
4231 Bassist College
4093 Columbia Christian College
4079 Concordia College
4384 Lewis and Clark College
4496 Multnomah School of Bible
4900 Oregon Health Sciences University
4504 Pacific Northwest College of Art
4617 Portland Community College
4610 Portland State University
4654 Reed College
4847 University of Portland
4595 Warner Pacific College
4979 Western States Chiropractic College

Roseburg
4862 Umqua Community College

Saint Benedict
4491 Mount Angel Seminary

Salem
4745 Chemeketa Community College
4956 Western Baptist College
4954 Willamette University

PENNSYLVANIA

Allentown
2079 Cedar Crest College
2424 Muhlenberg College
2222 United Wesleyan College

Annville
2364 Lebanon Valley College

Aston
2628 Neumann College

Beaver Falls
2273 Geneva College

Bethlehem
2365 Lehigh University
2418 Moravian College
2573 Northampton County Area Community College

Bloomsburg
2646 Bloomsburg University of Pennsylvania

Blue Bell
2445 Montgomery County Community College

Bradford
2935 University of Pittsburgh – Bradford

Bryn Athyn
2002 Academy of the New Church

Bryn Mawr
2049 Bryn Mawr College
2287 Harcum Junior College
2022 The American College

Butler
2069 Butler County Community College

California
2647 California University of Pennsylvania

Carlisle
2186 Dickinson College

Center Valley
2021 Allentown College – Access

Chambersburg
2979 Wilson College

Chester
2642 Widener University

Cheyney
2648 Cheyney University of Pennsylvania

Clarion
2649 Clarion University of Pennsylvania

Clarks Summit
2036 Baptist Bible College of Pennsylvania

Collegeville
2931 Ursinus College

Coopersburg
2718 Pinebrook Junior College

Coraopolis
2769 Robert Morris College

Cresson
2420 Mount Aloysius Junior College

Dallas
2087 College Misericordia

Doylestown
2510 Delaware Valley College of Science and Agriculture

East Stroudsburg
2650 East Stroudsburg University of Pennsylvania

Easton
2361 Lafayette College

Edinboro
2651 Edinboro University of Pennsylvania

Elizabethtown
2225 Elizabethtown College
2243 Elizabethtown College – Continued Education

Erie
2215 Erie Business Center
2270 Gannon University
2410 Mercyhurst College

Gettysburg
2275 Gettysburg College

Glenside
2039 Beaver College

Grantham
2411 Messiah College

Greensburg
2812 Seton Hill College
2936 University of Pittsburgh – Greensburg

Greenville
2910 Thiel College

Grove City
2277 Grove City College

Gwynedd Valley
2278 Gwynedd-Mercy College

Harrisburg
2309 Harrisburg Area Community College
7811 State Board of Physical Therapy Examiners
2918 University Center – Harrisburg

Huntingdon
2341 Juniata College

Immaculata
2320 Immaculata College
2961 Villa Maria House Studies

Indiana
2652 Indiana University of Pennsylvania

Jenkintown
2260 Manor Junior College

Johnstown
2934 University of Pittsburgh – Johnstown

Kutztown
2653 Kutztown University of Pennsylvania

La Plume
2351 Keystone Junior College

Lancaster
2261 Franklin and Marshall College
2388 Lancaster Bible College

Langhorne
2661 Philadelphia College of Bible

Latrobe
2808 Saint Vincent College

Lewisburg
2050 Bucknell University

Lincoln University
2367 Lincoln University

Lock Haven
2654 Lock Haven University of Pennsylvania

Loretto
2797 Saint Francis College

Mahonoy City
9189 McCann School of Business

Malvern
2723 Pennsylvania State University – Great Valley

Mansfield
2655 Mansfield University of Pennsylvania

McKeesport
2707 Pennsylvania State University – McKeesport

Meadville
2006 Allegheny College

Media
2125 Delaware County Community College

Middletown
2708 Pennsylvania State University

Millersville
2656 Millersville University of Pennsylvania

Monaca
2126 Beaver County Community College

Monroeville
2122 Community College of Allegheny County – Boyce

Mont Alto
2710 Pennsylvania State University – Mont Alto

Nanticoke
2382 Luzerne County Community College

New Castle
2577 Erie Business Center School

New Wilmington
2975 Westminster College

Newtown
2066 Bucks County Community College

Oil City
7200 Clarion University of Pennsylvania – Venango

Philadelphia
2608 Antioch University – Philadelphia
2033 Art Institute of Philadelphia
2082 Chestnut Hill College
2150 Combs College of Music
2682 Community College of Philadelphia
2100 Curtis Institute of Music
2194 Drexel University
2280 Gratz College
2285 Hahnemann University Graduate School
2306 Hahnemann University School of Health Sciences
2297 Holy Family College
2363 La Salle University – Evening Division
2474 Manna Bible Institute
2417 Moore College of Art
2576 Northeastern Hospital School of Nursing
2674 Peirce Junior College
2645 Pennsylvania College of Optometry
2663 Philadelphia College of Pharmacy and Science
2666 Philadelphia College of Textiles and Science
2794 Saint Charles Seminary
2801 Saint Joseph's University
2906 Temple University – Main Campus
2336 Thomas Jefferson University
2903 Thomas Jefferson University College of Health Sciences
2926 University of Pennsylvania
2664 University of the Arts

Philipsburg
2687 Central Pennsylvania School of Nursing

Phoenixville
2579 Valley Forge Christian College

Pittsburgh
2029 Art Institute Pittsburgh

2421 Carlow College
2074 Carnegie Mellon University
2081 Chatham College
2156 Community College of Allegheny County
2025 Community College of Allegheny County – North
2201 Duffs Business Institute
2196 Duquesne University
2379 La Roche College
2676 Point Park College
2927 University of Pittsburgh

Radnor
2071 Cabrini College

Reading
2004 Albright College
2431 Alvernia College
2743 Reading Area Community College

Rosemont
2763 Rosemont College

Saint Davids
2220 Eastern College

Schnecksville
2381 Lehigh County Community College

Scranton
2373 Lackawanna Junior College
2407 Marywood College
2457 Mercy Hospital School of Nursing
2929 University of Scranton

Selinsgrove
2820 Susquehanna University

Shippensburg
2657 Shippensburg University of Pennsylvania

Slippery Rock
2658 Slippery Rock University of Pennsylvania

Swarthmore
2821 Swarthmore College

Titusville
2937 University of Pittsburgh – Titusville

University Park
2660 Pennsylvania State University
2691 Pennsylvania State University – Fayette

Villanova
2567 Northeast Christian Junior College
2959 Villanova University

Washington
2967 Washington and Jefferson College

Wayne
2955 Valley Forge Military College

Waynesburg
2969 Waynesburg College

West Chester
2659 West Chester University

West Mifflin
2123 Community College of Allegheny County – South

Wilkes-Barre
2353 King's College
2684 NPW Medical Center – School of Nursing
2977 Wilkes College

Williamsport
2372 Lycoming College

2989 Williamsport Area Community College

York
2991 York College of Pennsylvania

Youngwood
2968 Westmoreland County Community College

PUERTO RICO

Aguadilla
0983 University of Puerto Rico – Aguadilla

Arecibo
0911 University of Puerto Rico – Arecibo

Bayamon
0779 Caribbean University College
0840 University Central de Bayamon
0852 University of Puerto Rico Technical University College

Carolina
0883 Colegio University del Este

Cayey
0981 University de Puerto Rico – Cayey

Gurabo
0780 University del Turabo

Hato Rey
0856 Puerto Rico Department of Education
0797 University Politechnica de Puerto Rico

Humacao
0874 University de Puerto Rico – Humacao

Mayaguez
0912 University of Puerto Rico – Mayaguez

Ponce
0910 Catholic University of Puerto Rico
0836 Ponce Tech University College of University – Puerto Rico

Rio Piedras
0979 University of Puerto Rico – Rio Piedras

San German
0946 Interamerican University of Puerto Rico

San Juan
0873 Interamerican University of Puerto Rico
0913 University of Sagrado Corazon

Santurce
9563 Ramirez College of Business/Tech.

RHODE ISLAND

Bristol
3729 Roger Williams University

Kingston
3919 University of Rhode Island

Lincoln
3733 Community College of Rhode Island – Flanagan Campus

Newport
3759 Salve Regina University

Pawtucket
3464 Hall Institute

Providence
3094 Brown University
3465 Johnson and Wales University
3476 Katharine Gibbs School
3693 Providence College
3724 Rhode Island College
3726 Rhode Island School of Design
3923 University of Rhode Island – Providence

Smithfield
3095 Bryant College

Warwick
3738 Community College of Rhode Island – Warwick

SOUTH CAROLINA

Aiken
5037 Aiken Technical College
5840 University of South Carolina – Aiken

Allendale
5847 University of South Carolina – Allendale

Anderson
5008 Anderson College

Beaufort
5047 Technological College – The Low Country
5845 University of South Carolina – Beaufort

Central
5896 Central Wesleyan College

Charleston
5079 Baptist College – Charleston
7197 Charleston Higher Education Consortium
5108 The Citadel
5113 College of Charleston
5407 Medical University of South Carolina
5579 Rutledge College
5049 Trident Technical College – Main Campus

Cheraw
5095 Chesterfield Marlboro Technical College

Clemson
5111 Clemson University – Main Campus

Columbia
5006 Allen University
5056 Benedict College
5116 Columbia Bible College
5117 Columbia College
5097 Columbia Junior College
5374 King Memorial College
5552 Midlands Technical College
5584 Midlands Technical College – Beltline
5818 University of South Carolina – Columbia

Conway
5837 Coastal Carolina University
5305 Horry-Georgetown Technical College

Denmark
5744 Denmark Technical College
5863 Voorhees College

Due West
5188 Erskine College

Florence
5207 Florence Darlington Technical College
5442 Francis Marion University

Fort Jackson
7133 Coker College

Gaffney
5366 Limestone College

Georgetown
5298 Horry-Georgetown Technical College

Greenville
5065 Bob Jones University
5222 Furman University
5278 Greenville Technical College
5586 Rutledge College – Greenville

Greenwood
5363 Lander University
5550 Piedmont Technical College

Hartsville
5112 Coker College

Kingstree
5892 Williamsburg Technical College

Lancaster
5849 University of South Carolina – Lancaster

Newberry
5493 Newberry College

North Charlestown
5551 Trident Technical College – Palmer

Orangeburg
5109 Claflin College
5527 Orangeburg Calhoun Technical College
5618 South Carolina State College
5663 Southern Methodist College

Pendleton
5789 Tri-County Technical School

Rock Hill
5743 Clinton Junior College
5910 Winthrop University
5989 York Technical College

Spartanburg
5021 American Management College
5121 Converse College
5627 Spartanburg Methodist College
5668 Spartanburg Technical College
5850 University of South Carolina – Spartanburg
5912 Wofford College

Sumter
5665 Central Carolina Technical College
5418 Morris College
5821 South Carolina University – Sumter

Tigerville
5498 North Greenville Junior College

Union
5846 University of South Carolina – Union

SOUTH DAKOTA

Aberdeen
6487 Northern State University
6582 Presentation College

Brookings
6653 South Dakota State University

Huron
6279 Huron University

Kyle
6553 Oglala Lakota College

Madison
6247 Dakota State University

Mitchell
6155 Dakota Wesleyan University

Rapid City
6464 National College
6652 South Dakota School of Mines & Technology

Sioux Falls
6015 Augustana College
6149 Kilian Community College
6423 McKennan Hospital – Educational Programs
6651 Sioux Falls College
7827 Southeast Vocational-Technical Institute

Spearfish
6042 Black Hills State University

Vermillion
6881 University of South Dakota

Yankton
6416 Mount Marty College

TENNESSEE

Athens
1805 Tennessee Wesleyan College

Blountville
9946 Tri-Cities State Technical Institute

Bristol
1371 King College

Brunswick
7045 American Technical Institute

Chattanooga
7166 Covenant College – Quest Program
1084 Chattanooga State Technical Community College
3265 Edmondson Junior College
9202 McKenzie College
1818 Tennessee Temple University
1831 University of Tennessee – Chattanooga

Clarksville
1028 Austin Peay State University
7170 Clarksville Baptist College

Cleveland
1981 Cleveland State Community College
1401 Lee College
1799 Tomlinson College

Collegedale
1727 Southern College of Seventh-Day Adventists

Columbia
1081 Columbia State Community College

Cookeville
1804 Tennessee Technological University

Dayton
1908 Bryan College

Dyersburg
1187 Dyersburg State Community College

Gallatin
1881 Volunteer State Community College

Greeneville
1812 Tusculum College

Harriman
1656 Roame State Community College

Harrogate
1408 Lincoln Memorial University

Henderson
1230 Freed-Hardeman College

Jackson
1359 Jackson State Community College
1394 Lambuth College
1395 Lane College
1826 Union University

Jefferson City
1102 Carson-Newman College

Johnson City
1198 East Tennessee State University

Knoxville
1345 Johnson Bible College
1373 Knoxville College
1795 Pellissippi State Technical Community College
1843 University of Tennessee – Knoxville

Lebanon
1146 Cumberland University

Madisonville
1298 Hiwassee College

Martin
1844 University of Tennessee – Martin

Maryville
1454 Maryville College

McKenzie
1063 Bethel College

Memphis
1121 Christian Brothers College
3136 Draughons Junior College
1403 Lemoyne-Owen College
1511 Memphis College of Art
1459 Memphis State University
1730 Rhodes College
1746 Shelby State Community College
1725 Southern College of Optometry
1751 State Technical Institute at Memphis
7928 Union University – BMH Campus
1850 University of Tennessee at Memphis – Health

Milligan College
1469 Milligan College

Morristown
1488 Morristown College
1893 Walters State Community College

Murfreesboro
1466 Middle Tennessee State University

Nashville
5709 American Baptist Theological/Bible College
1042 Aquinas Junior College
1058 Belmont College
1161 David Lipscomb University
3261 Draughons Junior College
1224 Fisk University
1232 Free Will Baptist Bible College

1458 Meharry Medical College
1648 Nashville State Technical Institute
1803 Tennessee State University
1809 Trevecca Nazarene College

Pulaski
1449 Martin Methodist College

Sewanee
1842 University of the South

Tullahoma
1543 Motlow State Community College

TEXAS

Abilene
6001 Abilene Christian University
6268 Hardin-Simmons University
6402 McMurray University

Alpine
6685 Sul Ross State University

Alvin
6005 Alvin Community College

Amarillo
6006 Amarillo College
7875 Texas State Technical Institute – Amarillo

Arlington
6039 Arlington Baptist College
6013 University of Texas at Arlington

Athens
6271 Trinity Valley Community College

Austin
6759 Austin Community College
6127 Concordia Lutheran College
6280 Huston-Tillotson College
6619 St. Edward's University
6882 University of Texas at Austin

Baytown
6363 Lee College

Beaumont
6360 Lamar University

Beeville
6055 Bee County College

Belton
6396 University of Mary Hardin-Baylor

Big Sandy
6261 Ambassador College

Big Spring
6277 Howard College

Borger
6222 Frank Phillips College

Brenham
6043 Blinn College

Brownsville
6588 Pan American University – Brownsville
6825 University of Texas at Brownsville

Brownwood
6278 Howard Payne University

Canyon
6938 West Texas A&M University

Carthage
6572 Panola College

Cedar Hill
6499 Northwood University

Cisco
6096 Cisco Junior College

Clarendon
6097 Clarendon College

Cleburne
6285 Hill College

College Station
6003 Texas A&M University

Commerce
6188 East Texas State University

Corpus Christi
6160 Del Mar College
6849 Texas A&M University – Corpus Christi

Corsicana
6465 Navarro College

Dallas
6159 Dallas Baptist University
6199 El Centro College
6438 Mountain View College
5861 Parker College of Chiropractic
6607 Richland College
6660 Southern Methodist University
6686 University of Texas Health Science Center

Denison
6254 Grayson County College

Denton
6481 University of North Texas

Edinburg
6570 University of Texas – Pan American

El Paso
6203 El Paso Community College
6829 University of Texas at El Paso

Farmers Branch
6070 Brookhaven College

Fort Worth
6845 Tarrant County Junior College – Northwest Campus
6834 Tarrant County Junior College – South Campus
6820 Texas Christian University
6828 Texas Wesleyan College

Gainesville
6245 North Central Texas College

Galveston
6255 Galveston College
6835 Texas A&M University at Galveston
6887 University of Texas Medical Branch – Galveston

Garland
6140 Amber University

Georgetown
6674 Southwestern University

Harlingen
6843 Texas State Technical Institute

Hawkins
6319 Jarvis Christian College

Houston
6282 Houston Baptist University
6296 Houston Community College
6508 North Harris County College
6609 Rice University
6729 San Jacinto College – North
6824 Texas Southern University
6916 University of Houston at Clear Lake City

6922 University of Houston – Downtown
6870 University of Houston – University Park
6880 University of Saint Thomas
6888 University of Texas Health Science Center – Houston

Huntsville
6643 Sam Houston State University

Hurst
6837 Tarrant County Junior College – Northeast

Irving
6519 North Lake College
9873 Parker College of Chiropractic
6868 University of Dallas

Jacksonville
6317 Jacksonville College
6369 Lon Morris College

Keene
6671 Southwestern Adventist College

Kilgore
6341 Kilgore College

Killeen
6130 Central Texas College
6756 University of Central Texas

Kingsville
6822 Texas A&M University – Kingsville

Lake Jackson
6054 Brazosport College

Lancaster
6148 Cedar Valley College

Laredo
6362 Laredo Junior College
6838 Laredo State University

Levelland
6695 South Plains College

Longview
6344 Kilgore College – Longview Center
6365 Letourneau University
7557 Letourneau University – LEAP

Lubbock
6378 Lubbock Christian University
6827 Texas Tech University

Lufkin
6025 Angelina College

Marshall
6187 East Texas Baptist University
6940 Wiley College

Mesquite
6201 Eastfield College

Midland
6459 Midland College

Mount Pleasant
6531 Northeast Texas Community College

Nacogdoches
6682 Stephen F. Austin State University

Odessa
6540 Odessa College

Paris
6573 Paris Junior College

Pasadena
6694 San Jacinto College Central

Plainview
6930 Wayland Baptist University

Plano
1951 Collin County Community College

Prairie View
6580 Prairie View A&M University

Ranger
6608 Ranger Junior College

Richardson
6897 University of Texas at Dallas

San Angelo
6644 Angelo State University

San Antonio
6303 Incarnate Word College
6550 Our Lady of the Lake University
3730 Palo Alto College
6645 San Antonio College
7787 San Antonio Theological Seminary
6637 St. Mary's University
6642 St. Philip's College
6831 Trinity University
6919 University of Texas at San Antonio
6908 University of Texas at San Antonio
   – Health Science

San Marcos
6667 Southwest Texas State University

Seguin
6823 Texas Lutheran College

Sherman
6016 Austin College

Snyder
6951 Western Texas College

Stephenville
6817 Tarleton State University

Temple
6818 Temple Junior College

Terrell
6705 Southwestern Christian College

Texarkana
6206 East Texas State University –
   Texarkana
6819 Texarkana College

Texas City
6133 College of the Mainland

Tyler
6821 Texas College
6833 Tyler Junior College
6850 University of Texas – Tyler

Uvalde
6666 Southwest Texas Junior College
7862 Sul Ross State University – Uvalde
   Center

Vernon
6913 Vernon Regional Junior College

Victoria
6915 Victoria College
6917 University of Houston – Victoria

Waco
6032 Baylor University
6429 McLennan Community College
6577 Paul Quinn College
6328 Texas State Technical College

Waxahachie
6669 Southwestern Assembly of God
   College

Weatherford
6931 Weatherford College

Wharton
6939 Wharton County Junior College

Wichita Falls
6408 Midwestern State University

UTAH

Blanding
7212 College of Eastern Utah – San Juan

Cedar City
4092 Southern Utah State College

Ephraim
4727 Snow College

Logan
4857 Utah State University

Ogden
4751 Stevens Henager College – Ogden
4941 Weber State University

Orem
4870 Utah Valley State College

Price
4040 College of Eastern Utah

Provo
4019 Brigham Young University

Saint George
4283 Dixie College

Salt Lake City
4412 Latter-Day Saints Business College
4864 Salt Lake Community College
4920 University of Phoenix – Utah
   Division
4853 University of Utah
4948 Westminster College of Salt Lake
   City

Vernal
7654 Utah State University – Unitah
   Basin

VERMONT

Bennington
3080 Bennington College

Burlington
3291 Champlain College
3900 Trinity College
3920 University of Vermont

Castleton
3765 Castleton State College – Vermont
   Education Center

Johnson
3766 Johnson State College

Lyndonville
3767 Lyndon State College

Marlboro
3509 Marlboro College

Montpelier
3939 Vermont College of Norwich
   University

Northfield
3669 Norwich University

Old Bennington
3796 Southern Vermont College

Plainfield
3416 Goddard College
3546 Middlesex College

Poultney
3418 Green Mountain College

Randolph Center
3941 Vermont Technical College

Rutland
3297 College of Saint Joseph

South Royalton
3735 Royalton College

Waterbury
3286 Community College of Vermont

Winooski
3757 Saint Michael's College

VIRGIN ISLANDS

St. Thomas
0879 University of the Virgin Islands

VIRGINIA

Abingdon
5927 Virginia Highlands Community
   College

Alberta
5660 Southside Virginia Community
   College

Alexandria
5510 Northern Virginia Community
   College – Alexandria
5542 Protestant Episcopal Seminary
7830 Strayer College – Alexandria

Annandale
5515 Northern Virginia Community
   College

Arlington
5405 Marymount University
7831 Strayer College – Arlington

Ashburn
7833 Strayer College – Loudown

Ashland
5566 Randolph Macon College

Big Stone Gap
5451 Mountain Empire Community
   College

Blacksburg
5859 Virginia Polytechnic Institute

Bluefield
5063 Bluefield College

Bridgewater
5069 Bridgewater College

Bristol
5857 Virginia Intermont College

Buena Vista
5625 Southern Virginia Women

Charlottesville
5561 Piedmont Virginia Community
   College
5820 University of Virginia

Chesapeake
5707 Tidewater Community College –
   Chesapeake

Chester
5342 John Tyler Community College

Clifton Forge
5139 Dabney S. Lancaster Community
   College

Danville
5017 Averett College
5163 Danville Community College

Dublin
5513 New River Community College

Emory
5185 Emory and Henry College

Fairfax
5827 George Mason University

Farmville
5368 Longwood College

Ferrum
5213 Ferrum College

Fort Eustis
7735 St. Leo College

Franklin
5557 Paul D. Camp Community College

Fredericksburg
5398 Mary Washington College
7832 Strayer College – Fredericksburg

Glenns
5590 Rappahannock Community College
   – Glenns

Hampton
5292 Hampton University
5793 Thomas Nelson Community
   College

Harrisonburg
5181 Eastern Mennonite College
5392 James Madison University

Hampden-Sydney
5291 Hampden-Sydney College

Keysville
5669 Southside Virginia Community
   College

Langley Air Force Base
7840 St. Leo College

Lawrenceville
5604 Saint Paul's College

Lexington
5858 Virginia Military Institute
5887 Washington-Lee University

Locust Grove
5276 Germanna Community College

Lynchburg
5141 Central Virginia Community College
5385 Liberty University
5372 Lynchburg College
5567 Randolph-Macon Woman's College

Manassas
5774 Northern Virginia Community
   College – Manassas
7834 Strayer College – Manassas

Martinsville
5549 Patrick Henry Community College

McLean
7674 National Louis University

Melfa
5844 Eastern Shore Community College

Middletown
5381 Lord Fairfax Community College

New Market
7838 Shenandoah Valley Academy

Newport News
5128 Christopher Newport University

Norfolk
5864 Norfolk State University
5126 Old Dominion University
7826 St. Leo College
5867 Virginia Wesleyan College

Petersburg
5574 Richard Bland College
5860 Virginia State University

Portsmouth
5226 Tidewater Community College – Portsmouth

Radford
5565 Radford University

Richlands
5659 Southwest Virginia Community College

Richmond
5676 J. Sargeant Reynolds Community College
5243 Presbyterian School of Christian Education
5675 St. Luke's Hospital – Nursing
5569 University of Richmond
5570 Virginia Commonwealth University
5862 Virginia Union University

Roanoke
5099 College of Health Sciences
5294 Hollins College
5868 Virginia Western Community College

Salem
5571 Roanoke College

Staunton
5397 Mary Baldwin College

Sterling
5775 Northern Virginia Community College – Sterling

Suffolk
5380 Louise Obici School of Nursing

Sweet Briar
5634 Sweet Briar College

Unversity of Richmond
5341 University of Richmond

Vienna
7048 Averett College

Virginia Beach
5787 Tidewater Community College – Virginia Beach Campus

Warsaw
5583 Rappahannock Community College – Warsaw

Weyers Cave
5083 Blue Ridge Community College

Williamsburg
5115 College of William & Mary – Virginia

Winchester
5613 Shenandoah University

Wise
5124 Clinch Valley College

Woodbridge
5517 Northern Virginia Community College – Woodbridge
7835 Strayer College – Potomac Mills

Wytheville
5917 Wytheville Community College

WASHINGTON

Aberdeen
4332 Grays Harbor College

Auburn
4337 Green River Community College

Bellevue
4029 Bellevue Community College
4042 City University

Bellingham
4947 Western Washington University
4974 Whatcom Community College

Bremerton
4583 Olympic College

Centralia
4045 Centralia College

Cheney
4301 Eastern Washington University

College Place
4940 Walla Walla College

Des Moines
4348 Highline Community College

Edmonds
4618 Puget Sound Christian College

Ellensburg
4044 Central Washington University

Everett
4303 Everett Community College

Issaquah
4408 Lutheran Bible in Seattle

Kent
7926 Valley College

Kirkland
4447 Cogswell College – North
4541 Northwest College

Lacey
4674 Saint Martin's College

Longview
4402 Lower Columbia College

Lynwood
4307 Edmonds Community College

Moses Lake
4024 Big Bend Community College

Mount Vernon
4699 Skagit Valley College

Olympia
4292 The Evergreen State College
4578 South Puget Sound Community College

Pasco
4077 Columbia Basin College

Port Angeles
4615 Peninsula College

Pullman
4705 Washington State University

Remond
7568 Lake Washington Vocational Technical Institute

Renton
7744 Renton Technical College

Richland
4369 Joint Center for Graduate Studies

Seattle
7585 Antioch University of Seattle
4801 Cornish College of the Arts
4741 Seattle Central Community College
4694 Seattle Pacific University
4695 Seattle University
4738 Shoreline Community College
4759 South Seattle Community College

Spokane
4330 Gonzaga University
4739 Spokane Community College
4752 Spokane Falls Community College
4374 Trend College
4953 Whitworth College

Tacoma
4597 Pacific Lutheran University
4103 Pierce College
4826 Tacoma Community College
4067 University of Puget Sound
4949 Washington Baptist Teachers College

Toppenish
4344 Heritage College

Vancouver
4055 Clark Community College

Walla Walla
4963 Walla Walla Community College
4951 Whitman College

Wenatchee
4942 Wenatchee Valley College

Yakima
4993 Yakima Valley Community College

WEST VIRGINIA

Athens
5120 Concord College

Beckley
5054 College of West Virginia

Bethany
5060 Bethany College

Bluefield
5064 Bluefield State College

Bradley
5034 Applachian Bible College

Buckhannon
5905 West Virginia Wesleyan College

Charleston
5419 University of Charleston

Elkins
5151 Davis and Elkins College

Fairmont
5211 Fairmont State College

Glenville
5254 Glenville State College

Huntington
5396 Marshall University

Institute
5903 West Virginia State College

Keyser
5539 Potomac State College of West Virginia

Logan
5446 Southern West Virginia Community College – Logan

Montgomery
5902 West Virginia Institute of Technology

Morgantown
5904 West Virginia University – Main Campus

Parkersburg
5519 Ohio Valley College
5932 West Virginia University – Parkersburg

Philippi
5005 Alderson-Broaddus College

Salem
5608 Salem College

Shepherdstown
5615 Shepherd College

West Liberty
5901 West Liberty State College

Wheeling
5520 Ohio Valley Medical Center
5942 West Virginia Northern Community College
5906 Wheeling Jesuit College

Williamson
5447 Southern West Virginia Community College – Williamson

WISCONSIN

Appleton
1217 Fox Valley Technical College
1398 Lawrence University

Ashland
1561 Northland College
1270 Wisconsin Indianhead Technical College

Baraboo
1996 University of Wisconsin Center – Baraboo/Sauk County

Beaver Dam
1433 Moraine Park Technical College – Beaver Dam

Beloit
1059 Beloit College

Cleveland
7574 Lakeshore Technical College

De Pere
1706 St. Norbert College

Eau Claire
1913 University of Wisonsin – Eau Claire

Fond du Lac
1443 Marian College of Fond du Lac

1499 Moraine Park Technical College
1942 University of Wisconsin – Fond du Lac

Green Bay
1046 Bellin College of Nursing
4190 Northeast Wisconsin Technical College
1859 University of Wisconsin – Green Bay

Janesville
1043 Blackhawk Technical College
1998 University of Wisconsin – Rock County

Kenosha
1103 Carthage College
1243 Gateway Technical College
1860 University of Wisconsin – Parkside

La Crosse
1914 University of Wisconsin – La Crosse
1878 Viterbo College
1087 Western Wisconsin Technical College

Ladysmith
1512 Mount Senario College

Madison
1202 Edgewood College
1536 Madison Area Technical College – Madison
1432 Madison Business College
1846 University of Wisconsin – Madison
1863 University of Wisconsin Medical School
1903 Wisconsin School of Electronics

Manitowoc
1300 Silver Lake College
1890 University of Wisconsin Center – Manitowoc

Marinette
1891 University of Wisconsin Center – Marinette

Marshfield
1788 St. Joseph's Hospital School of Nursing
1997 University of Wisconsin – Marshfield/Wood County

Menasha
1889 University of Wisconsin – Fox Valley

Menomonie
1740 University of Wisconsin – Stout

Mequon
1139 Concordia College

Milwaukee
1012 Alverno College
1100 Cardinal Stritch College
1448 Marquette University
1519 Medical College of Wisconsin – Nursing
1475 Milwaukee Area Technical College
1476 Milwaukee School of Engineering
1490 Mount Mary College
3617 Stratton College
1473 University of Wisconsin – Milwaukee
1513 Wisconsin Lutheran College

Oshkosh
1236 Fox Valley Technical Institute – Oshkosh
1916 University of Wisconsin – Oshkosh

Platteville
1917 University of Wisconsin – Platteville

Racine
1255 Gateway Technical College

Rhinelander
1549 Nicolet College and Technical Institute

Rice Lake
1772 University of Wisconsin – Rice Lake

Richland Center
1662 University of Wisconsin – Richland

Ripon
1664 Ripon College

River Falls
1918 University of Wisconsin – River Falls

Sheboygan
1393 Lakeland College
1994 University of Wisconsin – Sheboygan

Stevens Point
1919 University of Wisconsin – Stevens Point

Superior
1920 University of Wisconsin – Superior

Watertown
1945 Madison Area Technical College – Watertown
1563 Northwestern College

Waukesha
1101 Carroll College
1999 University of Wisconsin Center – Waukesha

Wausau
1579 Northcentral Technical College
1995 University of Wisconsin Center – Marathon

West Bend
4174 Moraine Park Technical College NB
1993 University of Wisconsin – Washington County

Whitewater
1921 University of Wisconsin – Whitewater

WYOMING

Casper
4043 Casper College

Cheyenne
4415 Laramie County Community College

Gillette
4680 Sheridan College – Gillette

Laramie
4855 University of Wyoming

Powell
4542 Northwest College

Rawlins
7956 Carbon County Higher Education Center

Riverton
4115 Central Wyoming College

Rock Springs
4957 Western Wyoming College

Sheridan
4536 Sheridan College

Torrington
4700 Eastern Wyoming College

Appendix D
What Your CLEP Score Means

Student's Score Report

Your score report shows the total scaled score for each examination you took. For the General Examinations, total scaled scores fall between 200 and 800, and for the Subject Examinations, between 20 and 80. For most Subject Examinations, you will also find a percentile rank on your score report. Percentile ranks indicate the percentage of students who scored at or below a given score.

To compare your performance to that of college students completing a course covering the same subject as the CLEP examination you took, refer to the tables that follow. Table 1 shows how the scores of college students in the sample are related to their final course grades. Tables 2 and 3 show the percentile ranks for these students for the Subject and General Examinations, respectively.

Because scales and percentile data for CLEP examinations are based on the performance of different groups of students, a score on one examination cannot be compared to a score on an examination in a different subject. Nor are CLEP scores comparable to Scholastic Aptitude Test (SAT) scores or scores of other tests that use similar scales.

CLEP scores are computed by tallying the number of correct responses and subtracting a percentage of wrong answers from this total to discourage random guessing. Omitted questions are not counted as wrong. If your examination had questions offering five choices, one-fourth of your wrong answers was subtracted. If your examination questions offered four choices, one-third of your wrong answers was subtracted.

The resulting score was converted to the CLEP score scale, which provides an unchanging measure of achievement regardless of which version of a particular examination you take or when you take it.

If you have a question about a test item, your score report, or any other aspect of a CLEP examination that your test center cannot answer, write to: CLEP, PO Box 6600, Princeton, NJ 08541-6600.

Table 1

Relationship between CLEP Scaled Scores and Final Course Grades*

Examination	Mean Scaled Score by Final Course Grade**					No. of Semesters for Which the Test Was Designed
	A	B	C†	D	E	
Composition and Literature						
American Literature	57	50	46	41	—	2
Analysis and Interpretation of Literature	61	55	49	41	40	2
English Literature	60	50	46	45	40	2
Freshman College Composition	54	49	44	42	42	2
Foreign Languages						
College French (Levels 1 and 2)						
Level 1 (two semesters)	49	43	39	36	37	2
Level 2 (four semesters)	57	50	45	41	40	4
College German (Levels 1 and 2)						
Level 1 (two semesters)	48	44	40	37	37	2
Level 2 (four semesters)	61	54	48	38	—	4
College Spanish (Levels 1 and 2)						
Level 1 (two semesters)	50	45	41	39	33	2
Level 2 (four semesters)	60	54	50	47	42	4
Social Sciences and History						
American Government	58	55	47	44	37	1
American History I: Early Colonizations to 1877	59	52	45	43	41	1
American History II: 1865 to the Present	57	53	45	38	36	1
Human Growth and Development	58	52	45	37	36	1
Introduction to Educational Psychology	58	52	47	41	39	1
Principles of Macroeconomics	57	49	44	39	39	1
Principles of Microeconomics	54	47	41	39	37	1
Introductory Psychology	57	52	47	44	42	1
Introductory Sociology	57	52	47	41	38	1
Western Civilization I: Ancient Near East to 1648	58	52	46	41	42	1
Western Civilization II: 1648 to the Present	59	52	47	43	40	1
Science and Mathematics						
Calculus with Elementary Functions	60	51	47	42	42	2
College Algebra	58	51	46	41	39	1
College Algebra-Trigonometry	60	53	45	39	35	1
General Biology	55	50	46	41	39	2
General Chemistry	58	52	47	41	39	2
Trigonometry	62	54	50	46	41	1
Business						
Information Systems and Computer Applications	60	56	52	48	44	1
Principles of Management	56	52	46	43	43	1
Introductory Accounting	59	52	47	43	40	2
Introductory Business Law	63	57	51	44	38	1
Principles of Marketing	61	55	50	45	41	1

*Data are not available for the General Examinations. The American Council on Education recommends that institutions set their minimum for receiving credit within the scaled score range of 420-500 when institutional data is not available.

**These are the average scores of college students completing courses in each subject in the year indicated in Table 2.

†The American Council on Education recommends that the minimum score for awarding credit should be the mean test score of students who earn a grade of C in the respective course.

The scores that appear in bold type in the center column of this table are the credit-granting scores recommended by the American Council on Education (ACE). *Each college, however, reserves the right to set its own credit-granting policy, which may differ from that of ACE.* If you haven't already done so, contact your college as soon as possible to find out the score it requires to grant credit, the number of credit hours granted, and the course(s) that can be bypassed with a satisfactory score.

Table 2
Percentile Ranks for the Subject Examinations (Total Scores)

Examination	Date	No. of Students	Selected Scaled Scores													Mean	Standard Deviation
			80	75	70	65	60	55	50	45	40	35	30	25	20		
Composition and Literature																	
American Literature	1971	659	99	99	98	93	83	70	51	33	18	6	1	1	1	50	10
Analysis and Interpretation of Literature	1964	541	99	99	98	94	85	65	46	33	18	8	2	1	1	50	10
English Literature	1970-71	1,023	99	99	98	91	82	69	53	34	17	6	1	1	1	50	10
Freshman College Composition	1993	1,112	99	99	99	92	82	68	50	33	18	7	1	1	1	50	10
Foreign Languages																	
College French (Levels 1 and 2)																	
Level 1 (two semesters)	1990	2,293	99	99	99	97	95	90	82	65	42	19	5	1	1	50	10
Level 2 (four semesters)	1990	655	99	99	98	92	83	69	51	31	15	6	1	1	1	50	10
College German (Levels 1 and 2)																	
Level 1 (two semesters)	1975	502	99	99	99	99	97	90	80	57	33	8	1	1	1	44	7
Level 2 (four semesters)	1975	321	99	99	98	89	68	51	30	18	11	2	1	1	1	54	9
College Spanish (Levels 1 and 2)																	
Level 1 (two semesters)	1975	1,124	99	99	99	96	92	83	69	49	25	9	2	1	1	46	9
Level 2 (four semesters)	1975	663	99	99	96	87	71	52	29	13	5	1	1	1	1	55	9
Social Sciences and History																	
American Government	1965-66	921	99	99	98	94	85	66	49	31	17	8	2	1	1	50	10
American History I: Early Colonizations to 1877	1979-80	1,091	99	99	96	91	85	72	55	34	16	4	1	1	1	50	10
American History II: 1865 to the Present	1979-80	822	99	99	97	93	84	67	52	34	17	6	1	1	1	50	10
Human Growth and Development	1976-77	1,009	99	99	99	94	82	67	47	31	18	9	2	1	1	50	10
Introduction to Educational Psychology	1990	1,957	99	99	98	93	83	69	52	32	17	7	2	1	1	50	10
Principles of Macroeconomics	1993	1,084	99	99	98	96	90	83	71	53	33	12	2	1	1	50	10
Principles of Microeconomics	1993	1,104	99	99	99	98	93	87	75	60	42	24	8	2	1	50	10
Introductory Psychology	1992	1,798	99	99	96	91	84	71	54	36	16	4	1	1	1	50	10
Introductory Sociology	1974	3,235	99	99	99	94	83	67	49	31	17	8	3	1	1	50	10
Western Civilization I: Ancient Near East to 1648	1979-80	793	99	99	98	92	83	70	51	34	18	6	1	1	1	50	10
Western Civilization II: 1648 to the Present	1979-81	703	99	98	94	90	84	74	59	38	14	1	1	1	1	50	10
Science and Mathematics																	
Calculus with Elementary Functions	1977	1,728	99	99	96	92	83	70	52	36	16	4	1	1	1	50	10
College Algebra	1993	1,042	99	99	99	95	86	75	61	43	27	12	3	1	1	50	10
College Algebra-Trigonometry	1979	1,116	99	99	98	91	80	65	49	33	21	12	6	1	1	50	11
General Biology	1977	2,207	99	99	97	92	82	69	52	36	18	4	1	1	1	50	10
General Chemistry	1978	3,016	99	99	97	92	84	69	52	33	17	6	1	1	1	50	10
Trigonometry	1979	1,517	99	99	94	85	71	53	36	22	10	4	1	1	1	54	10
Business																	
Information Systems and Computer Applications	1990	1,990	99	99	96	91	83	70	55	35	17	3	1	1	1	50	10
Principles of Management	1993	1,207	99	99	99	95	85	72	54	35	20	11	6	2	1	50	10
Introductory Accounting	1976	3,404	99	99	97	92	84	70	50	32	17	6	1	1	1	50	10
Introductory Business Law	1970	1,116	99	99	98	92	78	62	47	29	16	6	2	1	1	50	10
Principles of Marketing	1992	1,248	99	99	99	93	83	68	47	32	18	7	2	1	1	50	10

Table 3
Percentile Ranks for the General Examinations (Total Scores)

Examination	Date	No. of Students	Selected Scaled Scores													Mean	Standard Deviation
			800	750	700	650	600	550	500	450	400	350	300	250	200		
English Composition	1993	1,748	99	99	98	92	82	69	51	33	18	6	1	1	1	500	100
Humanities	1978	757	99	99	99	98	93	85	70	49	27	9	1	1	1	460	85
	1963	678	99	99	96	93	84	69	54	35	16	4	1	1	1	500	99
Mathematics	1978	1,214	99	99	99	97	93	86	71	52	27	7	1	1	1	460	83
	1972	1,552	99	99	98	92	82	68	51	34	18	6	1	1	1	500	100
Natural Sciences	1978	883	99	99	98	95	88	79	67	51	32	13	4	1	1	460	103
	1963	633	99	99	97	93	83	70	54	35	18	6	1	1	1	500	99
Social Sciences and History	1978	794	99	99	99	99	97	89	72	48	21	6	1	1	1	460	71
	1963	607	99	99	97	92	83	69	54	34	17	5	1	1	1	500	99

NOTE 1: The pre-1978 reference data (based on national samples of college sophomores) that are included in this table along with the 1978 data (based on students completing courses in the subject at selected institutions across the country) are given because many colleges and universities prefer to continue using the earlier data to interpret General Examination scores.

NOTE 2: Effective July 1, 1993, all scores on the General Examinations will be reported on a three-digit scale with a zero as the last digit.

18511-03108 • Y44M75 • 284244

528